THE ANALYST'S
PRECONSCIOUS

Victoria Hamilton

THE ANALYTIC PRESS

1996   Hillsdale, NJ   London

Published by The Analytic Press, Inc.
Editorial Offices: 101 West Street, Hillsdale, NJ 07642

Library of Congress Cataloging-in-Publication Data

Hamilton, Victoria
  The analyst's preconscious / Victoria Hamilton.
  p. cm.
  Includes bibliographical references and index.
  ISBN 0-88163-221-X
  1. Psychoanalysis. 2. Transference (Psychology)
3. Countertransference (Psychology) I. Title.
RC504.H29 1996
616.89'17--dc20   96-20093
                                                   CIP

Printed in the United States of America
10 9 8 7 6 5 4 3 2 1

Contents

Acknowledgments

I embarked on this project in 1985 when studying for a doctorate at the Psychoanalysis Unit, University College London. Following a brief period of respite after obtaining my degree in 1990, I began to rethink my way through the research findings and to formulate various questions in the context of some philosophical writings as well as from the viewpoint of contemporary developments in the field of psychoanalysis. My thanks reflect the two stages of the work.

First, I thank the 65 analysts in America and Britain who gave so graciously of their time and who engaged in such thoughtful and creative ways with the research. I wish I could name personally those who encouraged and inspired me on the way. I hope that the interview excerpts in the book reflect the range and depth of these psychoanalysts' thinking about the field of psychoanalysis as well as their clinical practice.

For the five-year period at the Psychoanalysis Unit London, I am most grateful to Professor Joseph Sandler and Professor Peter Fonagy for their teaching, and to the members of the unit who participated in the development of the research design. Joseph Sandler was the first psychoanalyst I had met who had a thorough grasp of international psychoanalysis and who was able to speak the languages of different psychoanalytic cultures. His brilliant translations of the forms of discourse of the three groups in the British Psychoanalytical Society as well as of the many American schools were invaluable, as was the information he supplied based on his knowledge of the history of psychoanalysis throughout the Western world. Peter Fonagy's ability to think about the overall design of the project, as well as the lightning speed of his thought, was always inspiring and often entertaining.

Special thanks also go to the members of the unit, Jill Miller, Bruna Seu, Mary Levens, Sira Dermen, and Miranda Wolpert, for many hours of discussion and attention to detail at all stages of the project. In contacting the 65 analysts for the interviews, the following persons were particularly helpful: Priscilla Roth, Professor Sandler, Drs. Arnold Cooper, Ed Corrigan, and Pearl-Ellen Gordon in New York, Professor Louis Breger in Los Angeles, and Dr. Robert Wallerstein in San Francisco.

I would also like to thank colleagues at the Tavistock Clinic who participated in the pilot studies and design of the questionnaires; a special acknowledgment is due Penelope Crick for her grasp of the methodological problems. I also enjoyed many informal discussions with Dr. John Bowlby until his death in 1990; he provided encouragement, interest, and support throughout the study. He was particularly taken with the idea of "psychoanalytic cultures," the title he favored for the book. Arnold and Frances Tustin, both of whom died in 1994, also entered enthusiastically into the development of both the research project and the book. Thanks also to many generous friends who have urged me to continue through many exhausting drafts and revisions: Al and Anne Alvarez, Penelope Crick, Stephen Grosz, Juliet Hopkins, MarySue Moore, Valerie Sinason, Harold Stewart, and Judith Vida. MarySue Moore has given much thought throughout all stages of the work. I am also grateful to the candidates at the Institute of Contemporary Psychoanalysis in Los Angeles who participated in a philosophy and psychoanalysis seminar in the summer of 1995 and gave me invaluable, up-to-date feedback on some of the chapters. Lastly, I thank my husband, Nicholas Tufnell, who has lived with the ideas expressed in the book; he is an exacting editor, demanding that ideas be expressed in the richness of ordinary language.

My final thanks go to the editors and publishers who have backed the book. First, to my dear friend and colleague Cesare Sacerdoti at H. Karnac Books in London. Mr. Sacerdoti read many drafts of the Ph.D. thesis and the book and sustained me throughout by his strong belief in my work. I cannot think of a kinder publisher who cares for his authors in a personal way that has become rare in modern times. Thanks also to editors at H. Karnac Books who worked on early drafts of the book: Eric and Klara King, and Graham Sleight. John Kerr, Associate Editor at The Analytic Press, has provided unerring support, advice, scholarship, and editorship. His encyclopedic knowledge of both the history of psychoanalysis and the contemporary debates has reshaped the organization of the book. His inexorable logic has forced me to think out distinctions and clarify inconsistencies. My thanks also to Paul Stepansky, Managing Director and Editor-in-Chief of The Analytic Press, for including me amongst his authors. And, finally, my thanks to Eleanor Starke Kobrin for her careful copy editing of the final manuscript.

Chapter 1

Introduction

It is as if one saw a screen with scattered colour-patches, and said: the way they are here, they are unintelligible; they only make sense when one completes them into a shape.—Whereas I want to say: Here *is* the whole. (If you complete it, you falsify it.) [Wittgenstein, 1980a].

In calling this book *The Analyst's Preconscious*, I wish to draw attention to an area of the mind that has been neglected in discussions of the work of practicing psychoanalysts. My interest in the preconscious level of analytic practice arose from two sources: a historical study of the concepts of transference and interpretation in the works of Freud and post-Freudian authors of different theoretical orientations, and an empirical investigation into the varieties of transference interpretation of contemporary psychoanalysts practicing in different psychoanalytic cultures. Thus, my initial inquiry into the transferences of patients as these were reported and interpreted by their analysts evolved into a study of analysts' interpretive practices. What do analysts draw on in order to enter into and elucidate the minds of others? My basic contention, following from these investigations, is that an analyst's preconscious contribution to the understanding of transference is not fully captured in the concept of countertransference. This is true even when the conceptualization of countertransference is expanded to include the analyst's theoretical orientation. For example, Samuel Stein (1991) discusses the unconscious influence of theory on the psychoanalyst's countertransference. In my view, another term is needed to describe the area between more deeply unconscious (private) beliefs and conscious (public) declarations.

If we follow the history of psychoanalytic concepts, we find that the conceptualization of the analyst's methods and skills is often preceded

1

by developments in the understanding of dynamics attributed to the patient. For instance, Freud's introduction of the terms countertransference and counterresistance followed his "discoveries" of his patients' transferences and resistances. But the idea that the analyst's preconscious might be worth attending to seems to be an exception to this basic rule. During the heyday of the topographical model, Freud had much to say about the preconscious when describing the workings of his patients' minds. (It is important to note that Freud used the term "preconscious" in two ways: first, to refer to an area of the mind on a par with the Systems Conscious and Unconscious and, second, as a qualifier of mental states.) Nevertheless, although references to the analyst's unconscious abound in Freud's writings on countertransference and counterresistance, he never really pursued the potential contributions of the analyst's preconscious to the psychoanalytic situation. This task was left to later analytic investigators. As the bipolar concepts relating to his uncovering of a second drive "beyond the pleasure principle" and the tripartite structural model increasingly influenced Freud's theorizing, the fluidity and degrees of vivacity captured in the idea of preconscious mental states disappeared. The ego of the structural model cannot be seen as a correlate of, or substitute for, the preconscious of the topographical theory.

Later psychoanalytic thinkers, notably Michael Balint and Donald Winnicott, however, did describe an area similar to the preconscious, although they did not tie their ideas to Freud's concept. Balint (1957) and Winnicott (1953) discussed a "third" or "intermediate" area of the mind. Although Balint and Winnicott focused their attention on the third area in the mind of the patient, they implied that the accessibility of an intermediate space was crucial to the analyst's functioning. Winnicott talked about the "overlap" of two play areas, or the "transitional" space, between conscious and unconscious thinking and between the primary and secondary processes. I apply these ideas to the mind of the psychoanalyst in the belief that every analyst has a preconscious, whether or not he or she attends to it.

The central aim of this book is to delineate those dimensions of technique existing in the analyst's preconscious that either are shared by, or are unique to, analysts practicing in a limited number of psychoanalytic cultures. I do not examine the foundations of psychoanalysis or the unifying principles of psychoanalysts' technique; I attempt instead to systematize the beliefs and actions that are typical of practicing American and British psychoanalysts today. The thrust of the book is away from parsimony, from the goal of discovering a few simple ideas or universal keys to our understanding of the mind. It is in the area between avowed theoretical orientation—"I am a Freudian," "I am a Jungian"—on one hand, and therapeutic actions in the "here-and-now" exchanges of the clinical situation on the other, that analysts reveal the muddled overlaps and uncomfortable, precarious coexistence of parts of belief systems.

By retrieving Freud's concept of the preconscious, I hope to focus the reader's attention on the mind of the psychoanalyst, on the clusters of beliefs, neither unconscious nor fully conscious, that make each inter-pret and practice in his or her individual way. The third, or "in-between," area is hard to articulate and is not easily represented in the languages of either the primary or secondary processes. Other terms capture the use to which I put Freud's concept: the "organizing princi-ples" of the intersubjective psychoanalysts; Joseph Sandler's "interpre-tive schema"; George Kelly's "personal constructs." These concepts come from psychology (Sandler and many of the contemporary inter-subjectivists, such as Robert Stolorow, were psychologists before they became psychoanalysts). But, within the discipline of psychoanalysis itself, we have a concept that is underused, namely, the preconscious. In, first, linking Freud's preconscious to the concepts of later psycho-analysts such as Balint and Winnicott and, second, using these con-cepts to describe the minds of practicing psychoanalysts, I expose another aim: I propose that these and related concepts can help to pro-tect the analyst's imaginative capacities and efforts, as these have been curtailed and undermined through psychoanalysis' scientist leanings and aspirations to become a more cohesive, homogeneous discipline.

These aims are consistent with the pluralistic situation that now exists within psychoanalysis. One of the unexpected results of my research into contemporary analytic practices was that a natural or log-ical link seemed to pertain between pluralism (as distinct from rela-tivism), on one hand, and the psychoanalytic notions of the preconscious and of a third, or intermediate, area of mind on the other. Analysts who subscribe to this third area commit themselves, even if unconsciously, to pluralism, diversity, overlap, balance—what philoso-phers such as Isaiah Berlin (1992a) and Richard Rorty (1991) describe as an "uneasy" or "precarious" equilibrium. In "Priority of Democracy to Philosophy," Rorty argues for a position of tolerance of equilibrium in philosophy, thus keeping the discipline in line with the politics of lib-eral democracy as opposed to religious fundamentalism. The same prin-ciple could be applied to the practice of psychoanalysis. Strife is rife amongst psychoanalysts of different persuasions, each arguing for the "right" developmental theory and therapeutic action. The main out-come of the research described in this book is that, with the exception of two "schools" or orientation groups, analysts think and practice

much more loosely than they publicly claim. They are guided preconsciously by many dimensions.

Pluralists, in particular, will look for overlaps between two interpretations of events rather than pronounce one real and the other unreal.
The pluralist must think imaginatively, for to interpret a radically different mind or community is to exercise an effort of imagination so that the
interpreter enters into the hopes and fears, loves and hates, fights and
desires, of the other individual or culture.

The analyst's preconscious model of his field and his professional
self will also influence his interpretive practices. Does he think of
himself as a scientist or a humanist? What sort of interpreter does he
imagine himself to be? Is psychoanalysis a science or a branch of
applied philosophy? What sorts of answers and what sorts of questions
does psychoanalysis address? Do analysts believe that psychoanalysis
is progressing toward a convergent goal in which we will finally
understand the workings of the mental life of man? Has psychoanalytic knowledge accumulated since Freud? Or, on the other hand, is
psychoanalysis akin to philosophy in that philosophy asks perennial
questions to which there are no final solutions? Or, perhaps, are there
some parts of the psychoanalyst's working model that, like chemistry,
can be answered empirically and in which knowledge is cumulative
and convergent?

One realm in which there is greater evidence of cumulative knowledge and agreement is the area of developmental theory. Finally, in the
last decade, 30 years of infancy research have percolated into the psychoanalytic theory of development. Freud's psychosexual theory is, if not
challenged, at least expanded. And Freud's amoeboid, autistic infant is
no longer seen in most of the Western world as the cultural norm.
Accumulated empirical observations of mother–infant and parent–child
relationships are biased toward man's need for attachment, for belonging
to a community throughout all stages of the life cycle.

But, I suspect, there are other areas of psychoanalysis that are not
like physiology or astronomy and in which knowledge is not cumulative. In discussing the question of progress in philosophy, Berlin
(1992a) points out that philosophy does not advance in the same way
as do other subjects. You cannot say of Plato or Aristotle, as you might
say of Archimedes or Bacon, that there is no need to read their work—
that it is, if not obsolete, at least totally superseded. Berlin observes
that the questions Plato asked are still being asked today: "The major
ideas, outlooks, theories, insights, have remained the central ideas of
philosophy" (p. 25). In like vein, we can say that no advances in tech-
nology or replicable experimentation will be able to tell us of a whole

body of work: Yes, Freud was wrong; Ferenczi was right—so we no longer need to read Freud (the attitude taken by many psychoanalysts toward Jung's work). One of the purposes of psychoanalytic inquiry might be to attempt to answer questions for which there are no empirical or logically necessary solutions. Perhaps no empirical investigation could tell us why the unconscious seems important, why the mind–body problem may never be answered, or why the issue of innate ideas cannot be finally settled. There are many answers to such questions and no accepted technique for establishing which is the right answer or, indeed, the right method of enquiry.

The systematization of the interpretive practices of analysts working in different analytic cultures helps to articulate the implications of the new pluralism for psychoanalysis. On one hand is the question, what does the contemporary ideology of pluralism amount to? And, who, if anyone, can practice pluralistically? On the other hand, one is led to ask whether even the most consistent monists practice more loosely than they claim. Since many psychoanalytic concepts have links with ordinary language, it is impossible to coerce these concepts into a purely technical vocabulary. A concept, such as "empathy," "envy," or "identification," which has become part of a specific technical approach and vocabulary, keeps spilling over so that the owners of that concept then have to redefine it in relation to what it is not. They keep having to spell out what is special, not ordinary, about its usage. In addition, it is often difficult to describe the ways we use a concept even though we are able to use it without difficulty. Wittgenstein (cited in Budd, 1993) pointed out that, although we are trained or encouraged to master the use of words, we are not taught to describe that use. He gave many examples of how "the possession of one ability does not guarantee the possession of a related, higher-level ability" (p. 5). Wittgenstein offered the example of how we might imagine that we could find our way around a city extremely well and easily take the shortest route from one place to another, and yet we could not draw a map of that city. And when we do try to draw a map, we go completely wrong. Thus, the maps or theoretical models that analysts construct of the ways they use specific concepts can be misleading.

In approaching these questions, I draw on material from interviews I conducted between 1988 and 1990 with psychoanalysts practicing in America and Britain. It seemed to me that examining what analysts say about what they think and do might flesh out the published, largely theoretical debates on the ways beliefs relate to one another and are enacted in clinical practice. Analysts were asked to describe their use of specific concepts. As Wittgenstein might have predicted, this proved to be a difficult task. Many were familiar with the particular concept under discussion; they knew, and might even have been taught, what it was supposed to mean. But they found it very hard to gather up the scattered uses of that concept throughout their current practice.

What I have called an analyst's preconscious consists of various descriptions of the maps or sketches analysts drew of the routes they followed in their daily practice. (These maps are reflected in the chapter topics of this book.) This preconscious is culled from a reading of analysts' definitions as these were presented in the interviews along with examples drawn from clinical material. The analysts I interviewed entered into the task of describing, by way of definition and illustration, their use of a number of central clinical concepts. Many of them involved themselves in the project with considerable interest, concentration, and reflectiveness. Some were surprised by their own thoughts. Many told me that they had really enjoyed the interview because it made them "think about things I usually don't have a chance to think about." One analyst remarked, "I wish there were more opportunities like this. Nobody ever asks me these sorts of questions."

Illustrative material and information used in this book are drawn from two sources. The first consists of the 65 interviews with psychoanalysts of varying orientations working in four American and British cities: Los Angeles, New York, San Francisco, and London. I selected the 65 analysts so as to represent variations in orientation, age, experience, and seniority in local institutes. During these "semidirected" interviews, which lasted from 45 minutes to two hours, 27 central psychoanalytic topics and concepts were discussed (an abbreviated list of the topic headings and the full interview protocol are shown in Appendix 1). Since statistical measures were to be applied to the results, the interview protocol had to meet the minimum standardization criteria for an empirical study in psychology. Obviously, the same list of questions had to be addressed in each interview. In selecting my sample, I restricted myself to analysts who were members of institutes within the American Psychoanalytic Association (A.P.A.) and the International Psychoanalytical Association (I.P.A.). I made one exception to this rule and interviewed three analysts of an interpersonal orientation in New York. Although this orientation has for the most part been ignored by British psychoanalysts, many American analysts acknowledged their debt to Sullivanian ideas; a few urged me to include interpersonalists in my study.

The second source of information was a questionnaire concerning the nature and degree of influence on the analysts of a number of key thinkers, and/or schools, in regard to analytic technique and orientation. This questionnaire is called the Psychoanalysts' Orientation Questionnaire (P.O.Q.) (see Figure 1). The P.O.Q. speaks for itself: it is a fairly simple questionnaire aimed at eliciting information concerning the influences that make up a publicly declared or official orientation—self psychology, independent, or Kleinian. This questionnaire was filled out by 64 of the 65 analysts and expresses their conscious beliefs about specific influences on their clinical work.

The interview protocol and the orientation questionnaire are the end result of several preliminary pilot surveys and experiments. I will start with the rationale for devising the P.O.Q. This questionnaire was designed after I had completed my interviews with 31 psychoanalysts in the British Psychoanalytical Society. In Britain, psychoanalysts train within three orientations: Contemporary Freudian, Independent, and Kleinian.[1] The three distinct groups are represented both in teaching and on all committees of the Society. I interviewed 10 or 11 analysts from each group. This tripartite system was set up in the British Society at the end of World War II by Sylvia Payne, the Society's first woman president, to resolve the "Controversial Discussions" between Anna Freud and Melanie Klein. The British Society seemed to represent a unique example of a pluralistic society operating within one institute, indeed the only institute in the country. No such system exists in America. Moreover, unlike in Britain, where training is centralized in the London institute, many American cities have several institutes. The absence of a straightforward orientation classification based on group affiliation such as exists in Britain meant that I had no ready-made way to associate avowed theoretical orientation with the many aspects of clinical practice discussed in the interviews. Since I had grown up in the British analytic system, I initially imagined that I would look for relationships between the different approaches to interpretation (the 27 dimensions shown on the Appendix) and the three orientation groups in the British Society. The idea that a second questionnaire focusing on finer distinctions within an orientation had not crossed my mind. But, once I had embarked on the American interviews, things became a lot more complicated. Unlike many of their British counterparts, American analysts seemed unwilling to describe their identities in group terms. For instance, at the end of the interview with an analyst whom I and others initially categorized as Freudian, the analyst said, "Oh, you must interview Dr. X; he is really classical." Most

---

[1] Contemporary Freudian, Independent, and Kleinian are official designations of the British Psychoanalytical Society and Institute.

Figure 1
Psychoanalysts' Orientation Questionnaire

Please rate the extent to which these orientations/frameworks have influenced your technique. Please make sure that you mark each category, even if the influence has been negligible. Place an X in the appropriate box and return the form to me in the enclosed stamped addressed envelope as soon as possible.

	Not at all	Very little	To some extent	To a considerable extent	To a very great extent More than any other
1. Anna Freud					
2. Freud: Drive Theory					
3. Topographic model					
4. Structural model					
5. Ego Psychology					
6. Mahler et al.					
7. American object-relations theory (Jacobsen, Loewald, Kernberg, etc.)					
8. British object-relations theory other than Klein (Winnicott, Balint, Fairbairn, Bowlby, etc.)					
9. Klein					
10. Post-Klein/Bion					
11. Sullivan/Interpersonalist					
12. Franz Alexander					
13. Kohut					
14. Self psychology/post-Kohut					
15. Lacan					
16. French analysts other than Lacan					
17. Contemporary developmental theory: Stern, Emde, attachment theorists					
18. Gill					
19. Schafer/action language					
20. Hermeneuticists/ Spence et al.					
Other (Please specify)					

American analysts wanted to project an image of themselves as "eclectic" and unfettered by group affiliations and loyalties.

With the collaboration of some of the American analysts, I drew up an extensive list of key figures and theoretical orientations. It was at this point, for instance, that I was urged by analysts both in and outside New York to include the influence of the interpersonal school. In retrospect, I think the acknowledgment of Sullivanian ideas at that time (five years ago) points to the interpersonal or relational direction to which many analysts were drawn preconsciously. The final list of 20 sources of influence shown on the P.O.Q. was then sent to all the analysts involved in the study, those in Britain and those in the United States. I discovered that a more detailed examination of orientation influences exposed a new and fascinating range of differences among the analysts in each of the three orientation groups in the British Society. It seemed to me that these were *preconscious* influences that had been drawn out of the woodwork, as it were, by the task of filling out the P.O.Q. Most analysts filled in this questionnaire with relative ease and speed, although a few obviously pondered the various categories, modifying them by including individual thinkers, often teachers, within a particular category.

At a much later point in the study, after all the interview material and the P.O.Q. scores had been rated by me and four independent raters, I was introduced to cluster analysis as a way of statistically controlling for types of response. What was fascinating about the results of this statistical analysis was that it delineated subgroups within a particular orientation group. For instance, in the British Society, two of the groupings that resulted from the statistical analysis replicated the respective memberships of two postgraduate clinical seminars that were run by powerful senior analysts. Another cluster linked a subset of analysts within one orientation, all of whom had been either analyzed or supervised by the same analysts.

The reader will note that the analysts were asked to rate themselves with regard to both the *source* of influence—for example, Anna Freud—and the *degree* of influence. With regard to the latter, analysts could choose among five alternatives on a simple five-point scale: 1) not at all, 2) very little, 3) to some extent, 4) to a considerable extent, and 5) to a very great extent. The analysts responded to the individual items on the score sheets. I don't think that many of them reviewed the overall pattern of their preferences. When I began to receive the completed questionnaires, however, I was struck by the differences in the patterns of response. On some score sheets, there was a scattering of positive responses across the five points, whereas, on others, the range of positive influences was extremely narrow, for example, "influenced to a great extent" by Klein and Bion but "very little" by any other thinkers or schools. I then started to focus on the patterns of response, for example, what was the ratio of "5s" to "1s"? Did strong beliefs in a particular orientation (point 5), exclude many other influences (point 1)? If so, which were the powerful belief systems? What proportion of the 20 scores tended to fall into the midrange? What did these scores indicate about the kinds of influences that make up a wide-ranging set of beliefs? Thus, what had started out as a simple questionnaire about the content of analysts' beliefs developed into an instrument for ascertaining the force of those beliefs.

When, at a later date, I became engrossed in the question of pluralism in psychoanalysis, it occurred to me that the various results of the statistical analyses of the P.O.Q. might throw light on the contemporary debate on pluralism and unity within the discipline. I had been able to use the results to determine the patterns, content, range, and strength of analysts' preconscious beliefs. What sorts of beliefs do pluralists hold? Are they strongly influenced by a number of thinkers and ideas, or do they take a more moderate approach to a wide variation of theories? Do some beliefs preclude a pluralist attitude?

BACKGROUND AND DEVELOPMENT OF THE INTERVIEW PROTOCOL

This protocol—the 27 dimensions of technique shown in Appendix 1—which I used to organize the semidirected interview/discussions with the 65 analysts in Britain and the United States, constituted the main focus of study and research, both historical and methodological. By comparison, the P.O.Q. was a short, subsidiary task. For two years I pursued a chronological reading of everything I could find on transference and interpretation from 1895 until 1988. I spent one year of this period reading Freud's writings on subjects relating to transference. As discussed in the chapters that follow, Freud held many views on transference. Like many later authors, he oscillated between the historical and the relational dimensions of transference. Sometimes he focused on the unconscious origins of transference that sprang from instinctual impulses within the individual; at other times, he emphasized the patient's powerful relationship to her or his doctor.

Of course, I soon found that it was impossible to read exclusively on transference. My reading branched into all the concepts that are represented by the 27 headings that I used in the interview/discussions with the 65 analysts. Prior to the selection of these 27 central dimensions, I had drawn up a preliminary list of 12 main categories of transference with approximately 120 subcategories reflecting refinements in both the definition of the concept of transference and the use and technique of transference interpretation in clinical practice. To simplify this list, I then drew a map of what I called "clusters of belief." This map is shown on Table 1. During my literature search, I noticed that particular ideas or concepts were frequently associated. For example, when I read a paper on, say, the transference neurosis, I would find myself reacquainting myself with the same literature that I had covered when reading a paper on the treatment alliance or on transference as resistance. Groups of concepts were linked with specific kinds of interpretations. My preliminary research revealed five sets of "family resemblances" or networks of concepts and the implications of these for interpretive practices.

To this point, my research had been largely of a theoretical nature. I then conducted a number of pilot studies to explore both the methodology that might organize my investigation and the kinds of response I might expect from contemporary psychoanalysts. The search for a suitable methodology led to a review of a number of empirical studies of transference from the mid-50s to the present. Here I was looking at the kinds of quantitative measures used by researchers. I found that these empirical studies could be classified into four groups: 1) studies of the degree of agreement among judges as to the presence of transference where transference was defined in terms of repetition; 2) studies of the similarity between a patient's experiences of his parents, on one hand, and of his therapist on the other; 3) studies of the relationship between the presence of transference and/or transference interpretation, on one hand, and therapeutic outcome on the other; and 4) more recent studies of the relationship between the patient's transference and the therapist's countertransference. This last group of studies paralleled the shift that was already taking place toward a more relational perspective on how psychotherapy works.

One problem pervaded these empirical studies relating to the ratable unit of study. Definitions of transference were either too narrow or too general to apply to the clinical data. The lack of clarity in the initial definitions of transference and interpretation contributed to the ambiguity of many of the results. These definitional problems, however, only confirmed my interest in finding a way to elicit information about the ways analysts formulate their clinical interventions, that is, their preconscious, or implicit, definitions of what they do. My next task was to experiment with various methodologies that might be appropriate to this kind of exploratory study: for example, questionnaires, directed or

Table 1
Clusters of Beliefs/Theoretical Concepts

NON/EXTRA TRANSFERENCE	TRANSF. & OBJECT-RELATIONSHIPS	TRANSFERENCE AS MANIFESTATION OF DEATH INSTINCT	HERE & NOW TRANSFERENCE	NARCISSISTIC TRANSFERENCES
TREATMENT ALLIANCE	TRANSFERENCE SITUATION/SETTING V. TRANSF.	NEGATIVE TRANSFERENCE	TRANSFERENCE IN SYSTEMS CS. & PRE-CS. PRESENT UCS.	SELF-OBJECT TRANSFERENCES
TRANSFERENCE NEUROSIS	RELATIONSHIP (DWW, Balint, e.g., holding)	PRIMITIVE ORAL TRANSFERENCE	TRANSFERENCE & CENSORSHIP	TRANSFERENCE AS REPRESENTATION OF DEFICIT
POSITIVE TRANSFERENCE	TRANSF. OF EARLY MOTHER–INFANT RELATIONSHIP (Spitz, DWW)	TRANSF. OF EARLIEST RELATION TO MOTHER AS BREAST	ALLUSIONS TO TRANSFERENCE	TRANSFERENCE AS RESPONSE TO FAILURES OF EMPATHY
UNOBJECTIONABLE FRIENDLY TRANSFERENCE	TRANSF. & BORDERLINE/PSYCHOTIC PATIENTS	TRANSFERENCE AS PROJECTIVE IDENTIFICATION 2 types: evacuation communication	TRANSFERENCE & CONFLICT	COUNTER-TRANSFERENCE AS ANALYST'S FAILURES OF EMPATHY
TRANSFERENCE AS DISTORTION (Greenson)	TRANSFERENCE & CORRECTIVE EMOTIONAL EXPERIENCE	TRANSFERENCE & AVOIDANCE OF TRUTH	TRANSFERENCE & RESISTANCE (Gill)	COUNTER-TRANSFERENCE AS ANALYST'S NARCISSISTIC TRANSFERENCE
TRANSFERENCE AS DISPLACEMENT (Ferenczi)	TRANSFERENCE & DEVELOPMENTAL DEFICIT	PSYCHOTIC/BORDERLINE TRANSFERENCE	TRANSFERENCE V RECONSTRUCTION	TRANSFERENCE & INTERSUBJECTIVITY
TRANSFERENCE AS DEFENSE	TRANSFERENCE & ROLE REVERSAL	TRANSFERENCE OF PART-OBJECT RELATIONSHIPS		TRANSFERENCE AS DERAILMENT OF DEVELOPMENT
TRANSFERENCE OF DEFENSE	TRANSFERENCE & ACTUALIZATION OF ROLES	EFFECTIVE/CORRECT INTERPRETATIONS		
DEFENSE AGAINST TRANSFERENCE	COUNTER-TRANSFERENCE AS OBJECT RELATIONSHIP	EROTICIZED TRANSFERENCE		
TRANSFERENCE & EXTERNALIZATION	RECONSTRUCTION OF EARLY FAILURES IN MOTHERING			
TRANSFERENCE & RESISTANCE	EXTRATRANSFERENCE			
RECONSTRUCTION AS HISTORICAL TRUTH				

Practical Implications
Analyst's Interpretations

REF. TO 'REAL' RELATIONSHIP BETWEEN ANAL. AND PT.	INTERPS. AIMED AT CREATION OF ANALYTIC ENVIRONMENT OR HOLDING ENVIRONMENT	INTERPS. OF DESTRUCTIVE FANTASIES TOWARD ANALYST	INTERP. TO ACHIEVE NARRATIVE COHERENCE	INTERP. OF NARCISSISTIC RAGE AS RESPONSE TO ANALYST'S FAILURES
EXTRA-TRANSF. INTERPS.	INTERPS. ADDRESSED TO INFANTILE/PSYCHOTIC PT.	INTERP. OF PUTTING FEELING/THOUGHTS INTO ANALYST AS AVOIDANCE OF PAIN	RECONSTRUCTION TO DISSOLVE HERE & NOW TRANSF.	INTERPS. ADDRESSED TO DEFICITS IN STRUCTURE OF SELF
INTERPS. TO PT.'S EGO, RATIONAL PART	USE OF SILENCE	INTERP. OF PUTTING FEELINGS/THOUGHTS INTO ANALYST AS COMMUNICATION	INTERP. AT POINT OF RESISTANCE	INTERPS. OF POLARITY BETWEEN GRANDIOSE AND DEFICIENT SELF
INTERPS. ADDRESSING PT.'S IDENTIFICATION WITH ANALYST	INTERPS. OF ENACTMENT OF WHAT PT. IS TRYING TO DO TO ANALYST AND GET ANALYST TO DO	INTERP. OF PARTS OF PT.'S SELF	INTERPS. AIMED AT PLAUSIBILITY FROM PT.'S POINT OF VIEW	INTERPS. AIMED TO CREATE SELF-OBJECT TIE
INTERPS. FOSTERING TOLERANCE TO UNDESIRABLE PTS. OF SELF, ID IMPULSES	INTERP. OF AGGRESSION AS REACTION	USE OF COUNTER-TRANSF. AS RESPONSE TO PROJECTIVE IDENTIFICATION	INTERPS. OF SHAME, SELF-ESTEEM, HUMILIATION	EXTRA-TRANSF. INTERPS. OF OTHERS AS MIRRORING OR DISRUPTING PT.'S SELF-EXPERIENCE
INTERPS. AIMED AT ESTABLISHING WORKING ALLIANCE LEADING TO TRANSF. NEUROSIS	INTERP. OF ANALYST'S FAILURE	INTERP. OF PT.'S FANTASIES OF PROCESS OF INTERP. (e.g., swallowing)	INTERPS. AIMED AT PT.'S RESPONSES TO ANALYST'S INTERPRETATIONS (Gill, Racker)	INTERPS. AIMED AT BUILDING PSYCHIC STRUCTURES
INTERP. OF INFANTILE WISHES	USE OF COUNTER-TRANSFERENCE	INTERP. OF ACTING-OUT IN SESSION	INTERPS. OF PT.'S CONFLICT OVER TRANSFERENCE	
INTERP. OF INFANTILE IMPULSES	RECONSTRUCTION OF PAST AS ENACTED IN ANALYTIC FAILURE	INTERP. OF ACTING IN		
INTERPS. OF RESISTANCE TO TRANSFERENCE	ACTUAL HOLDING & GRATIFICATION	INTERP. OF AVOIDING TRUTH AND UNDERSTANDING		
INTERPS. OF EROTIC IMPULSES		INTERP. OF SILENCE AS AVOIDANCE		

open-ended interviews, or the ratings of selected excerpts from case reports demonstrating transference interpretations. In the final protocol for the semidirected interview, I used the findings from one of these pilot studies; in this study, analysts were asked both to rate samples of transference interpretations drawn from American and British psychoanalytic journals and to give examples of interpretations from their own practices. The interview protocol aimed to bridge the gap between theoretical constructs and interpretive practices as reported in the literature and in clinical discussions.

These empirical studies (including my own pilot studies), however, did not address the analysts' working models of what they believe and do. Thus the final questionnaire addresses two levels: 1) the analysts' attitudes toward central dimensions of technique and 2) the details of what they say and do. For example, the question in which analysts were asked whether they prefaced their interpretations with a "perhaps," "maybe," "I think," or "I wonder if" threw further light on more theoretical positions on whether interpretations were aimed at the identification of psychic truth or reality or were put forward as hypotheses. Here I was aiming at the articulation of a third, preconscious level of organization, spanning theoretical and technical attitudes and therapeutic actions.

My experiences interviewing analysts of different orientations in the four cities of the two countries increased my awareness of cultural differences over and above those elicited by the topics discussed in the questionnaire. For example, the British Kleinian analysts and many of the older analysts in New York and San Francisco were quick to respond to my letters inviting them to participate in the project. The interviews with the British analysts and the older American analysts were also more leisurely, often taking place in the evening or during the weekend. In Los Angeles, where the majority of analysts work on a 45-minute hour and often see patients "back to back" without a break, the interviews were more rushed and sometimes took place over two sessions. The majority of the American analysts who had contributed to the field by writing books or papers referred to their work during the interview, with the clear expectation that I would be familiar with their publications. None of the British analysts expressed these expectations, even when they had made important contributions to the field. Although the atmosphere of some of the American interviews was more pressured, the American analysts appeared to be more widely read and more articulate than many of the British analysts. They tended to be familiar with the British literature, whereas the majority of British analysts were not conversant with the American psychoanalytic literature. On balance, the elderly and more senior American analysts seemed to be more interested in the research project than were the younger American analysts. This was not so in Britain; there, younger analysts expressed much greater interest in research than did senior members of the British Society.

Finally, a rating scale was developed by a number of colleagues and me. The 65 interview transcripts were given to four independent raters who had undertaken psychoanalytic training and had academic backgrounds in clinical psychology. All 65 interviews were also rated by me. A reliability study of the 27 rating scales that were used to rate the 65 interviews showed a high degree of interrater reliability. (The pooled coefficient based on the Spearman Rank-Order Correlation measures was 0.88.) The raters were asked to assess the analysts' responses to questions as these had been discussed throughout the *entire* interview. Thus, the raters scored the discussions on the basis of an overall estimate of several statements and examples. For instance, when talking about specific questions, many of the analysts gave clinical examples of their interventions that amplified, but at times contradicted, earlier responses. Again, I believe we were "tapping into" preconscious levels of thinking.

The ratings of the interviews and the answers to the P.O.Q. were then subjected to a number of statistical analyses. Univariate and multivariate statistical analyses were performed on the ratings of both the interviews and the P.O.Q. With respect to the P.O.Q., the influence of both declared orientation and geographical location was examined on each of the 20 items (the sources of influence), using one-way analyses of variance. Principle components analysis was then applied in order to identify the main components of variability. The factor structure that was then extracted was further subjected to a varimax rotation so as to maximize unique factor loadings. To examine further the extent to which the individual analysts could be meaningfully grouped according to their responses to the P.O.Q., a cluster analysis by cases was performed. (Cluster analysis is based on a matrix of Euclidian distances between "cases" and an algorithm that aims to form clusters on the basis of the two closest cases; the distance from the two closest cases is then gradually increased to include all the cases in the cluster. In the context of my research, the term "cases" refers to the individual analysts in the sample.) The results of the cluster analysis confirmed those of the factor analysis in that two groups of analysts, those of a Kleinian/Bionian orientation and those of a Kohutian/self-psychological orientation, appeared to be the most cohesive groups, acknowledging much less influence by any other sources of influence. The cluster analysis also highlighted differences between American and British analysts.

Similar statistical analyses were also performed on the rated inter-view/discussions with the 65 analysts. The results of the two different sets of data were also examined to delineate associations between orien-tation and aspects of technique discussed during the interviews. For instance, one-way analysis of variance was used to find out whether the principle dimensions that emerged from the factor analysis of the P.O.Q. were associated with each of the 27 items on the interview rat-ing schedule. For example, what were the respective attitudes of analysts of a Kleinian/Bionian orientation and those of a Kohutian/self-psycho-logical orientation toward the treatment alliance or the interpretation of dreams? Each of the 27 items was also analyzed in relation to geo-graphical location. What do Los Angeles analysts think of the clinical relevance of the death instinct? Multivariate analyses were also per-formed on the results of the two sets of data to clarify the interrelation-ships between analysts' theoretical models and the explicit as well as implicit (preconscious) working models underlying distinctive patterns of technique. Here both group orientation and the influence of individ-ual thinkers and theories were associated with patterns of technique as these emerged from the analyses of the interview discussions. For instance, the cluster analysis revealed patterns of association between individual analysts that were not just dependent on declared theoretical orientation. Geographical location, experience, and training with key figures played an important role in articulating attitudes toward specific areas of clinical practice and technique. To provide further confirma-tion of the factor and cluster analyses of the two sets of data, a third sta-tistical analysis, a Canonical Correlation, was performed. This analysis demarcated similar patterns of association between theoretical influ-ence and interpretive technique.

In broad overview, the univariate analyses of the two sets of results emerging from the two data sources (the P.O.Q. and the interview rat-ings) distinguished specific patterns of ideas, linked with the historical and geographical influences from which the individual psychoanalytic "cultures" have evolved. The multivariate analyses identified the interrelationships between specific theoretical influences and techni-cal practices and, moreover, distinguished the comparative power of individual sources of influence. Needless to say, the statistical proce-dures provided an invaluable check on more impressionistic readings of the interviews and the P.O.Q. score sheets. Moreover, in several instances, the results of the data analyses suggested new connections that either had not occurred to me or had not otherwise been noted in the literature. Chapters 2–5 of this book reflect those sets of concepts which contribute most strongly to the differentiation of the groups of analysts. In the chapters that follow, however, distinctions between groups become progressively less defined and more complex. From chapter 6 onward, the focus is on descriptions of preconscious networks of beliefs as these organize analysts' interventions.

In presenting the results of this research, I have elected for the most part to concentrate on the interview data themselves, rather than on the statistics. For ultimately it is in what analysts say about their use of concepts that we can discover the preconscious connections between different ideas. Thus, except where otherwise noted, the statistical analyses enter into my presentation rather as guides to the organization and selection of the complex topics discussed in the interviews. The results of these analyses are embedded in the various groupings and subgroupings presented in the text and are not reported in the book. The reader who wishes to review the statistical material can contact me.

It will be apparent that I have written the book with a number of different questions in mind. And readers will find their own ways, depending on their particular interests. The interviews could be explored in terms of their testing of a number of hypotheses: for example, do the statements of these 65 analysts conform to any of the basic tenets of psychoanalysis, principles such as the rule of free association, Freud's rules of dream formation, and the universality of the Oedipus complex? Intersecting with this approach, other questions arise concerning the history of psychoanalysis and the ways in which the field has changed over the last 100 years. The information conveyed in the book can also be read as a descriptive account of the diversity that exists in psychoanalytic practice today. In this way, the book directly addresses the pluralistic nature of psychoanalysis as well as the monistic theories within that pluralism. The interview excerpts invite readers to meet the analysts and to appreciate their thoughtfulness; the interviews are a testament to the complex and individual ways analysts think about their work. The title, *The Analyst's Preconscious*, describes my attempt to capture some of the philosophical beliefs, the personal relationships, the important psychoanalytic theories and experiences, that animate therapeutic responsiveness. Much of the day, analysts work on the fly, with little space to reflect on the questions discussed in this book. So, perhaps, the book provides some information about therapeutic efficacy—about what analysts are actually doing, how they respond, and why, given the chance to reflect, they do speak and think in their own unique ways.

A final note about the characters you will meet while reading this book. The analysts whose views are followed throughout the book have been given fictitious names so that readers can build up profiles of the ways in which individual analysts integrate a number of discrete topics. To protect the anonymity of individual analysts, lengthy, direct interview quotes are not given. Other analysts are referred to but are not named, since their views are quoted to illustrate the consistency of a particular viewpoint. The recorded discussions show clearly the plurality and diversity of beliefs and practices that exist within the profession. Some beliefs or systems of belief conflict; some are incompatible; others are incommensurable. For sure, there is no underlying, unifying master plan or descriptive metalanguage. And yet there are many consistencies and agreements both because analysts participate in a particular culture and because they use psychological concepts that are part of our ordinary language. It is these preconscious networks of belief and practice that are described in the following chapters.

Chapter 2

．₴₴．

Pluralism and Belief

The current debate on pluralism versus unity, divergence versus common ground, in psychoanalysis relates to beliefs—conscious, unconscious, and preconscious—concerning truth, objectivity, and reality (Hamilton, 1993). The positions we take on convergence and divergence, as supporters of solidarity versus incommensurability, have much to do with the ways we construe truth. Since Robert Wallerstein (1988) opened this debate in 1987 at a Congress of the International Psychoanalytical Association held in Montreal, the topic of "One Psychoanalysis or Many?" has been widely discussed both at conferences and in leading psychoanalytic journals. I shall not attempt to marshal and summarize all the arguments, as a thorough literature review would compete with the aim of this investigation; but I shall refer to some of the key positions and players as they contribute to the exposition of how central concepts are used both in the consulting room and when psychoanalysts discuss their work with one another.

It was natural that discussion of the desirability and/or actuality of pluralism and unity in psychoanalysis rekindled interest in the truth-value of psychoanalytic propositions. Pluralism—connoting many, numerous, a multiplicity—is often confused with relativism. While pluralism can be given fairly exact definitions, definitions of relativism tend to be looser, reflective perhaps of the term they define! A relativist stance can mean that truth is relative to a belief system; or that any belief is as good as another; or that, since truth is equivocal, belief systems are self-referential and, as such, incommensurable. Relativism and pluralism are easily confused since both positions deny that there are universal truths and methods of inquiry. Both oppose

19

grand, overarching, monistic systems of thought. Nevertheless, the two are distinguished in a number of important ways. Although pluralists, such as the German 18th-century thinker Johann Gottfried Herder, emphasize that "each culture has its own center of gravity" (cited in Jahanbegloo, 1992, p. 35), many also believe in a common core of values that cross cultures: values such as courage, a sense of belonging, a need for security have been embraced by societies throughout history. Pluralism has limits; it stops short of cynicism. Pluralists are unlikely to reside within one world view and are skeptical of those who do. They are not romantics, impassioned by one ideal. Different goals and cultures can present alternatives of equal value. Conflict and compromise are constitutive of the pluralist position. Ways of life compete with one another and cannot be combined so that, very often, uncomfortable choices have to be made. Yet, by and large, pluralists tend to believe that we have a primary conception of the external world, of something independent of, and other than, ourselves. They do not believe in the primacy of subjective reality. Nevertheless, that they believe that there is a world out there independent of mind does not imply objective knowledge of that world.

The frank espousal of pluralism and/or relativism by psychoanalysts seems to many to threaten the basic assumptions of the unity of science as well as standards of verification, replicability, and objectivity traditionally associated with the sciences. To sort out these problems, a number of analysts have turned to philosophy, borrowing philosophical theories of truth—notably, the "correspondence," "coherence," and "pragmatic" theories of truth. According to the coherence theory, truth derives from the internal consistency of beliefs rather than from a correspondence with facts that are external or independent of mind. The correspondence theory holds just the opposite. There are several versions of the pragmatic theory of truth: truth means assertibility or justifiability or expediency but does not derive from the representation of, or confrontation with, facts external to mind. Psychoanalysts have applied these philosophical theories to all levels of psychoanalytic discourse: to the highest metalevel of theory, to theories of technique, as well as to specific interpretations made by psychoanalysts in the clinical situation.

The discussion of pluralism comes at a time when the truth-values of psychoanalytic propositions are separately undergoing scrutiny. Adolf Grünbaum's (1984) critical work The Foundations of Psychoanalysis challenged the scientific respectability of the psychoanalytic enterprise, specifically Freud's theory of repression. Psychoanalysts who were interested in examining their discipline from another intellectual perspective were disturbed by Grünbaum's arguments. I will not grapple here with the complexities of his reasoning except to point out the unique impact he has had on philosophically minded psychoanalysts. No other philosopher is quoted to the same degree. Since 1984, however, a number of philosophical and psychoanalytic critiques of Grünbaum's approach have been published (Hopkins, 1988; Wollheim, 1993). These authors focus their criticism on what they believe to be a misunderstanding of psychoanalysis, particularly the "elasticity" of psychoanalytic concepts and their links with "the ordinary, the commonsense, conception of the mind" (Wollheim, 1993, p.92). Arguably, Grünbaum's reasoning has, in turn, been misunderstood by analysts. Nevertheless, Grünbaum-like standards of verification have motivated a significant number of analysts to abandon correspondence standards of truth—where individual statements or whole theories must face the tribunal of facts that are independent of mind and language. Instead, these analysts have taken up a looser, less confrontational, hermeneutic theory in which truth derives from the internal coherence, thematic affinity, and consistency of a large number of propositions. For instance, a web or cluster of coherent propositions can constitute a valid theory as well as the "narrative truth" of a patient's associations. The problem of facts, of externality, is simply dropped.

If, for a long time, the correspondence theory guaranteed the unity of psychoanalysis, the coherence theory seems to have undermined faith in convergence. During the last 10 years or so, there has been a thrust toward finding a metanarrative, or overarching, theory to encompass the many competing theoretical perspectives. Thus, the last three International Congresses of Psychoanalysis have focused on themes relating to finding a common ground. Viewed historically, this search for commonality can be seen as a response to the uncertainty about the status of psychoanalysis both as an intellectual discipline and as a mental health profession. The crisis has been particularly acute in North America, where, until recently, the medical establishment has controlled the selection and training of future practitioners. As various central concepts sacred to psychoanalysis as science have fallen out of favor, through either direct challenge or disuse, psychoanalysis has fallen prey to fears associated with relativism: if there is no objectivity, no causality, no regard for human beings as objects, no uncontaminated neutrality of the observer, no explanations of motivation as being drive derivative, then what is left? Is there nothing above or beyond a hodgepodge of solipsistic, internally coherent schemas? Must we choose between psychoanalysis as science and as metaphysics? Without some semblance of convergence and parsimony, aspirations to join the scientific community are frustrated, and the organizational-administrative structure of psychoanalysis is threatened. Confusing pluralism with relativism, psychoanalysts—especially those involved in the administration of psychoanalytic institutions—fear that psychoanalysis will degenerate into anarchy.

The fix in which psychoanalysis finds itself is not unique to the discipline. In the recent history of ideas, relativism and pluralism made their appearance within the same time span. The complexity of the issues involved is well described by the historian of ideas Isaiah Berlin. In an illuminating account of the historicist ideas of Johann Herder and Giambattista Vico, Berlin discusses the emergence of relativism and outlines some of the distinguishing features of pluralism. His discussion is highly pertinent to current debates on divergence and convergence in psychoanalysis. Berlin observes that, with the rise of the new nation-states in the 16th century and the Reformation, when both the universal authority of Roman Law and the universal authority of the Church of Rome were called in question,

> the spectre of relativism makes its dreaded appearance, and with it the beginning of the dissolution of faith in the very concept of universally valid goals, at least in the social and political sphere. This was accompanied, in due course, by a sense that there might be not only a historical or political but some logical flaw in the very idea of a universe equally acceptable to communities of different origin, with different traditions, character, outlook, concepts, categories, views of life [quoted in Berlin, 1992a, p. 33].

Berlin also notes that the implications of this shift in the belief in universal values were not fully spelt out, largely because of the enormous triumph at that very time of the natural sciences. With so many revolutionary discoveries in the areas of mathematics, physics, geology, and astronomy by such men of genius as Galileo and Newton, it seemed possible to imagine that a chaotic mass of observational data could be explained by a limited number of laws, which would determine precisely the movement and position of objects in the material world. It was hoped that the same methods could be applied to human matters—to morals, politics, and the organization of society—so that all observational data could be organized into a single, coherent, perfectly orderly system (Berlin, 1992b). Even the Romantic thinkers who reacted against the central ideas of the Age of Reason affirmed the belief in a universal "natural man." For, beneath the covers of reason and civilization, we find "man" in a state of nature.

The "spectre of relativism" appeared early in the history of psychoanalysis because of the close connection between transference and hypnosis. Fears of suggestibility and suggestion as a causal agent were closely linked to fears of relativism. Since Freud, psychoanalysts have made concerted efforts to purify the field and their professional lives of this unwelcome "contaminant." Ultimately, these efforts have meant that some psychoanalytic practitioners have attempted to rid the psychoanalytic encounter of its relational—that is, emotional or affective—properties. The contemporary philosopher Jonathan Bennett (1985) has defined "part of the philosopher's task" as the capacity "to take warm, familiar aspects of the human condition and look at them coldly and with the eye of a stranger" (p. 619). Here, a parallel can be drawn between Bennett's view of one aspect of the philosopher's task and Freud's view of the "neutral" psychoanalyst as epitomized in contemporary accounts of the American "classical" analyst, accounts, to be sure, that are often carried to the level of caricature. If human beings can be described objectively and impersonally, then perhaps we can be rescued from "the spectre of relativism."

A historical study of how central psychoanalytic concepts, for example transference and resistance, have been shaped by the fear of relativism suggests not only that "the eye of a stranger" can misperceive, but that 100 years of practice have demonstrated the hopelessness of the task. The fear of the "human," the emotional, relational, cultural nature of psychoanalysis created unrealistic and unrealizable goals. It is as if we have been trying to study human beings as if they were not human beings but, rather, mental structures, underlying principles, biological forces, or affective outbursts. We have been attempting to study them by nonhuman methods. Indeed, this search for something meta or latent, beyond the immediate, has led psychoanalysts to introduce a whole set of extra, "nonanalytic" ideas, such as the "real relationship," the "holding environment," "parameters," "supportive" techniques, to account for what most of them find themselves doing and saying, their theories notwithstanding. These extra-analytic concepts aver the relational aspect of psychoanalysis, whilst keeping the conceptual armamentarium of core beliefs uncontaminated.

But that is only one side of the story. Throughout the history of psychoanalysis, including in Freud's writings, there have been swings away from rationalism toward a more romantic, emotional, and passionate position. Recently, American psychoanalysis has witnessed a new backlash against the rationalism of the "classical" practitioners. Many self psychologists, for example, passionately defend the passions, and many intersubjectivists reject the idea of objectivity. If the unity of psychoanalysis cannot be maintained through appeal to neutral, scientist standards and the field cannot live with the spectre of relativism, then surely some sense must be made of pluralism. Much of the trouble with current arguments over unity and pluralism in psychoanalysis stems from the *polarization* of positions and the either/or framework in which questions are asked. Consider, for example, the statement that the diversity exemplified in clinical practice nevertheless converges at the highest metapsychological level. Leo Rangell (1988), a strong proponent of this position, has described it in terms of his concept of "total composite psychoanalysis." Psychoanalysts who favor this stance often subscribe to Freud's instinct theory, in which all derivatives can be traced to the "black box" of the basic organizing principles of the life and death instincts. There is a master plan that represents and explains what lies at the root of our being.

Then consider the alternative position that theories are "metanarratives" or "mere metaphors" whose diversity need not affect the putative commonality that exists at the empirical level of clinical practice. (Versions of this view have been proposed by Heinz Kohut and Robert Wallerstein.) In my view, both positions are irrational in that they imply a severance of belief from action; moreover, neither conforms to the ways most analysts practice. For this is not how belief works. Beliefs seep into experience. Beliefs rarely exist in isolation; complex interrelationships connect beliefs with one another; in addition, I cannot *choose* my beliefs in the simple sense that I might choose to eat meat or fish for dinner. Moreover, beliefs depend on social connections. They are linked to people with whom we have formed strong ties, both loving and hating.

Thus, although many psychoanalysts agree that pluralism is here to stay, it is not easy to spell out the connections between the ideology of pluralism and its application in clinical practice. Psychoanalysis has developed into a conglomerate of monistic systems that compete with one another, each advancing itself as the most comprehensive explanation of human pathology and development. The avowed commitment to pluralism is a very recent development. It is fired in part by a weariness with the recurring ideological wars that have plagued the growth of psychoanalysis. Clearly, pluralism cannot promote one theory, leader, or school. By comparison, bipolar theories, theories that are more black and white, seem to have greater appeal than theories with grey areas.

The development of psychoanalysis in Britain provides a unique example of the politics of a pluralistic society. There, for almost 80 years, three distinct groups have worked together, albeit discordantly at times, in one society. Many of the early British pioneers were pluralists.

In keeping with their academic and social backgrounds and their political beliefs, pioneers such as James Strachey, Marjorie Brierley, and Sylvia Payne brought to psychoanalysis an undogmatic, liberal, and pragmatic attitude. Thus, in England, we find pluralism at the level of groups and, within that context, a "middle group" that can be said to embody pluralism as a world view. Pluralism, however, does not have the mass appeal of bipolar systems, and the "middle group" of psychoanalysts, which developed into the contemporary British Independents, has not sustained an authoritative voice within British psychoanalysis. (The other two groups are formally designated as Kleinian and as Contemporary Freudian.) For, even in a pluralist society, monism tends to win out. Independents do not offer a grand explanatory scheme, and their force in the British Psychoanalytic Society has tended to be a mediating one between the Freudian and Kleinian systems. They have been called "terminally open minded." Eric Rayner (1991) describes this attitude more favorably: "it is the empirical tradition of open-mindedness which provides a core inspiration and ethic for the British Independents" (p. 9). This tradition goes hand in hand with a dislike of extremism. Reyner notes the traditional British antipathy toward both "complex, closed systems of theory" and the "enthusiastic ideology" of Romanticism and other charismatic movements (p. 8). Incidentally, my research results clearly indicate not only that Independent or eclectic analysts are not "terminally open minded," but also that specific influences organize and restrain their thinking. I use this example of the British Psychoanalytical Society to demonstrate the problems of survival for the pluralist position as it is lived out within a particular analytic institution at a particular period of history.

There are complex associations that link beliefs into a coherent point of view. Public statements do not necessarily reflect this complexity. For example, a psychoanalyst attending a conference on "One Psychoanalysis or Many?" is away from his patients (unless he is a training analyst!). He is not required to act, to make interpretations. He is at several removes from his daily work. Like the armchair philosopher, he can use his mind to set out arguments, clarify important questions, give reasons, and eliminate circular arguments. In sorting out muddles, he applies rules of logic that underlie ordinary language—laws such as those of the excluded middle and implication. (The coherence theory depends on applying basic logical rules such as *either x or y*—otherwise no theory would be excluded—and *if x, then y*—believing y follows from x.) Back in the consulting room, analysts do not always enjoy this liberty. They speak, act, and respond emotionally. Experiences are organized under different descriptions, many of which are not logically consistent with one another. A fully consistent position, encompassing all levels of the analyst's theoretical, practical, and collegial life, is probably the mark of an ideologue. But less than complete consistency does not mean that clinical practice is adrift from theoretical belief.

Imagine, for example, an analyst who interprets with the same degree of scepticism or scrutiny that he might convey at a psychoanalytic conference. "As a Kleinian, I find myself thinking that you are doing something to me, trying to make me hate you . . . but, as a self psychologist, I think you are taking an adversarial position with me in order to more clearly delineate yourself." A therapist without an anchor, with only shifting perspectives at her disposal, will be of little use to someone who has lost his way in the world. Some of the analysts I interviewed described strange and disorienting experiences of personal therapy with analysts who changed orientation: although the outcome was sometimes beneficial, what mattered to the analysand was the experience of the analyst's courage and strength of conviction, his or her faith in the new belief-system, not the system itself.

When an analyst changes orientation—no longer a Kleinian, he becomes a Kohutian—he gives up a whole network of beliefs, amongst which are a number of central or key beliefs. Central beliefs are the most resistant to change; as long as these remain unchallenged, the analyst may continue to work within a particular system. For Kleinians, central beliefs might include innate envy and destructiveness, and reparation. It would be difficult for a Kleinian who might give way on other concepts to surrender these central beliefs without becoming a non-Kleinian. A central belief that might make someone a non-Kleinian is the belief that destructiveness is reactive. It is only when central beliefs are shaken that an analyst will openly question his allegiance to a particular orientation group. As he moves over to another belief-system, he may or may not make a conscious effort to drop the peripheral concepts that cluster around the central core. These changes usually take place at different levels and can occur preconsciously. Because of the complex interrelationships that connect beliefs with one another both centrally and peripherally, change occurs slowly and often outside of conscious awareness. By the time a person is able to make an explicit statement about his change of belief, it may seem to him and to his colleagues that he has undergone a conversion experience. In the popular, Kuhnian vernacular, a "paradigm-shift" has taken place. Central beliefs are the last to go, and, when they do, the results can seem sudden, dramatic, and total.

If, as the foregoing discussion might suggest, it is difficult to work one's way out of a system of beliefs, it is also challenging to work one's way in to a network of concepts that one does not use. An effort of imagination is required to grasp the actions and ritual forms of speech of a different analytic culture. Pluralism makes demands on our imagination. For, to imagine or enter into someone else's point of view, I have to imagine that person doing and saying very specific things. Vague imagination does not count. The more deeply I enter into the life of another person, the greater the demands on my imagination as my projective powers are restricted. To imagine *myself* being X feeling certain emotions and acting in specific ways is different from imagining *being* X feeling and acting in these ways. At a certain point, this imaginative exercise may reach a limit. (This distinction between identifying myself with X, through introjection or projection, and imagining *being* X is explored more fully in chapter 8, on countertransference.)

For example, in discussing the usefulness of Klein's concept of envy, a self psychologist in Los Angeles declared that he had never seen a case of envy in his consulting room. What did he mean? He meant that there was no way, using the language of self psychology, that he could describe the behaviors of his patients in terms of envy. In addition, I assume, he was saying that he did not want to, or could not by any effort of will and imagination, enter into the mind of a psychoanalyst who would describe his patients that way.

Pluralism makes demands on our ability to tolerate "uneasy equilibrium," it tests our linguistic competence, it stretches our interpretative skills. Also, as Berlin (1992a) has observed, pluralism builds on, and fosters, a level of scepticism that curbs Romantic ideals that all will be answered. Berlin points to the negative, as well as positive, "heritage of Romanticism" when he describes the ways in which romantic ideals have inspired extremist political movements as well as liberal ones. In the history of psychoanalysis, new ideas often have a romantic appeal and these sometimes rigidify around a charismatic leader. It seems that healthy scepticism is an essential ingredient of pluralism.

In discussing the art and science of psychoanalysis, John Bowlby (1978) pointed out the two very different mental attitudes required of the psychoanalyst in his roles as scientist and practitioner. He describes these attitudes as *scepticism* and *faith*. To be effective, the psychoanalytic practitioner must have faith and hope; such qualities are therapeutic. This means that the practitioner is prepared to act as though certain principles were valid. Though open to correction, he must nevertheless have conviction. The absence of these qualities may make an excellent research worker but one ill suited to therapeutic work. Conversely, as scientist, the psychoanalyst must exercise a high degree of criticism toward the beliefs on which he acts. He stands apart, using everyday logical and rational arguments, sometimes attempting to survey one set of beliefs from the position of another set of beliefs, much as a nondogmatic Kleinian might attempt to restate his interpretations of a patient's deadness in terms of maternal failure rather than envious spoiling. But, once the therapist is back in the consulting room, these basic beliefs tell him *what* is so, not the reasons *why* he thinks or says what is so. In practice, for much of the time that the analyst interprets, something holds firm for him and judgment of his beliefs is in abeyance. He would not say, nor does he feel, that he *chooses* to believe that certain things are so.

When, however, people are invited to question their beliefs, as they were in responding both to the P.O.Q. and the semistructured interviews, they may find themselves articulating attitudes of which they were not fully aware. As described earlier, in filling out the P.O.Q., analysts engaged in the conscious execution of a task. They responded to questions about specific sources of influence but did not consider the nature of their beliefs as a whole. The research results indicate that some analysts are highly consistent in their range of beliefs, some are widely influenced, and some fall in between. The pattern of belief—that is, the degree of circumscription or breadth—can be distinguished logically from its content. Nevertheless, some beliefs seem to invite greater consistency than others; some theories are more compelling.

LINKS BETWEEN PATTERNS OF BELIEF AND PUBLICLY DECLARED ORIENTATION

What are the practical implications of the current trend toward pluralism as these are reflected in analysts' patterns of belief? The design of the P.O.Q. allows for a fairly simple discrimination between range, content, and force of a person's beliefs. Statistical measures can be applied that identify consistency of belief independently of content. This means that we can think of pluralism operationally as well as substantively, focusing exclusively on the range of beliefs that an individual allows himself to entertain. Having first established range as a baseline, it is then possible to consider whether some belief systems invite greater, in the sense of narrower, commitment than others. The empirical data can also be used to assess the extent to which an avowed commitment to pluralism, as implied by the position of British Independent and American eclectic analysts, is reflected in a broadened scope of influences. In the context of pluralism and monism in

clinical practice, the patterns of response of those who openly acknowledge a change in theoretical orientation are particularly illuminating.
It appears that a change of belief is unlikely to widen the range of a person's beliefs. And the degree of self-consistency that a person shows
may or may not relate to a particular set of beliefs.

Statistical analysis (factor analysis) of the responses to the P.O.Q.
yielded five distinct groups: developmental Freudian, classical
Freudian, Kleinian, Independent, and self-psychological. I refer to the
factor analysis here since the results reflect the five most coherent
groups in the sample of 65 analysts. It was, however, possible to make
much finer discriminations on a case-by-case basis using the analysts'
self-scores on the P.O.Q. Although the factor structure of the questionnaire identified collections of psychoanalytic ideas that do indeed
commonly go together, the univariate and cluster analyses showed
that analysts of common declared orientations find their way to such
"labels" by slightly different routes. The empirical examination of the
questionnaire responses can be seen as a step in the direction away
from the common stereotyping of theoretical groups that goes on
within psychoanalytic circles. Analysts bring a particular analytic history to the group with which they are affiliated at a particular point in
time. For instance, the Independent cluster includes, as one might
expect, members of the British Society who formally designate themselves as belonging to the Independent group. But the cluster also
includes five members of the British Society who formally designate
themselves as Contemporary Freudian, three New York interpersonalists, as well as some Americans who consider themselves to be eclectic.

This internal discrimination and refinement of group labels was
exemplified by differences within the Freudian group. For the sake of
clarity, it is important to note that, for the last 15 years or so, British
Freudians have formally referred to their group as Contemporary
Freudian. The change reflects the relational and developmental, as well
as Kleinian, influences on contemporary Freudian thinking in Britain.
The shift can be traced to a key paper by Anne-Marie and Joseph
Sandler (1978). "On the Development of Object Relationships and
Affects." Although the British Freudians subsequently adopted the
label Contemporary Freudian in order to distinguish the group from a
more traditional Freudian position, a number of older British Freudians,
trained by and loyal to Anna Freud, fit the "classical Freudian" designation of this study. The labels "developmental" and "classical"
Freudian that I applied to the two Freudian groups that emerged from
the statistical analyses reflect differences in both the American and the
British Freudian groups. To avoid confusion in this presentation, I will

simply refer to analysts in the official Freudian group of the British Society as British Freudians rather than Contemporary Freudians.

Focusing first on range, I checked the questionnaires for three types of response: 1) a *narrow* range of theoretical influences; 2) a scattered or *wide* range of influences; and 3) the content and degree of influence acknowledged by analysts who are known to have *changed* their orientation. Having first classified the P.O.Q. score sheets according to range of beliefs, I then examined the links between publicly declared orientation and specific influences, that is, the 20 key thinkers/orientations listed as influences on the P.O.Q. This second analysis revealed distinct patterns of belief that crossed the boundaries of the analysts' declared orientations. In other words, it was possible to discriminate within publicly declared orientation groups and to trace individual patterns of influence. As noted, a few of the younger British Freudians were included in the independent cluster. Another portion of the British independents clustered on the edge of a Kleinian subgroup organized around one particular leading Kleinian analyst. It was then possible, using statistical measures, to look for associations between groups identified in the first analysis as narrow or broad and groups identified in the second analysis as belonging to specific subgroups reflecting unique patterns of influence by key figures or theories. In this way, associations between range and content could be demonstrated at the empirical level. Members of specific orientation groups, notably Kleinian and self-psychological, seemed to concentrate almost exclusively on the literature of their own orientation. A secondary and unexpected result of these empirical studies showed a marked difference in the range of influences acknowledged by the American and British analysts. Contrary to popular belief, American analysts read more widely than British analysts.

NARROW RANGES OF THEORETICAL INFLUENCES

I took as my starting point the two endpoints on the five-point scale. First, I selected those analysts who had high scores on the "not at all influenced" point of the scale (Point 1). My hypothesis was that an individual who categorically declared that he was unaffected by a large proportion of thinkers or theories might believe strongly in one or two highly consistent theories—for example, the ideas of Klein and Bion. A small group of four analysts declared no degree of influence by 13 of the 20 thinkers/orientations. This group can be said to represent the most highly consistent, or circumscribed, thinkers of the total number of 64 analysts who returned the P.O.Q.

Having identified the subgroup of four analysts who were not at all influenced by 13 of the 20 sources, I looked at the responses of these four analysts to the remaining seven items on the P.O.Q. Did their scores fall in the mid-range, indicating some degree of influence by seven different sources? Or did they fall toward the other end of the scale (Points 5 and 4)? How many sources influenced these analysts "to a very great extent"? If the scores indicated strong influence by one or two closely related beliefs (for example, American and British object relations), then associations might be found between the force of one or two central beliefs and the range of a person's beliefs. To answer this question, I used the scores to build profiles of the four analysts classified in the most highly consistent range. Since one of the four had changed orientation, his views are discussed in the next section. The range and content of the three other analysts from this subgroup are described in the following paragraphs.

Dr. Matheson is a senior training analyst in the British independent group. As might be expected, she was influenced to a great extent by one source, those of her own group. She was influenced to a considerable extent (Point 4) by all three Freudian models, as well as by Bion and Klein. (These accounted for the remaining 30% of her responses.) This somewhat classical set of influences in part reflects the formative years of training. Dr. Matheson trained in the late 1950s and early 1960s. She was one of the third generation of British analysts (many of whom had personal connections to Freud) who read Freud's writings with a freshness and interest that has waned today. Melanie Klein's ideas were highly influential and hotly debated in the British Society during the 1950s, and Dr. Matheson also attended Bion's clinical seminars. Since qualifying, this Independent analyst had worked in National Health Service settings and currently works at the Tavistock Clinic, where the majority of colleagues speak in Kleinian-Bionian terms.

The second analyst is a younger, more recently qualified member of the British Kleinian group. Predictably, she was influenced to "a very great extent" by the ideas of Klein and Bion. No other ideas had a strong effect on her thinking although she was somewhat influenced (Point 3) by all three Freudian models and by British Independent ideas.

The third analyst, also a Kleinian and one of the younger training analysts in the group, shows a similar profile. What is interesting about this analyst's responses is that she is the only Kleinian analyst to give the same weight to Freud's theories as to the ideas of Bion and Klein. Her interest in Anna Freud's ideas is also unique. These influences accounted for the six responses that fell outside the "not at all influenced" category. Thus, the content of her scores suggest that, within a narrow range, she used a repertoire of concepts different from that of other Kleinian colleagues. The majority of Kleinian analysts did not value Freud's topographical model but affirmed the usefulness of Freud's drive theory; this influence reflects the way contemporary Kleinians, following Melanie Klein and her successors Betty Joseph and Hanna Segal, use the concept of the death instinct in clinical practice. Very few Kleinians acknowledged British Independent ideas and, with two exceptions, they ignored the ideas of Anna Freud. These three profiles describe analysts who hold *circumscribed* sets of beliefs. The scores help to delineate the "monistic" thinkers in the sample of 65 analysts, those who tend to use one or two master texts and seem unfamiliar with, or uninterested in, new or foreign ideas.

To explore further the associations among range, force, and content of belief, I looked at the profiles of analysts whose scores fell just below these highly consistent thinkers. The group of four analysts referred to earlier (which included the analyst who had changed orientation) were those who declared no degree of influence by 13 sources. An additional five analysts stated that they were "not at all" influenced by between 10 and 12 sources. In other words, 50% to 60% of their responses scored on the first point of the scale. Three of these five analysts also had high scores on Point 4 of the scale—that is, the "very little influenced" category. The combined scores (on Points 4 and 5) of these three analysts showed that 80% of their responses were negative with respect to range of influence. The profiles of these three analysts were very similar to those of the subgroup of analysts described earlier as holding the most circumscribed sets of beliefs. With respect to the content of their strong beliefs, this second group selected the same five sources of influence: Klein, Bion, British Independent thinkers, and Freud's drive and structural theories. These five sources seem to characterize the theoretical stance of the classical British analyst. This "classical" analyst might be of an Independent or Kleinian orientation. The unifying characteristic of the profiles is that they portray a group of analysts who remain steeped in what might be called the master texts of psychoanalysis.

The profiles of the other two analysts with slightly lower scores in this second group of circumscribed thinkers are rather different. One, a more recently qualified British Kleinian adult analyst, was also a child analyst. She had trained and worked at the Tavistock Clinic. Like all the child analysts in this sample, she acknowledged a wider range of influences than any of the adult analysts in the Freudian and Kleinian groups. Although Klein, Bion, and Freud's drive theory had by far the strongest impact on her work, she was influenced to some degree by Freud's structural model, the work of Margaret Mahler (though not Anna Freud), by British object relations theory, and by Daniel Stern. As noted, very few British Kleinian analysts acknowledged any influence by independent thinkers. In the case of this child analyst, however, it is possible to surmise that, since John Bowlby spent 40 years of his life at the Tavistock Clinic, his work on attachment infiltrated the preconscious thinking of those who worked there for any appreciable length of time.

The second analyst, Dr. Friedland, is a senior Freudian training analyst in San Francisco. He is the only American analyst, and indeed the only self-identified Freudian analyst, to be classified in the group of "monistic" thinkers although his was the lowest score. His inclusion in the "narrow" group is explained by his exclusive focus on Freudian ideas (all three models, as well as Anna Freud). Additional but weaker influences were ego psychological ideas and those of Margaret Mahler, Merton Gill (who lived and worked in San Francisco), and Roy Schafer. These analysts are, of course, American. Totally negative responses were given to British ideas (British object relations, Klein, and Bion), to French ideas, and to developmental and hermeneutic ideas. Innovative American thinkers, such as Harry Stack Sullivan, Franz Alexander, and Heinz Kohut, also appeared to have had zero impact on this highly consistent analyst.

What is striking about these highly consistent profiles is the forcefulness of three theoretical influences: Freud, Klein (and Bion), and, in the case of the two British Independent analysts, British independent ideas. It appears that the Kleinians read very little other than Freud and, not surprisingly, were most influenced by his later drive theory (the death instinct) and by his post-1923 and 1926 structural model of the mind, in which the ego is envisaged as "the seat of anxiety." Outside their own orientation, the two Independents read only Freud and Klein. And the "narrow" American Freudian seemed to read "classical Freudian" works, as well as the writings of American thinkers who have expanded Freud's works whilst staying within the bounds of the American psychoanalytic establishment (for example, the early, but not the later, works of Merton Gill). Another striking feature of the "monistic" group of analysts is that, with the exception of Dr. Friedland, all are British. The seven British analysts seemed to read only British authors; the one American analyst in the highly circumscribed group also seemed to read exclusively within his own culture. In summary, this group of highly consistent thinkers was composed of five Kleinians, two British Independents, and one San Francisco Freudian. The three other analysts with high scores in the circumscribed range had changed orientation. This suggests that the ability to change belief does not necessarily correlate with expansion of thought.

CHANGES IN ORIENTATION

Four of the analysts interviewed were known to have changed orientation. Three of them scored in the highly circumscribed range. Three practiced in Los Angeles. Of the three Los Angeles analysts, two had shifted from a Freudian, to a Kleinian, to a self-psychological orientation. The third Los Angeles analyst was more "eclectic"; though remaining broadly within an Anglo-American object relations perspective, he had shifted from a more classical Freudian to a Bionian-Kleinian perspective. He was the only analyst of those who had changed orientation who was not classified in the highly circumscribed group. The fourth analyst, a British analyst named Dr. Shaw, had moved from the British Independent to the Kleinian group. Thus, of the four analysts who had changed orientation, three scored within the narrow range. The profiles of these three analysts show the kinds of beliefs that are associated with a change in orientation and are experienced as mutually exclusive.

Of the first analyst's responses, 80% were on the first two points of the scale: thus, this analyst was "not at all" or "very little" influenced by 16 of the 20 sources. She had trained at the Freudian institute in Los Angeles and was later supervised and taught by Bion and other leading Los Angeles Kleinians. In filling out the P.O.Q., however, she acknowledged no influence by Klein and very little by Bion. The strongest influence on her work was self psychology, with "considerable influence" by Kohut and contemporary developmental theory. Only one of her scores fell within the medium range of the scale, British object relations.

The second analyst, a senior training analyst in Los Angeles, had trained within a classical framework and had been very close to Bion and other Kleinians who came out to Los Angeles in the late 1960s and early 1970s. Unlike most of her Los Angeles colleagues, she declared no influence by Franz Alexander; neither French and hermeneutic ideas nor the work of Roy Schafer had any influence on her thinking. She rejected Freud's drive and structural theories in their "concrete" form but was influenced to a minor extent by Freud's topographical model. The one very strong influence was self psychology and to a lesser extent Kohut; however, unlike the first analyst just described, she did acknowledge "some influence" by Klein and to a lesser extent Bion and other post-Kleinian authors. She also acknowledged "considerable influence" by British object relations theorists and contemporary developmental theory.

Dr. Shaw, the British analyst who had shifted from the Independent to the Kleinian group, gave the narrowest range of responses of all the analysts interviewed. Like the British analysts described in the foregoing section on narrow ranges of theoretical influences, this analyst indicated zero influence by non-British thinkers and very little influence by Anna Freud. These negative responses accounted for 70% of his responses. Dr. Shaw was influenced by Kleinian and Bionian ideas to a very great extent, and somewhat influenced by all three Freudian models and by British object relations theorists other than Klein.

The scores of a fifth analyst, a member of the British Independent group, are interesting in that they indicate an incipient change of orientation from the Independent to the Kleinian group. Since this study was conducted, a number of Independent analysts have told me that this analyst, though still officially independent, is "to all effects and purposes" a Kleinian. He worked at the Tavistock Clinic and, like most of the Independents who worked there, showed strong Bionian-Kleinian leanings. In fact, in filling out the P.O.Q., he affirmed a greater degree of influence by Bion's work (Point 5 on the scale) than by the ideas of other British object relations theorists. It is interesting to note that, like the patterns of belief of three of the analysts who changed orientation, his was highly circumscribed. As with the other highly consistent British analysts, American and French ideas seemed to have had no influence. In this case, the statistical results correlated not with publicly declared belief but with implicit, or preconscious, associations between theoretical beliefs, participation in clinical seminars with leading Kleinian analysts, and affiliations with colleagues in a public health setting.

None of the four analysts who had officially changed orientation fell within the "widely influenced" or eclectic range. Two had the highest scores in the "narrow" range. We can speculate whether a circumscribed set of beliefs reflects, on one hand, the character or personality of the believer in that, irrespective of content, highly consistent thinkers tend to hold strong beliefs, or, on the other hand, the nature of the beliefs held. With respect to content, Kleinian-Bionian and Kohutian-self-psychological beliefs held a central position in the network of beliefs of three of the four analysts who had changed orientation. If we also include the analyst who was incipiently changing orientation but remained officially within the independent group, these two belief-systems appear to be mutually exclusive.

WIDE RANGES OF THEORETICAL INFLUENCES

In this section, I use the P.O.Q. score sheets to delineate profiles of analysts who can be classified as pluralist or "eclectic." (In America, analysts tended to describe nonclassical colleagues as eclectic; in some quarters, however, this term can have unflattering connotations. In the chapters that follow, this group will be simply referred to as eclectics.) Statistical analyses placed 13 analysts in the wide range, 12 of whom were American. I have selected for discussion here the nine analysts who acknowledged the widest range of influences. Their scores are very different from those described in the previous two sections. Whereas 75%–80% of the responses of the "monistic" thinkers fell into the "little" or "not at all influenced" category, this type of response accounted for only 10% of the responses of the eclectic analysts. As we would expect, eclectics exclude very little.

If we now turn to the other end of the scale—"influenced to a very great extent"—seven of the nine analysts gave zero responses. This means that very few of the eclectic analysts were influenced exclusively by one thinker or theory. When I combined the scores on Points 4 and 5 of the scale ("to a very great extent" and "to a considerable extent"), a very different pattern of responses emerged from that of the circumscribed group. The combined scores show that these nine analysts were influenced to a considerable or great extent by a minimum of five sources; some were influenced strongly by as many as 11 sources. In other words, over 50% of their responses indicated associations between force of belief and a wide range of influences. In addition, all nine analysts showed scores of between 8 and 13 on the median point of the scale. Thus, these analysts were influenced "to some extent" by about 50% of the total number of sources listed. Again, this pattern is markedly different from the ratio of responses that fell in the medium range of the "monistic" group; the highly consistent analysts were influenced "to some extent" by only one or two sources.

The profiles of these eclectic analysts potentially throw further light on the connections between range, content, and strength of belief. What sorts of ideas combine in a wide network of beliefs? Let us look first at the profiles of two analysts, one in Los Angeles and the other in San Francisco, who acknowledged a very similar set of influences. Both declared considerable influence by ego-psychological ideas, by American and British object relations, and by contemporary developmental theory (Bowlby, Stern, Emde, attachment theory). The San Francisco analyst was more influenced by Freud's topographical and structural models than was the Los Angeles analyst, who, not surprisingly, was more influenced by Kohut and self psychology. These minor differences reflect local concerns.

Let us next look at the profiles of two eclectic analysts who had very little in common. The first profile is of the only British analyst in the eclectic group. This analyst, Dr. Stevens is a member of the Independent group. He was "influenced to a very great extent" (Point 5 on the scale) by one source, British object relations theory, and "not at all influenced" (Point 1 on the scale) by the work of Merton Gill. He was, however, "considerably influenced" by Freud's drive and structural theories, by Margaret Mahler, and by contemporary infancy theory (notably Bowlby's attachment model). When compared with those of his British colleagues, his responses were unusual in that he declared "some influence" by American object relations theory, ego psychology, Sullivanian and interpersonal ideas, Franz Alexander, Kohut, Schafer, as well as by French and hermeneutic ideas. This profile suggests that, unlike most British analysts, this analyst read widely in the literature of other cultures.

The second analyst, Dr. Furnham, was a very senior, pioneer analyst in Los Angeles. He was greatly influenced (Point 5 on the scale) by nine sources; these included Anna Freud, Freud's topographical model, ego psychology (specifically the work of Rado, Kardiner, and Horney), Sullivanian and interpersonal ideas, Franz Alexander, contemporary developmental theory (specifically Bowlby), and Schafer's action language. Like most American analysts, he appeared to be ignorant of, or uninterested in, French and Lacanian ideas.

With the help of the statistical results, I traced the common theoretical biases of the nine analysts with high scores in the widely influenced group: all acknowledged "considerable influence" by American and British object relations, by contemporary developmental theory, and by Freud's topographical and structural models. In contrast to what was reported by the British "monists," Freud's topographical and structural models were clearly more useful to these analysts than was Freud's drive theory. Differences within the widely influenced group were for the most part small, and those which did emerge reflected historical influences in the local psychoanalytic culture. For instance, the two San Francisco analysts gave more weight to Freud's ideas than to those of either British authors or important figures in the Los Angeles area—for example, Franz Alexander, Bion, and Brandchaft and Stolorow. The two New York analysts were clearly more influenced by interpersonal ideas, by French analysis, and by British object relations theorists than were most of the West Coast analysts. The majority of the analysts in the eclectic group were more influenced by the works of

Kohut and by self psychology than by the works of Bion and Klein. These two sets of beliefs, however, were not mutually exclusive, as they were in the case of the analysts in the Kleinian and self-psychological orientation groups previously described. It seems that the use of American and British object relations theory and contemporary developmental and infancy studies, as well as Freud's structural and topographical models, reflect or foster open-mindedness and eclecticism.

When I compared the five orientation groups (that emerged from the cluster and factor analyses) with one another, the self psychologists and the Kleinians formed much tighter clusters than did the other three groups, that is, the Independents (comprising both British Independents and American eclectics) and the two Freudian groups. Of interest is that, in this sample, no analysts reported changing to either Independent or Freudian orientations. Of course, "independence" speaks for itself, although it is possible to be both independent and yet not widely influenced by different thinkers, as exemplified in the profile of the British Independent analyst Dr. Matheson. Although analysts filled out these questionnaires at a particular moment in time so that their responses reflected their current interests and enthusiasms, it is interesting to observe that there seems to be no correlation between change, and widened scope, of belief. This finding suggests that orientation is the outcome not of cumulative learning, but rather of a sort of immersion in a new, alternative system.

One group seems to have eluded the three types of belief described in this chapter: the Freudians. Only one Freudian, Dr. Friedland in San Francisco, was included in the circumscribed range, and no Freudians fell within the wide or eclectic range. As noted earlier, statistical analyses divided the Freudians into two groups, reflecting two distinct sets of influences: "classical" and "developmental." To some extent, these two labels distinguished the American Freudians from many of the British Freudians, and the adult analysts from the child analysts. For instance, only one of the Freudian analysts who were also child psychoanalysts stated no influence by Winnicott, Bowlby, and contemporary infant researchers such as Daniel Stern. These thinkers were clearly important to all the other child analysts in the sample. The "classical" Freudian group was highly cohesive, in that members assigned to it demonstrated very similar patterns of belief, and included most of the San Francisco analysts, two New York analysts, and four older senior analysts in the British Society who had trained with Anna Freud. None of these analysts used attachment theory or contemporary developmental models, although all were strongly influenced by Anna Freud and, to a lesser extent, Margaret Mahler. Which influences accounted for these differences within the Freudian group? Which influences limited the range of sources and suggested a more "classical" Freudian profile?

Nearly all the British Freudians acknowledged "some" (Point 3) influence by British Independent ideas (particularly the work of Winnicott), by Kohut, and by Klein. Nearly all the American "classical" Freudians acknowledged "some" influence by British object relations, Kohut, and Klein, but no influence by Bion or self psychology after Kohut. It is possible to infer that these "classical" analysts (most of whom were in their 70s) read "classical" texts as well as American authors such as Gill and Schafer, but were not interested in the relational and developmental trends in contemporary psychoanalysis. If we compare their scores with those of the five British Freudians classified in the British independent group, a marked difference emerges in the emphasis placed on Freud's drive theory by the "classical" group. The five British Freudians classified as Independent gave more weight to Freud's structural and topographical models than to the theory of drives. They were influenced to the same extent by British independent ideas, contemporary developmental research, and the ideas of Freud and Anna Freud. It is possible to speculate that the "independent" British Freudians, who were also younger than the majority of those in the "classical" group, were affected by their active involvement in public health institutions, specifically, the Anna Freud Centre and the Tavistock and Portman Clinics.

The effects of institutional affiliation, particularly outside the main regional psychoanalytic societies, have been underestimated in public discussions on theory–practice links. It is in clinics such as the Tavistock, however, that analysts participate in clinical and diagnostic discussions linked to decision making. When colleagues work together in a community service setting, they are forced into close proximity with each other's way of working. They also observe which of their colleagues is effective, which concepts and techniques seem to work. Kleinian ideas will rub off on Independents working at the Tavistock Clinic just as Freudian ideas rub off on Independents working at the Anna Freud Centre or the Portman Clinic. As we do not choose our beliefs in a simple, clear-cut way, we may be quite unaware that a thinker we thought of as peripheral to our core beliefs has crept into a central position.

The separate scrutiny of range, content, and force of beliefs indicates that patterns of belief show a degree of coherence, although cohesion is reached by individual pathways that are largely preconscious. In the next few chapters, this preconscious coherence is explored in regard to distinct aspects of technique that are not ordinarily thought of as interrelated.

Chapter 3

·:§·§:·

"One is Not Neutral About Psychic Truth"

I n this and the next two chapters, I focus on what psychoanalysts say about psychic truth and reality and what they say or imply about public reality and truth. Although psychoanalysts rarely make their beliefs about the external world explicit, nevertheless the existence of these beliefs is revealed in statements about "distortion," "illusion," and "displacement," particularly as these occur in discussions of transference. For what is it that confronts or mismatches the psychic reality of transference? From a logical and practical point of view, psychoanalysts need and indeed use the idea of an external world.

Freud made a distinction between "psychic truth" and "psychic reality," on one hand, and "material reality," on the other. In so doing, he freed psychoanalysts to get on with the job of trying to understand individuals without undue concern for the standards of conventional reality. Arguably, however, the distinction has lingered long after its initial purpose was achieved and has accrued a host of additional meanings. A simple distinction between private and public has been generalized (as it was by Freud) to separate the mental and the physical, imagination and fact, madness and sanity, delusion and truth, fantasy[1] and reality, narrative and history, the romantic and scientific, the false and the true.

Can psychoanalysts really mean what they say when they declare or imply a lack of concern with external reality and ordinary standards of truth? Why use the words "truth" and "reality" at all when talking about psychic phenomena? And if "psychic reality" characterizes and

---

[1] As an editorial convention, fantasy has been spelled with an f except where the speaker is self-identified as a Kleinian. This is for the sake of easy readability and does not reflect the particular preferences of some of the individual analysts quoted here.

41

demarcates the domain of psychoanalytic enquiry, what are the consequences for the status of psychoanalysis when compared with other disciplines? How do we judge the findings, premises, and beliefs of a discipline that has no truck with our ordinary external world, with shared reality, and with the search for, and assumption of, objectivity?

Freud's concept of "historical truth" can be seen as a version of the correspondence theory, whereas his notion of indirect confirmation through thematic affinity is close to the coherence theory—the "narrative truth" of psychoanalysis. And yet, as I demonstrate by examples from interview discussions, analysts do not use the words "truth" and "reality" lightly. These words serve an important purpose. They carry a special weight and meaning, much as they do when we talk about external truth and reality, and the qualifiers "psychic," "subjective," and "internal" do not detract from the simplicity of these terms. When an analyst talks about "psychic truth," he means that a privately held belief holds true. Otherwise, the analyst might as well use the words fantasy or story. True means something nonrelative, just as reality means something beyond, or independent of, the private.

How might these higher order concepts of truth and reality affect the way in which interpretations are offered? Although these are topics of public debate, we find few examples in the literature of how analysts translate these concepts in their clinical work. Consider the question whether psychoanalytic interpretations are hypotheses—akin to Freud's (1937a) "constructions," each of which is no more than a "conjecture" or "preliminary labour" (pp. 260–261)—or declarative statements. One analyst says, "You are doing such and such"; another analyst says, "Maybe . . ." or "Perhaps . . ." or "I wonder if you are feeling such and such." One form tells the patient explicitly what the analyst thinks he or she is doing; the other invites the patient to consider the analyst's opinion. The second is more tentative than the first and suggests a more open-minded, flexible approach. The formulation indicates "a moment of hesitation" (Winnicott, 1941), leaving room for the exploration of difference (Bollas, 1989). But, as Freud (1937a) pointed out, there are no simple tests of validity in psychoanalysis. A "yes" may stand for its opposite. A "no" may simply communicate a "resistance" to an unconsciously or preconsciously held belief.

The psychoanalyst needs to give reasons for supposing the truth of certain beliefs, his own or those of his patient, that do not take the form of evidence. Notions of validity that depend on direct evidence do not make sense when we are talking of unconscious processes. Freud (1937a), of course, recognized this problem, and the last paragraphs of that "Constructions" paper focus on "the fragment of *historical truth*"

(p. 265–269) attached to the patient's delusions as well as the role of thematic affinity—"associations that fit in with the content of a construction" (p. 264)—in the justification of constructions by "indirect confirmation" (p. 264). The problem with psychoanalytic concepts is that, like all psychological terms, they carry uncertainty. Psychological states vary greatly; human behavior is unpredictable. Therefore, as Wittgenstein (1980) noted, the language of psychology must be indefinite and flexible if it is to describe the endless diversity of human expressions. But the fact that we do not have exact rules for applying psychoanalytic concepts does not mean that there are no criteria at all. What is surprising is both the degree to which we do understand each other and that we are not all that opaque to one another.

What I am proposing is that the concepts of truth and reality, as well as ideas on processes of validation, interconnect preconsciously in the minds of analysts at work. Further, I am suggesting that differences in these preconscious systems of belief lie at the heart of the pluralist state of contemporary psychoanalysis. Interestingly, the results of the research support these propositions, while adding some new puzzles.

In this chapter, I examine analysts' responses to four particular topics that interrelate with these basic concerns and were explicitly discussed in the interviews. Considered together, these four topics elucidated the most widely divergent opinions of any in the survey.[2] The first three of the topics listed below were salient during the interviews as seeming to distinguish different groups of analysts in a way that confirmed my initial hunches based on several readings of the interview transcripts. The fourth, however, emerged directly out of the various statistical analyses as connected to the other three. The unique loading of this topic, the clinical concept of the death instinct, on what was called the "psychic truth" factor was strong. It was when I went back to the interviews, rereading them with the data analysis in hand, that I began to make sense of why this fourth topic was indeed centrally related to the others. (Again, the statistically minded reader

---

[2] The statistically minded reader will appreciate that the topics of this and the next chapter loaded highly on the first two factors that emerged from the principal components analysis of the rated interviews. The factor analysis was combined with additional rotational techniques, in this case varimax. The first two factors accounted for 50% of the variance. Thus, the two principal factors can be interpreted as signifying the most distinguishing dimensions of analytic technique for analysts in this sample. Correlations with the individual items on the P.O.Q. and the principal factors that emerged from the factor analysis of the P.O.Q. revealed that the two main factors that emerged from the analysis of the interview discussions also contributed maximally to the differences between the different orientation groups of analysts.

will appreciate that, whatever the methodological limits of factor analysis, this is one of its real pleasures, that is, that it can suggest possible interconnections that the researcher had not previously considered.) The four topics are:

1. The concept of "psychic truth" and the use of the word "true" in interpretations
2. The concept of analytic neutrality
3. The formulation of interpretations as working hypotheses (Freud's "preliminary labours") or as direct statements
4. The clinical use of the death instinct.

When I began this research, I was stimulated in part by a belief that the positions analysts take in regard to truth and objectivity would reflect deeply held assumptions and have wide-ranging effects on how they organized a number of other beliefs. In general, I had a hunch that, interconnecting preconsciously with these ideas, I would find other ideas relating to the process of validation and to the style of interpretation. More particularly, I supposed that analysts for whom the ideas of psychic truth and psychic reality were focal would tend to make interpretations in a more probing, as opposed to tentative, fashion. That tendency, in turn, might well have some bearing on how they construed the concept of "neutrality" and, moreover, on whether it held a central or peripheral place in their model of analytic technique. In these suppositions, I was guided by prior reading and also by certain philosophical assumptions as to the necessity for a certain degree of coherence in a person's belief structures.

In fact, as I conducted the interviews, it did seem that attitudes with regard to these three areas of the analytic endeavor—psychic truth, tentativeness or definiteness of interpretation, and analytic neutrality—cohered in the responses of many of the interviewees. What I did not initially expect was that these three terms would be joined by a fourth, namely, the specific clinical concept of the death instinct. This connection became apparent only as a result of the subsequent data analyses.

It seems that analysts who aim their interpretations at the identification of psychic truth are more likely to formulate interpretations as direct statements: "You are doing this," "I think you are trying to make me think that." Since the aim of analytic intervention is to help the patient face the truth and reality of his situation, his psychic reality, it is unlikely that the analyst will be concerned with maintaining a neutral attitude, or "equidistant" stance, between conflicting agencies and structures within the patient. Interventions will be more pointed or probing.

But why, I ask, does the concept of the death instinct connect with interpretive practices involving the identification of psychic truth and reality? As suggested earlier, the terms "psychic truth" and "psychic reality" carry a special weight; interpretations correspond with and denote something independent of the interpreter. For the interpreters of psychic truth, standards of coherence, internal consistency, and thematic affinity are not stringent enough. Interpretations confront something. And where do analysts look when they wish to tie down formulations that lack the qualities of hard data? They look inside, to the bedrock or "black box" of the instincts.

The following quotations illustrate the contrasting ways in which two thinkers use the concept of instinct. The first, from the work of the American psychoanalyst and philosopher Charles Hanly (1992), uses philosophical theories to bolster the Freudian concept of instinct.

> Pattern making by the analyst is not required so long as resistances and defenses are interpreted in such a way as to allow the intrinsic forces at work in the psychic life of the patient to make themselves known. These forces will determine the pattern as they will determine the transference. The forces in question are the drives, their vicissitudes, and their derivatives. The ideas of pattern making, of theory-bound observation, and the like may serve as rationalizations for countertransferential resistance to the threats posed by the drives—that is, by the instinctual unconscious. Psychoanalytic theories that repudiate the drives tend to employ coherence as a concept of truth [p. 20].

Hanly is a proponent of the correspondence theory and critic of the coherence point of view. At the same time, like many analysts of different persuasions, Hanly is more concerned with psychic than with outer reality. To what, then, do interpretations correspond? The instincts, or drives, are the "black box," the x, the latent forces, to which the interpretations correspond. The drives confront the interpretations and determine their truth value. As Hanly observes, analysts who look for coherence and consistency are less likely to believe in the theory of drives. In my view, they are also more likely to put forward interpretations in a hypothetical manner.

Quite a different attitude toward instincts is taken by Gregory Bateson, the well-known anthropologist and systems theorist and one of the originators of the double-bind theory of schizophrenia. The following is one of Bateson's (1972) famous "metalogues." In it, a father and daughter struggle to make sense of the concept of instinct.

Daughter: Daddy, what is an instinct?

Father: An instinct, my dear, is an explanatory principle.

D: But what does it explain?

F: Anything—almost anything at all.

D: But that's nonsense, Daddy.

F: Yes, surely. But it was you who mentioned "instinct," not I.

D: All right—but then what does explain gravity?

F: Nothing, my dear, because gravity is an explanatory principle.

D: Oh . . . Daddy, is an explanatory principle the same thing as a hypothesis?

F: Nearly, but not quite. You see, a hypothesis tries to explain some particular something but an explanatory principle—like "gravity" or "instinct"—really explains nothing. It's a sort of conventional agreement between scientists to stop trying to explain things at a certain point. . . . There's no explanation of an explanatory principle. It's like a black box.

D: Oh . . . Daddy, what's a black box?

F: A "black box" is a conventional agreement between scientists to stop trying to explain things at a certain point. I guess it's usually a temporary agreement.

D: But that doesn't sound like a black box. . . . Daddy, what is an instinct?

F: It's a label for what a certain black box is supposed to do . . . [pp. 38–40].

Bateson's metalogue elucidates the way in which the concept of instinct is linked quite differently to philosophical notions of truth by correspondence. Whereas Hanly believes that an instinct can be directly apprehended through its derivatives in the transference, Bateson tells us that the concept of instinct, like Kant's "noumenon," is empty. It seems to me that, for an analyst with Bateson's attitude, there is nothing specific to confront within, a black box being by definition unknowable. That being the case, the task of interpretation is to allow the complexity of the inner life to emerge in all its manifold interconnections. This is what Bateson (1979) used to refer to as "the pattern that connects" (p. 8). Translated analytically, such a view would seem to invite both neutrality and tentativeness of interpretation. It is this approach that analysts such as Hanly (1992) deny, interpreting it away as "rationalizations for countertransferential resistance to the threats posed by the drives" (p. 20). It is the force of the drives, rather than any patterning in the minds of analysts, that determines the pattern of the patient's psychic life.

VIEWS OF HIGHLY CONSISTENT PSYCHOANALYSTS

On rereading the interview material, I was fascinated to find (or forge) new links between *range* of belief and the four core concepts listed earlier. Highly consistent thinkers—those with the highest scores in the "narrow" or "circumscribed" range of responses to the P.O.Q.—held the strongest opinions on the four topics discussed in this chapter. Cluster analysis identified these same thinkers as situated at the center of their respective orientation groups. Here I present the views of three highly consistent thinkers, two of whom were described in chapter two. These are Dr. Matheson, the independent analyst with the "classical" profile; Dr. Friedland, the one "narrowly influenced" American Freudian analyst; and Dr. Roberts, a British analyst close to the center of the Kleinian cluster. Incidentally, in reporting their views, I have italicized some phrases to draw the reader's attention to particular concepts. Here, and throughout this text, the reader should be aware that such added emphases are mine and not necessarily reflective of any verbal emphasis given by the speaker.

Dr. Matheson:

"I would very rarely talk about truth. But, sometimes, you can point out to a patient, when you can detect it, that their defense is to avoid looking at facts. But, avoiding the truth . . . it is always a big word, always a bit moral, you usually use it when you start to get angry!

"I have no use for the death drive. It doesn't help me in the slightest. Particularly because the death instinct isn't object-related, it's a narcissistic instinct to start with. It's not directed against an object; it's directed against the self at the beginning and becomes object-related secondarily.

"Yes, I do use 'perhaps,' 'maybe.' I don't have any qualms about it. I think it is essential to keep interpretations as hypotheses, as 'perhaps' or 'maybe.' But not always. Sometimes, and particularly with patients who end up being so negative, people don't want to listen. And, then you may have to be forceful and keep the 'perhaps' and 'maybes' out of it so as to try to get through to something."

These views contrasted with those of Dr. Roberts. (Again, let me remind the reader that emphasis in his remarks has been added):

"Although it is quite difficult with some patients to talk about truth, nevertheless I do think one is trying to get them *to face psychic reality*, and psychic reality is really the truth I am trying to get at. I mean like patients who have never discovered what they really thought about their parents. Well, I don't know the truth about their parents. But I do try to help them to see how they have avoided seeing what they thought, and what they now are really capable of thinking about. But I am not saying that is the truth, but it is as near as I can get to their truth."

In trying to elucidate for myself the idea of psychic truth and its connections with correspondence and coherence theories of truth, I asked Dr. Roberts if he meant something like trying to get to what a patient is avoiding feeling or thinking about. What was the truth that he felt patients should face or confront? He replied,

"I think so, I think it is more psychic reality, their own internal reality and truth that I am after. And that should lead to the *real* truth in so far as one can."

When I then asked Dr. Roberts whether he used qualifying phrases when making interpretations he replied,

"No, I try to make them without qualifying phrases. I notice that most students use them an enormous lot, in a very tentative way. I think that they can't help it, but that they should be encouraged to try not to. I very often use the word 'I think,' but I very rarely use the word 'perhaps.' I think that either you have a suspicion that you are right, or you don't say it. I don't think there is much place for 'perhaps.' I say 'I think' or 'It is quite clear to me that you were angry. . . .' "

Dr. Roberts responded enthusiastically to the idea of the death instinct:

"Essential, absolutely essential clinically; without it I couldn't live! I really mean it, I cannot understand how you can manage without it. I can't understand how you really understand perversion, masochism, apathy, passivity without having some idea of the death instinct."

When I asked Dr. Roberts whether he meant something like "aggression turned against the self," he replied:

"You see, I think that is not good-enough, because the patient I am thinking of, he was dedicated to very, very near dying. That is different, it is not just aggression against the self, or against me. That is there too. But this absolute pull toward near-death. It is fascinating. One couldn't handle it just by talking about aggression, you see, the perversion, and the pull is so marvelous. And then you begin to see it to a much less degree in much healthier patients, and it is such a relief to them. I think that it gives patients enormous relief when you can tackle it, you can't do it without a concept of the death instinct. Somehow, it goes wrong, so I am really devoted to the death instinct. Or the life instinct!"

Those excerpts from the interviews show how these three concepts work for two senior analysts with highly consistent sets of beliefs. For the Kleinian, the death instinct, the identification of psychic truth, and declarative statements combine to form a particular analytic attitude. None of these ideas underlies the basic attitude of the Independent analyst. On the subject of analytic neutrality, however, the majority of British Independent and Kleinian analysts were in agreement. This is not surprising since, despite their differences, both orientations work within a relational perspective.

Dr. Matheson understood the term neutrality to mean "tolerance":

"The analyst who follows the other sort of neutrality, where the analyst tries to say as little as possible, is perceived as someone who doesn't give very much, somebody who is very dry and who perhaps is rather mean as well. That means that you can't have any situation in analysis in which there isn't some value put on it by the patient, no matter what you do. There is no situation of neutrality."

Like many Kleinian analysts whose reading of mainstream American literature seems limited, Dr. Roberts did not react immediately to the notion of neutrality.

"Neutrality . . . I am never clear what this thing called neutrality is now. Tell me again what are you asking me?"

I repeated my question, offering different formulations: an "attitude of tolerance," Freud's analogies of the "mirror" and "surgeon," the idea of

"equidistance" between ego, superego, and id. None of these definitions helped, and the term equidistance was unfamiliar.

> "No, to me it feels like not using what you have available in
> terms of interpretive understanding. And I think that can some-
> times be really dangerous to a patient. You can build up some
> really serious transference difficulties which aren't being spotted
> at all. So that the concept of neutrality simply seems to me to be
> getting away from the concept that transference is everywhere
> and has to be analyzed. And, of course one tolerates, I think that
> neutrality is right if you mean by that toleration, containing, and
> so on".

By contrast, the concept of analytic neutrality had immediate reso-
nance for Dr. Friedland, the third highly consistent analyst discussed
here. Cluster analysis placed Dr. Friedland at the center of the San
Francisco "classical Freudian" group. Neutrality is a focal part of
American training in technique, whereas the topics of psychic truth,
the death instinct, and the use of qualifying phrases seemed marginal.
First, neutrality:

> "Absolutely essential, being open to all the different things that
> patients are expressing and bringing. Neutrality about that, and
> about how these people are going to live their lives, and about
> what *you* want to accomplish. In a lot of case histories we read,
> what indicates success is that he or she has now found a suitable
> mate, has found a better job, now is working, has more friends . . .
> bla, bla, bla. Suitable according to . . . ? Clearly, these are objec-
> tives which the analyst feels are essential. I think it is nice if peo-
> ple are happy, I have nothing against people enjoying their lives
> and having better jobs, but that is not relevant to analytic work.
> That may be a by-product of it, but it may not. Somebody may
> lead a very different life from what one feels is the conventional
> indicator of happiness, and I think the neutrality of the analyst
> has to respect that. Going to college, getting a better job . . . that
> is not the business of analysis. And if the analyst and the patient
> brag about the fact that that is the result, there is something
> probably that has gone a bit awry and is not a part of the analytic
> process."

Dr. Friedland's attitude toward the interpretation of psychic truth was
skeptical and consistent with his views on neutrality.

"The primary task of interpretation is the articulation of resistances to conflict. Most patients do not have to be *told how they are*, that is simply condescension on a technical scale. Much more important is that one should not be distracted from what one presumably wants to do, which is to analyze the person's motivations for feeling something, which is not to say that they are simply crazy about what they are reporting, but that they are affected by their internal struggles, there is an important tendency toward feeling a certain way, perceiving a certain way, thinking a certain way. And to interpret those tendencies and the pull and attraction toward a certain view of the world and oneself, that is the important task. One does not have to say that it is absolutely and categorically that and you [the patient] may take my word for it, since nobody is going to take my word for any of it anyway!

"What I am listening for is what, on the basis of everything I know about somebody up until that moment, which might be five minutes or five years, what I feel with some confidence I can understand about what it is they are expressing in a vocabulary that we share. I may be able to say something about the struggles that that person is expressing, and I mean *expressing* rather than *talking about*. Because people talk about x, when they may be expressing y. After all, that is so much the hallmark of what we do—people frequently believe that they are discussing x, but they are expressing y and z, and the relationship between y and z. They choose to say, 'No, I am speaking about x.' I assume that on good days when I am interpreting what somebody is doing, I am interpreting in a vocabulary and on the basis of evidence being supplied to me and potentially to the patient at that moment. The patient might say, 'That's exactly right,' and I might find that that was only another way of saying, 'That was exactly wrong.' But none of us functions with a kind of expectation of corroboration or agreeability. I suppose that relates to another assumption I make, which is that what people do express at any moment and not simply in the room is their entire self, both that part of them which one can define as their neurosis and the rest of them as well. Therefore, if most people are pretty much the way I am, then I assume that we are expressing everything, though with varying degrees of observability, acceptability or decodability. Whether they like it or not, people are expressing their neuroses. It is observable to someone else to varying degrees, and it is expressible as an interpretation, depending on the relationship to that person, the background of that person, the demonstrability of what is being expressed, and the articulateness of both people."

Dr. Friedland's attitude toward the concept of the death instinct was likewise skeptical:

"If your central intention is to clarify the way in which the past is connected with the present, the way in which there is essentially a compelling self-deception because of anxiety and the history of anxiety, and a continuing conflict, then you are really hoping to help that person to integrate all that is within themselves, rather than attribute it to psychotic parts or to demons or to some other agency. The analysis is supposed to go, 'Look this is you . . . I am speaking to you as a serious adult.' One would be describing various motivations. After all, most of what we do is to describe conflicts within that individual, in which there are various desires and a variety of fears, and a desperate effort to reduce pain and increase pleasure—continually. And you are speaking to the impact of the *conflict* of those desires and fears on that person. So that it isn't just, 'You *are doing* all these terrible things,' but rather, 'You are struggling with them, and expressing them, and that's how we know about them,' not because I have a diagram of how they are. And they don't do it to spite me, but to avoid pain and possibly to attempt frequently and importantly to find some measure of pleasure."

The foregoing excerpts illustrate both the meaning and meaningfulness of psychoanalytic concepts for different analysts. Analysts for whom a concept had immediate currency both in clinical work and in collegial discussions gave a very different type of response to that of analysts for whom the concept is strange or redundant. The two types of response are illustrated by the two British object relations analysts and the San Francisco Freudian analyst. On one hand, we have well-articulated ideas that fill out the current meaning of a concept such as neutrality (as illustrated by Dr. Friedland's discussion) and, on the other, rather naive associations that nevertheless give us some idea about the ways a foreign idea is interpreted by an analyst working within a very different analytic culture (as illustrated by Dr. Roberts). For many analysts in the British Psychoanalytical Society who hear Kleinian presentations on a regular basis, the link between the aim of interpretation and the identification of psychic truth is familiar.

American analysts simply associated more loosely to the concept of truth. The framework of debate did not exist. The same situation can be seen in reverse when British analysts who do not read contemporary Freudian or American literature associate to ideas of neutrality. To amplify the effects of familiarity with a specific concept, I have selected excerpts, first, from interviews with Freudian analysts for whom the concept of neutrality is familiar and central and, second, from interviews with Kleinian analysts for whom the concept was strange and marginal. These excerpts are presented in the following two sections.

FREUDIAN VIEWS

The views of three New York Freudian analysts, all trained at the New York Psychoanalytic Institute, and one British Freudian analyst, Dr. Smith, an American who trained both in America and Britain, are particularly revealing. All four analysts made clarifying and expansive statements about neutrality and about the use of qualifying phrases. At the same time, most of their comments on interpretations aimed at psychic truth and the clinical relevance of the death instinct were dismissive. Unlike the British Kleinians, for whom psychic truth can be seen as the superordinate concept, analytic neutrality occupied a central position around which thoughts on the other three topics followed naturally and logically. This association is illustrated by the remarks at the end of the excerpt quoted earlier from the interview with Dr. Friedland. There Dr. Friedland points out that, according to the conflict model in which manifest behavior is always a compromise formation in which unacceptable thoughts and desires are disguised, there is no place for the sort of action language employed by many Kleinians. Patients are not *doing* things to the analyst "in order to spite" her or him. In the following excerpts, before summarizing approaches to psychic truth and the death instinct, I describe responses to neutrality and the use of qualifiers.

Dr. Braun, the first of the New York analysts, is an elderly training analyst of international standing:

"Analytic neutrality applies to the representations emerging from the different psychic systems. The analyst is getting a record of an internal debate, just like a political meeting. And people are all making statements about what they think is right, what they would like to have, what they think is practical.

There may be shifting alliances: if you favor this part of my argument, I favor that part of the argument. What the analyst has to
do is to make sure that each party in the argument's voice is
heard at some time. And in that sense, he remains neutral. It
doesn't mean that . . . to give an illustration that I think
Lowenstein gave: if the patient falls down at the threshold, it
doesn't mean that you don't offer your hand to pick him up, or
you don't say, 'Are you hurt?' or 'Are you all right?' It is not that
kind of woodenness, but the kind of thing that Anna Freud said,
of keeping equidistant to the three parts of the psychic apparatus. It is really like a debate: you have to be an impartial chair-
man and you have to permit each voice to be heard and point
out what each voice is saying. Some voices are very soft and subtle—you have to make sure that you hear them. That is my idea
of neutrality.

"Let me tell you a funny story about this. This was a friend of
mine who was a candidate in training, being supervised by Dr.
Lowenstein. He sneezed during the session and the patient said
'God bless you.' And the candidate didn't respond. The patient
said, 'Why don't you say thank you?' And he didn't respond.
The patient said, 'Well, that is not polite. Ordinarily when
somebody says God bless you! you say Thank you.' Well, the
analyst felt that this was getting nowhere, so he thought he had
better give an answer so as to get this out of the way. So he said,
'Well, you know, that is acknowledging a kind of superstition.
God has nothing to do with health and with sneezing.' But he
felt a little troubled about it because the patient wasn't satisfied
at all. He said, 'You were being impolite.' So the candidate took
it up with Dr. Lowenstein, and Dr. Lowenstein listened carefully
and said, 'You know, the next time you sneeze and a patient says
God bless you, you say thank you.' Now that was carrying neutrality too far."

Dr. Braun had this to say about his use of qualifying phrases:

"You can't make a general rule about it. But, in general, I avoid
it. Sometimes, under certain circumstances, I might say something like, 'It might be.' The point, however, is this: any kind of
intervention one makes has an effect, even if it is not what is
classically called interpretation—and I don't like the term interpretation; I like the term intervention. After all, what happens
in an analysis: you have the patient there on the couch, and you

are getting a certain record of the thoughts that are coming to his mind. Those thoughts, that conscious stream of thought, is the end result of a dynamic process in which impulse, defense, superego considerations all participate. And we see the interplay of these different elements. Anything that the analyst says or does may or may not have a dynamic effect upon the course of the patient's associations. So if you say to the patient, 'It seems to me that at that point, you felt like killing so and so,' the patient may or may not pay attention to the 'it seems,' depending on the balance of forces operative in him at that time. He may not even hear the 'it seems.' He may hear nothing but 'it seems.' The real test is what happens in the subsequent course of his associations. It is just the same as if the patient says 'yes' or a 'no'. The real difficulty with 'maybe' or 'perhaps' is with *obsessional* patients. Because they use it the same way—'perhaps' means 'maybe yes, maybe no,' so we can shelve it and forget about it."

The second New York Freudian analyst, also a senior training analyst, replied without hesitation:

"I think it is very important. There is *ethical* neutrality and moral neutrality. We try not to be moralistic or judgmental, but we do still have ethical responsibilities, one of which is not to evade ethical issues which arouse strong feelings of guilt. It can be very useful to explore both the dynamics and the historical sources of neurotic guilt. We can analyze these issues through interpreting conflicts over guilt as these appear in a dream while maintaining an atmosphere of moral neutrality. Whereas interpreting behavior directly is more difficult, because we do have feelings and judgments, and it is more difficult not to convey impressions of moral repugnance or exculpation. Often this can lead to very important memories of the childhood circumstances which contribute to the persistent sense of neurotic guilt. Of course, the psychoanalytic method possesses a morality of its own, *the analytic situation has its own implicit ethical structure*—to tell the truth as well as possible, to conceal as little as possible—but that is different from the imposition of the personal standards of the analyst.

"Also I think of the stance of analytic neutrality as one of interest, the *maintenance of curiosity about the workings of the mind*, including matters of conscience, guilt, self-deception, a sort of educated conscience. Calef and Weinshel used the term 'the conscience of the analysis.' There is the integrity of the contract, which is not to explain moral guilt away, or to collude or condone, or communicate through punitive interference. I think of the 'window of the dream' into memories of forbidden desires which contribute to the unexplained burden of guilt. This recovery and correction of memories can lead to a more discriminating, less punitive, and more effective conscience."

A third New York analyst, a generation younger than the two analysts just quoted, had had considerable exposure to British object relations ideas. Although trained at the New York Psychoanalytic Institute, he was now teaching at the "less classical" Columbia Psychoanalytic Institute.

"I trained at New York, which is classical Freudian, orthodox, where analytic neutrality was espoused. Columbia has much more of a feeling that it is grist for the mill. For example, if you teach at Columbia and you have a patient, an analysand, who is in your class, you still teach with that patient sitting in that class. This didn't used to happen, it was not allowed. I haven't had the experience yet, but I will. As I mature, I think the idea of total analytic neutrality is just nonsense. I could say the same thing about the people who analyzed me at the New York. My analyst who was classical and depressed and conservative had his office in the home. So the elevator would break down, and we had to go up in the service elevator and walk through his kitchen. And I saw all his antiquities on the way through, it was ridiculous, utter nonsense. My patients know a certain amount about me, by my imagery. I am a sculptor and I play tennis. I normally don't pick up the phone, but one day my wife was out of town and I had to. It was my close friend who plays with me. I mumbled something about 9 o'clock. The patient said, 'You have a tennis game.' From that point on, you can imagine the competition in the analysis to perform a tennis game, and the recurrent dreams of tennis. His tennis incidentally improved incredibly; he was a very good player. It was a very good analysis, I had a terrific supervisor. There are many ways the transference is played out. That patient was a good tennis player, when he was winning in tennis, his oedipal material was being worked through. So we could do the whole analysis at that point on the tennis game. How did he pick up that? . . . I am sure some place before I had used some tennis analogy. You can't be totally neutral."

About using qualifying phrases, this analyst commented, like Dr. Braun, that he used them with everyone *except obsessives*:

"If you put the conditional clause into an interpretation with a real obsessive, you are feeding their pathology. They are going through 'perhaps,' 'could be,' and what do you do? You give them an obsessional dance to play out. Otherwise, I would say it is very tactful and very useful in producing ideas with the right patients, they play with the ideas, to go back to Winnicott."

Throughout the book, we will be following the thoughts of Dr. Smith, the American analyst working in Britain and a member of the British Contemporary Freudian group. Dr. Smith had trained in both countries, and his views reflect this unique combination of influences.

"Neutrality doesn't mean a cold, surgeonlike indifference. It means a very benign, tolerant listening and sympathetic concern, where you don't impose your critical views. That's the Greenson, the old-fashioned, Freud's way of being neutral, and it is hardly what people today would call neutral. I think it's very unfortunate that changes have taken place in the thinking about neutrality so that it means this impersonal, relatively cold, and indifferent person. That isn't the old way at all.

"I do use qualifying phrases, but you've got to be careful that it doesn't become too routine. Sometimes, once you get familiar with a patient and you know that you are going into the 'we' relationship, you can say, 'Well, I think it very well might be that.' But, it sounds definite. But I would also be willing to correct it if it seems wrong. In defenses, I am more sure. It is pretty definite when it's a defense. Then, I can be more certain in saying, 'You're just not willing to accept that.' When it's a speculation about an unconscious fantasy or something, I'm a bit more waiting for a collaborative response."

The three New York Freudian analysts either had never heard the phrases "evading reality," "turning away from reality," or "perverting the truth" in analytic discourse, or simply answered "No," indicating that they personally never thought in these terms. One observed sardonically, "I'm not in the business of faking." Dr. Smith, the British Freudian analyst, of course was familiar with this terminology but stated that he would never use it "unless it was very specific." The rather vague or lukewarm responses of other American analysts toward interpretations aimed at the identification of psychic truth indicated that this was not a key issue for American Freudians.

The clinical usefulness of the death instinct concept, on the other hand, evoked strong negative responses. Another distinguished New York analyst, who had held high offices in both the American and the International Psychoanalytical Societies, replied:

> "*The death instinct has no place in clinical work.* It is a superordinate concept governing biology and psychology perhaps, in general, but has absolutely no relevance to psychoanalytic work, absolutely none. It is Freud's broadest philosophical speculation, and it doesn't mean anything; it is just another way of saying we all die, and when we die the structural integration which makes life is disorganized. So what! However, there is one danger in that, from this concept, Freud derived the idea of a repetition compulsion. I also find that irrelevant; it has no place; it doesn't do anything. You have a compulsion to repeat . . . Well, doctor, that is why I came. If I could have stopped this, I wouldn't have come to you. I have no use for the concept. Which doesn't mean that there aren't certain unexplained areas of mental functioning that are related to such a problem. Say the child has not resolved his conflicts during the oedipal phase, why is it that he keeps trying to work out again and again an unsuccessful compromise formation to a particular conflict? That is a good question, and I don't know the answer to it. But the repetition compulsion does not answer it."

When I described the ways some British Kleinian analysts used the concept—turning away from life, seeking a near-death state—Dr. Braun, the elderly, highly esteemed New York analyst, replied:

> "But that, again, is the *phenomenological fallacy.* What is going on in that individual's mind? Death does not mean the same thing to everybody. You have to find out what the unconscious fantasy is that is articulated in the conscious mental representation of I want to die. That is a good example of the use of the phenomenological error in interpretation."

Other New York analysts replied simply, "No, no use at all" or "totally unuseful . . . unequivocally, I think it has done us a lot of harm. I have no understanding of it at this point."

Dr. Smith had worked very closely with Anna Freud:

"No, I would hold the classical view, which is . . . you see, even in Vienna, hardly any of Freud's immediate circle of followers accepted it, only one or two, but that was rare. I find the concept an interesting speculation about the to-and-fro of organic–inorganic matter. I liked Freud's thinking about that. But as to the idea that it really gets displaced, gets into the mental system and functions, I'm very doubtful. I think it's just a speculation, and you can work much better with guilt, aggression, superego, anger. I don't find any need to use a very speculative concept."

KLEINIAN VIEWS

As a group, British Kleinians responded with immediacy to the notion of the evasion of psychic truth as well as to the clinical application of Freud's theory of the death instinct. Clearly, both were topics of current discussion. On the other hand, most Kleinians had little to say about neutrality, and many of the younger Kleinians were apologetic about their use of qualifying phrases. The following two examples are taken from discussions of qualifiers with younger though fully qualified Kleinians:

1. "Oh I do that, more than I should. I think it's because I have this terrible fear of being dogmatic, of sounding as though I know what you are thinking. . . . Actually this has come up in supervision, and the supervisor said to me, 'I think you are using perhaps, maybe, too much. It is sounding a bit wobbly.' I think probably with experience you use these terms less because you are more confident in your own countertransference."

2. "I do, I use them a bit too much. That's my personality. I think it's wrong. Sometimes I am too tentative; that's a weakness in me. It's my personality, not a theoretical or technical issue at all. It can be a kind of placating of the patient or making it a little bit too nice. But, on the whole, I wouldn't formulate an interpretation as an absolute statement, ever. That would be wrong, and in any case I don't see that I have reason to say that I know anything."

Another analyst of the same age and experience, who was also a training analyst, responded with more conviction:

> "I think this is completely a matter of personal style and not really something thought out. I probably don't qualify enough. I probably say what I think without prefacing it very much by 'I think,' 'Perhaps,' 'You might feel that.' That is just not the way I talk. Most of my patients just get used to the way I talk. You cannot get rid of your style.[3] With some patients, you have to be careful not to hurt their feelings. But I think, with most patients, they get used to the way you talk. For instance, I sometimes use sarcasm. It is sometimes for me the most effective way of getting a point across, to be extremely sarcastic. It is not terribly kind but it makes the point that the patient can understand and join with you for a second and that will get the point across."

Since the idea of interpretation as a "preliminary endeavor" or hypothetical construction is not central to the Kleinian theory of technique, responses of Kleinian analysts tended to be subjective and reflected experiences in supervision, teaching, and personal analysis. Many of the younger Kleinian analysts responded in a similar way to the notion of neutrality. When I gave illustrations from the literature, most agreed vaguely with the notion of tolerance. The one South American analyst in the sample discussed the relationship between neutrality and politics (a number of American analysts, closer to South American colleagues, made similar connections). He said:

> "Obviously I don't believe in neutrality. Of course, I do believe very much in engaging with the patient, and in any case I wouldn't know how to do otherwise even if I tried. I do try to convey as little as possible of my beliefs and tastes. But I think that the nearer patients are to you, the more these can come out for the wrong reason. I am just thinking of politics. One patient thinks I am a Thatcherite, and I have had two very right-wing patients who just assumed that their world view was right. The countertransference was a bit difficult. But then there can be the same difficulty with patients who have the same political views as me. That is a terrible mistake; I can see that the tone of my interpretation shows that I am agreeing with them. That is wrong. I

---

[3] It is interesting to compare this analyst's view with that of Roy Schafer (1992), who classifies "personal style" as "characterological countertransference" (p. 85).

would probably have to be more careful with them than with patients who are saying something completely preposterous. I think you should keep your views 100% to yourself. It's very seductive I think, not with a mad patient, but with a reasonably sane patient who is engaged in similar things, very easy to imply you are on the same side."

In contrast to questions about neutrality, questions about the death instinct elicited clear responses. Like Dr. Roberts, the senior Kleinian training analyst, the majority of younger Kleinian analysts agreed without hesitation that the death instinct was clinically valuable. Here are two examples that illustrate the practical effect of this concept on interpretation.

1. "I can think of one instance, a psychotherapy case. He is actually somebody who is really very ill in the sense that he has obsessional thoughts which take over his mind and stop him living. So I feel that there is something operating which is very antilife, which he recognizes but can't stop. Which is very upsetting for both of us. When you ask me these things, I think of my patients, but also in terms of myself as an analytic patient. There are moments when I have felt I have been full of a kind of death instinct, refusing to make a move that would get me out of that— terrible, terrible periods in my analysis, having to come to terms with something quite frightening in myself. Very difficult to get over and change. So I do think it is a useful concept."

2. "On the whole, with most patients, I don't really think about it, except when I am confronted with something that does feel to be very evil, something that is always against good. The concept is something I am a bit ambivalent about really, but when I read the newspaper, I do believe in it. I don't think in sessions, 'This is the death instinct.' It has to be a very crazy patient doing something terrible to themselves and one feels protective of anything alive in the patient and that one has to fight something completely horrible that is doing terrible damage to them. That's when I think about the death instinct. I do think it is something different from aggression turned against the self, which is a more ordinary superegoish thing, self-punishment, etc. This is knowing that you are in the presence of something really horrible, let's say with a psychotic patient, where the baby part of them is actually being tortured in a horrible way, connected with something perverse."

The preceding example draws out the distinction between a Kleinian view of aggression and that of a Freudian like Dr. Smith. In the excerpt quoted earlier, Dr. Smith states explicitly that the ideas of aggression, superego, anger etc. have greater clinical value than does the concept of the death instinct.

So far, I have presented the attitudes of three "highly consistent" thinkers—Drs. Matheson (independent), Roberts (Kleinian), and Friedland (San Francisco Freudian)—to the network of concepts under review. I amplified these individual profiles with further examples, demonstrating the ways that Freudians and Kleinians think about the core concepts of neutrality and psychic truth as well as the looser network of concepts that link logically with these two. The additional examples confirm the results of the various statistical analyses, which showed that Freudians and Kleinians hold contrasting positions on this set of concepts. In the final two sections of this chapter, I summarize briefly the views on these topics of analysts who hold "broad-ranging" beliefs as well as the views of analysts who have changed orientation.

VIEWS OF BROAD-RANGING ANALYSTS

Responses of British independent analysts to the concept of neutrality, the use of qualifying phrases, the death instinct, and the identification of psychic truth were fairly uniform. I here quote from the interview with Dr. Stevens, the British analyst I referred to in the previous chapter who was the only British analyst included in the eclectic or "wide-ranging" group of analysts.

"I think of neutrality not as the old, well-polished mirror, but in the sense that Shakespeare meant it—to hold a mirror up, as it were, to nature. I use it in that sense. Freud's well-polished mirror is rather a cold image. But the mirror, the whole idea of the child being the gleam in the mother's eye, that kind of mirroring, reflecting back to the patient as a mother does, that is a very important idea. But that idea is far from the cold, passive thing; it is much more active. And a related question . . . I don't believe analysts don't have standards. I think that is palpable nonsense. Every time you interpret defense, you're implying there is a more mature way of doing something. I think there is a developmental standard implied in the whole enterprise—mature is better than less mature."

Dr. Stevens also expressed strong views on the topic of qualifiers:

"I don't think interpretations should ever be made en bas, as if you know better than the patient. It's always that you are phrasing a hypothesis to the patient for mutual exploration. Making suggestions, speculations. I suppose it's what Winnicott was talking about. You are not doing analysis by making clever interpretations. It's a sort of squiggle game with the patient . . . you put it like this, or like that. You're building a picture of something together. I have very strong feelings about these things. I've had so much of it from my Kleinian colleagues. I've actually introduced whole meetings on the subject of 'Should one ever say perhaps?' Some Kleinians tell colleagues to never say perhaps. Just state it. That's an insult to people's intelligence. Maybe they have a point, which was Balint's point, which has to do with working with very disturbed or psychotic patients. These patients respond to the interpretation which appears to be very certain. Maybe they feel securely held by the ex cathedra interpretation. But I think the less disturbed patient would be insulted by such a style of interpretation. It's an unwritten paper that's been around. If you look at the literature, you find Kleinians saying, 'I told the patient that,' or 'I showed the patient that . . .' You don't find 'I suggested that' or 'I said perhaps . . .' "

Dr. Stevens did not find the concept of psychic truth useful and declared categorically that he never used such words as "evading" the truth or "avoiding" reality. He had a "lot of views" about the clinical relevance of the death instinct:

"I certainly don't believe in it, and it is curious how it arose. It is as meaningful as attributing difficulties to the devil. It's a nonexplanation. Sometimes we come across things we feel so awful about, we feel it must be the work of the devil. Something inexplicable. [Dr. Stevens's statements compare closely to Bateson's metalogue.] It's important to look at the history of how the concept arose. Why did Freud think of it so late in his career? How did something he tossed out as a speculation get taken up as a concrete reality? How was he affected by having cancer of the mouth? All these things must have come into it. But to then take it on as a reality is most peculiar. My framework would be a very broad evolutionary one. It's impossible to conceive evolutionarily how such a thing would be arrived at. Why turn that into an actual biological state?"

A German-speaking British Independent analyst took a similar position on the death instinct:

> "I think that this is a misunderstanding. Freud has designated to the death instinct total silence. And that is nowadays so much forgotten. Only when this death instinct causes anxiety, then part of it is directed outward and becomes a destructive instinct. There is no such a thing that anybody ever can see or perceive. The very definition of Freud's death instinct is that it is silence."

And about neutrality:

> "Well . . . if there is such a thing as a neutral analyst. But it is more than tolerance. I think it also means that you have an *interest in other people's value systems even if they are far away from your own.*"

Two British analysts, one Independent, the other Contemporary Freudian, expressed idiosyncratic and illuminating views on these four topics. The Independent analyst linked neutrality (qua Balint) with "unobtrusiveness":

> "I don't believe that you're ever totally neutral. That's a myth. I don't think you can be a mirror. But it's really an art to recognize when the patient is feeling you to be intrusive. Or when the patient is picking up things in you, and he is modeling himself on you without your being aware of it."

This Independent training analyst responded personally to the use of qualifiers:

> "I have my voice and everybody tells me that I'm too intimidating, especially as I grow older. So I just take refuge in using all these words . . . [laughs] I just learned it."

With reference to interpretations of avoiding reality and truth, he replied,

> "No, I don't use that kind of phrasing, because it means I am holding the truth, and I know what it is. I might say, 'Is that very rational?' Or I could say, 'That's not what you told me yesterday.' Or, 'Do you really think that's what's going on?' Something like

that. But to say you're avoiding reality, clearly I am the one who knows it. It's presumptuous."

In thinking about the death instinct, this analyst described his work with children in both child guidance and hospital settings:

"You have a sick mother, depressed or psychotic, and you have a child coming and wanting to cuddle the mother, and the mother cringes and pushes the child away. I'm one of those who believes that that child, if he is exposed to that repeatedly, he is going to come to the conclusion that for his love object to react like that, it can only mean that what he thought was love is, in fact, something very destructive. That kind of notion colors much of my work. I have to acknowledge that it is theoretically conceivable that there must be children who were born with all sorts of destructive, hostile, and what-have-you fantasies. I haven't seen them. I can imagine that they might exist. I would really like it if you could give me a concrete example. Then we could argue about it. I've heard so many students talking about their patient's destructive impulses, and to my ears there's nothing destructive in it. What there is is a fear of being attacked, or fantasy of destroying. Yes, we all have fantasies of wishing somebody dead and what have you . . . but I'm not sure if that's the same as talking about destructive impulses in the sense of a death instinct or anything like that. I think it's a marvelous thing that Freud came up with for God's sake what, and that Melanie Klein came up with for the sake of blaming her children."

An Asian analyst in the British Freudian group responded meditatively to the notion of the death instinct:

"I find it theoretically very interesting. I find the concept fascinating, but I don't find it clinically useful. It is more like . . . awesome is the word. It is a metaphysical idea, with awe, not something wrong or bad. But I must say if one sees the repetition compulsion, and trauma and traumatic anxiety, it has an inexorable quality to it, an unchangeable quality to it which is quite impressive. But to call it the death instinct, to use a label, is really another thing. But intractability, I am very struck by, and it is a puzzling thing."

When I asked this Freudian analyst whether he thought there was another explanation for intractability, connected perhaps with trauma, he replied,

"Yes, the inability to give up things, the adhesiveness of the libido, of the aggression, the relation that Freud talked about between love, hate and ambivalence, the balance between them. If something else could be put in place of the death instinct, then the idea could be interesting. But it is just not possible that a living organism could go for it, that life could be in the service of death. You can see self-destructiveness, you can self-destruct, but you can't use that as an aim."

These reflections are similar to those of a San Francisco analyst who had one of the highest scores in the "wide-ranging" group. She pondered:

"I toy with the idea. I think there are many primitive urges, and I think I can see the attraction Freud found in the death instinct idea. That is, in the metapsychological idea, where Freud had this kind of mathematics of transmutation, and the idea of decathexis and cathexis and neutralization. Unfortunately, I think that notion got us off into a kind of beautiful but excessively abstract and erroneous theory. But the idea that people want quiescence and to go to sleep and to die and to get away from the present state of affairs, this is a very powerful urge. I don't enlarge it into a death instinct. I think one has to distinguish between the urge to just be done with this and a biological tendency to age and die that is going to manifest itself in different ways. And it is going to affect the person's experienced energy levels and things like that. Freud got too adventurous in his theory, and it just doesn't work. But there is something going on. There are all sorts of puzzling and mysterious phenomena such as self-mutilation which give rise to such notions, and we need explanations, we don't have agreed upon ones, I would love to see some better ones."

In the last chapter I introduced the Los Angeles pioneer analyst, Dr. Furnham, whose responses to the P.O.Q. showed the strong effects of many theories and thinkers on his clinical practice. Dr. Furnham felt that neutrality related much more to moral neutrality than to a position of equidistance from intrapsychic agencies:

"One should attempt to be flexible in one's value-systems, neutral in the sense that we must allow patients to find their own way of dealing with life. However, I don't think any form of analysis is value-free. The moment you make an interpretation that something is healthy or unhealthy, neurotic or mature, infantile or adult, you are imposing a subtle value and fortunately, in most instances, the value systems of the patient and the therapist correspond. [Note that his views are diametrically opposed to those of the South American Kleinian analyst described earlier.] But there are times when a patient may be deeply religious, and the analyst may not be. It is important that the analyst respect the values of the patient, even though they differ from his. That's not so much neutrality as it is respect for differences, and that's important."

Dr. Furnham said that he deliberately used qualifying phrases:

"I do it deliberately because I never want to appear infallible, and I want to give the patient the opportunity to contradict me or to disagree or to qualify what I am saying. And I think that it is in the matrix of that kind of interaction that the patient grows and begins to acquire more self-respect, while, on the other hand, if I appear infallible and if I say, 'This is it,' I am not allowing the patient the ability to question me or to challenge me. And I want to be challenged, I think that in the process of being challenged, even if the patient is wrong, he has grown by virtue of being able to challenge an authority figure."

CHANGES OF BELIEF

In chapter one, I discussed the range and content of beliefs of two Los Angeles analysts who had shifted from classical Freudian to Kleinian to a self-psychological orientation. Both adamantly disagreed with Kleinian views on the death instinct and with Freudian views on neutrality. These excerpts show the ways in which analysts who change orientation tend not to "add on" new beliefs, but rather to go through a sort of "conversion" experience from the old to the new model. Of course, there may be rational and logical reasons for this shift of gestalt since central concepts in the old and new models may be incompatible and incommensurable.

1.   "No, the death instinct is a real aberration, and I think it is much more a derivative of the analyst's feeling of helplessness. It does not belong to the psychoanalytic method at all. It is the last-ditch defense on the part of the analyst."

2.   "I think it is a myth that any person is neutral. He has his own subjective framework. There is nothing wrong with that, but that doesn't mean that it is necessarily inimical or interfering, but it has to be recognized what the impact is."

In chapter one, I also described the content and range of beliefs of Dr. Shaw, a British analyst who had changed orientation from the Independent to the Kleinian group. When asked how the death instinct concept related to his clinical work, Dr. Shaw replied:

"I do think, just as Freud did, that there is something in addition to repressions and defenses in our reluctance to change. Irrespective of the desire to change, there is something very, very powerful, and it is not just defenses, which seem to attach to bad experiences, or repetitions of bad experience. I am very struck by how extremely powerful it is. And there are some patients where you see something very like what Freud described, some longing to go back into some state of fusion with a very deathlike fantasy. They would rather be dead and at one with you than be alive and have to experience their separateness. I do think that that is very painful."

About neutrality and the use of qualifying phrases, he said:

"I think I tend to use quite a lot of qualifying words. Whether I would advocate that is another matter. I think that the most effective interpretations are probably quite punchy and emphatic. I think it is probably something to do with a diffidence of mine rather than something I would advocate."

"If what you mean by neutrality is being nonjudgmental, I don't think it is possible to be nonjudgmental, I don't think any human being can be. One wouldn't be able to choose what to say. There is a sort of distinction between moral judgments and other judgments, but I think that that distinction is perhaps invalid. I would think that what an analyst needs to be concerned about is psychic truth, and that one is not neutral about psychic truth, and that there are things related to psychic truth about which one has inevitably moral attitudes. And that certain kinds of attacks on truth are regrettable, deplorable, and worrying, whereas other kinds of inability to face psychic truth, one has a morally favorable attitude toward, I don't think one can get away from that."

These excerpts provide information, explicit and implicit, about the ways ideas about truth, about telling and identifying the truth, permeate the analytic situation. Attitudes toward truth interweave with deep-seated and often unconscious beliefs about reality, raising epistemological as well as ontological questions. Is there an external world, and, if there is, are we as psychoanalysts concerned with it? How do we know it? If, on the other hand, truth is to be found in the inner world, then what sort of relationship do our beliefs have with it? Is psychic truth something we should be neutral about? Or is neutrality a precondition for the emergence of psychic truth? In this chapter, I have examined four topics that take us to one way of construing the role of reality. In the next chapter, I explore different ways of construing reality in analysis, as these are revealed in discussions of the "real relationship" and other topics. The focus is more on beliefs about the external world than on notions of truth.

Chapter 4

Objective Reality and the
"Real Relationship"
Freudian Views

I n orienting the reader to the idea of the analyst's preconscious, I
have focused on beliefs concerning the nature of truth and reality
as these organize attitudes toward many of the central concepts in
psychoanalysis. Ideas about psychic truth and instinct, on one hand,
and neutrality and tentativeness of interpretation, on the other, have
complex associations with the ways interpretations are formulated by
analysts of different persuasions. As noted in the last chapter, preconscious views on these topics create sharp distinctions between analysts
practicing in different psychoanalytic cultures. In particular, they discriminate between British Kleinian analysts and the different varieties
of Freudian analysts on both sides of the Atlantic who were interviewed for this project. I noted in the previous chapter that these topics reflected the second of the two principal factors that emerged from
the factor analysis. In making sense of the principal dimensions of the
factor analysis, I defined this second factor as "psychic truth versus
interpretations as hypotheses."

In this chapter and the next, I examine a different set of concepts.
This set of concepts corresponds with those which loaded on the first
factor to emerge from the factor analysis of the rated interviews. This
dimension is described as "total transference" versus "a relative view of
transference." "Total transference" describes analysts who focused
almost exclusively on the "here-and-now" transference relationship
between analyst and patient. "Relative view of transference," on the
other hand, describes analysts who defined transference as "distortion,"

"displacement" or "illusion," and who drew a conceptual distinction between the unreal and real aspects of the analytic situation. Their view of transference was circumscribed rather than all-embracing. This distinction had clear ramifications for technique.

The analysts' explicit and implicit views on this dimension emerge in discussions of a network of four analytic concepts. These are:

1. The concept of the real relationship as distinct from transference
2. Extratransference interpretation as an effective agent of psychic change
3. The concept of the treatment or therapeutic alliance
4. The concept of the transference neurosis.

Two other aspects of technique discussed in the interviews further elucidate the ways analysts use the four concepts under review: the analyst's validation of the patient's correct perceptions, and the analyst's acknowledgment of his or her own mistakes. Included in discussions of mistakes were other failures such as lateness, illness, holidays, and unplanned changes in routine. Views on these topics provided additional information on the ways that superordinate concepts—in this instance, the "real relationship"—translate into therapeutic action. Thus, in the network of concepts reviewed in this chapter, the "real relationship" can be seen as the central concept that has a number of significant operational consequences for analytic technique. Epistemological and ontological beliefs about reality are reflected in what might be called subsidiary or secondary concepts, such as the treatment alliance and the whole issue of the analyst's validation or invalidation of his patient's perceptions. Again, my emphasis is on the ways that implicit philosophical views concerning the nature of truth and reality affect analytic practice.

Correlations between analysts' responses to the topics of this chapter and theoretical orientation were high. The material presented in this and the next chapter is organized, therefore, according to group affiliation. The network of concepts surrounding the central concept of the "real relationship" is part of the currency of Anglo-Saxon Freudian culture and evoked fluent and informed responses from Freudian analysts. These ideas have a history of debate, particularly in the United States. Since most British Kleinian and Independent analysts have not participated in conferences where these concepts have been discussed, their responses seem simpler and more spontaneous. The views of British Independent and Kleinian analysts, and of

American eclectic analysts and self psychologists are presented in the next chapter.

In general, Freudians of all persuasions tended to be conversant with the idea of the real relationship and spontaneously organized their responses to related topics around this central idea. Most of them found it valuable. The exception was a small subgroup of classical Freudians, located in New York and San Francisco, who were so strongly committed to the idea of interpretation as a continuous *process* that they rejected as artificial any attempt to divide it into realistic and transferential components. The remaining group of classical Freudians resembled the group identified as developmental Freudians in valuing the idea of the real relationship. However, other differences emerged in the data analysis. In particular, developmental Freudians tended to be more influenced by the work of infant researchers. They also tended to place greater value on extratransference interpretation. The reason these two tendencies might be connected is discussed at greater length at the end of this chapter. Here, let it just be noted that analysts who work regularly with children and/or immerse themselves in research pertaining to the actual quality of the mother–child bond may be more inclined to put emphasis on those portions of the patient's experience that lie beyond the treatment relationship.

Beyond these general patterns, geographical location and institutional affiliation played a key role in selecting and discriminating the responses of the Freudian analysts, specifically the two original Los Angeles institutes affiliated with the American Psychoanalytic Association (the Los Angeles Psychoanalytic Institute and Society and the Southern California Psychoanalytic Institute) and The Anna Freud Centre in London. These institutional links are not surprising since the concept of the "real relationship" was described by Anna Freud and elaborated by Ralph Greenson, as was the concept of the "working alliance".[1] Freudians in London, Los Angeles, New York,

---

[1] The reader will find that analysts refer to the "working," "treatment," and "therapeutic" alliances interchangeably. However, it is interesting to note what Greenson (1967) said about these concepts: "Terms like the 'therapeutic alliance,' of Zetzel (1956), the 'rational transference' of Fenichel (1941) and the 'mature transference' of Stone (1961) refer to similar concepts. The designation working alliance, however, has the advantage of stressing the vital elements: the patient's capacity to work purposefully in the treatment situation. It can be seen at its clearest when a patient is in the throes of an intense transference neurosis and yet can still maintain an effective working relationship with the analyst. . . . The working alliance comes to the fore in the analytic situation in the same way as the patient's reasonable ego, the observing, analyzing ego, is separated from his experiencing ego" (p. 192).

and San Francisco who had been influenced by Greenson and, in the case of the New Yorkers, by interpersonal ideas responded enthusiastically to the idea of the "real relationship." Indeed, with respect to this network of concepts, Greenson's influence clearly divided the Freudians into a more "classical," older (in age) group, and what could be called a more relationally minded, "contemporary" Freudian group. The British Freudians who used this concept were either child analysts or analysts who had trained and worked with Anna Freud. As Ralph Greenson was a close friend and supporter of Anna Freud and a regular participant at the annual colloquia held at the Anna Freud Centre, his ideas are part of the conceptual currency of analysts linked with the Centre.

The following four sections present excerpts from interviews with Freudian analysts in four cities: London, New York, San Francisco, and Los Angeles.

LONDON FREUDIANS: "CONTEMPORARY" AND "CLASSICAL"

To avoid confusion over the different subgroups of analysts within the Freudian group, I remind the reader that all British Freudians officially belong to what is now called the Contemporary Freudian group of the British Society. According to both my understanding of the interview discussions and the statistical results, even British Freudians divide up into a minimum of two groups. One subgroup, the smaller group, consisted of older analysts who had trained with Anna Freud and who held many of the same views as the American "classical Freudians." The other subgroup, consisting of the younger analysts, expressed more "contemporary" approaches in that this group was strongly influenced by relational perspectives, specifically those of British Independent colleagues. In terms of orientation, analysts in the second subgroup either were rated as falling on the edge of the British Independent cluster or as belonging to the "developmental Freudian" group, which included many of the American Freudians.

A few of the more "contemporary" or "developmental" Freudians spontaneously connected the network of concepts under review. In making these links, they seem to demonstrate the ways that concepts are associated in the analyst's preconscious conceptual repertoire. Although a number of Freudians expressed negative attitudes toward the concept of the "transference neurosis," nevertheless the concept continues to play a role in Freudian thinking. As is explored in the next chapter, neither British Independents and Kleinians nor American interpersonalists and self psychologists referred to the concept. In the interviews with the Freudian analysts, however, the concept of the transference neurosis emerged in discussions of the treatment alliance as well as of the real relationship. It seems that, for those analysts who discriminate between transference and reality, the two concepts go hand in hand. In other words, perhaps the treatment or working alliance is required to counterbalance the fantasy distortions and illusions of the transference neurosis.

The following excerpts from the interview with one of the more widely influenced and eloquent British Freudians exemplify this approach. Incidentally, this analyst was one of the few British analysts to have studied Kohut's work and to have applied his ideas clinically.

"I see transference as universal, but also as an artifact in every analysis, and it can very much reflect the *personality* of the psychoanalyst. In a way, I disagree with the classical Freudian position. I mean, Freud warned us that we should not feel that transference has anything specifically to do with us, but I have a feeling you can't get away from the personality aspects. If you take on patients in second and third analyses, you see this in a very obvious way. I have taken on somebody recently who was with a very austere and cold analyst, and I think I am not like that. It is a dramatic difference.

"I have always felt that Greenson made a very big impact with that paper "The Non-Transference Relationship and the Real Relationship." I especially feel this because of being a member of the British Society, where you do see one group, the Kleinian group, that pretends to interpret transference virtually the moment that the patient walks into the door. And I have always felt that a sort of language develops in those analyses where transference becomes not only part of the interchange, but also is what is expected by people who then anticipate a particular kind of analysis. Of course, the same is true for the Contemporary Freudian analyses; people often come *not* expecting transference interpretations. But things have changed now because everybody, even the Americans, are very alert to transferences.

"I think that it is very important to allow transference to *develop*—this may not be in line with what your research is about—but, you see, there was a time when there was a great deal of talk about the *treatment alliance*. And analysts, especially classical analysts, were thinking they must try and evoke a treatment alliance because that is what everything depends on. My feeling is that, were Greenson or Elizabeth Zetzel writing about these things now, they would not get heard at all because most good analysts should not be looking to try to evoke a treatment alliance—it is a bit seductive you know. It is easy to be nice to people and build that up. The problem is that the people who need the treatment alliance or therapeutic alliance most of all—borderline patients— are the very ones who can't actually use those sorts of interventions. Whereas the ones who need it least—the neurotics—and who will develop transferences anyway are the ones with whom you should not be creating an alliance.

"The author who most impressed me about this is Merton Gill. I feel that he was very strong on delineating how a treatment alliance that is forced is actually a highly transferential type of organization. You can't easily separate it. Whereas the real relationship, I think that really is different. The treatment alliance can become a *terrible resistance*, really a deep transference resistance which you might never be able to overcome in analysis. When I did my training, I really spent a lot of time on "Be nice to the patient." I had two supervisors: one was a very old, classical analyst who was very warm and caring; I learned an enormous lot. But the second supervisor was a really brilliant clinician. He was able to judge these things to perfection at the clinical level, a really outstanding clinician. He very quickly picked up that I was interpreting in a very inhibited way. I was learning to interpret in this sort of packaging, by name, in such a way that I didn't have any impact at all. He really got me back to where I should have been."

When I asked this analyst to elaborate further on his view of the real relationship as distinct from transference and the treatment alliance, he answered:

"I do have some feelings about it. I think that Greenson was very exhibitionistic in the way he expressed this. He sort of paraded it in such a way that if the patient told him he talked too much— which was one of the things the patient noticed he did—he would admit that he talked too much, and then look for associations. I would go along with that up to a point. And he would have made the same point—that, of course, you don't *burden* the patient with whatever it is about you. I am a little less inclined to make a virtue of it, if you like. It is something to bear in mind. If you make a mistake, it is proper to say, 'Perhaps I got that wrong.' But not to make a meal out of it. You see I am a great believer in the *quality of the relationship*. If the quality of the relationship is good, you don't have to parade these things because it is so obvious from the reliability, the consistency, and so on. And, if the quality of the relationship is good, then you don't have to be a brilliant interpreter. If the quality is bad, it doesn't matter how brilliant the transference interpretation is; it can meet with insurmountable resistances. I think that that in a way was Greenson's point. But I think that analysts have held the transference interpretation as being the most sacrosanct. It is. One can't do without it, but it isn't much good if the quality of the relationship is poor. That is my feeling.

"I believe in the fairly detached classical, silent beginning of the analysis. I think that that stands the best chance of developing a transference neurosis; a proper transference neurosis can really develop only where there is a nonintrusive, noninterfering type of analyst. Of course, there are exceptions, because from time to time you see a patient where it becomes an emergency to interpret the transference even in the first session. But the best chance of developing a transference neurosis is if you interfere as little as possible. Not to behave coldly or austerely, since I think the analyst has to give a bit of the nontransference relationship as well—that is, greet people coming in the door, shake hands— behave in a proper way."

The views of Dr. Smith, the Contemporary Freudian analyst from America who had trained with Anna Freud, are unique in that his historical perspective comprises both American "classical" and British "relational" influences:

"This has been talked about by, let's call them, the Viennese "classical" analysts because Freud, in places, made the distinction between transference and a more realistic, positive relationship. This distinction was made clearer by Richard Sterba and Anna Freud and then well articulated by Greenson, whose view is close to mine. There's a kind of interpenetrating of what you might call the *therapeutic relationship*, the actual helping relationship where you're doing a technical-type job, which is the *working alliance*; and then there's a *real relationship* or an *ordinary relationship*, which is in the background, which is two human beings that are in an unusual situation but they're two real human beings and certain aspects of the interaction are just ordinary. Gradually, the transference relationship starts flooding or permeating the analytic situation. As I see it, you've got three complicated, differentiated levels all the time, with different weights on them, and I would always be paying attention to all three, and taking up whichever was the most therapeutically effective at the time.

"And is there a question about *extratransference interpretation*? Because I see that as a little different to these three levels which always exist. This gets us into another realm, because a lot of my analytic interventions would be interpretations, reconstructions of the person's developmental past. And that's not using the immediate transference; that's trying to construct an understanding of what happened to them in their childhood, in their development, and I would even use present-day relationships if I saw they were transferring from the past into their work relations or family. So I would interpret those too, and I think, by English standards, that would be called extratransference because it's not me as the analyst. And interpreting dreams, I think of that as sort of extratransference because I would be interpreting the dream as an *intrapsychic*, a sort of very complex message from the person's unconscious which I would see as relatively independent of me, as it is in thousands of people that are dreaming but who are not in analysis. It's the old Freudian thinking about interpreting the unconscious as it emerges in dreams."

Dr. Smith associated the interpretation of the transference element in dreams with the development of the transference neurosis "stage":

"That's fundamental to my approach, and, of course, that comes from working with neurotic patients and not highly disturbed patients where it takes a different form. If I happen to be referred, or a patient becomes, a very disturbed patient, then I take a different model, more a holding kind of Winnicottian approach, or an ego-supportive approach. But if the patient is in, let's call it, the normal neurotic range, which is quite broad, then—it's really from Freud—you leave it alone until it becomes a resistance and a major interference, or, rather, major phenomenon, in the analysis. So it is based on what I would call the growing plant model—you know the neurosis is there, and you know the fantasies were originally there, and you hold them in your mind because you want the thing to grow and become a very powerful, central force in the analysis. It may take months."

I asked Dr. Smith how the transference neurosis "stage" might relate to the therapeutic alliance:

"The alliance would be more of a *passive* approach, listening, trying to keep the patient free associating and bringing in more material, feeling safer and trusting in the situation so that more unaccept-able memories and thoughts come out. I would see that as the cru-cial thing in the beginning, not doing brilliant insight transference interpretations even if they're obvious. It's a very different model than the English one and the Kleinian influence on Englishmen. It is a little bit old, the old Viennese or 1930s–1940s Viennese way."

Another analyst, who had trained with Anna Freud and worked in the Wartime Nurseries, talked personally about the ways she under-stood the "real relationship":

"I think it is very important, and very much denied and neglected by some of our colleagues at the moment. This is a very interesting issue with people who deny that the present-day reality about the analyst matters. There are two areas in my life where I have seen it and watched it quite consistently. One was when I was pregnant, very many years ago, and I was taught at the time that the reality of the analyst is not really what matters. And the second is now, when I am so old, there are the transference fantasies that are influenced by the fact that I am old and by the way I look. The other thing that from the very beginning always seemed important to me is whether the analyst is male or female. With aging, the fear of loss and death is very much more intense and comes out even more sharply in patients with whom, in their childhood and life-time, the ideas of loss and the loss of a parent have *not* played a big part. For instance, I have a patient who, each time I answer the door, says, 'Oh, you are here.' At first, it sounded as though he thought I had forgotten his appointment, but it was clearly about the idea that 'she might not be alive anymore.' And with him, it was possible to link the idea with a great deal of fantasy, largely of hostility, and wishes that his mother would die.

"I also feel that the treatment alliance is extremely important. Where there isn't one, one must really think about all the hostil-ity that is expressed by not being allied. Is that something that can be analyzed? With some severely disturbed people you read about, and where you can see that an alliance never really devel-oped, the analysis comes to an end. This is what is often referred to as the *negative therapeutic reaction*. I have experienced it myself with people who find the idea that the analyst is superior, in the sense that the analyst has been able to help and the patient is therefore second-best, quite unacceptable. I have seen one person who has stopped analysis three times with different analysts at the very time when it was quite clear that there was great improvement. But the idea that the analyst helps or has ideas and knows something the patient doesn't know is unacceptable. Then the alliance is gone. I find the alliance so important with children. I don't create it first, as Anna Freud did early on, but I have worked so much with teenagers and it is extremely difficult with some teenagers, just because it coincides with the time when they want to be separate. And so it is so important to say, 'We work together.' You don't get very far if the alliance isn't there."

Another British Freudian analyst, who also had trained in child analysis with Anna Freud, focused on different aspects of these concepts. Many of his views were closer to those of Kleinian colleagues:

"I see the real relationship more as being polite, civilized, and as a counteraction to analytic interpretation, which can be persecutory, and like a constant attack. But I don't think there is much efficacy in the concept though—Well, you are a nice person—the humanity comes across, but that is not analysis. I don't feel it is necessary to have a treatment alliance in the sense that you set it up. In fact, I also don't feel strongly that a patient should be psychologically minded. It is a balance between the different forces within the personality, within the person. If those factors are missing, then it is harder to work, that's all. For instance, my psychotic patient, he was one where the alliance was not there, but he was clinging to me for his life, and on that we built something. He was using me so as to be less afraid of what was going on in his mind. But that is not an alliance in terms of working with. And that can be a defensive thing too. To me the important thing is more about the patient being able to work in analysis, much more important than the concept of therapeutic alliance.

"Also I don't think it is useful to acknowledge or apologize for, or explain, mistakes. I have done it in the past, but I am not happy about it. I would not do it now. Now, I think it is better if the patient can experience the failure.

"I think we work mostly with the transference neurosis. It is a useful concept, but it has become so general that it no longer has much

of a distinctive quality. I think now it has to do with the interpretation of anxieties, which starts right from the beginning, not after the
structure is set up. And this is because of the kind of patient we are
seeing; there are borderline and character deficiencies and self-dis-
orders, which aren't so well organized as the neurosis."

NEW YORK FREUDIANS:
"CLASSICAL" AND "DEVELOPMENTAL"

Senior members of the New York Psychoanalytic Society expressed little interest in the concepts of the real relationship and the treatment,
or therapeutic, alliance. Most subscribed to a loose concept of the
transference neurosis as representing habitual ways of feeling and perceiving. Unlike those of British Kleinians, however, negative attitudes
toward the nontransference elements of the analytic relationship did
not imply that everything was interpreted within the transference.
The views of Dr. Braun show the subtlety and complexity with which
older New York analysts understood these newer developments:

> "It would be easy to answer the question of the real relationship if
> you did not mention Greenson's views. There is a real relation-
> ship—namely, that the analysand comes into treatment with the
> expectation that the doctor can help him. But into that anticipa-
> tion he brings with him all sorts of preexisting hopes and dreams
> and fantasies so that it is impossible, at any particular moment, to
> isolate the transference from what might be called a real relation-
> ship. But the real relationships are minimal. Since you mention
> Greenson, I will comment on that. The analyst has a real person-
> ality. The patient may or may not recognize aspects of the real
> personality, depending on the strength of their transference
> needs. So that, in actual practice, one has to be very creative to
> draw the line as to what is the real relationship, other than, of
> course, the assumed professional responsibilities and the transfer-
> ence relationship. Greenson's distinction is projecting too much
> of the analyst's interests and self-image."

Consistent with these views on the real person of the analyst, Dr.
Braun observed:

> "I don't find any specific usefulness in either the treatment
> alliance or the transference neurosis. If the patient comes and

keeps on coming, then he has allied himself at some level. If his resistances are so great that you can't make any progress, then you have a difficult problem. But I don't think that having a preparatory situation does anything to change it. I don't find the concept of the transference neurosis useful as such because, if one wants to be strict about the use of the term, then you would have to have a situation in which the symptoms of the neurosis now become the symptoms of the interrelationship between the analyst and the patient. That does not always happen in that form, and transference always occurs in many, many other forms. Transference is transference, but you analyze all the forms as they appear. A neurosis is a relatively structured concept, something of that sort may happen in the course of analytic treatment or it may not; all events, transference neurosis or nonneurotic aspects of the transference, they all have to be analyzed.

"Whether the patient's perception is correct or not is really irrelevant. What matters is the evocative power that a particular perception has had for the patient's thinking, what dynamic effect it has had upon the patient's associations and the emergence of material."

Addressing the contemporary focus on transference interpretations, Dr. Braun stated:

"I am completely against this idealization of here-and-now transference interpretations. What one does in an analysis is make connections and give meaning to the flow of the patient's associations. To be able to demonstrate from what the patient has said, and the configurations and the contexts and the manner in which the material has appeared in sequence, to demonstrate how certain unconscious forces representing experiences and unresolved conflicts from the past are embedded in the present and are causing the patient difficulties in the here and now. It is not always a transference interpretation that is necessarily mutative, and some transference interpretations are not immediately mutative but are mutative later on after a certain dynamic has taken place in the course of the patient's work at the analysis. So I take issue with Strachey's position completely."

Three senior New York training analysts of the next generation, affiliated with both the New York and the Columbia Psychoanalytic Institutes, gave less consistent responses to this network of concepts.

Unlike the older analysts, all agreed on the value of the real relationship as separate from transference.

The first analyst in this group referred to a research project undertaken 20 years ago by himself and his fellow candidates:

"We interviewed senior analysts such as Phyllis Greenacre, Edith Jacobson, Rudolph Lowenstein, all of whom had undertaken a large number of second analyses. Very interesting what came out. Most of them were European-trained analysts, and they thought that many American analysts—at that point analysis was in full swing in this country—had taken over a rigid and judgmental, almost puritanical, attitude in their work. And this was in contrast to the less judgmental demeanor of the European analysts. That would be particularly true of Jacobson, a very accepting lady. I think that is the kind of stuff you don't find written up. I think there are certain analysts who do better with certain patients beyond any interpretive stance. There are other people who have a judgmental bias and it leaks in. Americans may have it more than first-generation European analysts.

"In this context, extratransference interpretations can be helpful—especially with patients who are lawyers, who have a great deal of difficulty in accepting transference interpretations. You have to interpret outside. This is a problem particularly with beginning analysts; they are so obsessed with showing us as supervisors that they know it is transference, and God forbid we think that they haven't seen it, that they almost bombard a patient. The patient tells them, 'You are a fucking egomaniac.' Now, that patient happens to be correct. The interpretation is probably correct, except that it has lost impetus. If you want a musical analogy, you can't play one theme without some kind of variation. We become sort of Johnny-One-Notes."

This analyst responded enthusiastically to the concept of the real relationship:

"Oh, Greenson. Absolutely. You can't deal with *termination* effectively if you don't acknowledge the real relationship. For example, a patient—another attorney—who has been reworking through a grief about his father's death which he couldn't deal with 20 years ago. He comes in today and says, 'You know, beyond what you mean to me, you have been a very real person to me, I know a lot about what you like, you like art, etc., and this has been a unique experience with somebody who is willing to hear things that nobody else is interested in. I am sure that when I leave, I will not be interested in sharing feelings with people because in my life I never have, all my life I have been a private person.' What are the criteria for termination? One of them used to be the resolution of the transference neurosis. I don't think we use that any more. We are talking about the working through of transferences, or a diminution in the intensity of the transference. And here the real relationship is crucial.

"I think the therapeutic alliance is vital. I think that it is the climate of the analysis, and that is what these senior analysts in our research sample were talking about. In a sense it is the holding environment. But it is more than that, because to my mind the holding environment in its imagery is a passive role which is fine for certain people. Therapeutic alliance is a *bilateral, active, complementary role*, you and the patient. I use it all the time when somebody says, 'Well, you know, you know the answer' and I say, 'No, I don't. But with your help both of us might understand what is going on.' But you can't do analysis with one hand clapping. It is a much different role, and I think that, if you haven't established it at a certain point, you never work."

The second analyst in this group of three also commented on the way "transference interpretations had been greatly overplayed":

"Looking back on my experience over the years, I can think of a number of patients where I would be hard-pressed to say that successful work had been done within the transference but where a great deal of work was done on extra-analytic transferences which had powerful results. And, of course, there is a real relationship. Patients pay bills, come on time, have consensually validated perceptions of what is going on which can be recognized as such. But that does not mean that none of that is interpretable or that it does not have transferential aspects. So I think it is an error to think that everything the patient is doing is transference as some analysts imply. On the other hand, accurate perceptions are also interpretable. I don't agree that we only interpret distortions; we also interpret the patient's correct perceptions, interpretations, etc. For instance, today I am tired; I am not as receptive as usual. It is not a distortion, but nonetheless it has a particular meaning. Yes, sometimes I think it can be enormously important to validate. For instance, with patients who are already burdened with loads of guilt because they think bad things about people, they ought to know that they were right. Yes, they saw you on a bad day or when you were sick.

"On the other hand, I don't really have much use for the concepts of the treatment alliance and the transference neurosis. Obviously, to do analytic work, you and the patient need some mutual understanding as to what you are doing together in the room, but that seems to me fairly primitive and basic and not in itself deserving of attention. I think transference covers what I need. I think the transference neurosis is dead, it is a useless and meaningless concept and it has posed an ideal of something going on that is not going on—one of those concepts we should drop."

The third analyst in this group linked transference with prejudice in everyday life.

"Prejudice resides, it seems to me, in the inability to correct a stereotype based upon an individual interaction. I would see the neurotic distortion in transference as a fixed view, reflective of that same inability to correct a distortion. Now, how does this relate to transference in the analytic situation? The analytic situation is designed, through a certain technical stance, to create a situation in which distortions will express themselves in a situation of regression where they will not be so readily corrected by immediate responses on the part of the analyst as in everyday life.

"Now, I also think about transference from two other points of view. One is the view of Phyllis Greenacre and Leo Stone about primary or 'primordial' transference,' i.e., transference in a formal sense that is a substratum for psychoanalysis. And I think if the substratum of trust in the relationship does not exist on that level, then analysis is not possible in important ways. However, there is also a second aspect which I have been interested in, and that is the real relationship between the analyst and the patient; that is a substratum that is potentially experienced. Unlike the primal transference, which is fundamentally a very primitive unconscious phenomenon, this is something else, a positive relationship that also is subject ultimately to analysis. It is probably best expressed as a sort of wishful, good parental transference that becomes apparent at the end of the analysis and is then subject to discussion. It is reflective not only of the analytic stance but also of the actual interaction that really does go on, certain modes of behavior, the ambiance, the way people talk. And this is also what I meant by the real person. Every relationship with a patient you know well has special characteristics. And you talk to no two people the same way. No two patients talk to you the same way. This is something we tend to ignore. Also the serendipitous encounter with a person who resonates, with whom you can talk. And it is enormously valuable and very hard to predict. I do a lot of referrals and consultations and try to find someone with whom a person will resonate. Also, you know, things do change because patients are also very much affected by what is going on in their current lives, and that stimulates new transferences. Change does not all have to do with what used to be called the transference neurosis."

I asked this analyst how he distinguished this real relationship from the treatment alliance:

"Well, the therapeutic alliance is a concept that I do find useful, some don't, but I think there is a sort of alliance when working in effective analysis that is sometimes disrupted but goes on for the most part. It has to do with one level of the patient's perception of the analyst as a person who is contributing with them to the analytic process, facilitating the analysis, facilitating free association in the way Tony Kris talks about."

I picked up on this analyst's reference to *free association* since this was a topic I had included in my original interview protocol but that, because of the lack of responsiveness on the part of British analysts, I had subsequently dropped.

"Don't drop that question. It is an essential aspect of the analytic process. The aim of analyzing defense and resistance is to facilitate free association so that the patient has the experience of discovering associations and putting them together—the 'Aha' phenomenon—that is, the experience of an awareness that has meaning, where the affective component is very important."

During the interview, I experienced this analyst as one of the most free-associative analysts in the sample, a quality that perhaps reflected his interest in the lives and development of artists.

It is interesting to observe that third-generation New York analysts were more open to the "real" aspects of the analytic relationship and, in this respect, linked back to analysts of the first generation who, like

Freud, had social contact with their analysands. Second-generation analysts, such as Dr. Braun, on the other hand, had fought for the acceptance of psychoanalysis as a legitimate branch of medicine and, accordingly, were concerned with the objectivity and neutrality of the psychoanalytic encounter. Another third-generation New York training analyst, a member of the IPA-affiliated New York Freudian Society, also responded enthusiastically to the concepts of treatment alliance and real relationship:

> "I can't tell you how useful I find this distinction between transference and nontransference. There is a transference, 'as-if,' relationship that derives from relationships in the past, but the patient also has a very clear picture of the analyst. Freud made this distinction in his own work, in the five technical papers, without realizing it, and in the anecdotal records of his work. I think Greenson's paper is very valuable. I have it on my courses. And I find the concept of the treatment alliance enormously useful too, the quality of psychological mindedness. I see it as distinct to transference, more as Greenson sees it, he also links it to the real relationship. I think the therapeutic alliance works on the basis of some very deep knowledge of the analyst as a real and useful person."

SAN FRANCISCO FREUDIANS

Whereas there is considerable divergence in the views of the London and third-generation New York Freudians with respect to the cluster of concepts surrounding the concept of the real relationship, the responses of the San Francisco analysts were highly consistent. The majority focused on the *process* of analysis and expressed an unwillingness to divide up this process into transference and nontransference elements. Let us look first at the responses of Dr. Friedland, the "highly circumscribed" classical Freudian described in previous chapters:

> "The central interpretive work in analysis concerns the connection between the past and present that is expressed in a person's life, and the anxiety and resistance against seeing that connection and making that integration. I find all these distinctions—extratransference, real relationship, treatment alliance—completely trivial from the point of view of technique. I would say that Greenson made rather too big a deal out of something which does

not in fact have much consequence for one's technique. The distinction is obvious and gratuitous and is not worth the trouble that has been taken over it conceptually. As for validating a patient's perceptions, that is also trivial and probably obstructive in that it expresses more the analyst's anxiety than the patient's.

"Whatever you are trying to describe by putting these labels of therapeutic alliance or containment, or holding environment, or something or other . . . I find them all trivial. Not that it is trivial to be supportive and helpful and therapeutic and to intend to be so in some responsible way, but I find them all trivial as concepts offering any technical usefulness. They don't inform as much as they seem to. In addition, I wouldn't even try to say what I understand, say, the therapeutic alliance to mean, because then the proper patent-holders would say, 'Well, that is just nonsense and gross and is not what we mean.' So I will speak English and say, yes, there has to be an intention on both parts, and the capacity for that intention, to solve a very serious problem in one of those person's lives. Presumably the analyst is equipped to do that and the patient has the resources to tolerate that kind of investigation, which is why they put up with the idea of coming to an analyst rather than a fortuneteller."

Dr. Friedland raised doubts similar to those described in the next chapter by Kleinian analysts concerning the "working" alliance:

"It becomes a bit ambiguous when people talk about *working* together. The patient is suffering and the analyst is trying to understand. But, once you get onto this 'work' problem, then analysts frequently get derailed into discussions of whether this patient is 'working properly,' I mean *really* free associating. You must get them to free associate. Well, that's nuts, to use a technical term. It just isn't what it is about. People do what they can do, and if an analyst is thinking, 'Well, this person just isn't working'—well, that is the analyst's problem. There is no other way to get people to, quotes, 'work' than to continue to try to show them not what they are *not* doing, but what they are doing. So, again, the working together, that is a sort of happy little phrase, working together sounds like a good democratic thing to do."

"A transference neurosis doesn't *develop*. What develops is its *observability*. The longer you have an opportunity to observe another person, the more observable and visible the neurosis will be, particularly when you have the opportunity of interpreting what that person is doing. People express their neuroses intensely and intensively with someone that they are seeing several times a week and in a situation in which they have the opportunity to say what comes to mind. So the kind of needlessly complicated way of stringing out reality, or insisting on the existence of a transference neurosis which was not there and which then gets resolved, that seems wasteful, and I mean conceptually wasteful."

The following excerpts from interviews with the San Francisco analysts demonstrate the overall consistency of the San Francisco Freudian group:

1. "I make no distinction between the real and transference. I see it all as transference, very close to Gill's current point of view. Actually, Gill was my first supervisor, some 30-odd years ago. He was a training analyst at our institute; he lived in Berkeley. At that time, he followed strictly the mirror view and did not put much emphasis on the interpersonal. I remember, in a continuous case conference, someone said 'Dr. Gill, what do you do if, when the patient is leaving your office, he smiles at you?' Dr. Gill said instantly, 'Just maintain your serious demeanor and not reveal any kind of responsiveness.' You know, the fear then was of distorting the transference, confusing or manipulating it. He's changed 180° on that. He would always admonish us, 'That's an interaction, be careful.' Now, he would be much more comfortable with the analyst being relatively spontaneous and then analyzing the patient's reaction to that."

2. "I certainly want to emphasize my feeling that there is no distinction between the real relationship and the transference, and I don't even make too much distinction between negative and positive transferences or the nonobjectionable transference. I just think all aspects of the transference should be analyzed as well as one can in the service of the analytic process. Very early on, when I was a candidate, I was impressed by some of the ideas about the therapeutic alliance, the real relationship, the positive, unobjectionable transference . . . Zetzel's ideas. But then quickly, through teaching and learning from others and experience, I just think of the transference significance of whatever comes up. I use the term resistance in analysis, resistance patterns. It's the individual's attempt to *maintain equilibrium to avoid*

anxiety by not revealing an affect or fantasy or impulse that is anxiety provoking. I think the terms treatment alliance and transference neurosis are used to communicate sometimes between colleagues—'Yes, we have a good working relationship'—not as a technical term. Used more descriptively, it means that the process is moving along. I don't ever think of transference neurosis, unless somebody brings it up, say, in a scientific paper or discussion."

American analysts who were active participants in meetings of the International Psychoanalytical Association tended to hold more varied views on concepts that have played a central role in the debate, as well as in the training, of American analysts. This more cross-cultural approach is illustrated by the following excerpt. Although statistical analysis of the overall responses of this analyst placed her in the classical Freudian group, her views approximate those of the younger, third-generation New York Freudian analysts. During the interview, she spontaneously linked the therapeutic alliance, the real relationship, and the holding environment as forming important aspects of the nontransference component of the analytic relationship.

"As you know, everything in our field tends to get polarized, and I think one can see the transference component in every aspect of every relationship. But nonetheless I think there is some usefulness in going along with the thinking of Zetzel, Greenson, Loewald, Stone, Gitelson, and others who have said, 'Well, look, there is a value in looking at those non-transferential aspects of the relationship and at what is called the therapeutic alliance.' Where I found a special value in these aspects has to do with Freud's original distinction between the nosology of the actual neuroses and transference neuroses, on one hand, and the narcissistic neuroses on the other. Freud turned out to be quite wrong about this. The narcissistic neuroses—pre-Kohut, of course—had to do with what we today call the psychoses, the schizophrenic illnesses, and the manic–depressive illnesses. Freud said that transferences could not be established and therefore these illnesses could not be treated. He was clearly proved wrong in this. Frieda Fromm-Reichmann and many others have said that the problem was not that there were no transferences, but that the transferences were so violent, so fluctuating, so unpredictable, and chaotic that it was much more difficult for the therapist to manage and control them than with the neurotic. With the neurotic, the intensity of the transference can be contained within the situation for the most part and within the parameters of a good, sustaining therapeutic alliance, so that the patient can walk out of the hour and say, 'I hate your guts. I hope I never see you again.' And you will know what they are saying as they walk out, but also that they will come back the next hour. They know that, regardless of their transference feelings, they are with somebody who is benevolently interested in them. That sustains the process. With sicker patients, the therapeutic alliance is weaker because of this inability to establish a firm object attachment with a benevolently interested, neutral outsider.

"Now, about the therapeutic alliance, I see it as having two components. I gathered this from my reading of Stone and to some extent Loewald. On one hand, it is based on the highest level secondary process, logical functioning—one uses one's intelligence, learning, experience of the world to pick out in every field by the best criteria one has available the expert in whom one can have confidence and whom one believes will be benevolently interested in doing the best for one. On the other hand, to be able to do that and to entrust oneself to somebody, to be willing to be a surgical patient and have anaesthesia and be unconscious while somebody tinkers with your heart or your brain, you have to have a capacity for a real, fundamental, elemental trust in other people—Erikson's concept of basic trust. So, it also rests on the establishment early in life of that capacity, which is among the most fundamental, archaic, and primitive capacities, that either one can trust the general goodness of the world, or not. And that is the failing in those who later become psychotic, in the earliest stages of their infantile relationships—they couldn't establish that basic trust. Thus, the therapeutic alliance rests on a combination of a capacity for that basic trust, together with the use of one's most highly organized intelligence and capacities and abilities.

"I agree with those like Charles Brenner and Martin Stein who say you should not let anything go by automatically and that there can be a lot of hidden resistances in the so-called therapeutic alliance. But that does not vitiate the usefulness of the concept for me. Nor do I see it as something totally separate from, or that it would have to be established before, transference. I think the boundaries are porous and transference infiltrates every aspect of the alliance. Bion's and Winnicott's ideas on containment and the holding environment are variant expressions of the therapeutic alliance. At the same time as Winnicott developed these ideas, others in America were developing similar ideas but under different names. Most Americans of my generation who did analytic training never read anything by the British. Nothing of Melanie Klein, that is sure, or the whole Independent group. We never read a single paper by Ian Suttie, Fairbairn, Guntrip, Bowlby, Balint. Winnicott, yes, but only a few papers, the 'Transitional Object' paper, the 'Hate in the Countertransference' paper, probably no others. And of the Anna Freud group, we read only Anna Freud, not Willi Hoffer or anybody else. So basically you could be fully educated psychoanalytically in this country and have read only Anna Freud's 'The Ego and the Mechanisms of Defence' and one or two papers by Winnicott."

The one "widely influenced" analyst in the San Francisco sample discussed this network of ideas as follows:

"I distinguish between social alliances, transferences, and therapeutic alliances. All of them are based on the person's repertoire of schemas of themselves and others, although they are not all realistic concerning the actual properties of the situation. The idea is for the working alliance and the real relationship to get realler and realler. I don't think the analyst is some kind of neutral, unknown personality; the patient gets to know more and more accurately—if the patient gets better—what the analyst's personality is like—or at least a sector of it.

"The transference neurosis concept is extremely useful and of central importance to analysis. The task and prototype of analysis is to evoke a regressive transference neurosis. I think psychoanalysis is a procedure for evoking transference and you work on it in relation to a therapeutic alliance. But I do think the whole idea of resolution is up for reexamining. *I don't think people ever erase their schemas*; they may learn new ones and override others, but the idea of resolution somehow came from the energy model. The entire idea is now translated into the idea that you need to develop a repertoire of flexibly used schemas for all kinds of situations, both for satisfaction and for avoiding threat. So resolution of transference means no more than that you both let yourself know what your transferences are and that they are psychologically real, but that they are not interpersonally real."

LOS ANGELES FREUDIANS AND ECLECTICS

It is not surprising that the Los Angeles Freudians, many of whom had been colleagues of Ralph Greenson, took a favorable view of the distinction between the transference and nontransference elements of the analytic relationship. The views of two older Freudian analysts, members of the Los Angeles and Southern California Psychoanalytic Institutes, are described here. The first replied:

"I think it is an important distinction, and I know that many people, especially in the past, have simply ignored the real world and I don't believe that you can. I think it is important to see the analyst not only as all the things implied by transference, but also as a meaningful person in the patient's life who can be depended on and who is perhaps a role model in terms of integrity and that sort of thing. I also think it is important to validate correct perceptions as well as to acknowledge mistakes or failures. Sometimes one is caught up in some personal, internal goings on, and the patient may remark, 'You look tired, you look stressed, you sound angry.' And then I will become aware of an edge to my voice that I had not been aware of, and I will say, 'You're right.' I do acknowledge mistakes, but I think it is important how you do it. It's not right to put the burden on the patient by saying, 'It's all your fault; look what you made me do.' But I wouldn't apologize, I think there is enough blame to go around. That would not be my way. I always look to myself, because we are in the power position and we have to take that responsibility.

"I would wait until the alliance was established before making transference interpretations. That is why the so-called Kleinian techniques always felt alien to me. A person comes into a first session and gets a deep interpretation; my feeling is that probably most of those patients go out and say, 'Who is the crazy person in there?' That may be unfair but that is my feeling. I don't like the idea of working together against resistances, as if we were adversaries. I think that is a very negative way of looking at it. I want the patient to know that I am on his side. I do think there is a difference between transference and the transference neurosis which is the reenactment of the past, it is an intensification and the focus becomes somewhat different. Ideally, the transference neurosis should be resolved by the end of the analysis."

The second analyst was trained and analyzed by Ralph Greenson:

"I think it is important to distinguish reality from the patient's response in order to show him that his response is irrational, and then to try to explain what that irrationality is. For example, I think of a borderline patient I saw yesterday who came in and spent a half hour describing her hurt and pain because I hadn't smiled at her when she came in. We tried to look at that. I didn't have to tell her that I was unfriendly; she came to recognize that this was her fragile state. So, in talking about it but without actually stating it, she came to recognize the real way I am in contrast to her fear that, unless I smiled, I was an enemy of hers. I think the relationship is very important and that the real relationship can very often have a profound therapeutic effect on the patient. It's another way of talking about the therapeutic alliance. The alliance is a relationship that is built up between the patient and the therapist, based on a working relationship in which the patient comes to feel that this person is there to understand him, and to help him and to clarify for him what is going on with himself. And the more effective this is, the stronger the therapeutic alliance. So, whenever you are able to help clarify or interpret what is going on in the patient, you are building the therapeutic alliance."

Another Los Angeles analyst, who was also a child psychoanalyst, talked personally about the stress of transference on the analyst and the need for communication outside the transference:

"I guess you can always relate a person's material to what is going on between the two of you. I just can't think that way though. Practically speaking, I can't stay with that all the time. There is a real life and if you don't pay attention to that as separate from what is going on between the two of you, then it gets to be an oppressive situation. And there is something else: the burden of the analysis is sometimes very great not only on the patient but also on the analyst. At the same time as you are there as an analyst, you are a kind of friend and you do and say things that would be in that realm. For instance, a lot of analysts will recommend a movie, or a patient of mine is taking a trip to Prague and he knows that I went to Czechoslovakia and he said, 'Gee, I would like to get some advice from you about places to go,' and I probably will tell him. But I won't necessarily see that as the real relationship, but as something going on in the context of the analysis. I also don't use the concept of the treatment alliance much. When there is resistance, I don't think the patient is fighting against you; they are fighting to maintain a degree of equilibrium and *they are terrified that the homeostasis is going to be lost.* That is not a resistance, but a desperate need to hold together."

DISCUSSION

The conclusion to this chapter includes a digression into a topic that was not discussed during the interviews and was not one of the 27 items on the interview protocol: the subject involves the relevance of infancy research to clinical practice. An interest in studies of an observational nature has implications for analysts' conscious and preconscious beliefs about the external world as well as standards of objectivity. When I examined the P.O.Q. scores of the American analysts presented in this chapter, the influence of infancy studies (Bowlby, Emde, Stern et al.) was clearly associated with positive responses to the idea of the real relationship and, to a lesser extent, the therapeutic alliance. It seemed to me that here was an example of a preconscious logical link between beliefs in the existence of an external or public reality, on one side, and the validity of observational studies on the other. Responses to the two questionnaires drew this association "out of the woodwork."

How, then, might infant observational studies fit with analysts' preconscious beliefs in the external world as these are reflected in discussions of the real relationship? During the last 10 years, we have witnessed a radical shift in the attention given by psychoanalysts to the findings of infant research. This focus can be explained, in part, by the promise research holds out for greater objectivity within the unsystematized, relativistic, somewhat chaotic discipline of psychoanalysis. Of course, the interest in infant observation is not entirely new to psychoanalysis. In some European psychoanalytic training institutes, observational courses of infants and young children have formed an integral part of the core curriculum for a long time. In Britain, the four analytic training centres—The British Institute of Psycho-Analysis and the three child trainings at The Anna Freud Centre, the Society of Analytical Psychology, and the Tavistock Clinic—have always placed the infant observation course at the beginning of training because of its profound affective as well as diagnostic impact on new candidates (Brafman, 1989). But these observational trainings for future psychoanalysts do not have the same goals, nor are their results put to the same use, as the observational studies of Mary Ainsworth, Robert Emde, Lou Sander, Daniel Stern, Colwyn Trevarthen, and others. Apart from training candidates' observational, memorizing, and recording skills, no attempt has been made by the psychoanalytic institutes to systematize the method and results of the observations. In the last decade, however, audiovisual equipment has revolutionized what can be observed, and a wealth of observational material has filtered from academic settings into the developmental models of all but the most "classical" adult analysts. Thus, analysts are increasingly affected during training by the new views of infancy, in particular the contribution of the developing infant to his own destiny.

Arguably, the resurgence of attachment theory is currently shifting the boundaries of the field of psychoanalysis. Concepts that described instinctual behavioral patterns organizing attachment were totally ignored by psychoanalysts when first introduced by John Bowlby in the 1950s and 1960s. Bowlby's (1958) paper on the child's tie to the mother, based on both observation and clinical work, was scorned on both sides of the Atlantic: in the United Kingdom, by Anna Freud, Melanie Klein, and Donald Winnicott; in America, by Margaret Mahler and Rene Spitz. Bowlby's work received some attention during the 1970s, when more traditional psychoanalysts such as Margaret Mahler started to change their model of development. Using accepted concepts such as symbiosis and separation-individuation, these thinkers provided a bridge so that psychoanalysts could consider the motivating power of attachment in contrast to drive satisfaction.

Another stimulus for interest in interactional studies is the intersubjective point of view put forward by contemporary self psychologists. There is considerable clinical overlap between the intersubjectivists and the attachment therapists, although the two models develop from very different premises. In the psychoanalytic literature, the qualifier *inter*subjective refers to the overlap between *two* minds—the analyst's and the patient's—and the term does not usually have the wider public significance it carries in other disciplines (for instance, in developmental psychology, the philosophy of science, attachment theory, and existential psychotherapy). Indeed, the concept of intersubjectivity was introduced by a number of leading self psychologists to achieve a specific purpose: to emphasize both the irrelevance of the objective or real world and the overriding importance of subjective experience and psychic reality. We would expect, then, that analysts who use the concept of intersubjectivity do not subscribe to the correspondence theory of truth. Intersubjectivists usually subscribe to the coherence theory and take a relativist position on truth.

We can also conjecture that some of the attraction of current infancy studies is that they fit the common-sense idea that there is a world to be observed that is independent of our enquiries—an objective world, perhaps, that is highly relevant to the clinical domain of "psychic" or "internal" reality. The relative autonomy of this world from our individual assumptions or prejudices is supported by the commonality of its effects on group behavior. In its effort to free itself from the "myth" of the objective, where objectivity is linked to material nonhuman reality, some psychoanalysts have tended to overlook the important role that causal explanations and communal beliefs play in ordinary human discourse. A first step in this direction was taken by Freud when he drew the distinction between material and psychic reality. The second step was to define terms like objectivity and causality within the framework of material, that is, nonhuman, reality. Using a distinction made by philosophers at one time between reasons and causes, some analysts went on to jettison the whole idea that causality has a place in the psychic domain.

When psychoanalysts restrict the use of causality to the concept of linear causality that once prevailed in the physical sciences, it follows that reasons do not cause mental events. As a number of modern philosophers have observed (Hopkins, 1988; Cavell, 1993), however, reasons *are* causes. Although reason-explanations do not have the same degree of generality or predictive power as causal explanations in the physical sciences, nevertheless motives play a causal role in explaining human action. These thinkers argue for the weaker concept of "causal relevance." The 17th-century philosopher Gottfried von Leibniz distinguished between causes that *necessitate* and those that *incline*: in reasoning about morals and politics for the purpose of discovering the causes of human actions, Leibniz (c. 1689) observed, "We avail ourselves tacitly of the same assumption that there is always a reason or cause which inclines the will. . . . There is always a reason, that is to say, a greater inclination, for what has in fact been chosen. . . . This does not master freedom although it inclines it" [p. 113].

When we say that reasons are causally relevant to mental states and human action, we mean that we can trace complex webs of association among conscious, preconscious, and unconscious beliefs and desires and the actions these incline.

In my experience, this inclination toward intersubjective agreement is borne out in conferences in which mother–infant interactions are observed by the audience. Audiovisual presentations of mother–infant interactions seem to occasion (Leibniz's "incline") similar reactions in large audiences. When an infant's crying is ignored by a mother, the audience winces, moans, leans forward as if to do something. When an infant smiles and looks eagerly at her or his mother's face, the audience smiles and "aahs," and sits back. Later discussants may differ over their interpretations of what the cry or smile *meant* to the mother. But, in the many presentations I have attended, audience responses are nearly always uniform and seldom discrepant. Surely, then, some beliefs must cohere with one another since we do not simply react "affectively," irrespective of what we believe. We enter into the emotional world of the child because we interpret his or her actions and expressions in similar ways. Crying makes us want to do something, to reach forward and stop the distress. Smiling and laughing make us smile and laugh. There are behavioral patterns, or predictable sequences of behavior, that we designate "basic" or "hard-wired" (for example, Bowlby's five "fixed action" patterns of neonatal development) because our responsiveness to them is highly regulated and predictable. Other behaviors are more difficult to interpret and do not express themselves that clearly. For instance, we ascribe insincerity, lying, deceit, and pretense to behaviors that do not fit together in a more transparent way. One behavior cancels out the other, leaving us wondering what the person is "really" saying. We seem to feel a more direct relation, however, with such behaviors as smiling and crying. These behaviors do not feel as if our response to them needs to be mediated by sophisticated rules of interpretation. We would feel that the person who does not react with immediate concern to, say, a baby's radiant smile or searing distress lacks sensitivity, or that his or her natural kinship with others is disturbed.

It appears that infant studies offer an alternative route to objectivity other than reliance on instinct. We seem inclined to respond with a degree of convergence not far from the unanimity with which we might say, "Yes, the grass is green." Intersubjective agreement is high. In contrast, descriptions of the various manifestations of Freud's "death instinct"—for example, turning away from life, conservation of energy, persecutory anxiety, fear of extinction, evil, the perversions, the nirvana principle—lack consensus even among those who value the concept. Whereas we feel little need to justify our responses to a crying baby, most non-Kleinian analysts find Freud's death instinct unintelligible; the belief seems unjustified. These analysts would surely agree with Gregory Bateson when, in the metalogue quoted in chapter 2, he tells his daughter that an instinct is nothing more than a "black box."

To turn now to the results of the two empirical studies presented in this book (the P.O.Q. responses and the interview discussions), strong associations occurred between the explicit interest in infancy studies and both group affiliation and clinical practice. As noted earlier, analyses of the rated interviews with the Freudian analysts distinguished two groups: 1) those analysts who see infants and children in their practice and who follow the developmental literature (developmental Freudians) and 2) those who work exclusively with adults (classical Freudians). The classical analysts were strongly influenced by Freud's instinct theory but did not read contemporary developmental authors such as Bowlby, Stern, and Trevarthen. A similar lack of interest in or acquaintance with the developmental literature was displayed by the Kleinian adult analysts, who also held strong beliefs about the explanatory power, and clinical manifestations, of the death instinct. That these beliefs and practices are linked makes good sense. Instincts are known through their derivatives; they are not observed directly. Their derivatives manifest themselves in "psychic reality." Instincts do not confront the tribunal of external reality. Analysts who view interpretation as a skill for understanding the hidden psychic truths of human nature have no need to cast their eye outward into the public sphere.

CONCLUSION

My primary aim in this chapter is to look at analysts' attitudes toward the nontransference elements in the analytic relationship as these reveal philosophical assumptions about the nature of reality. It seems logical that we find greater enthusiasm for observational studies amongst analysts who do not focus exclusively on the "psychic reality" of their adult patients and who distinguish between transference and nontransference, and between the "illusory" and the "real." Child analysts necessarily interface with the child's environment; they observe the parents in a number of external contexts—for example, at the initial consultation, in the waiting room, when making arrangements, over the telephone—and they also observe them from within the child's world as this is played out in the therapy room. The child analyst works at the interface between the family, the school environment, and the internal world. The therapist not only mediates but observes these forces in action; to the child, the therapist offers himself both as a transference figure, playing out the dramas of home and school, and as a person, a supporter, sometimes even a competitor, within the family and school situation.

Further, it seemed that the preconscious link between observational studies and the delineation of reality from illusion was borne out when I reviewed the interviews with analysts in a particular psychoanalytic community in which the idea of the real relationship between analyst and patient was part of common analytic debate. Many Los Angeles analysts had discussed Greenson's clinical papers in which Greenson presents examples illustrating both the real relationship and the importance of validating his patients' correct perceptions of himself. In Los Angeles, analysts of all persuasions knew, or had heard of the work of, Ralph Greenson. One might hypothesize that Los Angeles analysts were preconsciously determined to take an interest in observational studies. With one exception, all the Los Angeles analysts in this sample were influenced by the work of John Bowlby and Daniel Stern. With the exception of the two most senior, second-generation Freudian adult analysts in New York, the New York analysts also acknowledged considerable influence by infancy studies. These New York analysts also declared strong influences by Greenson, Sullivan, the New York interpersonal school, and British Independent authors. Of course, the real relationship addresses the interpersonal dimension of the analytic situation, and this is captured in the title of Stern's (1985) ground-breaking work, *The Interpersonal World of the Infant*.

San Francisco analysts, on the other hand, acknowledged very little influence by contemporary infancy research. In contrast to the younger British Freudians and many of the Los Angeles and New York Freudians, none of the San Francisco analysts were classified as developmental Freudians. Only one of the San Francisco Freudians was classified in the "widely influenced" group of thinkers that emerged from the statistical analyses of the P.O.Q. Cluster analysis placed this analyst in the American eclectic cluster. He was unique in stating a strong degree of influence by infancy research. The only other San Francisco analyst who declared some degree of influence by infancy studies (Point 3 on the P.O.Q.) was a child analyst. As noted earlier, child analysts of all orientations formed a distinct subgroup. Thus, it seems that preconscious links can be discerned between reading the infant developmental literature, the experience of child analysts who work at the interface between the child and his or her environment, and positive attitudes toward the concept of the real relationship and, to a lesser extent, the treatment alliance.

By contrast, it seems that analysts who view analysis as a *process* related to free association and resistance are highly unlikely to divide the analytic relationship into transference and nontransference aspects. Most of the San Francisco analysts, as well as the older New York Freudians, were dismissive of Greenson's work on the real relationship and the therapeutic alliance. Like the London Kleinians, they felt that the process of analysis was not accessible to subdivision. They were not concerned with distinctions between "material" and "psychic" reality. They felt that the so-called reality of the analyst, his position as arbiter of the patient's reality and perceptions, and other factors obstruct or sidetrack an unfolding analytic process. As we will see in the next chapter, however, the absence of this distinction has different effects on the clinical practice of analysts in the different orientation groups.

Chapter 5

Objective Reality and the "Real Relationship"

British Independent, Kleinian, and American Self-Psychological Views

The British Kleinian analysts and the American self psychologists shared similar views on the concepts of the real relationship, the treatment alliance, and the transference neurosis. Both groups of analysts had little need to distinguish the real from the transference relationship, and neither group found the idea of the transference neurosis useful. Surprisingly, however, the two groups showed much less consistency in their approaches to extratransference interpretations. Attitudes toward the value of interpretations outside the transference follow logically from more general and fundamental beliefs in the distinction between transference as distortion and reality. Clearly, analysts who believe in the existence of a real relationship outside the illusory transference relationship are more likely to value extratransference interventions. In this chapter, extratransference interpretation assumes greater significance since many British Independent analysts felt that extratransference interpretations had intrinsic mutative value, quite distinct from interpretations of the transference. We can hypothesize that, for British Independents, the concept of extratransference interpretation plays a role parallel to that played by the concept of the real relationship in the work of American analysts.

Extratransference interpretation was not a central concept in the repertoire of either the British Kleinians or the American self psychologists. The majority of the analysts in both groups indicated a clear preference for the "total transference" approach, although some did not

103

dismiss extratransference comments if these culminated in transference interpretations. Younger Kleinians seemed to feel that, although they made extratransference interventions, these should be minimized if not excluded; like qualifying phrases, nontransference interpretations were seen as signs of weakness or fear aroused by the prospect of making the more probing and mutative transference interpretation. I suggest that those analysts of a self-psychological perspective who incorporate extratransference comments in their interventions do so because this type of intervention links preconsciously with positive views of the role of validation in technique. It is with respect to issues of validation of the patient's subjective experience that differences emerged in the technical approaches of Kleinians and self psychologists.

These two orientation groups differed radically in their approaches not only to the validation of the patient's perceptions but also to the acknowledgment of mistakes and failures. This contrast between Kleinian and self psychological technique follows logically from the intersubjective context in which self psychologists interpret and communicate understanding. The views of analysts in both groups on the real relationship are presented by group in the first two sections of this chapter. The views of both groups on the associated ideas in this network of concepts are discussed in the subsequent section. Approaches of American eclectic and British Independent analysts to this network of concepts are described in the final section.

KLEINIAN APPROACHES TO THE REAL RELATIONSHIP

I first present some of the ideas of Dr. Roberts, the senior analyst described in previous chapters, before discussing excerpts from interviews with Kleinian analysts in the younger group. These interview excerpts illustrate the fundamental belief shared by most Kleinians in the pervasiveness of transference. The widened concept of transference to cover the "total situation" is incompatible with the concept of the real relationship. Dr. Roberts:

> "Very rarely, I think the idea of the real relationship may be of some use right *at the end of an analysis*, but otherwise I am very doubtful about it, very doubtful. And, about validating perceptions, I think that is a problematic question. Because, if a patient says, 'I think you look very tired and worn today,' I would not validate that I am tired or worn. I would assume that it has come from inside the patient. But if I know I actually am, I would be

careful not to what I call *interpret away*. I would take very seriously the patient's observation, but I would neither validate nor invalidate—unless there was a terrible denial and I was all brown and sunny and the patient said, 'You look very pale.' There, I would not validate, but I would very much question.

"If I made a mistake, for instance if I was late or made a mistake on a bill, I would certainly point this out to the patient but I would not explain why. If I made an interpretation that the patient thought wasn't right, I would say, 'Look, when I said this and this, I don't think you thought I was quite right.' And if the patient had not dared to say he thought the interpretation was wrong, or he thought I was getting narcissistic, or I was covering up, I would absolutely show him—'I think you thought I wasn't right.' That is the way I would like to handle it, without in any way making it a point of laughter or denial. But it is awfully easy to say that kind of thing with a little giggle, and not take it seriously and not let the patient take it seriously. It is a very important thing to take it seriously.

"With failures in understanding—beware, beware, do not call your own mistakes other people's! It depends what you mean by mistakes too. If you get impatient with a patient, it may be your impatience but at the same time there may be something going on which the patient brought with him or her and which one has acted out with them. That is terribly important to notice, and again not to blame the patient because it was one's own fault for fitting in. I call this *acting in*. I have one patient who has a wonderful capacity to stir up a kind of impatience. Now, if I get impatient with that patient, I think I am acting in, that is real acting in. Or if I get flattered by another patient and get carried away with the beauty of my own thoughts, I would think that is acting in too. She is nudging me and flattering me. . . . The analyst acts in, in that way, and—very, very important—the patient acts in *all* the time, but then she should. We used to think the patient talked. And now we think, or I think, that most of the patient's talking is accompanied by acting and activity. But the analyst can also act in and that is where the analyst has to be careful."

Some examples from the younger group of Kleinians:

1. "No, I wouldn't think about it in that way at all. If something real is happening that the patient perceives, I wouldn't

ignore it. For instance, if the patient says, 'I notice you look terrible today,' and it corresponds to a reality, I wouldn't pretend that that didn't exist. But I wouldn't say, 'This is the real me' either; I would say that the patient perceived something and then see what the patient made of it. Because, of course, what the patient made of it probably has nothing to do with the *correctness* of perception. Say the patient notices that you look pale and horrible, it might be because you have a cold but the patient thinks you are dying.

"With mistakes and the like, I would always think of the meaning of it, but I would be terribly careful not to blame my patient for any nonsense of mine. I would acknowledge that, but the way I would then interpret the mistake would depend very much on the patient. You know, if you have a completely mad patient, you would have to be very careful how you acknowledge a mistake, how you phrased it, so as not to create too much paranoia, too much triumph or whatever."

2.   "No, not for the sake of saying, 'You're right.' There are many patients who are very apt to pick up anything and everything very accurately about the analyst. But the point about that is to see it in the context of the ongoing transference relationship. To me the transference is so pervasive, so much *a total feature of the analysis*, that to talk of what's real and not real is unreal to me. The patient can't distinguish the two, and the analyst can't either. I would hope I would never *explain* a mistake. I think there are times when I would acknowledge a mistake, but there is a tendency to see explaining yourself as something very virtuous."

3.   "No, I wouldn't say what is real, or what is right and what isn't. Say, for instance, that the patient's transference is maximal in those areas where they are busy with something real about you, and *they project into something that is really there*. I don't find much use for the distinction except that, obviously, the patient would distort what is there. There may be a grain of truth in it, but it may have been changed quite dramatically so that you have to take up the way it emerges. But, *for myself*, the distinction has some use. I would like to be able to sort out how much is real and how much is distorted in what the patient is observing."

SELF-PSYCHOLOGICAL APPROACHES TO THE
REAL RELATIONSHIP

The first excerpt is from the interview with a leading self psychologist in the Los Angeles area who has developed his particular self-psychological approach over a period of time, as opposed to shifting from a radically different sets of beliefs:

"Well, you could read Stolorow's paper on what is reality in psychoanalysis. I agree with that. I don't believe in the distinction. I think there is only one kind of reality in psychoanalysis, and that's psychic reality. So the idea that some aspects of the relationship are more real than others doesn't make any sense to me. If you think of transference as distortion, then you think of something as being more real which the analyst has privileged access to, which is not part of my thinking.

"I would not directly validate because a patient's need to be validated may emerge as a central theme in the transference, in which case I think I would want to investigate that and understand that. But the concept that it is the analyst's task to validate, I think that is another one of these things that elevates, that gives privileged access to, the analyst's psychic reality. What I would say is that you bring out into the open and investigate the correspondences or disparities between the two worlds of experience but without indicating in any way that one is more correct than the other. And so the fact that the patient and the analyst might see things the same way doesn't necessarily mean that they have arrived at truth."

Although the analyst just quoted is a well-known self psychologist, statistical analysis (cluster analysis) did not place him at the center of the Kohut-self psychology orientation group. The three analysts who were closest to the center of the self psychology cluster had changed first from a Freudian to a Kleinian orientation, and subsequently to a self-psychological-Kohutian framework. Their views were more circumscribed than those of the self psychologists whose views had evolved over time without a major break with previous traditions. The following excerpts are taken from interviews with those who had *changed* orientation:

1. "I don't think there is a real relationship. I think it is all part of an experience that isn't divisible in that way. I wouldn't

validate, not at all. I would say that the perception was correct insofar as there is something that the person is reacting to, whether or not I am aware of it, and I would be interested in the meaning for that person. But with people not in analysis—and this happens very rarely—who are quite ill and need validation of that sort and feel desperate about it, I might say something like, 'Well, yes I am aware of it, I was irritated or feeling tired today.' "

2.   "First of all, I don't think that transference necessarily is a distortion. And I don't think the analyst has the access to the reality that the patient does not. I don't hold with that distinction. I mean, I think the person brings their relationship to the analysis, that there is this organizing experience and then there is the actual experience which is going on and these two may or may not coincide."

3.   "I think that transference consists of the present and the past and, further, that my view differs from all the definitions that have shaped psychoanalytic thinking for all these years in that it departs from the notion of inappropriateness of transference experience, and from the notions of displacement or projection or distortion. It takes the person's subjective experience as the focus of interest without superimposing upon it a judgment as to the superiority or inferiority of the reality that is being experienced. The point is to view the patient's experience consistently from within his or her own subjective framework, from which real and transference has no meaning whatever—it is meaningless.

"About Greenson's idea of the real relationship, he was off to a very promising start. What remains valid and what he discerned and identified was the importance and significance of the impact, unconscious or unwitting or conscious, of the analyst on the patient. The importance of this he then called the real relationship. And he even extended it to—it was first in terms of acts, humane acts, and so forth—the doctrine of abstinence and neutrality, which were inimical to his own nature. He wasn't that sort of person; he tried to make it fit, but he couldn't. And that led him to the clue that the relationship with the analyst was having an impact and that what was important was to restore the bond. He also correctly recognized, although he did not articulate this, that the usual way of taking up such experiences was cruel, or inhuman or unfeeling or uncaring. He felt that when these experiences are taken up as grist for the mill, it had the important side effect of undermining the patient's perceptual set. So, operating from his own framework, now easily understandable, he tried to avoid this additional damage. The problem was that he couldn't get beyond the problem of 'real' and 'distortion'—but, again, he made a substantial leap forward. He couldn't get there. If he had lived longer, he might have and, certainly, if I had had the experience and talked to him, I think I could have shown it to him. His purpose in restoring the bond was to bring the patient back to understand the transferences that were involved and were representative of the childhood neurosis. That approach kept him then from being able to grasp the significance of the pathology that was being expressed, experienced, the damage to the self, the damage to the bond, and so forth. It led him away from his greatest skill which would have been to really investigate that.

"I think it is most important to investigate mistakes and failures. That is the most important focus in my opinion. The analyst has to get over his feeling that these are *objective* failures. This is a misconception that self psychologists also have and that others have about self psychologists—the idea that empathic attunement is based on a model of there being no disruptions in the dialogue, that the patient is right, and so forth. This is a mistake; the focus is not on the validity of the patient's experience. Of that there should be no doubt, the unquestioned and unquestioning acceptance of the patient's experience of the error or intrusion. The focus is on turning to what that meant to the patient and why it meant what it did mean. My preference would be not to validate but to bring about a setting—although sometimes it does not proceed as smoothly as one would like—in which the patient would come to recognize that the validity of her experience was not in doubt. I would not burden them with my own perspective. But that is the kind of environment I would be striving for, and if it did not happen, I would raise the question, 'Now, is there some question in your mind that I have a different perspective about this than the one you are having?' I would try to get at that rather than attempt to assure him. I am a much stricter psychoanalyst than most psychoanalysts. That is why I object to everybody saying that I have abandoned psychoanalysis."

The foregoing excerpts clearly illustrate the different approaches of Kleinians and self psychologists to the interpretation of failures and mistakes. Although both groups felt that the distinction between transference and distortion was irrelevant and both focused on the meaning or psychic reality of patients' responses to mistakes and disruptions, the Kleinians did not view failures as providing a fertile area for analysis and psychic change. And despite the internalist position of both orientations toward reality, Los Angeles self psychologists focus on the *inter*subjective in contrast to the *intra*subjective context in which failures accrue meaning.

Though neither group used infancy research to bestow objectivity on their interpretations, it is interesting to note that the three Los Angeles self psychologists who had changed orientation acknowledged the considerable influence of infancy research on their thinking. The attention given by self psychologists to the disruption of the bond in analytic work clearly reflects central concepts in the many infancy studies that have developed out of Bowlby's original theory of attachment. The primacy of the attachment bond and the kind of interpersonal exchanges that occur between mother and infant were taken as a model for therapeutic intervention and understanding. The three Kleinian analysts in the study who acknowledged some degree of influence by infant studies were child analysts in the younger age group. All three worked part time at the Tavistock Clinic, where, despite ambivalence toward Bowlby's work, regular departmental meetings force colleagues from different disciplines and orientations into proximity with one another.

TREATMENT ALLIANCE, TRANSFERENCE NEUROSIS, AND EXTRATRANSFERENCE INTERPRETATION

In this section, I look at the attitudes of Kleinian analysts and self psychologists toward the concepts of the treatment alliance, the transference neurosis, and extratransference interpretation. The fact that, for organizational purposes, I place discussion of these concepts in a separate section from that of the real relationship reflects the way that non-Freudian analysts do not link these concepts either consciously or preconsciously. In the previous chapter, in which I presented Freudian views, all these concepts tended to cluster around the central concept of the real relationship. When I was talking with Kleinians and self psychologists, on the other hand, each topic was introduced by me and discussed as a discrete entity.

With one exception, analysts of both groups gave uniformly negative responses to the concepts of the treatment alliance and the transference neurosis. From a logical and conceptual point of view, these responses are highly predictable. Again, I first present excerpts from the interview with Dr. Roberts in which he states his views clearly and categorically. The responses of most of the Kleinian analysts, particularly those in the younger group, were brief and unexpansive, in part because of their unfamiliarity with the concepts. Although these Kleinians elaborated on the notion of a therapeutic alliance because of ordinary, common-sense associations to the word alliance, they answered with a simple "no" or a doubtful "no, not really" to the concept of the transference neurosis. The concept evoked few associations since it is not part of Kleinian conceptual currency. Dr. Roberts spoke dismissively of the treatment alliance:

"You mean the idea of the observing ego? I think one does eventually aim to talk to that, but not to begin with. I think one is trying to find *a bit of the ego that can for a moment listen to you*. But I expect to lose it very quickly. I don't think that that is important, any more than I think this whole notion of therapeutic alliance is really meaningful. I don't like the word therapeutic alliance. It sounds as if the patient ought to side with the analyst, or part of the patient ought to. Whereas I think that at times, if you have *relieved anxiety*, the patient can feel something, can look at something, can observe and feel gratitude—or not. At that moment, you have something which you can work with and which is on your side. But I don't care if it disappears in a minute. I really don't mind about therapeutic alliances. I think it has become a kind of moral thing. [I interjected, "Really."] Yes, like some people use the word 'work'—'you are not working properly.' All this seems to me to be something the analyst has to struggle with, and we ought not to talk about alliances. And to establish it first, I think, is nonsense. If you make a helpful transference interpretation, you get a bit of the patient gathered up with you for the moment."

Unlike with the younger group of Kleinian analysts, there was no hesitancy in Dr. Roberts's response to the transference neurosis since this was a concept with which he was obviously familiar:

"Well, no, I don't any longer—although on another level, I do. What I mean is that I don't see what you mean by transference unless it includes neurotic parts, psychotic bits, humor, everything else. I mean everything is in the transference . . . and how do you distinguish whether something is neurotic or not? So I really feel that that concept has got something terribly rigid about it—another of those rigidified structures. Say you have got an obsessional patient, he will be an obsessional patient from the word go, he will be obsessional about the way he comes to analysis. Is that a transference neurosis? Or is it just transference, character, or whatever you like?"

The responses of younger analysts were more hesitant but were markedly consistent with one another. For instance:

"The transference neurosis . . . I don't . . . I suppose . . . I can't think of any way of embellishing that, I suppose the reason why I don't agree with that approach would be that I think that one is trying to respond to the patient's need and wish to be understood. I do think that is a very inherent human characteristic and that is really what one is engaging in. I think of the treatment alliance as connected with the patient's 'observing ego.' But, the problem with things like therapeutic alliance is that it can be used defensively. You can sort of *seduce* a pseudoadult into a relationship when in fact it is quite pseudo and *as-if*, and then you can call that therapeutic alliance when in fact it's probably resistance. I would never foster an alliance. Either it is available or it isn't, and I think then you may have to interpret why it isn't available. But I would be careful, especially in the as-if area. I think it is easy to think about it in basic Kleinian terms, that is, in terms of paranoid-schizoid and depressive positions. If depressive, there would be a wish to work, and that can be during any session really; it can develop in a session. But I think you can think about it as both depressive and defensive, because the adult relationship can be at the expense of everything else, of the relationship with the infantile. You would have to keep that in mind because you can be talking to an adult *about* a baby and it would again be completely split off. One could unconsciously do that with apparently very cooperative, submissive patients; you could just be engaged in this relationship which is antianalysis. So I think it is quite a dodgy kind of concept."

When I referred to Richard Sterba's technique of using "we" in interpretations, this analyst laughed, commenting "that can be such a seduction." The following two excerpts are also from interviews with the younger London Kleinians:

1. "As far as I am concerned, the treatment alliance is built upon the patient's experience of the analyst's interpreting, rather than being built upon a sort of notion that we are friends."

2. "Um . . . yes . . . I think you have to have an idea of the alliance in your mind, but I don't think one would use it as something distinct from transference. I would, if possible, make transference interpretations with the idea of somehow making an alliance with some part of the patient that is available."

The responses of a "nonconformist" Kleinian analyst, Dr. Martin, are instructive in that his views on this network of concepts diverged from the more critical stance of Kleinian colleagues. Dr. Martin is an adult and child analyst who has worked in National Health Service settings, including the Tavistock Clinic. In answering the P.O.Q., Dr. Martin had acknowledged a much greater range of influences than had other members of the Kleinian group. With respect to the network of concepts under review, he supported the distinction between transference and extratransference interpretation. He viewed analysis as a process in which extratransference interpretations play a part and have mutative value. His responses show marked similarities to those of some the San Francisco Freudian analysts described in the previous chapter, many of whom focused more on the *process* of psychoanalysis than on the analytical relationship:

"My own attitude is that an extratransference interpretation is a stepwise progression to something. In my clinical work with a patient, I'd be listening, first of all, to what the patient is actually saying about the external person. And I would be thinking, does this relate to myself, in terms of what happened in the week, or what I did last session, or whatever? Or I would think, does it relate to a person in their own reality, say, a parental, or, if you like, superego figure? Or does it relate to the intrapsychic conflict with a bit of themselves which they have *externalized* and are having some sort of battle with in the outside? Now it may be that I can see, at that point in time, one of these alternatives more clearly than any of the others, and given the feel of the session, I might make some intervention or some interpretation about whichever one I could see most clearly. It may be that, as the session progressed and the patient said more, I would be able to see how this linked with me in the transference situation, either directly or with some variation.

"I do not think that everything should be taken up in the transference. I think that just to think immediately of transference as a projection detracts from the subtlety of analysis. I mean lots of things are projections, but there are all sorts of other things that are happening at the same time. One needs to have a sense of clinical astuteness and sensitivity towards what might be going on in the process, I want to see what happens to it. How does the patient actually deal with what I'm doing? And, if I feel that I've put in an interpretation involving myself which is not taken up by the patient, then I would be thinking, well, was I right? Was the patient defensive? Or was I wrong? Or was I wrong at this particular point in time in that that bit of me that is involved is so far away from the patient's struggle with what is going on outside, that, from the patient's point of view, it is really quite irrelevant to bring myself in.

"And in connection with that, my major thought about analysis is that it is a process between yourself and the patient, and an interaction that is going on all the time. It's not just something that *I am doing to the patient or the patient is doing to me*. The interesting thing about analysis is the *process* and the response to what one says, not just that one has made a correct interpretation."

It is interesting that, in this discussion, Dr. Martin used the Freudian concept of externalization in place of the more common Kleinian concept of projective identification; though the two terms describe a similar action, nevertheless they evoke different connotations due to the network of concepts with which they are linked. The basic distinction between transference as the "total situation" and transference as one dimension of the analytic relationship has logical implications for the network of concepts under review. Dr. Martin's use of extratransference interpretation is consistent with his more Freudian views on the related concepts of the treatment alliance and the transference. Examples from these parts of the interview with Dr. Martin follow. All the interviews started with a general discussion of transference in which the analysts talked about transference as a specific phenomenon within analysis and as a phenomenon of everyday life. In this initial part of the interview, Dr. Martin spontaneously associated to the concept of the "transference neurosis":

"My own view is that transference does go on generally, but that something really quite specific happens within the analytic situation. With some patients you see it more clearly than with others; transference occurs as always, but then you do seem to get to what one might call the *transference neurosis*, which is specifically *within* the analytic situation. As originally described by Freud, it is the transference neurosis which really brought up the blocks to the free flow of associations. This is different from the transferences which occur everywhere. That would be my basic thinking about transference."

In that excerpt, Dr. Martin spontaneously associated the transference neurosis concept with free association. As stated in the previous chapter, the idea of analysis as related to a free-associative process had formed part of my interview protocol. Since the term seemed to draw a blank from many Independent and Kleinian analysts, the topic was dropped. Dr. Martin went on to comment favorably on the concepts of the therapeutic alliance, neutrality, and the real relationship:

"Again, I would see the alliance much more in the sequential way. I think that, unless there is some bit of treatment alliance, the patient actually doesn't come. There has to be some sort of treatment alliance, but it may be a very peculiar one, or a very perverse one, or a bizarre one, or it may be a positive one. It comes and goes—sometimes patients don't want to come. And, yes, I do aim to have an attitude of neutrality; I think it is terribly important for doing the work of analysis. I know that when I find I am disturbed by something in the patient's material, it's a sort of safety net for me to drop back into, to say to myself I have to be neutral about this and understand it in terms of what the patient is doing. I find it's like a handrail or a bannister to steady yourself on when the going gets a bit rough.

"I suppose there is another meaning of neutrality that has to do with doing analytic work—that the analytic work is to analyze and, beyond that, that analysis is a good thing. This is an ethical point of view, and, in that sense, there isn't a neutrality. There is a feeling that analysis is a good thing to be doing and that by the hard, painful work the patient is going to be better off at the end of analysis than they were at the beginning. But that is different. In clinical work, there is a particular kind of neutrality and two reasons for being neutral. One is so that the patient feels they can actually produce any material and you can analyze the superego, the guilt, the anxiety, the persecution, the shame, etc. The other is that it is a protection for the analyst so that, when you are dealing with very difficult material, you can cling to your seat and to yourself and say, 'I've got to be neutral. What is all this about?' If you are dealing with very perverse material, very upsetting material, it gives you an anchor. A number of things that Freud talked about in terms of technique were *protection for the analyst* as well as concern for the patient. I think that's important. Such a lot comes over not just in what you say, but in the tone you say it. If you just have a robotic neutrality like Mr. Spock in *Star Trek*, then of course you can't be in touch empathically with the feelings—the pain, distress, conflict, triumph, disaster—that are going on in the patient and in yourself. In *Star Trek*, this is wonderfully portrayed; he just can't understand what these other people are going on about. To call that neutrality is a misuse of the need for neutrality."

BRITISH INDEPENDENT APPROACHES TO THE REAL RELATIONSHIP AND RELATED CONCEPTS

Since the views of British Independent analysts on extratransference interpretation, the real relationship, validation of perceptions, and approaches to mistakes and failures were mixed, I will briefly comment on general trends before presenting some unusual responses. Most Independent analysts made frequent extratransference interpretations, clearly focusing less exclusively on here-and-now transference interpretations than do analysts of a Kleinian or self-psychological orientation. Some thought that extratransference interpretations and the real relationship had mutative value.

Dr. Matheson, the British Independent training analyst described in previous chapters, responded emphatically:

"Yes, an extratransference interpretation might have to do with a fear of making transference interpretations. It could be. But then making a transference interpretation can equally be the analyst acting out and being afraid of making a nontransference interpretation. Transference, psychology, is a sword which cuts both ways. I don't like these rather dogmatic statements made on the basis, I think, of a failure to have a look at what is actually happening clinically. To me, that is the real issue rather than trying to fit everything into the procrustean bed of a transference interpretation—Strachey's kind of mutative interpretation. Don't forget that the Strachey type of interpretation is based upon the idea of conflict in a sort of dependency relationship, the conflictual relationship with the analyst. But there is also another type of relationship, which also includes conflict but which is, more importantly, the narcissistic form of relationship in which transference interpretations can go wrong. Here, conflict and interpretations have a very different shape and form from the Strachey type.

"I think both the real relationship and the validation of the patient's reality are vitally important. Vitally important to recognize what comes out of the patient, how much it applies to you, and being able to corroborate, if the patient does see something about you, that their perception is accurate. They are reality testing, and this is particularly important with patients with faulty reality testing. When they do see something accurately, that's something which needs to be commented on and ratified. And also this is particularly important if, say, I was ill or tired and this was interfering with the analysis, particularly with more disturbed patients. And any lack of attention on the part of the analyst which impinges on the patient and causes blockages, if you see that it is causing a blockage or impasse in the analysis, it is very important to acknowledge what they are seeing, but then to take it up and see what it means to them."

In discussing the handling of mistakes and failures, several Independents referred to Winnicott's work on the importance of the analyst's failures as these reflected early environmental failures which could then be reexperienced, understood, and modified within the analytic relationship. Others felt that it was also important that the analyst should not blame himself—a mea culpa attitude—since this could easily burden the patient with explanations. Dr. Matheson expressed the dilemma as follows:

"If you do get into a mea culpa sort of position, it sounds like, what a hopeless person I really am [laughs]! Maybe that works; the patient feels stronger if the analyst feels weaker! But you can burden the patient with guilt—why is it that this analyst is always asking What am I doing to him? In that sort of case, the patient won't get better."

The ideas of Independents on the concepts of the treatment alliance and the transference neurosis were pretty uniform. Several thought that the treatment alliance was an important aspect of analytic work, but the majority had little use for the concept of the transference neurosis. Some, particularly in the younger group, showed the same hesitancy as the Kleinian analysts:

1. "Transference neurosis . . . that's a very old-fashioned idea, isn't it? No . . . I don't use it, haven't heard of that one."

2. "It's a historical idea really. People don't talk about it so much nowadays—that's the idea that the infantile neurosis is repeated in relation to the analyst, isn't it?"

3. "No, I don't think I have an encapsulated view like that. Don't we think more generally now, that all major character conflicts may be repeated in relation to the analyst which, I suppose, is another way of saying the same thing? We talk about a transference character neurosis, rather than a specific transference neurosis."

In reading through the interviews with Independent analysts, it was possible to discern patterns of response that reflected institutional ties connected with training and work. The two most prominent sources of influence were, of course, Anna Freud and Melanie Klein, reflecting training or work at the Anna Freud and Tavistock Centres.

Two Independent child analysts discussed the relevance of the treatment alliance to work with children:

1. "Let me take this up from a slightly different angle. I'm going to start with children and then come back to adults. Thinking of an under-five: if one has a good enough relationship, whatever else is happening, the child is going to be *learning* from one because children learn from adults. So do adults, but it's easier to see with children. And, in that sense, what is going on isn't transference in the sense of reexperiencing. It can be a problem, of course, if one doesn't want to see oneself in the role of teaching. But, on the other hand, what is one doing in analysis? One is helping someone to see something and you could say that, in a way, one is in a role that might be understood as some sort of teaching role."

2. "The treatment alliance? You bet I believe in it. The moment it stops, the patient doesn't come. I think it's a non sequitur. You can't have a patient attending and paying fees unless there is a treatment alliance. I don't think you can explain

the patient's paying you the fee on the basis just of the psychotic or neurotic transference. To me a transference is essentially and primarily a distortion—there isn't a transference unless there is a distortion of reality. Unless you are going to say, 'O.K., from now on, we'll say transference is everything the patient feels about me.' I would rather differentiate the therapeutic alliance to refer to where there is no transference going on; if you like, there are just two human beings dealing with each other. One charges, the other pays. And what you then call transference means that the patient has lost a sense of reality—momentarily, temporarily, or persistently. It's a long-standing joke in England, it always has been, about Americans' fear of interpreting the transference. But you can turn it the other way around: I think Americans have a point when they say it is crazy to interpret transference the moment the patient walks into the room. Virtually every word I said to you about transference, I meant something like a transference neurosis or psychosis. It's a distortion of reality."

In preceding chapters, I referred to Dr. Stevens, the only British analyst whose responses to the P.O.Q. indicated an extensive range of cross-cultural influences. In addition, he was the one British analyst who was classified within the American eclectic cluster. Commenting on the distinction between transference and extratransference interpretation, Dr. Stevens stated:

"That distinction is too narrow in that it does not cover the many types of intervention analysts make. When you just speak of transference interpretation, you are dignifying the particular word interpretation. Do you mean by that intervention? Suppose you are commenting on the way somebody has reacted to their boss, which seems a bit like the way they felt about their parents. Is that a transference interpretation or not? One not only makes a nontransference interpretation—if that is a nontransference interpretation, i.e., an interpretation about transference phenomena occurring outside the consulting room—but one makes all kinds of interventions which don't involve notions of transference at all. I've a general bias against people dignifying the word interpretation. There are many other things that analysts do, and people often say, 'I interpreted that,' when they mean 'I said,' or 'I suggested,' or 'I commented.'

"About transference and countertransference and therapeutic alliance, I think all have a general and a special sense. We have a working alliance with the milkman, or the postman—an ordinary, reliable kind of professional relationship. I would have thought you shouldn't have to work at that. I always think that talk of promoting understanding and empathy in therapists is wrong. What's wrong is, why doesn't the therapist have warmth and understanding to begin with? You would think it was part of ordinary professional relationships—good architects, solicitors, anyone ought to be good at promoting something called a therapeutic alliance. It is about the way you welcome somebody, the way you deal with someone and make contact on the telephone. Yes, they immediately have a transference and may complain; even if you think you're being friendly and professional, they'll think you're being forbidding or seductive or something. I think both things are inherent from the beginning before therapy starts, both a working alliance and an incipient predisposition for transference. So it doesn't seem to me that you need to go out of your way to work at it. Nor do you have to remain silent for six months like the French in order to promote transference."

Independent analysts were the only British group to indicate strong influence by infancy studies—principally Bowlby's work on attachment, the films on childhood separation by James and Joyce Robertson, and the work of Daniel Stern. Only three of the older Independent adult analysts declared no influence at all. The remaining eight obtained high scores. Unlike in the Freudian and Kleinian groups, this interest was not just reflective of training in child analysis. British Independent analysts have always focused on the early mother–child relationship, both the fantasied internal object relationship and the ways that these fantasies represent actual experiences. The works of Winnicott, and to a lesser extent Balint and Fairbairn, are central to the thinking of Independent analysts, as are the larger evolutionary, social, and cultural theories of such thinkers as Charles Darwin. (Both Bowlby and Winnicott wrote that Darwin and Freud were the most formative influences on their intellectual development.) A number of the pioneer British analysts had backgrounds in social psychology and philosophy as well as in literature. For instance, Marjorie Brierley, Edward Glover, and Ernest Jones were strongly influenced by the British academic psychologist William McDougall (both Brierley and James Flugel, a founding member of the British Society, were pupils of McDougall) and by the Scottish philosopher John Macmurray. Their ideas also influenced later thinkers, such as Fairbairn, Harry Guntrip, Ian Suttie and, more recently, Charles

Rycroft and Anthony Storr. British instinct theory is not dualistic; there are many instincts, simple and compound, and each of these is experienced with its own specific affective quality. For Independent analysts, the individual is always situated in the context of a specific environment and network of relationships.

AMERICAN ECLECTIC ANALYSTS

Finally, I present excerpts from interviews with two elderly analysts who had worked with Franz Alexander and pioneered psychoanalysis in the Los Angeles area. Both were rated as belonging to the American eclectic group. The first analyst, Dr. Furnham, was described in chapter 2. He obtained the highest score in the "widely influenced" group, scoring influence "to a very great extent" (Point 5) on 9 of the 20 sources.

"I do make a distinction between transference and nontransference. I think the task of the analyst is to help the patient understand distortions in his or her perceptions wherever they occur. But the tendency to direct every distortion to the analytic core is in itself a distortion. I think that is an iatrogenic distortion which often intensifies the unrealistic aspects of the individual's relationship to the analyst. So I believe in the value of transference interpretations within the transference situation, but the whole importance of that lies in the ability to apply these interpretations and to generalize them to relationships outside. And when we see transference distortions on the outside, it is important to make those clear. Sometimes, it is possible to say, 'And you know you do the same thing in your relationship to me.' So that we can take a nontransference distortion and show the patient how it operates also within the transference, within the analytic process. And I also think that a transference neurosis is an iatrogenic artifact. There are transference distortions and neurotic transference attitudes that take place all the time in the patient–therapist relationship, but when you create a specific transference neurosis in the classical analytical sense, that is an iatrogenic artifact. It does not have to happen."

Dr. Furnham's responses to the ideas of the real relationship and the treatment alliance were highly consistent with the attitudes previously described.

"Very much so. I believe that not everything that goes on, not every perception, within an analytic relationship is a transference perception. For example, if the analyst behaves coldly or with a lack of interest and the patient perceives and reacts to that, that is not necessarily a negative transference. There is a real relationship that is going on based on the realities of their mutual relationship in addition to the transference distortions. Very often, the patient's reactions are a perfectly valid and realistic judgment of the situation and analyst. I think the working alliance is part of the realistic aspect of the relationship. The transference–countertransference phenomena may sometimes get in the way of it and have to be worked through, but what helps the patient stay with it and work through these problems is the existence of a reality-based relationship that is founded on mutual trust and mutual respect, and that is the essence of the working alliance.

"And, yes, the analyst should confirm the patient's correct perceptions. Absolutely, absolutely, it is important that the analyst be honest with his patient and not make pretensions to infallibility as unfortunately analysts do. That creates additional problems for the patient because it makes him doubt his own perceptions. But I don't believe in analyzing oneself in front of the patient. I think that is an indulgence and it often creates great problems for the patient. It is enough to say, 'I think I was wrong about that. You are right in criticizing me.' But to change it into an analysis of you by the patient becomes a very messy situation and I don't think that it is helpful. We must be guided at all times by what is in the best interests of the patient."

The second pioneer analyst, Dr. Nathan, responded with equal enthusiasm to the ideas of the real relationship and the analyst's validation of correct perceptions.

"Very much so, very much so. In fact, I probably feel more intensely about that than a great many analysts. I believe that the actual experience that the patient has with the analyst and the real person of the analyst, the kind of interaction they have, plays a tremendous role, a very, very prominent part, in the therapeutic process. I consider validation very important. It is very important that the analyst constantly monitors, scrutinizes, himself and really tries to be aware of what he is really doing in everything he does. Because, you see, we are constantly communicating covertly our attitudes and the patient is frequently reacting to communications that are covert.

"And also it is very important that *we accept the patient as an equal and a grown-up and that we are collaborators*. I see the therapeutic alliance as consisting of two grownups with a common aim and functioning as collaborators and equals. The psychoanalytic encounter is a collaboration between two consenting adults. Each one has his job to do . . . but their common aim is for the patient to get an increasing awareness of his own inner psychic processes and they collaborate in the effort to achieve this. Patients make observations about us that are frequently quite realistic and valid; and we owe it to them, when they make an observation, to scrutinize and examine it and, when we see it is valid, to admit it. With exceptions. At times, we accept that it is better not to admit it, and then we lie. We know that we are lying, but we decide that it is best for the work and for the treatment. But, otherwise, it is vital to look inside and admit whatever it is if it is true. Because when all is said and done, the kind of experience that that patient has with an analyst or therapist is what I would call *a new parental figure*. We are in fact in a parental role. Now, how many analysts frankly face that fact that we are in an actual, real parental role? Anyone that is in the role of being a helper in a helping profession is automatically in a parental role. Our attitudes and our feelings toward our patients are parental. We care about their welfare, and we don't expect or need or want them to care a great deal about our welfare. But that is a parental attitude.

"Now, the kind of experience the patient has with this new parent figure makes a tremendous difference to the patient's ability to grow and develop into more maturity. That is why it is important to be as honest as you can because, after a while, you become a model for your patient. You are asking the patient to reveal everything. We have a contract that the patient reveals everything and that we are free to exercise our choice about what we wish to reveal. And that choice, of course, has much to do with the personality of the analyst. Some are more reserved than others, some don't like to reveal personal things, and others do it even when it isn't asked for by the patient. They have a need to be more personal. I see all these things as coming into the category of technique because whatever we do is also technique, because we are functioning as professional technicians."

My experience of interviewing Dr. Furnham and Dr. Nathan was of being in the presence of two analysts who were at home with themselves both outside and within the psychoanalytic encounter. Perhaps their links with first-generation analysts in the Los Angeles area gave them the sort of personal freedom to engage with patients that characterized the kinds of interactions described by Freud and the early Viennese analysts. Unlike the more classical, second-generation Freudian analysts, whose focus is on analytic neutrality in the service of the unfolding of a purely intrapsychic process, Dr. Furnham and Dr. Nathan stressed the interpersonal, bilateral dimension of psychoanalytic treatment.

CONCLUSION

In this chapter, I have described the similar approaches of British Kleinians and American self psychologists to the notions of the real relationship and the treatment alliance. This consistency of attitude between analysts of the two groups would not be predicted on the basis of theory alone. On the face of it, Kleinians and self psychologists seem to hold diametrically opposed sets of beliefs. One might be characterized as an exclusively intrasubjective approach, the other as strongly intersubjective. The marked difference between the two groups of analysts emerged in discussions of the interpretation of mistakes and failures and, to a lesser degree, of extratransference interpretation. In contrast, British independents and American eclectic analysts discriminate nontransference aspects of the total analytic situation, and, in this respect, their views are more consistent with those of their Freudian colleagues presented in the previous chapter. As noted earlier, extratransference is valued by British Independent analysts in much the same way as the real relationship is valued by many of the American Freudians and eclectics. These two concepts serve the function of acknowledging the interpersonal dimension of the analytic relationship.

This chapter concludes discussion of the themes of truth and reality as these contribute preconsciously to the use of a number of central analytic concepts in clinical practice. In the previous four chapters, I trace preconscious and logical links between these clinical concepts, suggesting that networks or clusters of beliefs guide the content and form of analysts' interpretations. Although these links are prompted by theoretical orientation, geographical location, institutional affiliation, and proximity to powerful and inspiring figures, nevertheless epistemological and ontological notions about reality and truth generate a number of implicit, often logical, associations.

In the chapters that follow, notions of truth and reality no longer play a central role in discriminating distinctions between the networks of clinical concepts. Chapters 2 through 5 tackled the stronger and more encompassing beliefs of contemporary American and British analysts. Now the reader is asked to shift gears and to focus less on the reality or truth of the analytic enterprise and to think more about the qualities of relatedness that are peculiar to the analytic relationship. We can see that ideas about the real relationship and the value of extratransference interventions open the way to those aspects of the analytic relationship that lie beyond the hallowed transference interpretation leading to insight. We are going to follow analysts' thoughts on such topics as holding and containment, on psychotic or borderline kinds of mental functioning, as well as on issues of analyzability. Our attention moves to the analysts' contribution to the analytic situation.

Chapter 6

Containment and the Holding Environment
American Analysts

The subjects of this and the next chapter—the analytic situation as providing a holding environment, the analyst as a container, interventions with borderline patients, and the interpretation of primitive psychotic or borderline parts of the personality—are of relatively recent interest in the 100-year history of psychoanalysis. Starting in the 1950s, a number of leading analysts in the United Kingdom and the United States—Wilfred Bion, Melanie Klein, Ronald Laing, Masud Khan, Marion Milner, Herbert Rosenfeld, and Donald Winnicott in England; Frieda Fromm-Reichmann, Robert Knight, Harold Searles, Harry Stack Sullivan, and Otto Will in America—pioneered the psychoanalysis of "primitively organized" patients, including hospitalized psychotics. The widening scope of the application of psychoanalytic principles paralleled equally innovative developments in the psychotherapy of children, families, and groups. In the view of many of the pioneers of this movement, moreover, psychotic processes were at the core of both individual and group functioning.

Many psychoanalysts have noted that in psychoanalytic theory building, theories about particulars—for instance, specific patient populations, diagnostic categories, stages in the life cycle—tend to become generalized. Thus, theories that initially attempt to explain the behaviors of schizophrenics, hysterics, narcissists, two-year-olds, or three-month-old babies are readily applied to everyone. Since orientation groups tend to compete with one another, particularly if they have a growing constituency, each part-theory expands into a total

127

explanatory system. Do we all have a "primitive" or borderline area of functioning? If yes, does this mode of functioning lie at the core of our being; or, rather, is it an alternative system that can take over temporarily under the influence of specific conditions? Does structural change through the psychoanalytic method hinge on the analysis of primitive anxieties? Discussion of these questions bears on analysts' beliefs about man's "essential" nature, as well as reflecting differences in analysts trained in science, medicine, and the humanities. Statistical analyses indicated significant associations among beliefs in a universal "psychotic" core, the death instinct, and interpretations aimed at the identification of psychic truth. Discussion of diagnostic and treatment procedures also highlighted contrasts in analysts' academic backgrounds. Fields in which expertise depends on the refinement of diagnostic skills promote different attitudes toward problem solving than do disciplines that converse through argument, criticism, and imagination.

Although these ideas are not as hotly debated as they were 40 years ago, they nevertheless reveal important differences in analysts' views of the "normal personality" as well as the local context in which the analytic dialogue develops. Discussions of Winnicott's concept of the holding environment provided by mother and analyst, and of Bion's concept of the mother and analyst as container of the infant's projections and communications demonstrate the local "narcissistic overvaluation of small differences" (Balint and Balint, 1939). For analysts who are not involved in the divisions between the British Independent and Kleinian groups, these two concepts do much the same job. But for British Kleinians, on one hand, and Independents of a pro-Winnicottian bent, on the other, the differences between these two concepts are important. Excerpts from the interviews show how analysts in one psychoanalytic culture can be intensely preoccupied with theoretical and technical matters that are of no interest to analysts in a society where esteemed figures are personally unknown and where their work has not been transmitted by students and admirers. For instance, Bion's influence lingers on in Los Angeles because of the influential people he analyzed and supervised, whereas references to his work are rare in the New York Psychoanalytic Society or in the San Francisco Institute. Similarly, the differences that are hotly debated at self psychology conferences in the United States between Kohut's colleagues and more contemporary intersubjectivists are of no interest to British analysts simply because no important colleague or analysand of Kohut has permanently settled in the British psychoanalytic community.

VIEWS OF AMERICAN ANALYSTS

The analysts' views on the topics under review are organized according to geographical location and theoretical orientation. Marked differences emerged between American and British analysts, although at least two-thirds of the analysts interviewed were extremely respectful of Winnicott's work. Most used his concept of the holding environment to describe the essential background conditions for interpretive work, although many observed that the concept assumed a foreground position when they were working with more disturbed patients. Nearly all the American analysts, all the self psychologists, independent-eclectics, and interpersonalists, as well as many Freudians, responded in this way. Several American Freudians associated Winnicott's term with familiar concepts in their own culture and orientation—specifically, the real relationship, the therapeutic alliance, and Joseph Sandler's (1960) concept of "the background of safety." Only the most "classical" of the New York and San Francisco Freudians rejected Winnicott's concept; these same analysts found the concept of containment even "more useless."

Of the three American cities I visited, Los Angeles is unique in that it is the only North American city to have seriously entertained the ideas of Klein and Bion and to offer Kleinian-Bionian training within an I.P.A.-approved institute (The Pacific Center of California). In Los Angeles, a Kleinian phase was followed by an equally fervent, although larger and expanding, Kohutian movement. Thus, it is possible to examine the effects of new ideas on different members of a psychoanalytic population, including those who appear *not* to have been influenced by the new thinkers. For example, the responses of Los Angeles Freudians who did not join Bion or Kleinian study groups are nevertheless significant. In the following three sections, excerpts are given from interviews with analysts in each of the three American cities: Los Angeles, New York, and San Francisco.

LOS ANGELES

The self psychologists were most enthusiastic about Winnicott's ideas, which they perceived as relating to "the provision of an empathic milieu." Many of the Los Angeles self psychologists also responded positively to Bion's concept of containment. Those who did not had not participated in any of the study groups organized by Bion and his disciples during the 1970s prior to the advent of self psychology. These attitudes underline the importance of charismatic figures in the exchange of concepts. Those who felt appreciative of, or loyal to, Bion found affinities between his concepts and those of Kohut. At the same time, in marked contrast to British analysts who admired Bion's work, the Los Angeles self psychologists, particularly those formerly identified as Kleinian, were strongly anti-Kleinian. To them, Bion was not a Kleinian. Self psychologists strongly disagreed with Kleinian developmental theory and with clinical assumptions concerning the ubiquitous nature of psychotic functioning.

The following excerpts convey the ways in which the self psychologists, who had actively participated in Bion study groups, incorporated the ideas of Bion and Winnicott into their current framework. One of the Los Angeles self psychologists, who had changed from a Kleinian to a Kohutian orientation, clearly demarcated the two concepts:

"I certainly agree with the holding environment. This involves the recognition by the analyst of a state of disturbed regulation experienced intuitively by the patient. Winnicott was intuitive, and he came from a fund of experience with classical and Kleinian analysis, and he followed Mrs. Klein in taking up the primitive anxiety. But he recognized intuitively from his practice as a pediatrician that, when a patient is in a state of disturbed regulation, then he or she is not able to assimilate an intervention from the outside. That would call upon the *cognitive* abilities of the patient; Winnicott recognized that was not right. The concept of the holding or containing environment gives the patient the experience of a nonintrusive, empathic person. And this experience facilitates the recovery from the disturbed state. This would be followed by a process of investigation into what produced the disequilibration.

"In terms of containing, many people have their own interpretation of Bion. Whether Bion would agree with these interpretations, I have great doubts. It should not be taken as Bion saying this. One then has to investigate what the person means by the process of the container. Because, if it includes the concept of projection into—which it usually does—then I would say the empirical evidence needs to be presented. If containment involves an interpretation about the projected contents, then I would say that that further traumatizes the patient. We have to understand the patient's experience and what the traumatic state was about. And the idea of projection bypasses consideration of these factors.

"About borderline patients, I see them in analysis, but I mean a different thing by analysis. What is meant by analysis? I preserve what I consider to be the fundamentals of the psychoanalytic procedure in terms of the facilitation of transference, the recognition and interpretation of whatever the resistances are to the increasing engagement and deployment of developmental longings. I respect those. I don't try to hurry the patient into some posture, or some experience, that he is not prepared for. And that might take a very long period of time. From this definition of analysis, the establishment of a particular bond is perfectly possible with a borderline patient. It is very difficult, not at all easy.

"The whole idea of parameters is itself judgmental. I don't feel that analysis of any kind should be limited to interpretation. That is artificial, and I don't think anybody sticks to it. The interventions, responses, posture of the analyst have to be geared to facilitate the development of an atmosphere of trust. If you interpret the patient's first experience of disruption as splitting, the analysis never gets to the point of an environment of trust. Any trust that is established on that basis is founded on idealization or compliance, on the hope that everything will turn out for the best if you believe what he says."

In contrast, a younger self psychologist who had had no connection with Bion during the 1970s stated:

"You know, I have a sympathetic response to holding. Containment makes the analytic hairs on the back of my neck bristle, which may be my own subjective experience and not anything that Bion intended by the term. I would understand containment more as maintaining the patient's cohesiveness. But holding to me seems to be an experience consonant with the patient's feeling of being understood and having their affective experiences accepted as meaningful."

Discussions of the treatment of borderline patients and "psychotic" areas of functioning were particularly revealing. Self psychologists, like Kleinians, are not strong supporters of the medical-diagnostic bias in psychoanalytic treatment. Neither orientation group divided the analytic relationship into the "real," on one hand, and the "distorted" or transference on the other. Both groups focused on the here-and-now transference relationship, differing, of course, in the emphasis placed on the intersubjective versus the projective nature of this two-person relationship. Thus, when discussing treatment interventions with borderline patients, Kleinians and Kohutians alike tended to follow their usual technique without introducing special "parameters." In the following excerpts, Los Angeles self psychologists address these questions:

1. "I use the same technique. I only know one. Parameters— much too complicated. Some people are more into borderline or psychotic experience than others. I think the same person can certainly seem borderline to one person and not to another, depending on the nature of the interaction."

2. "I think the basic stance is the same. The idea of a parameter isn't a concept that I would accept anyway. It implies that an analyst that is not using a parameter is a neutral or nonexistent presence, which I think is ridiculous. It also implies that the analytic field should be a pure one, which is not an idea I accept. I would reframe the question and say, 'Well, to what extent does the patient feel sufficiently provided for by the analyst's analyzing activity versus to what extent does the analyst need to introduce nonanalytic provisions?' But this is a question that comes up in every treatment, not just with borderline or psychotic patients."

A number of senior Los Angeles analysts who had been influenced by both Bionian and Kleinian ideas in the 1970s and self psychology in the 1980s were rated as American eclectics in contrast to self psychologists. These "independents" were not known to have publicly changed orientation, which suggests that, in their case, learning new approaches resulted in a more pluralistic, less monistic approach. In the interview discussions, these eclectic analysts were not particularly concerned with differentiating Bion from his Kleinian interpreters. Presumably, they felt less need to disown previous allegiances than did those who had undergone a total shift in orientation. For example:

"Both concepts are very closely related. One comment of Winnicott's that has always impressed me was his statement that it is an achievement just to survive with certain patients. If you can just *survive* all the attempts of certain patients to destroy the link or the relationship between themselves and you, a lot of that involves holding, being able to maintain the bond during a period when the patient is so threatened by the relationship.

Containing goes with that because these patients cannot tolerate their feelings so you need to contain them."

It is interesting to compare the foregoing response with those of a second subgroup of eclectic analysts: analysts in this second group had *never* been involved in Bion or Kleinian study groups in Los Angeles:

1. "I find containment less meaningful than Winnicott's idea. In my terms, Winnicott is referring to the provision of a stable and secure environment for the child, the kind of environment that Bowlby talks about where a mother is protective when the child needs protection, and yet is able to let the child move away—a secure base."

2. "I use the Winnicottian term with more zest; he talks more my language except when he is biologizing. To my taste, I find Bion pretentious and obscurantist. He seemed to relish the Delphic role. He said, 'Abandon memory and desire.' Freud said, 'Start every session as though you are starting anew.' That is the same statement to me, I don't see anything original in Bion's statement. The trouble with container/contained is that it is a little too hydraulic and mechanistic. The holding environment, after all, borrows more from an embrace than from an oil can. It humanizes. The model of the mother as the first interpreter, her fantasies and feelings about her child that are conveyed to the child—there is more and more reciprocity as development matures, each interpreting to the other just as patient and analyst interpret to one another. I think the holding environment, the "good-enough" mother, absorption of aggression, the child kills the mother—the mother survives and then the child learns he does not have to split off aggression, and then split off the self— those ideas are very valuable to me, and I think that they are essentially the base for much of self psychology. Interpretations constitute an expression of the intersubjective process."

With regard to the treatment of borderline patients, the American eclectic analysts took a more inter*related*, less inter*subjective*, stance than the self psychologists did. Interpersonal responsiveness seemed to involve a more confrontative, social style:

1. "I work with borderlines face to face. I see them more or less often, depending on the dynamics of each case. I don't find

putting them on the couch, four or five times a week, and interpreting primitive material helpful."

2. "Yes, I do think they need special sorts of intervention. I am
seeing a borderline five times a week, and she needs much more
than the usual analytic patient. She needs some concrete provisions, but within an analytic context. She uses the answering
machine, I don't know whether you can call that a parameter.
But she can express herself at night and during the weekends.
She used up all my tapes at one point, and I got angry. We went
through all kinds of limit-setting. Yes, I think you do different
things. I would let her know my feelings. Absolutely, because
often she knows my feelings before I know my feelings. She will
tell me, and often I will realize that I have disavowed a feeling
and she is really right. If I didn't confront that, I would feel that
I was crazy-making but, more importantly, she utilizes this kind of
intervention, she uses it in an analytic way and takes it further."

To turn now to attitudes toward the belief in, and interpretation of,
a psychotic core or part, most American analysts disagreed with this
notion. They felt that the idea of a psychotic core was very largely a
matter of definition. With the exception of the Los Angeles analysts
who had been influenced by Bion and Klein, this idea sharply divided
British Kleinians from American analysts. The following excerpts
illustrate the more diverse approaches of the Los Angeles eclectic
analysts:

1. "I would have to do a lot of work on definitions. These terms
are used so differently not only across the ocean but even here in
our community. Are we talking about the same patient population? Are we talking about borderline personality organization?
Are we talking about borderline disorders? I wouldn't agree that
we all have a borderline part if that implies the presence of identity diffusion, the use of primitive mechanisms with a basically
intact capacity for reality testing. But that we are all capable of
primary-process thinking at times, yes."

2. "I am not surprised any more when a delusional element
comes out in analysis. I use Kleinian concepts. I regard myself as
very eclectic, and I use whatever is available. I am not involved
in any particular school. I have had exposure to all kinds of
points of view. Early in my career, I was very influenced by Franz

Alexander, his corrective emotional experience. That is not just being nice to the patient. Alexander would tell stories, he would be pretty rough on certain patients, and the patients really responded because their parents never seemed to care enough to be strict or concerned enough to deal with certain issues in life. He really tried to determine what a particular patient needed, and he conformed himself to that. Some analysts talk deprecatingly about his play acting. He didn't really play act; he tried to fashion himself into the best instrument in order to help a particular patient."

3.   "I don't think I am borderline or psychotic, but you know, in recent years, I think I have seen more so-called borderline characteristics in myself. It has taken me a long time to be able to use or even think about concepts like splitting. And I am beginning to see that maybe I have done splitting . . . it is really chastening that, in my dotage, I am starting to recognize my borderline characteristics. But better late than never. But I don't think that is the answer you want. I would put it that probably everybody can become disorganized, given enough stress. But psychotic, that means an organization that is psychotic rather than disorganized. I think people can become paranoid with sufficient guilt over sexuality and aggression—but whether these people are psychotic, I don't know."

As stated at the beginning of this chapter, the majority of Los Angeles Freudian analysts, especially those who had trained with Ralph Greenson, used Winnicott's concepts but showed little or no familiarity with the idea of containment. Only one Freudian analyst, also a child analyst, made use of both concepts; his more diverse responses are consistent with those of other child analysts:

"I see the holding concept as being very helpful. I also like the idea of someone being able to use the analyst as a container in Bion's sense of projective identification, where the analyst becomes the container of the affects in the way that a normal mother helps her baby. A defective, deficient patient has never had that kind of containment. You act as a buffer, as a holder, the way that Bion puts it in terms of normal projective identification. The other aspect, I see as different—that is, the container as a wastebasket, dumping ground. All the crap comes into you and somehow magically it has left the patient. They feel fine and you

end up feeling like shit. That kind of projective identification I
see as different, and that is also very helpful. I don't see it as being
put into you. I don't believe that kind of stuff, but I really feel
something is happening to me."

SAN FRANCISCO

The responses of San Francisco analysts to this set of concepts illustrate how the destiny of ideas is tied to key figures—in this case, Bion
and Klein. The San Francisco analysts were the most cohesive of the
four communities and, at the same time, the most respectful of each
other's differences. The majority of the analysts interviewed were
widely read and eager to participate in my project; many were actively
involved in research and traveled internationally. It is interesting to
speculate whether their balanced perspective results in part from the
fact that, unlike Los Angeles, the analytic community has neither
been challenged by a new psychoanalytic movement (Klein and self
psychology) nor been "invaded" by foreign ideas (Bion and other
British Kleinians).

San Francisco analysts who responded positively associated
Winnicott's concept with familiar concepts in the American literature: the therapeutic alliance, the real relationship, and Joseph
Sandler's "safety principle." Many commented that they knew very little about Bion; they found his writings impossible to understand. "I
tried to read something of Bion once and got about halfway through
and gave up." Or, "Now, you have gotten to a point with me where I
am not well read. I suspect that I conduct my analyses in some way
consistent with them, but frankly I have no working familiarity with
the concepts." In contrast, the following three excerpts from interviews with analysts active in the I.P.A. show the ways that analysts
working with more disturbed patients relate to the concepts of holding
and containment:

1.   "There is only one little Kleinian enclave in the U.S., and
that I guess was due to Susan Isaacs-Elmhirst and Bion. It was
never clear to me what made L.A. the place that the people from
London went to, but it took hold and influenced a whole group
of people there. It has remained relatively restricted to Los
Angeles, and then it has waned in Los Angeles with Kohut's rise.
The only other influence the Kleinians have had in America is
through the internationalization of the I.P.A. and the fact that,

although the *International Journal* is not the journal of the I.P.A. but the journal of the British, it has always made an effort to be international in character. And, in the last 10 years, I would say, the Americans are more willing to read the Kleinian papers in that journal. So the names of people like Elizabeth Spillius, Betty Joseph, and Eric Brenman are a little better known in the U.S. now. In terms of Winnicott's holding, there must be a dozen terms that can be used in different areas, and I don't know which best fits the concept. I like the holding idea, I think Phyllis Greenacre called it the 'primal transference,' and I think people ignore the nonanalytical support that comes from just coming four or five times a week. Whatever you want to call it, holding is as good as any."

2. "I am not that sophisticated about Bion, maybe slightly more about Winnicott. But I see containment as relating to the negative affects that are generated in the analyst and the analytic field. You know, there is anger in the room and the patient is incredibly furious and resentful. I become a hero in my mind's eye by thinking of Bion or Winnicott and just saying I am holding them [the patients], or this is fantastic, we are going to get some place with this. I have a kind of presentiment of, this will work; by my holding onto this, something will be repaired. Let's say a person has been talking nonstop and I have been talking with them, and then suddenly they are silent and they are troubled by the silence. And I am troubled by it too. Holding that, just being there and letting myself be a little lulled into feeling I can just wait, there is no hurry, we are here together, we don't have to talk. But often what is going on is anger, or boredom, these two things. And so, over the years, I have become much less negative in my thinking and much more exploratory about my own anger or boredom in relationship to patients. I have had some help through reading and just by introspection. What is very interesting is how often the boredom wards off a very strong libidinal attachment, much more than anger actually. So I get a little excited when I get bored or the patient starts getting sleepy. I think, 'Oh, what's next?' So that has been helpful with more seriously disturbed patients; it is always hard. I tend to see, at least I have the reputation of seeing, people that are more disturbed than others, or I tend to be more of a reactive analyst. So the way my reports go, or the way my patients go, it sounds like there is a lot of action and *sturm und drang*.

"So the diagnosticians might think, 'Well, is this person neurotic, or is there something about your interactive style that is making this person look more disturbed than she actually is?' My answer to that is, 'Well, is there something about your deadening style that makes the patients appear more put together, they are going through the motions with you of being polite? They may get something out of it, but maybe less than what I have to offer.' These are my competitive notions. I had a candidate in a long analysis, just finished. I saw him as being very seriously narcissistic, a very disturbed character. With this guy, I would see something clearly and I would put it together in what I would call a brilliant interpretation. He would say, 'You really got me with that one, didn't you? You notice how you raised your voice, how excited you were.' And he was right. Then he noticed, when I finally got hold of it, that I was just speaking in a more casual way. It was a bit more boring, not the same excitement that I had to pin him down. And one day he said, 'You know, I don't think I am getting to you as much lately. I think you understand me more, it feels better somehow.' He said this clearing his throat; he was very moved. He felt that I had stopped jumping in to get in my two cents, and he had figured it out for himself.

"I don't use parameters, but there are people I don't put on the couch because I am scared. I used to think of borderlines as a separate category, and I used to sit them up. Calef and Weinshel attacked Kernberg in a devastating way. But now I have been stimulated by Tom Ogden, who has elaborated on Winnicott's idea of potential space. Not many people think in those terms here. Erikson wrote a paper, which he never published, in which he talks about how the patient has to have the capacity to play in terms of recognizing the 'as-if.' The patient has to know that the transference is both real and not real—the capacity to fantasize and yet experience your fantasizing as real. For instance, I have one patient, a brilliant woman who functions very well, who has her own transitional object in her adult life. She has a teddy bear and she still goes in and pets it. And she has identified me as her transitional object. She has said, 'You know this will offend you, but I just don't want you to talk, just be there waiting for me. It sounds like my teddy bear, doesn't it? Would you mind if you were my teddy bear?' It is playful; it is quite regressed but it is not borderline per se."

3. "Borderline, yes, I have 10 analytic patients: two are severely borderline, both in the profession, one a psychiatrist, the other a social worker. They have never experienced anything psychotic in their lives, but they have typical feelings of emptiness and incredibly terrible interpersonal relationships and terribly difficult problems with rage. They themselves call themselves borderline. Although, in the long run, his formulations lack some depth, nevertheless descriptively I don't think there is anyone better than Kernberg on the borderline. Now, some of my colleagues would shoot me, and my good friends Calef and Weinshel wrote a seething long critique of Kernberg. But, descriptively, Kernberg is just excellent on this. I think they are very difficult to treat. Even at best, after many years, they don't integrate to as high and smooth level as less disturbed people. For example, I have a patient with a terrible negative transference. Eventually I say, 'Why are you coming? You are not doing analysis, and you don't like to come.' He replies that he doesn't think about himself. He is always saying to himself, 'You are thinking such and such . . . you want me to . . . ' So I say, 'What do you think?' Three seconds later, he is back to what I think. So I say, 'Why are you coming here? You are analyzing me, spending all this money figuring me out!' He says, 'Oh, I am getting better.' And he is. I don't really know how except through some identification with my working ego, my analytic ego. So I think I am helping, or else I really would discharge him. But it is not the same as other analyses; it is a different kind of process and it reaches a different level."

The majority of the San Francisco analysts, however, felt that interpretive techniques, particularly transference interpretations, should not be used with borderline patients. Several observed that the British were far "too loose" about diagnosis and treatment. When correlations were made between the rated interview responses and responses to the P.O.Q., analysts at the center of the San Francisco Freudian cluster acknowledged minimal influence by American and British object relational ideas and by contemporary infancy research. After Freud, the strongest influences on clinical practice were Margaret Mahler, Merton Gill, and Roy Schafer. Self psychology and Kohut had no impact. Of the three Freudian models listed on the P.O.Q. (Freud's drive theory, the topographical, and the structural models), the "hard core" Freudians were more strongly influenced by Freud's *drive* theory than by his structural model (or by ego psychology), and they were least influenced by Freud's topographical model. These core Freudians argued forcefully against the softer concepts of technique used by the more eclectic American Freudians and the British Contemporary Freudians. The views of Dr. Friedland, the highly consistent San Francisco Freudian described in previous chapters, are presented in the following excerpt:

"Well, it is a little bit like the real relationship. I find it difficult to see how these ideas pertain to anything that would significantly affect one's technique of analyzing. If your central objective is to help someone to understand themselves in ways which would keep them from repeating the past endlessly, anxiously, and conflictually, then to speak of the holding environment or containment is irrelevant. It's like a lot of Kernberg's views. Analysts begin by talking about people who are especially vulnerable and end up including everyone. So we are all borderline characters. It may be that in somebody's world we are all borderline characters, but it just seems like a measles epidemic that has gone amuck. The technique of being in some sense supportive is not to be argued. I mean, you are there to help, you have agreed to help, you are taking money to help, and it is known between the two of you that you are, or intend to be, helpful. So, yes, some wish to help and make some provision of a situation or an atmosphere or relationship in which someone has reason to trust this other person with their thoughts. Is that a holding environment, or does it imply something more active in technique?"

Although less dismissive than Dr. Friedland, other San Francisco Freudians expressed similar views:

1.   "I agree with Anna Freud. By and large, I have a very narrow view of analyzability. I've seen the pendulum swing back and forth, and I've never been convinced. Even as a resident, when Fromm-Reichmann and others were treating psychotics, and when that was the big thing at the Menninger Clinic, I was always very skeptical. In my view, only a very narrow segment of people can benefit from analysis. In my practice and in my supervision, I find my judgment has been sustained. Although I agree that everyone has a psychotic area, I would not use those terms. Yes, everyone uses psychotic thinking, defenses; everyone regresses. All of this occurs in the framework of the healthy ego. I know that the idea that regression serves the ego is old fash-

ioned, but that is what my thinking would be. There is a terrible arrogance amongst therapists—you know, 'We're the healthy ones and they're the sick ones.' But what it really hinges on is whether there is a healthy ego that can encompass all of this and make it work. So what you might think of as a psychotic thought or a regression can in fact be adaptive and enriching, you can bounce back."

2.   "I differ from my good friends like Otto Kernberg. The treating of overtly psychotic patients analytically requires the heroic approach of a Frieda Fromm-Reichmann, who is willing to devote not just five, six, or seven times a week but Sundays and the availability of a kind of protected setting, a sanatorium like Chestnut Lodge or Austen Riggs or the Menninger Foundation. With modern drugs, that is now less necessary. There are people in this town, like Bryce Boyer and Milton Wexler in Los Angeles, who have treated very sick patients by giving enormously of themselves. Of course, the English have been doing it all along, people like Margaret Little. But I am much more on the side of Anna Freud and Leo Stone. Stone wrote about how, originally, psychoanalysts treated neurotics; then Federn came along and said we could treat psychotics; Aichhorn said we could treat delinquents, and Alexander said we could deal with psychosomatic cases. In the Menninger Project, Kernberg looked at the same patient population as Wallerstein—the 42 lives. Kernberg said they could have unmodified psychoanalytic treatment. Wallerstein said that, very clearly, there were supportive parameters in the treatment but that Kernberg was consigning all those supportive elements to others. And, therefore, Kernberg could say that the work within the sessions could be as analytic as possible because others were managing the patient's life. But I don't make that kind of separation. If you are part of the apparatus that is managing the patient's life, then it is not an unmodified analysis, because in true analysis the patient is a totally autonomous individual.

"Take the example of a surgeon in analysis. This surgeon had the most bloodthirsty fantasies that came out on the couch and were potentially in his mind when he was in the operating room with a scalpel, fantasies such as, 'I could make an incision and destroy a patient.' He was a very skilled and competent surgeon whom everybody sought out. He was able to keep his fantasies in the room and go out and operate at a high level of skill. You need the capacity to make that split to have a real analytic patient. If you couldn't rely on that and you had to intervene in all kinds of ways, that is not analysis; it is a modified treatment. I know this is a much more American outlook, not the way the English feel at all. Certainly, many of the Kleinians say the reason their analyses are so long is that they need to reach the psychotic core which is in everybody. What do I think about that? Well, look, everybody dreams at night. And in our dreams, logic, space, and time are thrown akilter. If we had those experiences in waking life, they would be psychotic. To that extent, we all have primary-process capacities. And even those of us who have solid neurotic character organizations can be driven toward the most primitive aspect of themselves in extreme traumatic circumstances. And a psychotic transference can arise under the impact of the analytic procedure in a clearly neurotic character. The transference loses the 'as-if' quality and takes on a more delusional quality. The analysis can be carried through successfully with parameters and modifications. That does not mean that in every analysis one routinely gets to a psychotic core. Far from it, one gets to it in those who have more fragile ego organizations."

NEW YORK

The views of the San Francisco core Freudians were very similar to those of the New York Classical Freudians. Statistical analysis placed both groups at the center of the "Classical Freudian" cluster. It appears, therefore, that the issue of the analytic treatment of borderline patients, together with the use of Bionian-Winnicottian concepts of containment and holding, clearly discriminated between "classical" and "contemporary" Freudians. Contemporary Freudians integrate developmental theory as well as relational concepts into their clinical approach. Dr. Braun, the elderly, distinguished New York analyst, declared both concepts "completely useless":

"You go by what the patient says. Now, there are some patients for whom the conflict of the couch, the feeling of rubbing up against something, the security of the room, the fact that nobody else is there, the sounds, someone who is very comforting, etc.— these people may have a fantasy-wish to be held by the mother. Fine. But what matters is the role that fantasy plays in stimulating conflict or in evoking conscious derivatives that are of significance to the patient's problem. I have thought of these ideas [holding and containment]; they are interesting, true about certain stages of development unquestionably, but largely irrelevant in actual clinical experience and certainly irrelevant in theory formation about pathogenesis.

"I cannot answer your question about the treatment of borderline patients, except from a theoretical point of view, perhaps because I have been a successful analyst in the sense of having being able to pick and choose my patients from the beginning. I have had very few borderlines, and only three psychotic patients. I would think you would modify the procedure, I can't give any strong guidelines; for that I would refer you to my good friend Otto Kernberg. And the notion that everyone has a psychotic area is, of course, a phenomenological fallacy. What do you mean by psychotic? We are all irrational a good deal of the time, we can all be dominated by primary-process thinking."

By contrast, the New York analysts of the next generation expressed attitudes similar to those of the more "eclectic" Los Angeles analysts. Not surprisingly, statistical analysis placed these younger, third-generation analysts on the edge of either the developmental Freudian or the American "eclectic" cluster. These analysts were influenced by the interpersonal ideas of Harry Stack Sullivan, an early pioneer in the treatment of schizophrenia. For the most part, they used Winnicott's concept but were completely unfamiliar with Bion's ideas. For example:

"Very useful. I think Winnicott was marvelous. I think the space to play in is so important. I am not a child analyst, but I have some background working with children. When I was a resident, Eleanor Galenson gave the child development course. And we all took it. If you have kids, you learn a lot, I don't know how anyone could think that Winnicott is not very relevant. I think Arnold Modell has made a career of this. I think a lot of things he says are very sensitive and very true. But it is not enough, I don't think you can cure people or change them by holding them. On the other hand, I don't think they are going to listen to you if you don't have a holding environment. You know Winnicott's last book—Holding and Interpretation—where he describes practically verbatim the analysis of a patient who could not be reached except by some extraordinary measures. I read that one summer vacation, and I was astounded by how adept Winnicott was, and very intellectual. My picture of Winnicott was radically changed by this book. I thought, "My God, this man is really taking a very scrupulous intellectual attitude. He is interpreting all over the place." Obviously he condensed a lot, but it was not my picture of somebody holding somebody. So obviously he went beyond the position that he was simply providing a holding environment; that is what I object to, there are people who think that chicken soup cures. It doesn't.

"In terms of treatment of psychotics or borderlines, I think you British have a lot of guts to take on these cases. Many people do it here, but we are not equipped. Kernberg could do it because he had the backup of the social work staff at Menninger. I am also not a fan of DSM-III, and I think that putting on labels is a political move to do with the medicalization of psychiatry and third-party payment. I am on the admissions committee at Columbia; candidates present two or three cases to us. Most of the labels are a mixed characterological disorder; nobody is pure. Mixed obsessional, depressive, hysterical features, etc. I think diagnostic labels are most useful with affective disorders, where there is a bipolar disease with a depressive feature, or certain classical post-traumatic stress disorders. Kernberg has done a lot of clarifying, yet his narcissistic characters are much different than Kohut's because they are much sicker. A different population, but the same label. Now, do I think every patient has a psychotic core? No. There may be pockets of primitive thinking in every well-functioning neurotic. That does not mean the healthiest person does not have crazy thoughts, but they do not persist."

One of the New York eclectic analysts, who had held high offices in both the A.P.A. and the I.P.A., replied:

"To me, they are totally different. And the idea of a holding or facilitating environment is very important and part of the core that analysis is about. I certainly agree with Winnicott. In fact I am more and more inclined to think that interpretation is less important than the interaction and experience of the patient with the analyst. Interpretation is only one phase of that. The idea of the analyst as the container of the patient's feelings, I find concrete nonsense. I wish it would disappear from the literature. I don't see severe borderlines or psychotics, no. My years of experience have demonstrated that analytic work with psychotic patients does not get far. The British feel differently, but I have never seen any data that convinced me that it worked. I can't imagine putting a psychotic patient on the couch. I don't see that many borderline patients; the few I have treated are on the couch, off the couch; but severe borderlines, I would be very hesitant to put on the couch."

A training analyst at the William Alanson White Institute responded:

"You see, I don't agree with the concept of parameter because that concept says that this isn't really analysis, this is sort of extra stuff; when you get to step 4, then the real analysis begins. I think you don't do exactly the same kind of work with a borderline and that you have to be a much realer person. For instance, an analytic patient of mine is grateful that I don't speak because she had a very intrusive family. She is grateful to have the space. But a borderline patient would probably not know what to do with that, however much they are pushing you away all the time. But, as a colleague once said, 'Those are the most gratifying patients. They make the most progress. They come from such a low place and, if it works, they leave you put back together; whereas your analytic patients may move half an inch.' The difference between borderlines and the rest of us is that we bounce back relatively quickly with less damage in the interim, whereas borderline people have no place to bounce back to. You know, panic is panic. I don't know that there are differences in panic states. It is a psychotic state, if you will. Your judgment has gone, your memory has gone, your reality testing is absolutely off the wall. With more neurotic people or character disorder people, they know how to seek out some help, but the borderline-psychotic does not, they just go further into the state. I guess I really sound like Sullivan's dictum: 'We are all more human than otherwise.' "

CONCLUSION

Discussion of this network of concepts elicited views about the scope of psychoanalysis and agents of psychic change, on one hand, and, on the other, the strong influence of charismatic figures, in this case Bion and Winnicott, on the development of different psychoanalytic communities. The responses of the Los Angeles analysts were particularly illuminating in this respect since the community has benefited from both

Bionian-Kleinian and Kohutian-self-psychological ideas. Because of the powerful presence of such thinkers as Bion in the 1970s and, more recently, Bernard Brandchaft and Robert Stolorow, it is possible to trace the different ways in which analysts in one community absorb (or reject) new ideas. With reference to the contemporary debate on pluralism, the Los Angeles "independent/eclectic" analysts exemplify a pluralist position in that many in this group had participated in study groups both with Bion and with Stolorow—and in earlier times, Franz Alexander, another charismatic figure—but these immersion experiences did not lead to a total shift of theoretical perspective.

Chapter 7

Holding and Containment
British Analysts

The majority of British Freudian and Independent analysts were very enthusiastic about Winnicott's ideas. Half of the Kleinians interviewed gave a lukewarm response to the concept of holding, and the other 50%, emphasizing the limitations of holding as compared with the competing concept of containment, were strongly opposed to Winnicott's concept. Strong feelings against Winnicott may result from criticisms of Klein in his later work. In terms of the theoretical influence of key figures and schools, statistical analysis indicated significant associations between the use of the concept of holding in analytic work and interest in the infancy literature and British Independent ideas.

All the Kleinians in this study found Bion's concept of containment extremely valuable, and a large proportion of the Independent group also felt positively about Bion's ideas. A number of British Freudians were either unfamiliar with, or disliked, Bion's theories; in this regard, they followed the American classical Freudians and the ego psychologists. Negative attitudes toward Bion's ideas were closely associated with the influences of Anna Freud, ego psychology, and Freud's structural and topographical models.

BRITISH FREUDIANS

Dr. Smith was the only British analyst to link Winnicott's concept with the concepts of the real relationship, therapeutic alliance, and background of safety.

147

"I don't make much of a distinction, but I would agree that, in a general sense, the whole analytic situation is a holding one. A person is becoming very vulnerable in talking about things they don't usually talk about or haven't even talked or thought about ever. I like Joe Sandler's term, *creating a safe situation*. Holding would come up when a patient gets into a very upset state. There I would switch gears, I'd switch over to a fusion of the therapeutic relationship and the real relationship. I would convey that it is understandable that you're very upset, or very sad about this. It would be an ordinary human communication. I wouldn't be trying to interpret during periods of great distress and anxiety, and this probably shows some of my American influence. If a person starts getting too upset, their functioning or some part of their ego is gone or has been overwhelmed. So, from my point of view, you need a functioning ego to work analytically. I would see the task as being to repair or to create a holding situation where patients can reintegrate themselves and then get back to work. So, frequently, I would ask them to sit up, maybe on the couch, and then say, 'Well now, perhaps you can lie down again.' Or, 'Tomorrow, we can get back to work.'

"It is different from trying to solve this through interpretation, which I am very doubtful about—the whole English view that interpretation will solve or even be helpful. I wouldn't have an absolutely closed mind on this, but I am just not comfortable with the idea that, when a person is that upset, you should try to give a deep interpretation. I do agree that if you can catch just the *right* interpretation about what triggered off the anxiety attack, then probably it is helpful. If you happen to be right with your interpretation, then it works, but it's a little risky. And if you're wrong, it makes everything worse."

Another senior British Freudian responded in a moving and personal way:

"Well, they were all my teachers, you see. Winnicott had these child seminar evenings at home where we discussed his cases when he had the new ideas about real holding, physically, with children in particular. I knew the Winnicotts very well, and I went to his seminars for many years. I have certainly been very influenced by him. I have lived and worked for five years with children who had no parents—their mothers visited, but they had no family life. Many of them were analyzed later in life. And that was Anna Freud's main achievement in the War Nurseries—children who were damaged in the first years but who got substitute mothers. They were always handled by the same people, not by anybody who was on duty. I still see one of mine—when the war broke out, she was an illegitimate baby with no family. She had a very good mother, who visited as much as possible, but the day-to-day attachment was to myself and A.A. when I went out. That is a good example of supplementing what was missing at the time.

"Now, Winnicott had the idea that there are certain patients who have missed out on being held and that one cannot give this to them verbally because they have missed out on a preverbal experience. He and Margaret Little, for instance, thought that, by holding the hand or touching the forehead, you can *replace* this experience to some extent. I have never done that myself. I have never been convinced about it, and I know why. At the time, several of the students were very influenced by this idea and tried it. But there is a very narrow line between giving the infantile satisfaction which has been missed in childhood and this experience becoming sexualized. The danger of the sexualization is something I never wanted to enter, because I have seen cases where this happened and the analysis came to an end. I don't think words will replace the experience either. But if you talk about it the patient becomes aware. And most patients are aware anyway: for instance, I have had children who were in Barnardo's homes for abandoned and orphaned children and who have known and thought about how there was nobody they could run up to and feel safe with. All I do really is to let them experience this in the transference; of course, the analyst becomes much more important. Weekends are very difficult to cope with, and some ring up because they want to hear your voice, at least.

"I never did see psychotics. I was in the same class as Herbert Rosenfeld. We were great friends. I admired his work and his courage very much. I felt that he had really found something that most of us could not do. He was very much ahead, and he had the courage to do it. But about the Kleinian view of psychotic parts, I have never been convinced about this. I think one gets closest to it with daydreaming or fantasying that are influenced by actual events in the external world that enter into one. Sometimes, I have seen a phase when there was a sudden unexpected shock, the loss of a child for instance; after the loss, there may be the conviction that the next child will also die. This is very close to some-

thing psychotic because it is a loss of reality testing, ego functioning, etc. But I don't think we all have this, as the Kleinians do."

The following examples illustrate minor differences perceived by
British Freudians between containment and holding.

1. "I do differentiate them. In my mind, holding has a greater
complexity to it than a container. A container is much more of a
solid object that things are put into. It is much more concrete
than holding. I lean more toward holding because I think it is an
experiential, fantasied sort of phenomenon."

2. "I think containment has much more of a psychic reverbera-
tion to me. You are actually containing the person's anxieties and
fantasies and craziness if you like, which quite often does happen
in terms of the transference of infant and child feelings, fantasies,
and wishes. Are the terms used synonymously? I suppose they
must be. I mean, after all, Winnicott was talking about—but
maybe Bion was as well—the early mother–child relationship. I
don't really know much about Bion at all. He has never particularly attracted me."

The more widely influenced Freudian analyst described in Chapter
4 who stressed the importance of the "quality" of the analytic relationship felt both ideas were crucial to analysis.

"I do think they are enormously important. I mean they are
basic, the bottom line, unquestionably. I haven't really ironed
out the differences. Bion's concept is probably much more
sophisticated than simply a holding situation because it includes
the idea of there being a receptacle for projections and for giving
these projections back in a certain way. So I think that is a more
sophisticated notion. But I don't really think that a classical psychoanalytical setting is correct for a psychotic patient. I have
never taken on a patient in analysis whom I knew to be psychotic; I wouldn't. I agree with Anna Freud and Leo Stone on
this. Anna Freud did have a point when she said that if analysts
stayed with the neuroses, we might rightly be known as the people who treat neuroses, instead of having the reputation of treating anything and everything that comes our way.

"But, on the other hand, I have had some successes with borderline patients. They are very attractive to take into treat-

ment; they are very challenging. I would be tempted to take on a borderline, depending on the balance of my practice. You usually end up with borderlines because you are known to be somebody who is interested in those patients or because you are starting off your practice. One of my training cases was a borderline. Mind you, I do see perversions, and many of them are borderline. I had one patient who had an acute psychosis during analysis; after seven years, out of the blue, one day she arrived psychotic."

Whereas most Freudian analysts understood these concepts from a developmental point of view, one British Freudian saw them as providing support for the analyst:

"These ideas have become sort of post hoc—that is, when you are anxious with your patient or you haven't been able to work with your patient, then you say, 'Well, I was holding him during that time.' What that means is that *you were pretty confused yourself.* So I don't know how much it is for the patient and how much for the analyst. Also, they are concepts about infantile development, and that is where I feel uneasy when there is a direct translation from child or infant observation to the analytic situation. The essential link is missing."

As some of the foregoing excerpts indicate, the British Freudians, in contrast to the American Freudians, expressed diverse opinions on the treatment of borderline patients and the ubiquity of psychotic areas of functioning. Positions on these topics also reflected work experiences with diverse patient populations in National Health Service settings, where the work environment provided exposure to colleagues of other theoretical persuasions. The following three examples illustrate the approaches of the analysts who had trained at the Anna Freud Centre and worked subsequently at the Brent Consultation Centre for adolescents, the Portman Clinic for delinquent and sexual perversions, and other child guidance clinics:

1.   "I don't think I would knowingly take on a psychotic for analysis, probably for no other reason than that I think it takes *a certain talent*, rather than a particular theoretical approach. Also, *a particular commitment* because psychotic patients make demands, particularly around breaks and separations, that neurotic patients do not. Personally, I don't think I have got the

talent and, second, I am not willing to spend holidays being available. Now, if you define patients who exhibit psychotic behavior as borderline, I would say, yes, I treat them all the time. And by psychotic behavior I mean those with perversions or who manifest violent behavior. I used to be very much of a hawk when it came to parameters; I was against them. And, while I still wouldn't introduce them myself, at least I consider them more than I did before. I'll tell you why: if, by way of definition, we take the perverse patient as a borderline, then the perversion encapsulates the psychotic anxiety or the psychotic organization. This is a working definition. In other aspects of their life, these patients can function fairly well, hold jobs, and so forth. But there is such a pressure that they bring to bear on extracting real gratification in the treatment that any alteration in orthodox technique is experienced as gratification. They may use crises or even ordinary kinds of excuses. There can be very gross and very subtle ways in which they try to manipulate the therapist.

"It is very tricky with these patients because of their mode of dealing with what they perceive as a *sadistic* object, or their way of dealing with their wishes to be sadistic toward the object. They eroticize aggression so they can get quite a lot of sexual gratification in a session just by exciting your interest. So changing their session time or increasing or reducing the number of sessions can be experienced in terms of your interest and excitement. Generally, I think that the more solid your technique, the more committed you can be to it; and the more you can retain the structure, the more the patient finds security. I think there is evidence that, when you are getting pressure to change the structure, it is a signal to the analyst that you are in some way on target and that the psychotic anxiety is in the session. The older I get, the less tolerant I am of acting out in the session. When I was younger, I used to put up with all kinds of shit."

2. "I started analysis with a paranoid-schizophrenic adolescent seven years ago when the patient was 17. She came five times a week, now twice a week. This is the only psychotic person I have had, so I can't pronounce on this subject. I was learning my way with her. What I did was out of sheer panic and anxiety. What I would say is that these patients can be treated, but it is something one learns as one goes along. *This is not analytic theory*. What I found with this patient is that initially you have got to

help the patient with her madness by making sense of it. She is caught up in it. She can't use this for a long time, but she can hold on to the idea that there is sense in her madness. As for parameters, no, I don't think so. The trouble with working with psychotics is that other people can share and learn from your understanding, but what you do in the situation is very ad hoc, not a technique that can be taught. Over many years, you live with the patient and live with that kind of anxiety, and you develop a certain way of working, that's all. And, yes, I do think that everyone has their psychotic bit. I work with children too, you know. But I don't see it in the way the Kleinians do, as a hygienic thing you have to remove. If these parts are not trou- blesome and the balance is right, then I wouldn't go after them in the way the Kleinians do."

3.   "I would look for a minimal observing ego in anyone I am talking to, but, then, I'm not heroic. But one doesn't always know whether someone is a borderline when one takes them on. They may present the neurotic part rather than the much more encapsulated, crazy part. So, yes, I would see borderline patients, but not too many in one analytic day because they wear you down something dreadful. I'm sure that we all have enormously crazy fantasies, crazy dreams, and experiences. But whether I would call these psychotic, I am uncertain. I find it terribly glib when I hear analysts say, 'But, of course, there are psychotic parts in each of us.' If they mean infantile, out of control, that is dif- ferent. But I never know what they really mean and I don't ask because I don't like to show my ignorance."

INDEPENDENT ANALYSTS

Although the younger generation of British Independent analysts tended not to differentiate between holding and containment, a few of the senior analysts who had known Winnicott personally clearly dis- tinguished between the two concepts. The first two excerpts are from interviews with younger Independents:

1.   "My immediate reaction is that I can't see a distinction between the two. But are they important? Yes, very much so, because if you don't have them, you can't interpret anxiety."

2. "I think they are important ideas. Any analyst who says that they are not important is denying something. Or any analyst who scorns supportive psychotherapy is denying the support of psychoanalysis: the regular times of the sessions, the lying on the couch, the lighting, the warmth of the room, all these features that create a tranquil and benign setting provide a holding and containing environment. There is a great literature on the non-specific factors in psychotherapy. That is something analysts hate to admit. But this is what patients very often recall after analysis. They don't recall interpretations."

The next two examples illustrate the ways in which senior Independent analysts distinguished these concepts:

1. "Bion's containment has to do with anxieties and with thinking. Winnicott's holding has to do with emotional quality. Bion's contribution is in the area of thinking, Winnicott's in the area of emotionality."

2. "The literature suggests that they were talking about the same things. But holding brings to mind the mother and the baby. What does the mother do? She holds the baby. We don't talk about the mother's containing babies. Winnicott goes for the whole object theory. Bion was talking about a part-process or a part-object. But I tell you the trouble with both concepts: like a lot of Winnicott's stuff, it sounds simple but it is highly complex. Take the holding environment: is it about the analytic situation? The answer must be yes. Is it about the interpretations the analyst makes? The answer is probably yes. Is it about the way the analyst makes the interpretation? Yes. And so forth. By the time you end up with those two concepts, I think you are talking about psychoanalysis and not just about a holding environment or containment."

Two other senior Independent analysts expressed skepticism about the way both concepts were used. Both emphasized the metaphorical nature of the two concepts.

1. "I think both of them are sort of half- baked. Because, actually, containing and holding mean exactly the same thing. When I say half-baked, what I mean is that they are metaphors, physical analogies. What seems to me important is what people are referring to when they talk about either containing or holding. What

are they in touch with? I like the idea of the environment because I believe in it. The so-called mother is not necessarily felt to be a specific person, but *an atmosphere* as much as anything. In analysis, you are certainly not holding the person physically, so these terms are just metaphors. But what is happening is that your thoughts and feelings are going along in tune with those of the patient; you are attuned and yet you are separate. Now, to contain or hold, you have got to be self-contained and self-disciplined in order to be able to identify with the other person and yet move out of that identification."

2. "The whole thing really has to do with Winnicott's wonderful idea that he knew how to look after his patients, together with his concept that you have a child and you have a mother who can give that child an environment where the child can develop his individuality. Bion paraphrases it. To my mind, he is saying the same thing: the analyst is containing or retaining the patient's projections and giving back the material divested of the hostile projections. It is all this idea of the analyst seeing himself as this marvelous giver. To my mind, this has all become rather farcical, because I don't see why good clinical practice should be glorified into something wonderful. Now, if you want to say between colleagues that you are seeing a very difficult patient but you are keeping him together or keeping the therapy going, that's fine. What you then call being a container makes sense when you are talking between colleagues. But, within the patient–analyst relationship, I think it defines a particular phase of treatment. You are dealing with the phase of the patient's development where articulateness doesn't count, all that matters is an experience of being kept going."

Like the majority of the Kleinians interviewed, Independent analysts were relatively unfamiliar with the extensive American literature on the diagnosis and treatment of borderline patients, particularly the concept of "parameters." "I haven't the foggiest idea" was a common type of response, especially among younger analysts. Two senior Independent analysts, however, trained in both Anna Freudian and Kleinian orientations and familiar with American diagnostic categories, gave clear responses:

1. "Yes, certainly, I would see borderline patients, provided they are not too thought disordered. I believe in schizophrenia as true schizophrenia in the sense that I make the differentiation

between patients whose defenses have broken down and who therefore show psychotic symptomatology and those patients who suffer truly from schizophrenia. If the latter, then there are ego damages in terms of ego functioning which are most likely permanent, and I doubt whether they can benefit from intensive individual psychoanalytic psychotherapy. I wouldn't introduce parameters because parameters should be provided by those who care for such patients in the outside world, be it the family or a professional setting. But, contrary to Rosenfeld, I would not give the same interpretation to an ego-integrated person that I would give to somebody whose defenses have broken down. I would be very careful and very clearly give only *mirror* interpretations, making absolutely sure all the time that the patient in that diminished ego-affective state can understand what I think. This is quite different from the the Kleinian approach.

"And, I certainly don't agree that everyone has a psychotic level. I find the idea of the level of the ego nuclei helpful; that idea is very close to Winnicott, although he never put his theories into structural terms. When he says that the infant experiences the instinct outside, that is Glover's structural theory. So I would say there are most likely dissociated ego nuclei which can break through at a certain point. But to call that psychotic, I object to strongly. Psychosis is reserved for people who suddenly show a dysfunctioning where they have been functioning and who do not start off life with pathology."

2. "Yes, I have seen borderline and psychotic patients in certain phases of my life. I think everybody uses other sorts of parameters. The Kleinians like to argue that you do the same analysis with everybody, but that is rubbish, just not true. You have to speak a language which is understandable. If you just use one language with everybody, you should check what you are doing. And about psychotic parts, it is theoretically obvious but in practice difficult to find out, because not many people let you see it. But theoretically, yes, we all have experiences of waking up from a dream and taking time to perceive that it was a dream. Or of having a near-miss when driving and taking about half an hour to shake off the experience: examples where you lose track of the boundary between the real and the imaginary. But I think that analysts who talk about working with psychotic material when they are working with the earliest phases are just using those words. For instance, analysts who believe they are interpreting the earliest phase at the

breast: they are not paying attention to whether the patient agrees or not. I know you haven't asked me, but I find it necessary to say that it is terribly important to me that a patient understands what I say. That is my basic assumption in doing analysis. It runs through all my answers to these particular questions."

KLEINIAN ANALYSTS

Older Kleinian analysts, trained during the 1950s, were exposed to the lively and heated discussions concerning the extension of psychoanalysis to different patient populations. Many had personal ties to Bion and Winnicott. Younger Kleinians, on the other hand, seemed to have had little exposure to, and therefore little use for, Winnicott's concept. The ways that these two concepts are used (or not used) also reflect preconscious beliefs about the nature of the analytic relationship, in particular the extension of the concept of countertransference (to be discussed in chapter 9). Since many of the Kleinians expressed strong opinions on the differences between, and comparative effectiveness of, the concepts of containing and holding, views on this topic are discussed in a separate section on the related concepts of psychotic or borderline parts of the personality.

Holding and Containment

Dr. Roberts, the senior training analyst at the center of the Kleinian cluster, expressed a clear preference for Bion's concept:

> "I must say Bion's idea of containment is most helpful to me because I feel the idea of the container has such a richness and is more ubiquitous than the idea of a holding environment, which is more limiting. I am just laughing because I have just been dealing with a child who was five last week and who drew huge, great fortresses. And I felt sure that was what I have got to be, a really strong fortress, and she said 'No.' But I think I am right! It is much easier to see that example in terms of a containing, than a holding, object. No amount of absolutely stable setting is going to take the place of correct interpretations. And, anyway, Balint didn't hold a steady setting."

The following four examples are drawn from interviews with Kleinians in the younger group.

1. "I never think of the words holding environment, *they have never crossed my mind.* I sometimes think that the patient's experience of coming five times a week gives a feeling that something is being contained, particularly if there is a tremendous amount of anxiety. I do not really know what a holding environment is, so I assume it is more or less the same."

2. "I am not sure. I suppose that containing isn't just listening; it includes interpreting, whereas holding—but again, *I haven't read much of the literature* so I don't really know. Perhaps it means holding on, saying to yourself, Hang on, I am prepared to wait."

3. *"I have never thought of holding.* Containing, yes, and I feel that I am doing that from the moment I wake up until the time I stop work, except when I slip or can't do it anymore. You are processing what people are feeling and saying to you, and giving it back to them in a form in which they can take it."

4. "I think they are different. The ideas come from very different personalities, and I think the personality enters in. Whilst it is nice if we can say that we agree with both of them, I think that is often phony. To me, the notion of a holding environment conjures up a kind of soft object which often blunts the sharpness of things, the pain, or hostility, or whatever. I feel the concept has a kind of cosy, evasive quality. That is different from the sense of somebody who is not going to let you down, take in what you are saying, where it might be relatively easy for them to transform it into something else, or it might be very difficult, but where there are all sorts of trials. The other issue I mentioned about the personality of the analyst has to do with how much the analyst actually digests these matters—I think it is too easy to equate containment with the holding environment, which means settling oneself into a certain position in the chair and assuming a passive posture. I don't feel that is justified."

Dr. Martin, the most "independent" or "widely influenced" member of the Kleinian group, described in chapter 5, discussed the two concepts in illuminating ways:

"I do think they are different. Containment is a psychological, psychic phenomenon where feeling states, affects have to be managed by the individual. If the ego structure is not there, then they are not managed or contained within the individual. Or, if one thinks of the individual as a child, then these feeling states are not contained within the parent because of the parent's ego structure. Holding I would see much more as a physical state which may have containment as one of its corollaries. For instance, take the mother who holds her baby but cannot contain his depression. So she can hold and hug the baby but cannot deal with the very complex process of projection-introjection which goes on from the mother to the child. This can be a very confusing picture. The child can feel physically held, but the affective state is not contained. And there, the mother is doing something which is really evacuating the depressive affect and replacing it with something else, which might be spurious cheeriness or excessive loving, or something else. For some mothers, the two things become synonymous—the mother is comfortable holding her infant and also feels that she can affectively contain the child's anxiety or depression or fury, and the two aspects are mutually enhancing. But they are not necessarily mutually enhancing."

Psychotic or Borderline Parts

Dr. Roberts's perspective on the relationship between psychic change and the analysis of psychotic functioning differs in some respects from the views of younger Kleinians:

"Well, I try to avoid seeing clearly psychotic patients, not being a medical analyst. But, if by chance, one of my patients turns out to be borderline—which I doubt I would say that any of them actually are—I would see them five or six times a week. Either five or six, or send them to somebody else for psychotherapy. Parameters, no. If I were to find myself treating a psychotic, I would certainly make the same kind of interpretations, but then I hope that I would have enough knowledge of very primitive mechanisms, so that my interpretations were really touching the patient. Sometimes one finds in supervision that students are landed for their first case with a psychotic or a borderline. Then I would absolutely encourage them to keep the whole situation the same, as far and for as long as possible. That is really about parameters, isn't it? Personally, I find it difficult to say a psychotic part. I think that everybody does have a certain area of anxieties which are perhaps of a psychotic nature or intensity. Whether it is right to call that a psychotic part, I am doubtful. I think it is a bit different."

The majority of the younger Kleinians were unconversant with the debates about the diagnosis and treatment of borderline patients. Again, this can be explained in part by their ignorance of the American literature and, in part, by the particular influences and controversies encountered during the time when they trained. A number of short excerpts demonstrate the high degree of consistency among the younger Kleinians:

1. "I don't know honestly whether a patient is borderline or not. Parameters? What do you mean? [I define.] Oh! . . . Well, if I did introduce other ways . . . now I am thinking about a particular patient that I lost where I did do that. But I think that, if I was really honest about that case, I did different sorts of things for my own sake rather than for hers—for example, avoiding things, taking things off the boil a bit. But, I would aim to carry on in my usual analytic way."

2. "Parameters, what do you mean exactly? I try to be as consistent as I can in maintaining the setting. If someone does change the setting, for example not paying their bill, that is all grist for the mill. It is a matter for interpretation, not for imposing authority. I would certainly not take on psychotic patients. Borderline? Again, everyone has a different definition. I am seeing people I would not call neurotic. But then I don't know that this category actually exists. I think most of my patients are borderline. I don't make this sort of categorization, only because I would always see the neurosis as a symptom, as a defense against some underlying psychotic anxiety."

3. "Sorry, what do you mean by parameters? [I define.] I think I would aim to use the same kind of technique. I think there are certain times when patients are going through a particularly difficult time when they need a kind of reassurance which is based upon the analyst's remembering good aspects of the patient's personality. All I can say is that every patient I have ever had has had areas of very intense primitive early anxieties. I wouldn't use the term psychotic although it boils down to that. It is very

important if these can be resolved in analysis rather than split off, but resolving these anxieties is not that easy."

4.   "I don't know, I haven't got any patients who I would say are neurotic and not borderline. I have never had to distinguish the two. I would just say there is a preponderance of one or the other. If I think of my patients, I would not be able to say this one is borderline, that one neurotic. One gets a big mix of the two in the same patient. I do think that the basic level of psychotic anxiety has to be reached. You could have an analysis that did not reach that level, but it would be incomplete."

5.   "I think there are not any special parameters. In fact, just the opposite. I think that sticking absolutely to the setting is mandatory. Although I would be more prepared to let a psychotic patient sit in a chair. But then I would never force any patient to lie down. And I do think the interpretations are different. You have to be much more careful because everything is taken as absolute concrete reality, you cannot talk in metaphors."

6.   "No, I wouldn't make different sorts of interventions with borderline patients. I would respond differently to them because they would be bringing different material, and some of that might be about how intolerable it is for them for you to speak. So interpretations might address questions about why they couldn't hear you, or they would be linked to issues about projective identification. But then that wouldn't be any different for any other patient; it just might happen more often. In my opinion, everyone does have a psychotic area, but not everyone is psychotic. Usually, one also has a more healthy side that one can talk to. But, although it is a huge job analyzing psychotics, one goes about it in the same way."

7.   "No, no, I would analyze exactly the same way. Anyway, I don't think these distinctions are so clearcut, I would think that everybody has a psychotic aspect. But some people have nicer psychotic aspects than others. I think in terms of the amount of destructiveness. One feels much more hopeful about some people that there is more sanity or love, more constructive things. There is regression and regression; it is really a balance of how much death instinct and aggression is involved. And, also, what is done with the destructiveness is obviously important, whether it is turned against the self or the object."

Finally, I present the views of Dr. Shaw, the British analyst who had publicly changed orientation from the Independent to the Kleinian group. The views of this British analyst seem to confirm the finding that change of orientation leads to immersion in an alternate theory in contrast to an expanded theoretical base.

"I would distinguish very strongly between the two because I think that emotional containment includes the availability on the part of the analyst to bear what the patient is communicating and projecting into them. Not only to bear it, but to think about it and to transform it. I think you transform it via interpretation, and I don't think the notion of holding involves that. Just being available is not sufficient. I think that containment is quite different. Some of the Independents who talk about holding actually deny the importance of maintaining the analytic setting and even advocate breaking it—for instance, by holding the patient's hand or giving them things to take away on holiday. That is breaking the setting. And that relates back to what we were saying about the death instinct. I don't think that what is wrong with neurotic and disturbed people is just that they have not been sufficiently held by the facilitating environment. That position always makes me feel absolutely aghast—and the parody of it by the patient. It is like saying, 'All you need is good soil and sunshine, and you grow up naturally straight and strong and beautiful.' And I always think, 'What about the weeds? What grows up? Is it all sweetness and light?' Don't we also have to select out what it is that is going to grow up, because you know very pernicious things can grow up and it isn't just the awful environment that is causing that to happen.

"I don't take on psychotic patients by choice. But, sometimes, patients reveal themselves to be more psychotic than I thought. I don't really know what the difference is between a borderline and a neurotic. I am very confused as to where the line is. I think of my patients as somewhere between the borderline and the extremely borderline. I would try to keep to the same form. I would intend to work as analytically as I could. I wouldn't say categorically that a psychotic area had to be reached, or that it was an illusion that some people do not have a psychotic part. But, if I come across people who think they don't have such areas, I am extremely suspicious of them."

CONCLUSION

The quotations from the interviews delineate two distinct attitudes toward the competing concepts of containment and holding, reflecting learning with, and loyalty toward, two innovative figures in the development of psychoanalysis in Britain: Bion and Winnicott. In the preceding chapter, I concentrated on the association between attitudes toward these two concepts and geographical location. I focused on how these "foreign" ideas were translated into the conceptual currency of American psychoanalysis, on one hand, and, on the other, the effects of charismatic figures on a particular local culture, that of Los Angeles. In Britain, by contrast, the two thinkers developed their ideas in parallel, over roughly the same time span, within the same culture. The concepts of holding and containment developed within two pre-existing theoretical frameworks, those of the nonaligned British "Middle Group" and Melanie Klein. In the selection of excerpts from the interviews with British analysts, generational differences emerged between those analysts with personal and training links with Bion and Winnicott and younger analysts who had studied the ideas of these two pioneers second-hand.

Chapter 8

———— ⋆§§⋆ ————

Do Patients *Really* Love Their Analysts?

L ove can break or win human hearts. What does psychoanalysis
do about love? Why is the literature on love so meager as compared with that on, say, narcissism? The psychoanalytic literature on love is dominated by fears of collusion and mutual enactment.
Even more platonic forms of love, as described in the literature on
idealization and the therapeutic alliance, are often thought to be per-
ilous to both analyst and patient. In general, expressions of positive
feelings toward the analyst by the patient have met with distrust on
the part of the analyst. Ultimately, this was Freud's solution to the
problem; it is a solution that has continued to the present day, as is
illustrated by many of the interview excerpts. And yet, as Freud realized, the conundrum is not easily solved. Freud took a long time to
clarify what he and others should do about love in general and the
erotic transference in particular. For, at the center of love lies an
essential ambiguity. Love, in various forms, is an irreducible ingredient in the patient's search for cure and in his sticking with analysis,
although these aims are counterbalanced by a formidable array of conflicting forces.

The ethical and technical difficulties of love in the therapeutic situation played a generative role in the development of psychoanalysis.
The psychoanalytic legend tells us that Anna O fell in love with her
doctor, Joseph Breuer, who, unable to cope with her passions and the
jealousy of his wife, fled the therapy. I say "legend" because this is how
the case of Anna O has been transmitted throughout psychoanalysis'
100-year history. If the story is true, Anna O's phantom pregnancy
exemplified a phenomenon that was widely recognized at the time—
namely, the tendency of hysterical women to form erotic attachments

165

to their physicians. Despite the efforts of contemporary historians to clarify matters, the Anna O-Breuer entanglement has not been fully settled. Indeed, Freud reported the episode decades after it allegedly occurred, and the circulation of the story by Freud and Jones served a polemical purpose: that Anna O had formed an erotic transference to her physician that had not been analyzed. Like other female hysterics of that time, Anna O was highly suggestible, but the fact that her suggestibility was based on transference escaped Breuer. And because the transference was not analyzed, it was enacted, finally escalating into the uncontrollable situation that Breuer fled.

The first question, then, that confronted Freud and his contemporaries was, what could the physician do about the patient's erotic passion? From the beginning, love appears in the literature as something requiring management. Like transference (a "mesalliance" or "false connection") and countertransference (a "blind spot"), the hysterical patient's passionate attachment to her doctor was first seen as an obstacle. But by 1910, Freud's model of the doctor was no longer that of an archaeologist picking over broken fragments hidden in the sand; instead, the physician unwittingly found himself at the center of an emotional storm. It is the "dynamics" of transference, as opposed to the "mechanism" of transference (Freud, 1912, pp. 104–105), that create the fire, the "catalytic ferment" (Freud, 1909, p. 51), through which past situations come alive in the "raised temperature of the experience of transference" (Freud, 1909, p. 51). The past that has caused the present neurosis should be treated "not as an event of the past, but as a present-day force" (Freud, 1914, p. 151). How, Freud asks is the physician to protect himself and the treatment from these forces? Unleashed emotions surely call for skillful handling within a "definite field" (Freud, 1914, p. 151).

Freud's realization that the "raised temperature" of the experience of transference could bring conviction to both patient and analyst concerning the pathogenesis of neurosis led to a reevaluation of enactment through transference. The experience of transference was valued in itself, not merely as a "replica" of the past. But transference experiences, particularly those of an erotic nature, were intense; consequently, a much greater burden was placed on the analyst's capacities for feeling and understanding. Between 1911 and 1915, Freud published six papers describing his "recommendations on technique." "Observations on Transference-Love" (Freud, 1915) is the last of the six. In this series of papers, Freud attempted to resolve publicly many of the conceptual anomalies and technical difficulties evoked by the power of transference.

Freud delineated three central technical concepts to address the problem of love in the analytic situation. The three clinical concepts are resistance, neutrality (*indifferenz*) together with abstinence, and transference interpretation. The professional attitudes described by these concepts furnish the doctor with tools to manage the emotional storms of transference. In contemporary criticisms of Freud, psychoanalysts tend to portray the concepts of neutrality and abstinence as ploys that enable the analyst to remain emotionally detached and aloof. They neglect the fact that Freud introduced these terms in order to protect both patient and analyst from the analyst's acting on his own passions. Such reciprocal actions are natural in ordinary life, but in treatment they become enactments that place the therapy in jeopardy. Abstinence captures the analyst's *renunciation* of personal wishes and self-serving desires. Renunciation describes a complex process, a giving up for a higher purpose that needs to be differentiated from countertransference character attitudes of denial, disavowal, or detachment.

Fortunately, the doctor was not just abandoned to his own devices to deal with the onerous task of managing his emotions. Freud's more cognitive concepts of resistance and interpretation bolstered the analyst's powers of thinking and encouraged an attitude of noninterference and impartiality. The physician's attitude of disbelief and distrust of the patient's "material" was already implicit in Freud's theory of dream formation. Within the topographical model illustrated in Freud's (1900) "Interpretation of Dreams," the manifest content of a session—the dream report, hysterical symptom, or declaration of love—did not really describe what was going on. Like the manifest dream, transference love was little more than a complex set of disguises.

> He [the analyst] must take care not to steer away from the transference-love, or to repulse it or to make it distasteful to the patient. . . . He must . . . treat it as something unreal, as a situation which has to be gone through in the treatment and traced back to its unconscious origins. . . . The patient . . . will then feel safe enough to allow . . . all the detailed characteristics of her state of being in love, to come to light; and from these she will herself open the way to the infantile roots of her love [Freud, 1915, p. 166].

Freud introduced the concept of transference neurosis to function as an organizer of unleashed erotic feelings. The transference neurosis provided the definite field in which the erotic transference as a recapitulation of the infantile neurosis could be played out without endangering the person of either the analyst or analysand.

The foregoing quotation directs us both to love's foundation and to the latent language into which the patient's manifest communication is to be translated. Freud's account of the nature and genesis of love gives the analyst a technical "out" from the situational discomfort caused by transference love. Since transference love is not "real," the doctor is under no obligation either to become, or to respond as, a "real" person: "He must recognize that the patient's falling in love is induced by the analytic situation and is not to be attributed to the charms of his own person" (Freud, 1915, p. 161). And, since the analytic enterprise is "founded on truthfulness," the doctor need have no compunction in spelling out the unreality of the patient's declarations of love. Unlike regular medical practitioners, Freud observes, psychoanalysts have no need to resort to lies and pretenses in order to placate their patients. Indeed, he should focus on the function of resistance that underlies manifest transference-love. Here, Freud describes the ways in which the patient endeavors to assure herself of her irresistibility in order to destroy the doctor's authority and bring him down to the same level. (I say "her" because Freud's cases of hysteria are women.) She would rather destroy her chances of getting better than devote herself to the task of analysis. The patient uses all the rational powers her ego can muster to keep the awareness of the infantile situation at bay. Although Freud emphasized the resistance in the patient that is disguised in transference love, he undoubtedly recognized the analyst's role in the apparently intractable love of hysterical female patients toward their physicians. If, in the treatment situation, love is by definition unreal, then enactments occur with the analyst's collaboration—that is, the analyst's conscious or unconscious countertransference or counterresistance. A number of the analysts interviewed in this study expressed a similar view, namely, that erotic transference manifestations are iatrogenic; in other words, they result from mismanaged countertransference.

In the foregoing passages, Freud emphasizes the discontinuities between real and transference love. These distinctions fortify the analyst against natural tendencies to reciprocate expressions of love and affection. Freud then tackles the topic of *normal* love, demonstrating that it too has its roots in the infantile situation. Although transference love is characterized by particular qualities that give it a special position, nevertheless "being in love in ordinary life, outside analysis, is also more similar to abnormal than to normal mental phenomena" (Freud, 1915, p. 168). Normal love, like transference love, is simply a display of the infantile neurosis. Transference love is on a continuum with normal love and both are based on illusion. This makes the doctor's task even clearer. He must neither gratify nor suppress and "steer away" the patient's erotic fantasies, but simply focus on the "truth" of the situation. Transference love, like ordinary love, is reduced to a dependent oral attachment. Both are unreal.

Freud also believed, however, that there is one portion of transference love that is a little less fraudulent and obstinate and, possibly, resistance free. This aspect refers to the affectionate, nonerotic love that the patient shows in his wish to cooperate with the analyst and the treatment. This portion Freud called the "positive unobjectionable transference." Later writers developed Freud's notion of the positive unobjectionable transference by introducing the concepts of the treatment and working alliance. This distinction between the objectionable and the unobjectionable aspects of positive transference can be seen as another solution to the central ambiguity of love in the transference relationship. As noted earlier, Freud needed the theory of transference to explain the patient's investment in treatment. For physicians of his era, suggestion functioned as the active and effective stimulus for the unleashing of unconscious forces. Freud's great insight, to which he remained attached throughout his career, was to reverse the relationship between suggestion and transference: transference was not based on suggestion; suggestion was simply an instance of the more general principle of transference. Whereas his contemporaries believed that suggestion was the key to understanding the hypnotic method, Freud emphasized that it was suggestion itself that was in need of explanation. The theory of transference fulfilled this function. But for transference to be harnessed into the service of treatment, Freud needed to distinguish the erotic and unconscious from the unobjectionable and conscious aspects of the positive transference. The unobjectionable part formed an alliance with the physician as healer rather than with the physician as an erotic stimulant.

Many analysts do not accept Freud's qualification. As indicated in chapters 4 and 5, analysts' views on the therapeutic alliance differ considerably. Indeed, Freud himself suggests that this apparently nonproblematic love is also a product of infantile love. Following the work of Martin Stein (1981), a number of classical Freudians link this type of transference to the chronic resistance of the "ideal analytic patient" who sets up a mutually admiring and seductive transference–countertransference interplay with his analyst. This alliance, to which training analysts and candidates are particularly susceptible, can obscure analytic exploration of hidden feelings of defiance and revenge.

Analysts' skepticism about patients' alliance with their analysts intersects with a general attitude of distrust toward feelings of idealization. Viewed under the category of positive transferences toward the analyst, idealization is as suspect as any of the frankly erotic or mildly friendly expressions of positive feeling discussed above. Freud's views on this topic are also ambiguous. Early on in the development of psychoanalysis, Freud recognized that erotic attraction could lead to idealization. At the same time, he noted, idealization could not be sustained unless erotic feelings were blocked. From the patient's point of view, idealization was at odds with sexual desire. Both could function as resistances; yet both could provide the necessary active ingredient that would keep the patient in treatment.

But this was not the main route that analysts, including Freud, have followed when discussing idealization. The literature on idealization develops out of a quite separate line of inquiry: the discussion of narcissism in both its positive and its negative aspects. Narcissism is a large topic that is embedded in complex conceptual networks that are distinct from and yet interweave with ideas on the erotic transference and the unobjectionable positive transference. Nevertheless, as in the case of the erotic transference, ambiguities run through the extensive discourse that developed over the concept of narcissism. Originally, narcissism was linked to the concept of the ego ideal and to ideas concerning the patient's feelings of self-worth. Though Freud first linked narcissism to the ego ideal, both he and Jones developed the theory of self-love as an alternative to object-love. Narcissism in both its primary and secondary forms conflicts with a more mature love of others.

In his first book, Kohut (1971) followed Freud in distinguishing two developmental lines: one was directed at the other person, the other at the self. This conceptual distinction between the two libidinal lines enabled Kohut to focus exclusively on a new understanding of the narcissistic disorders. Kohut later collapsed this distinction, and the theory of narcissism took off as an all-encompassing theory of normal development as well as pathology. Idealization involves specific transferences that are based on narcissistic deficits as well as normal strivings of the self toward realization. Kohutian analysts and contemporary self psychologists value the idealizing transferences as essential to analytic cure. Through these selfobject transferences, derailments are put back on track, and new experiences of empathic responsiveness are internalized.

On the other hand, a number of the early pioneers, for example, Abraham and Adler, focused almost exclusively on pathological forms of narcissism. This line of thinking culminates in Melanie Klein's work. Klein's views on narcissism are linked to her theories of destructiveness, primary anxiety, and the death instinct. Idealization of the analyst expresses manic defenses, including denial against essentially hostile impulses. Idealization and erotization point not only to the infantile neurosis but to primary destructive urges toward the mother. Contemporary Kleinian analysts view idealization in much the same way as they do the treatment alliance and Freud's unobjectionable positive transference. Collaboration masks aggressive, envious, and destructive feelings. Even in its more benign form, the positive affectionate transference is used to defeat the analyst and to nullify the impact of his interventions. In turn, the analyst is drawn all too easily into a mutual enactment in which he or she is flattered by signs of affection and appreciation and excited by the patient's progress and insight. It is probably true to say that, as much as Kohutian analysts welcome idealization, Kleinian analysts distrust it.

Despite this radical deconstruction of love, the Kleinian system has a place for an "unobjectionable" form of loving—the reparative and constructive urges that are set in train by the achievement of the "depressive position." Out of depressive states of concern for the mother and for the damage inflicted on her through earlier actions dominated by paranoid-schizoid states of mind, there springs a moral kind of loving. This grateful, atoning love, infused with depressive, in contrast to persecutory, anxiety, is divested of all traces of erotism and excitement. Freud and Klein linked mania with an inability to mourn. For Klein, mourning is a necessary condition of the development of the "depressive position." True love depends on a capacity to endure the complex affective states associated with mourning. Excitement experienced during mourning is perverse. The belief that love is associated with depressive states of concern implies that excitement in loving indicates perversion. Though Freud included perversion within his model of erotic love, Klein did not. For Klein, genuine love signifies concern for, and the wish to understand, the self and, by extension, its internal objects. This view of love is reiterated in Kleinian views on the therapeutic alliance; an alliance has truth when it grows out of depressive experiences of understanding and of being understood.

Interview discussions with analysts of all orientations bear out the tenacity of Freud's ideas on transference love in contemporary psychoanalysis. Narcissism, both as a separate line of discussion and as it intersects with the erotic and other types of positive transference, seems to elicit attitudes that are complex and contradictory. The responses of the analysts were often wide ranging though inconsistent. It seems that they inherited a number of conundrums surrounding ideas of love, friendship, collaboration, erotism, and idealization.

Like Freud, they attempt to resolve these ambiguities by using those concepts and theories that are associated consciously and preconsciously with expressions of positive feeling. Although narcissism was not a specific topic of the interview protocol, nevertheless discussions of the idealizing transference revealed an uneasy juxtaposition of concepts as well as ordinary ideas about narcissism. These stemmed from theories of the different developmental lines of narcissism as well as conscious and preconscious beliefs about the correct technical stance for the interpretation of idealizing transferences. Idealization was conceptualized by analysts of different orientations as derivative not only of narcissistic strivings but also of other, much less acceptable impulses. Ordinary moral attitudes also attach to images of narcissists as people who think only about themselves and not other people.

Although there is considerable divergence in the analysts' attitudes toward the patient's affectionate, collaborative feelings, the approaches of Freudians, Independents, Kleinians, and self psychologists to the erotic transference were remarkably similar. The independent raters of the interviews had some difficulty in rating responses to the concept of erotic transference because many analysts were unable to give a clear response. Several analysts, particularly in the British group, simply said, "I don't know really. I haven't really thought about it. I haven't really come across an erotic transference." Very few analysts distinguished between sensual erotic feelings and highly defensive, eroticized transferences that serve the resistance as well as the patient's defensive structure. Those analysts who distinguished clearly between the two types of erotic transference stood out as being particularly good looking or they were elderly. The views of two analysts in their 80s, one female and one male, are described later in the chapter. These elderly analysts had a youthfulness and grace, somehow conveying a natural ease and awareness of their bodies. They had been trained during an era when more ordinary, personal interactions were not prohibited by strict rules of abstinence and neutrality. With age, both noted the diminution of their patients' erotic transferences. Merton Gill has commented on a similar phenomenon. Referring to Freud's statement that erotic transferences may be particularly difficult for young analysts who have not yet formed strong family ties (a statement surely based on Freud's experiences with the young Ferenczi), Gill (1995) noted: "As an oldish analyst, it occurs to me that at least as much compassion might be extended to an analyst who is disappointed by the analysand's failure to observe an erotized transference" (pp. 114–115).

KLEINIAN VIEWS ON THE POSITIVE TRANSFERENCE, IDEALIZATION, AND THE EROTIC TRANSFERENCE

In discussing the attitudes of analysts in the different orientation groups, I first present excerpts from the interviews with the most consistent group, the British Kleinians. Without exception, the British Kleinians viewed expressions of positive feelings with suspicion: erotic and idealizing transferences were interpreted as highly defensive. Although these analysts tended to feel ambivalent about positive feelings in general and wished to maintain a balanced approach, nevertheless many expressed their personal discomfort with such feelings. Some were more willing to wait before interpreting the true feelings that underlie idealization. In contrast to the self psychologists, most of the Kleinian analysts believed that idealization did not lead to an expansion, but to a *depletion*, of the sense of self. Dr. Roberts's views are particularly cogent and were reiterated by the majority of analysts in the younger group:

"I think this is a terribly difficult area actually. Have you read Elizabeth Spillius's paper on this, the idea that Kleinians only take up the negative transference? I think this is a slightly old-fashioned view of the Kleinians. Sometimes it is just bad analysis, not just Kleinian analysis. I do think that taking up the positive transferences is terribly difficult, though, much more, in fact, than the negative transference. But, nevertheless, I always feel a bit suspicious. Mm, what is this? Is it idealization, or something funny going on, you know? It can be very destructive if one doesn't acknowledge something positive. It is an issue that isn't discussed enough. I think it is often much easier to express anger or hatred. And patients can use negative things so as not to say sorry, or when they feel they want to repair something. And for the analyst, it is also difficult. I am slightly suspicious of my own wish to be liked, so I worry about that—you know, the need to be told that you are doing well. But I do think that people have more difficulty with negative feelings. I think that aggression, resentment, and envy are the things that are causing so much trouble. If you pick those up, then you can get to the conflict involved in them. Provided you get the proper balance and don't leave out the rest of the personality.

"You can't stop idealization, but it needs analyzing. It had not occurred to me that one used the word erotic transference nowadays. I thought of it as an adjective, that the patient would bring sexualized feelings into the transference and that the transference would get erotized. So I wouldn't make a distinction between an erotic and an erotized transference. I was just thinking of a student who had not spotted that her patient, a woman, was developing a very lesbian relationship to her. I think that is going to be very dangerous. You might say, 'Well, but she has never been openly lesbian and expressed these erotic feelings, so perhaps it is a good thing.' But I think that is an irrelevant question. The point is that all the ambivalence within the lesbian development is coming into the analysis. Thank goodness, the student can handle it, but it is very tricky to handle."

The younger analysts seemed apologetic about the discrepancy they perceived between what they thought they should do and what they actually do. The tentativeness they expressed over the interpretation of erotic transference also stemmed from the fact that this concept is not central in the Kleinian conceptual repertoire. The following brief excerpts illustrate the highly consistent views of the younger Kleinians:

1.   "I hope I don't do that, but I think that's probably not true. *I focus more on the negative* not because that is what I prefer to do, but because the patients I see happen to find it easier to talk about positive things."

2.   "Well, often, as we know, it is really more difficult to take up people's positive feelings. I would hope that I take up both, but I don't think I succeed. *I think I take up the negative too much.*"

3.   "I think this must vary from patient to patient. The important thing is to try to bring the splits together, whether positive or negative. But I think I do focus more on the negative, whether that is because of my nature or—no, I shouldn't say that—my training. It is maybe more to do with me."

4.   "I am not sure that I know what Freud meant by the erotic transference, but I would think that the erotic transference refers to a more fundamental way of relating, whereas an eroticized transference would be a much more superficial thing."

5.   "I don't see the sort of erotic transference that Freud talked about so much. I don't see it in those terms. To be honest, I don't know. Certainly with one patient, at one point, she kept going on about how she felt I avoided talking about her sexual difficul-

ties. I think this had to do with her worries about her feelings about me. But I actually think I did avoid it a bit, perhaps because the patient was a woman. I think that idealization depletes the patient. My feeling about somebody idealizing me would be that it would actually frighten me, because then I would think there is going to be a horrible crash. I would want to get off the pedestal."

6.   "I would definitely take up an erotic transference as defensive. But with an idealizing transference I do think there are times when you let it exist for a little while until you get the measure of it and know precisely and specifically what it is defending against. You don't just come in and say 'That's idealization,' because that doesn't do the patient any good. You have to actually understand what it is serving to deny. You leave it alone temporarily while you understand it, but you don't allow it because it is a nice state. I would always regard it as completely defensive, regardless of whether I interpreted. For instance, I think of a patient who idealized me, though not in the sense that she thought I was wonderful. It had to do with what she did with an interpretation. She would become part of the interpretation in a sort of idealized at-oneness with it. That would lead eventually to a *depletion of the self*. I don't think idealization is necessarily a defense against envy, but that it leads to an omnipotence in the patient. There is a kind of control of the object and a kind of knowledge built on the falseness of idealization. Patients feel that as long as they can idealize you, you are actually being seduced and, therefore, it is actually very ugly, what is going on."

7.   "I am unhappy about whether one would 'allow' or not allow something, because I often don't feel that much in control of what is happening. But certainly idealization makes me feel uncomfortable and I don't think it is useful for a patient."

In earlier chapters, I referred to the idiosyncratic profile of a younger Kleinian training analyst who, in completing the P.O.Q., indicated that she had been influenced to the same extent by Freud's three models as by Bionian-Kleinian thinking. The explanations she gave for her technical approaches to the varieties of positive transference have a distinctly Freudian flavor:

"I don't think I veer more toward one than the other. It is true that early Klein papers focus on negative things. I have been teaching Klein's paper on manic–depression. I always find it hard to teach because she does interpret very negatively and there are many things in the paper which you could take up both positively and negatively. You could see the material as more reparative, more in the depressive position. I think she did interpret much more negatively—one doesn't know, of course, maybe it wasn't like that in the consulting room. Perhaps, in that paper, she wanted to get something across about the death instinct. The first time I read 'The Psycho-Analysis of Children,' I thought I'll never be a Kleinian in a million years. In the published papers, there is an emphasis on the negative side and also on the very primitive. But Kleinian analysts don't interpret in such primitive ways any more. You don't see anybody making interpretations about 'scooping out' for instance; I have never heard it, certainly not in adult analysis.

"I think of the erotic transference as mostly defensive. I think there is a very different feel to eroticizing defensively and perversely than actual true oedipal longings. Somebody with deep oedipal longings has a completely different feel. Eroticization is much more to partial object relationships and to perverse things, whereas the other oedipal form has much more to do with longing and sadness and wishes that are easier to tolerate. I would definitely think of idealization as one of the most primitive defense mechanisms. As well as depleting the patient, it creates something very imprisoning for the analyst. It creates states of mind which are terribly vulnerable and fragile. One of the things that can happen with very mad people who idealize in these total ways is that, in the countertransference, *the analyst has to feel in a state of paralysis.* These sorts of transferences develop in patients who are on the border between mania and depression. Some patients can only idealize or go paranoid. You know that whatever interpretation you make, it is either going to be felt as persecuting or idealizing. Obviously, idealization has to do with splitting and defensiveness."

Dr. Shaw, the British analyst who had changed orientation from the Independent to the Kleinian group, qualified all descriptions of positive feelings with words like apparent and apparently. Only positive feelings with a depressive quality were treated as valid:

"I think that, when the patient is actually able to be aggressive, the negative transference is more widespread and much less pernicious. What may appear to be a very idealized, apparently positive, transference may be indicative of a very mistrustful, negative transference. It depends what you mean by negative transference. For instance, I can think of patients who are apparently talking to you about whatever is going on in their lives, but they are actually walling you out. That is a destructive kind of transference. They may not be aware of it; it is just that you feel marginalized. I think there are patients who find it easier to express negative feelings than positive ones. But I think there are an awful lot of people who come to analysis because in their inner worlds there must be a predominance of bad objects over good ones. So one is going to be in the negative transference quite a lot. There are going to be a lot of very painful things that will have to be interpreted. But one of the things that tends to get overlooked in Kleinian theory is that, as well as the death instinct, there is the life instinct—*things like gratitude and reparation.* And, when they are apparent, they need to be recognized every bit as much as the negative side. That gives the patient more strength, and is very important in terms of giving the patient the feeling that they have the capacity to cope with the destructive aspects.

"I would tend to think of idealization as very defensive. I have read very little of Kohut, but I actually wonder whether he can really be included in the psychoanalytic tradition because he seems to think that development is possible without conflict, which I would think is fundamental to the psychoanalytic approach. Conflict is inevitable. I haven't come across the erotic transference much, perhaps because I see a predominance of female patients. One could get an erotic homosexual transference. I would think it is defensive. *I think it is a very powerfully coercive thing to do to somebody, to do to an analyst, to fall in love with them* and to insist on defining the transference as sexual. That is certainly my opinion anyway of the instances I have read about."

SELF PSYCHOLOGISTS

The views of the self psychologists on the positive transferences were also highly consistent. In contrast to the Kleinians, the self psychologists interpreted the positive affectionate, and idealizing, transferences as nondefensive and productive of psychic change. Like the Kleinian analysts, however, they did not distinguish between a libidinal or sensual, erotic transference and defensively eroticized thoughts and feelings. Erotic transferences were viewed as responsive either to inappropriate parental behavior in childhood or to countertransference enactments by the analyst in the present. The following excerpts illustrate these highly consistent attitudes:

1. "The view that an idealizing transference needs to be interpreted away . . . no, no, no. Nor do I think that a transference has to be completely resolved at the end of therapy. I think that to have a good feeling about the experience, and toward the person, is a good outcome."

2. "No, I don't agree with the view that an idealizing or idealized selfobject transference results from a primitive defensiveness. Very often, idealization and grandiosity are manifestations of selfobject transferences that were phase-inappropriately ruptured in childhood."

3. "About the negative transference, I tend to wait to make sure it doesn't have something to do with something I have done. I do a lot of self-reflection. *How much am I contributing to this?* How much has my interpretation contributed as well? I think there has been too much of an inclination towards the negative, towards making the patient feel like a child or like a child who spoils things. I find that is not helpful."

4. "My basic view is that negative transference is precipitated by *a nonempathic comment or behavior of the analyst.* It may be something as benign as wiggling one's toes which has some meaning for the patient. It's hard for me to separate negative transferences from the patient's experience of the analyst. I don't see it as a distortional experience of the patient. I would enquire as to whether something I had said or done had upset or bothered the patient."

One of the three Los Angeles self psychologists who had *changed* orientation replied:

"I think the interpretation of destructiveness as a motivational force is a large contributor to the negative therapeutic reaction. *Destructiveness is never primary,* and its interpretation as a primary motivational force always drastically limits the understanding of the observer and always has a negative effect on the possibility of any transformation taking place. On further investigation, such feelings are *always reactive to an experience of damage or humiliation*. Chronic rage is always the outcome of a preceding experience of helplessness in the face of a relentless assault upon one's own self-experience. Then the person says "Right," and goes on to inflict pain in order to overcome the feeling of powerlessness and helplessness. In the presence of rage, I would never interpret rage. I would do what I could to restrain my own self and my own reactions from being defensive and permit the full articulation of the state and let the disorganizing process that is taking place subside. Once the patient has expressed their feelings, I would look at what caused them. What are you experiencing from me, what did I say and what did I do, not in the sense that I did it, but rather, what did I do that produced that reaction?

"Most certainly, the erotic transferences that I have seen develop *in response to some posture or interpretation or cue on the part of the therapist*. This cue is experienced as seductive and is unrecognized. Erotic transferences which arise with minimal cue do so because experiences have been revived in which the child felt that only by pleasing the parent of the opposite gender, by titillating and exciting that parent, could they maintain any kind of interest or connection or attachment. In situations where a transference of affection becomes sexualized, the therapist must not give the impression that this is pathological or abhorrent. Why the change from an affectionate to a sexualized feeling? Is it some need for validation? As a product of long experience, I believe that there is no statement that can be viewed purely intrapsychically. It is always a product of the interaction of two subjectivities. It can be something as innocuous as putting flowers in the room."

AMERICAN AND BRITISH FREUDIANS

Although the views of the Freudian analysts were less consistent than those of the Kleinians and the self psychologists, many interpreted varieties of positive transference in the context of conflict and resistance. Their approaches to erotic feelings and idealization also reflected their work with different patient populations. The responses of the San Francisco Freudians and the older New York Freudians to

this part of the interview were fairly uniform, reflecting the homogeneity of these two groups. The following excerpts are from interviews with San Francisco analysts:

1. "I agree with the view that a lot of people have difficulty
with expressing positive feelings. It has gotten more fashionable,
you know, to express your aggressions. Let it all hang out which
is the Americanism for this. Some people are much more comfortable saying all the hateful things they can. I think that Kohut
has tried to be corrective of that. I think there are drives, aggressive and erotic, etc., and whenever they are expressed, they can
always be read from their defensive side. *Everything can be seen in
both the impulse and drive that are expressed, as well as what that
expression is defending against.*"

2. "I take an in-between position. *The deficit versus conflict argument is a spurious argument.* To me, there is always a conflict to
every aspect of functioning. I think that Kohut made a useful
contribution in focusing on the selfobject transferences, on the
idealizing transferences. He gave them a character and a definition. But I would still look at it from the point of view of the conflict that is being expressed in an idealizing or mirror kind of
transference."

3. "You deal with it like any other narcissistic phenomenon.
There is no question that there are idealizations both in the
course of development and in the course of analysis. I half-jok-
ingly say, 'You enjoy it as long as you feel it is O.K.' And then you
have to deal with it. Where I would differ in emphasis from
Kohut is that I worry about idealization because so often it is a
cover for a very intense anger. It really is pride before a fall. These
transferences are important though because they give rise to a lot
of countertransference in us. You want to believe it, even though
you know better."

The attitude of the New York classical Freudians was similar to that
of the San Francisco group and is well represented by Dr. Braun's
comments:

"Well, that is part of the self psychologists' approach as a
replacement therapy of psychoanalysis. The child didn't have
enough opportunity to idealize, so you let him idealize you.

Then you deidealize yourself. First of all, I think a lot of the idealization that goes on in the analysis self psychologists report
may be therapeutic artifacts. I haven't seen that idealization
constantly. Idealization is just like any other kind of phenomenon you get in analysis. Why do you get idealized at a certain
time? What is the meaning of it? It derives its meaning from the
context and the associations and the progress of the analysis.
The idea that this is now a recapitulation of an early phase, or
that the idealization takes place now because it hadn't happened before, how would you know that? You don't know that
for a fact. Self psychologists have no way of knowing what was
going on in those phases where they think idealization would
have taken place. *They have a certain schema of development,* a
certain theory of what should pertain, and then they find reca-
pitulations by analogies in the later situations. Now, a patient
can idealize you for many reasons. First, it may be a way of coun-
teracting hostile feelings. I had a patient at one time who was
saying, 'I think you are the greatest, I am very fond of you, I wish
I could be like you.' And, while he was talking, he went like this
[sign of slitting the throat], which is a sign we all recognize. So
idealization there served a defensive function. There is a good
paper by Melitta Schmideberg that nobody ever cites which is
called 'After the Analysis.' It has to do with the idealization of
the analyst and the analytic process. Idealizing transference is
just another form of transference; you understand it in its context. To bring it back immediately to some putative stage of
development, which is only a reconstruction, is a very hazardous
methodological procedure.

"I am not a Kohutian, clearly. On the other hand, I think there
are some patients that need that sort of support of their self-
esteem; they need to feel bathed in admiration in order to get any
perspective on themselves. I don't think it is a be all and end all;
I don't think people are cured with it. It certainly may be important in establishing a relationship with a patient, but it is just part
of our activities, I would not give it central stage."

Other New York Freudians were skeptical of Kohut's technical concepts, which they saw as reinforcing developmental attitudes from
childhood that were applied inappropriately to adult life:

"The selfobject tie and transference is a term I don't really understand. I don't know what the selfobject tie is, I have never been

impressed by the need for the term. But, yes, I do think that the idealizing transference is very important. But I do see it as defensive. I see it as a normal development in childhood, the idealization that is transferred onto the parent, but the persistence of that into adult life causes a lot of trouble. For instance, the patient believes that the analyst is solving their problem. It's not the analyst's problem. I am inclined to interpret it early on so that the world becomes more manageable for them, it is tied to a sort of omnipotence from childhood."

It is interesting to compare the Freudian perspective of the New York and San Francisco analysts with the approach of a classical Freudian analyst in Los Angeles. This analyst had been analyzed by Greenson and clearly associated aspects of the positive transference with the therapeutic alliance. In filling out the P.O.Q., he acknowledged the influence of Kohut on his technique:

"In general, you only interpret that which has become a resistance. I think a positive transference and an idealizing transference help the analysis move along because then the patient is more willing to work, more able to listen and to try to understand what is going on in himself. It becomes a resistance when the patient says, 'I love you so much. I can only think of you. I don't understand why you won't date me and go out with me. I don't see how I can get along without you.' This causes the patient to stop working. Then you use whatever knowledge you have about the patient in order to try to interpret this."

The views of the British Freudian analysts were less consistent than those of the American classical Freudians. In the first excerpt that follows, the analyst spontaneously distinguishes between the erotic, idealizing, and positive transferences. In addition, he distinguishes between a sensual erotic transference and defensive sexualization.

"I don't think that it is the positive transference per se that is a problem, but the sexualized transference. It is not the same with the positive transference involved in idealization. That is all right. One can work with idealization, but the sexualization of material can be defensive against very negative feelings. Nevertheless, *I think there is a place in infantile life for the passionate side*, and this is very much a part of the erotic transference. You might not always be able to get the patient in touch with it. So I find the erotic transference a very valuable concept and description. If you don't have it, you can't understand the infantile sexuality. The child wants to swallow you, or feels like squashing you; these can be loving feelings that are very erotic. You can call it sensual, but that is part of the infantile sexuality. You can't ignore it; it is very powerful. It is not just defensive eroticization. Freud's ideas about sexuality are very powerful within analysis, experientially. That has got lost now.

"But idealization is different. For instance, take this 17-year-old kid I mentioned earlier. I think she has an idealized image of me to the extent that it is an image that can't tolerate negative hateful aspects. I don't think the treatment would survive at this stage if that broke down. But, with most of my other patients, I would feel very uncomfortable with the idealized transference, and I would take up the defensive aspect of it. One of the things I don't quite understand about the self psychologists is that I think they seek to foster it. Unlike the self psychologists, I wouldn't think this is good in the sense that the patient can utilize my masculinity or my fatherliness or something to their own end."

IDIOSYNCRATIC RESPONSES

Several analysts discussed their experiences of the erotic and idealizing transferences in ways that did not reflect group orientation. In order to discriminate possible sources of influence on these individual attitudes, I looked at both content and range of influences as indicated in their responses to the P.O.Q. In terms of breadth of influence, all the analysts who believed in a nondefensive erotic transference were rated as falling within the "widely influenced" group. Within this subgroup, both the British Independent analysts and the American eclectic analysts were more influenced by Freudian than by Kleinian thinkers. The Los Angeles eclectic analysts had undergone Freudian training and, unlike the British Independents, were influenced by self-psychological ideas. Interestingly, however, none of these eclectic Los Angeles analysts had participated in Bionian-Kleinian study groups. It appears that analysts who view the erotic and idealizing transferences as nondefensive may have undergone a Freudian training and are unlikely to have been influenced by Bionian-Kleinian ideas.

The views of two younger *female* analysts, one a New York interpersonalist and one a Los Angeles eclectic, on the non-defensive erotic transference follow. Their responses contrast sharply with those of the younger Kleinian analysts:

1. "Absolutely a place for both, absolutely. I think with some patients it is very important to be able to experience these feelings, both the early, sensual relationship and, with some patients, a more genital and mature sexuality."

2. "I think, as a woman analyst, the erotic transference isn't usually as pronounced or as consistent. But I know, when I supervise a male analyst on work with a female patient, there are certainly times when there are erotic transferences that are quite specific and pronounced. But, in terms of myself, when I compare myself to five or ten years ago, I do interpret an erotic transference a bit differently since I do not always interpret oedipal material."

One of the San Francisco analysts (noted for his "good looks" by me and by others I interviewed) linked an erotic attachment to the analyst with the unique quality of analytic attentiveness. He was rated as falling on the border between the American Freudian and eclectic groups:

"I do think there is both an eroticized and an erotic transference. Sometimes, somebody is trying to distract me from a wish to be taken care of; they are trying to be very appealing. And what is underneath is a more oral wish, or a wish to be held, with no erotic component. Sometimes, it is the other way round. Someone will say, 'I am so glad to be here today because what I really need is support.' And that can be warding off a more exciting feeling. The most difficult part of the work is to be open minded about what is going on. I do think there is something in the psychoanalytic setting where somebody is lying down and relaxing and where they have the sense over a period of years that somebody is listening to them. That is very exciting. Where else would you get that in the world? *I mean who else loves you enough to listen to you for that length of time?* If that isn't the basis for an erotic attachment, what else is? The hardest thing about termination is that nobody else is ever going to listen to you again."

Earlier, I commented on the way that two elderly analysts, one female, the other male, perceived the erotic transference through its diminution.

"Let me explain that it is not always transference. Being the age I am, I have had the opportunity to observe how the erotic trans- ference has decreased as I have got older. There are two kinds, sure. One of them is just human. You know, you develop sexual feelings. Like, if I develop some sexual feelings toward one of my female patients, I don't call that erotic transference. I just call it the way I feel about attractive women. And what goes on in me when I see an attractive woman: I tend to develop some erotic feelings and thoughts. Then, of course, there is another situa- tion, where there are really very intense sexual feelings toward the analyst that are rather unrealistic. That can be a defense against something else, and, usually, I would say that it is a way to avoid the business of analyzing. Some patients do make real attempts to try to get you to engage in some sexual activity. That needs to be analyzed, especially when they are so insistent. It will often turn out to be a sign of not being loved, or rejected, or looked down on."

Dr. Furnham, the most "widely read" of the American eclectic ana- lysts and one of the first analysts to speak out publicly on the central- ity of the analytic relationship, observed:

"Well, I think an erotized transference is often a defense and a resistance. But a great deal depends on the nature of the rela- tionship. *Sometimes an erotic transference is stimulated by certain techniques on the part of the analyst.* For example, one of the most violently erotized relationships I observed was with an analyst who kept describing everything that happened to the patient as being related to himself. The whole significance of the relation- ship became extraordinarily exaggerated. The patient finally went into a violently erotic, erotized transference. But I have seen erotized transferences develop very early without stimula- tion from the analyst simply as a defense: 'Love me as I am. Don't try to change me.' This is the unconscious formula."

The one "widely influenced" San Francisco analyst in the sample emphasized Kohut's contributions on narcissism and the idealizing transferences:

"I think Kohut's concepts of the selfobject and idealizing transfer- ences were outstanding new observations. The big contribution made by self psychologists was to recognize these transferences and to allow them to develop. I think they were recognized before, but these things require illumination. It is too bad that Kohut and his followers had to enlarge these developments into a whole new theory and to discard a lot of stuff. Kohut's philosophy of science was that he did not quote! But I think that is understandable. I think he felt he had a short time to live, and he had a lot to write. He didn't want to spend his time on bibliographies."

Several American eclectic analysts emphasized the inevitable disillusionment that occurs in analysis and that affects the analyst's response to idealization:

1.   "You know, *usually the analysis really starts with the first major disappointment or disillusionment.* I don't think you have to worry; patients are going to change anyway. I think that the Kleinian approach that, if the analyst doesn't do something, the patient will just go on, that is the Kleinians' omnipotent phantasy. I don't have any doubt that patients will be disillusioned."

2.   "No, I used to interpret it defensively. But, through self psychology, I discovered that if you just let it develop, it changes. It is like the child with parents. When the child is four, parents are God. When the child is fourteen forget it!"

3.   "My experience is that if you interpret the idealizing transference, all you do is transfer the idealization. But I don't think of the idealizing transference as a new concept, Winnicott talked about it. Kohut is a man who writes without footnotes. Loewald also writes a lot on this; he is a very profound influence on my thinking."

A New York interpersonalist analyst expressed yet another point of view:

"Well, I don't get idealized so much. I guess I don't focus on it as much because it doesn't come up as an ongoing issue. It could have to do with the way I see analysis working: I really view it as a *cooperative* venture. And viewing it that way, there is a lot of back and forth, and that could well cut down on the idealization. It could be an artifact of the way I do therapy. Let me say one thing though. Years ago, when I was the object of an idealizing transference, I was very uncomfortable with it. I think in that sense Kohut is right. I felt very uncomfortable and so I wanted to disabuse the patient immediately of it. I was inexperienced and young. I certainly felt so far short of the ideal, that it would be deceitful. Now I think I would be much more accepting and try to understand it and go with it."

The British Independent analysts took a similar approach to the American eclectic analysts, although they used different technical concepts and brought a characteristic British irony to expressions of positive feeling:

1. "You can't undo an idealization just by interpreting it when you see it. An idealization has to be worked through. But I might say something in a slightly ironical tone of voice—'You seem to have the most wonderful analyst in the world.' Without slamming the patient, you let them know that you don't take it quite as seriously as they do. I would never let the patient go through a stage of idealization untouched."

2. "My interpretations are probably 60/40 in favor of negative over positive. It's not because I think people find it more difficult to talk about negative feelings, but because my practice has a predominance of *narcissistic* patients. And if you don't deal with the destructive side, you never get anywhere. I've been struck by Limentani's advice on technique with narcissistic patients: he says it is a bit like the cowboys in the Westerns where you knock the man down and then pick him up again in order to hit him again. So you sock him with something, but then you need to balance it because you have got to bring them back to consciousness again."

In previous chapters, I quoted from the interview with a British Independent analyst who had immersed himself in Kohut's work. He was also a close colleague of both Anna Freud and John Bowlby. He stated:

"Certainly with narcissistic patients, I only interpret a *mirror* transference, not conflict. I wouldn't necessarily interpret the selfobject tie or idealization in terms of a defense. That needs to be worked through. But I do think more in Winnicott's terms. We aim at *separation and a separate object relationship* in terms of the patient putting the analyst, the object, outside omnipotent control. The difference with Kohut is that Kohut only looks at the period beginning in the second year of life, whereas Winnicott places the releasing of the object out of omnipotent control during the first half year of life. I think erotic feelings are always eroticized because of anxiety. *If we don't have a transference neurosis, then we don't any longer have an eroticized transference.* This is because an eroticized transference is an unmitigated reliving of oedipal instinctual impulses. But this can only come about in a transference neurosis. And we no longer accept the transference neurosis concept."

Dr. Stevens, the British analyst who was classified in the American eclectic cluster, responded in a similar way to the Americans quoted earlier:

"I think I would have to respect and tolerate idealization at the start, but I would expect that it would give way to gradual disillusionment. I wouldn't start attacking it. It's like a developmental sequence. Just as the infant idealizes the breast—magical control and all that—so, in normal development, you expect gradual disillusionment to occur."

Dr. Matheson, the highly consistent, senior British Independent training analyst described in previous chapters, linked his interpretation of idealization to experiences during training:

"I think that the view that it is defensive is quite wrong. I remember when I was a student in a clinical seminar with Bion. I was presenting my case and saying how the patient was idealizing me and I felt I had to try to stop her being so idealizing. Bion said, 'Why?' I think this is very important, because the idealization will also stop by itself. It is very important for you to be able to tolerate being an idealized object, and that is an important thing that Kohut talks about. Some people can't tolerate being idealized because they see it as so seductive. They feel they lose their place, and also they feel that they have got to fit in with it somehow. They feel they have got to stop being an ordinary analyst and be this idealized analyst, rather than just letting the idealization go on. I don't think anything has got to be got rid of, quite frankly. If anybody gets rid of anything, it is the patient—when he feels it is appropriate to get rid of it, when he feels he has had enough of it and gets out of that place and passes on to something else. Your job is to help the patient to understand, and to let the patient decide. I mean, you set your limits, but within those limits, the patient has the utmost freedom to do what they want, and it is up to you to try to understand but not to try to stop them."

CONCLUSION

The interviews with contemporary psychoanalysts from the five main orientation groups in America and Britain indicate that ideas on love, especially passionate, erotic love, have changed very little in the last 100 years. Idealization, on the other hand, is viewed very differently by different orientation groups. Interpretive approaches to idealizing transferences reflect changes in the theory of narcissism and treatment of narcissistic disorders. As one type of positive transference, idealization does not present the same degree of difficulty as an overt erotic transference. Psychoanalysis offers a unique setting for the expression of agreeable and disagreeable feelings, and yet psychoanalysts still suffer a lack of technical and personal support when faced with powerful feelings of sexual longing. Using the available networks of concepts and theories in which ideas about positive feelings are embedded, contemporary psychoanalysts continue to wrestle with the ambiguities and puzzles that troubled Freud and his colleagues.

We have another concept, however, that of countertransference, which occupies an increasingly large place in the literature of analysts of all orientations. Many of the puzzles described in this chapter reoccur in discussions of countertransference. Approaches to countertransference are discussed in the next chapter. Freud's first public reference to countertransference occurred in 1910 although he had previously mentioned the term in a letter to Jung (McGuire, p. 231). The concept of countertransference provided the physician with another protective device in the management of transference. In the Freud-Jung correspondence, countertransference refers specifically to the physician's erotic attraction to the patient. Indeed, in the same correspondence, Freud notes that a paper on this topic could not be published, but only circulated privately. Originally, countertransference was viewed by Freud as symmetrical with transference. Both were erotic. But, once various enactments occurred among the early circle of analysts and their analysands, Freud felt it necessary to refine the theory of transference and its treatment in a number of ways. One consequence was that the openly erotic transference was viewed with suspicion. As noted earlier, the erotic transference was either a derivative of the infantile neurosis or a manifestation of resistance. Like normal love, it was based on illusion. Viewed symmetrically, the erotic countertransference was also an illusion and a manifestation of something unconscious. Enactment of the analyst's countertransference was a technical mistake and a demonstration that the deluded physician was responding to something in the patient that was not real. Countertransference was simply not meant to happen.

Thus, an asymmetry enters into the analytic relationship with respect to erotic thoughts and feelings. In its various ambiguous formulations, transference still contains the idea that the patient's erotic and loving impulses are a necessary ingredient of the patient's investment in the analysis. If the analyst is well analyzed and his analytic instrument is in good order, the patient's feelings can be harnessed to a beneficial result. They can be contained within a developing transference neurosis. Countertransference is of another order. The analyst's investment can never be powered by erotic or even frankly affectionate feelings. In the service of "truth," the analyst extends respect and positive regard toward his patient. But, if he is to be effective, the temperature of his feelings must be kept within limits. As with the surgeon, nothing should interfere with his skill in applying his instrument to the task in hand. The analyst's instrument is his listening. When the playing of this instrument is undisturbed by loud and intrusive emotions, listening is accompanied by free associations leading to insight. Unconscious countertransference feelings of a an erotic nature stem from the analyst's infantile neurosis. They are always a disturbance. With proper analysis, his infantile neurosis becomes conscious so that the analyst is freed from the threat of collusive enactment.

The exclusion of the frankly erotic and to some extent openly friendly feelings has had a paradoxical result. The first is that, until fairly recently, analysts simply did not discuss their erotic attractions to their patients. These feelings were something that the analyst needed to work through on his own or in the privacy of another analysis. The second result is quite different. Precisely because eroticism was publicly excluded from the analyst's countertransference repertoire, the concept of countertransference has taken off. As many analysts have noted, the concept of countertransference has been extended to include the analyst's total responsiveness to the patient. Countertransference is treated by many analysts as a valuable instrument in the analyst's technical repertoire. In the next chapter, I explore the many pathways that countertransference has taken in the minds of contemporary psychoanalysts. The interview excerpts testify to the wide extension of this concept in contemporary psychoanalysis.

Chapter 9

Chapter 9

Countertransference
Affective, Cognitive, and Imaginative Responsiveness

Conversations with analysts about the "nonanalytic" aspects of the analytic relationship (the real relationship, treatment alliance, validation of perceptions, acknowledgment of mistakes, holding and containment) were presented in preceding chapters. These "non-neutral" areas of analytic practice, which result from dividing up the analytic enterprise into the analytic and the nonanalytic, often reveal the analyst's personal qualities. Countertransference is another concept that flushes out the personal contributions of the analyst to the analytic situation. That the idea of countertransference exists at all, that it occupies an increasingly large place in the analytic literature and the minds of practicing psychoanalysts, testifies to the fact that the analyst is deeply involved in his patient's life, whether he likes it or not. Freud may have hoped that the field could be saved from the spectre of hypnotic suggestion by the discovery of transference, but it was not long before he came up against the contaminant of countertransference. What seemed like pure transference was only too easily affected, or infected, by thoughts, feelings, and actions originating in the analyst. The analyst's responsiveness was not that of a blank screen. In fact, in one of his last papers, Freud (1937b) commiserated with the "poor wretch" (p. 248). He recognized the beleaguered situation in which the analyst could find himself. The analyst was at the mercy of intense affects, from which he needed protection. New skills, quite unnecessary in everyday life, had to be acquired. As I learned from the interview experience, analysts still tend to feel shame about their ordinary human responsiveness.

191

It is impossible to classify the many approaches to countertransference, although theoretical orientation seems to play some delineating role. As one San Francisco Freudian analyst commented: "You can't get any agreement on countertransference. Every year, somebody writes a monograph or reviews the whole thing, but there is still no agreement. Isn't that your experience? We could talk for 10 hours about it. Isn't that what you hear from others?" The interviews confirmed this observation. Responses were often personal, and the contribution of theoretical orientation is not clear. The parts of the interview in which countertransference was discussed demonstrate a loose connection between theory and practice. Countertransference was also one of the topics that was particularly difficult to rate. In other words, the lack of clarity in the definitions of countertransference was reflected in the difficulties the raters encountered in applying the rating scale to the raw interview transcripts. In rating this part of the interviews, the raters complained that what seemed like a definite statement was often contradicted, or canceled out, by the next statement, or by the example given spontaneously by the particular analyst. For organizational reasons, I classify interview excerpts according to geographical location and theoretical orientation although associations between these factors and concepts of countertransference are not clearcut. (Distinctions based on the statistical analyses were of either no or low significance.)

For instance, analysts who took a more "classical" approach to countertransference, subscribing to the narrower definition associated with the analyst's "blind spots," did so for a variety of reasons. Not all the analysts who took the "narrow" view of countertransference as manifesting the analyst's blind spots belonged to the classical Freudian group. Whereas some analysts defined countertransference in the context of neutrality, others differentiated between countertransference, the real relationship, and the culture and personality of the analyst. Some viewed countertransference as a temporary aberration or obstacle; others saw it as omnipresent and part of normal conversation.

The role of theory is more easily appreciated if we have some understanding of the complex and somewhat muddled concepts that are available in the literature. The complexity of countertransference is reflected in the widening definition of the concept, particularly in the last 30 years. In the following survey of the literature, I explore psychoanalytic writings on countertransference from three perspectives: 1) the analyst's affective or emotional responses to his patients; 2) the analyst's cognitive processes, his use of theory and learning from colleagues; and 3) countertransference as an imaginative encounter, including the analyst's use of play. Whereas the first perspective has been covered extensively in the psychoanalytic literature, the second perspective, namely, the analyst's more cognitive or intellectual use of countertransference, features, though less conspicuously, in theoretical papers concerning this term. Definitional statements are many, reflecting the unease and unclarity that surrounds even conscious reflection on the analyst's contribution.

In clarifying the distinction between the affective and cognitive aspects of countertransference, we are led into a third area of thinking. Though barely discussed in the psychoanalytic literature, this third perspective seems to inform the thinking of some individuals. This area can best be described in terms of the imaginative encounter between analyst and analysand. In this intermediate area of mind, neither conscious nor unconscious, participating in both primary- and secondary-process thinking, in the passions and the intellect, in body and mind, analyst and patient communicate at a preconscious level. By recovering Freud's original concept of the preconscious, imagination can perhaps take a more central position in the analyst's use of himself in the analytic relationship.

COUNTERTRANSFERENCE AS AFFECTIVE RESPONSIVENESS

Of the three aspects of countertransference just listed, this aspect is undoubtedly the most familiar. Traditionally, both transference and countertransference were linked to the more primitive, id-like, unconscious exchanges of the analyst and patient; thus, we tend to think of them as conveying feelings, impulses, something raw, needing to be worked over by secondary-process thinking. For the most part, the literature on countertransference, its dangers and its usefulness, concentrates on the analyst's emotional response to the patient's material. As is well known, Freud initially believed that the analyst's difficulties arose from obstacles within himself, from his unconscious and unresolved transferences that were unfortunately evoked by his patient's transferences. In order to function as a mirror or incisive surgeon, it was the analyst's job to clear his mind of all contaminants that might blur his vision. Urges toward ordinary human relatedness were particularly dangerous since they might obscure the analyst's objectivity about his patient.

During the 1940s and 1950s, a number of innovative relational theorists, such as Alice and Michael Balint (1939), Donald Winnicott (1949), and Paula Heimann (1950), radically altered these unfavorable attitudes toward countertransference. Affects, of course, were seen as central and vital in all object relationships, and the analytic relationship was no exception. The result of this theoretical shift from a one-person to a two-, three-, or many-person psychology was that the transference–countertransference matrix was also interpreted in a relational context. The analyst was liberated not only to listen to his own feelings, but also to use them in the service of understanding the relationships that peopled his patient's internal world. In one of the first formulations of countertransference by object relations analysts, Michael and Alice Balint (1939) expanded on Freud's mirror analogy in ways that integrated cognitive, affective, and dramatic aspects. The Balints defined the analytic situation as "the result of an interplay between the patient's transference and the analyst's countertransference, complicated by the reactions released in each by the other's transference on to him" (p. 228). This definition has obvious echoes in the intersubjective approach of contemporary self psychologists. In addition, the Balints wrote, the analyst

> must really become like a well-polished mirror—not, however, by behaving passively like an inanimate thing, but by reflecting without distortion the whole of the patient. . . . The more clearly the patient can see himself in the reflection, the better our technique; and if this has been achieved, it does not matter greatly how much of the analyst's personality has been revealed by his activity or passivity, his severity or lenience, his methods of interpretation etc. [p. 229].

A search of the literature on countertransference also reveals a clear link between favorable views of countertransference and observations of mother–infant relationships. Many of the pioneer British object relations analysts were child analysts—for example, John Bowlby, Susan Isaacs, Melanie Klein, Marion Milner, and Donald Winnicott. Child analysts cannot ignore the mutual influencing of the parental environment and the development of the child; these clinical and observational experiences clearly affect analysts' internal working models of their patients, both adult and child. For instance, Winnicott's (1949) groundbreaking paper, "Hate in the Countertransference," arose from his work with very primitive and regressed patients; to these clinical experiences, he brought his pediatric knowledge of 30 years of work with mother–infant couples where communication and development had broken down.

Pearl King (1978) summarizes analysts' changing perspectives on the value of countertransference. She distinguishes between countertransference that emanates from the analyst's pathology (Freud's view), on one hand, and the analyst's affective response, on the other. She defines the latter as

> the perception by the analyst of feelings and moods, unrelated to his personal life, and which may even feel alien to his normal way of reacting, but which when placed in the context of the patient's material and the psychoanalytical setting, illumine and render meaning to those transference phenomena that are in the process of being experienced . . . by the patient [p. 330].

Many contemporary Kleinian analysts have taken up, and extended, a modified version of Paula Heimann's (1950) view of counter-transference as providing "one of the most important tools" (p. 74) for the analyst's understanding. Heimann had described the analyst's emotional responses as providing an "*instrument of research* into the patient's unconscious" (p. 74), italics added. The majority of Kleinian writers locate this instrument within a theory of object relationships in which the concept of projective identification plays a central role. If projective identification is viewed as a pervasive, primitive (i.e., nonverbal, evacuative, enacted) mode of communication to the analyst, then it is but a short step to suggest that the analyst's counteremotions are a direct response to what has been projected into him by his patient's actions.

Although this linking of projective identification and countertransference is logical from within this Kleinian framework, it was not part of Heimann's original formulation. Heimann stressed the researching value of the countertransference instrument. Interestingly, a few of the more senior British Kleinians have recently warned against the potential dangers of coupling projective identification with countertransference, since it is only too easy for the analyst to attribute his emotional responses to the actions and projections of his patient. These older Kleinians surely knew of Heimann's influence. Contemporary Kleinians, however, do not usually refer to her innovative views on countertransference since it was over these views that Heimann broke away from Klein's influence and joined the "Middle Group" of British analysts. By contrast, Heimann's work on countertransference is frequently cited by British Independent analysts and valued as a central contribution to the development of Independent technique. (Incidentally, it was Heimann who suggested the name Independent for the nonaligned middle group of British analysts.)

COUNTERTRANSFERENCE AND THE ANALYST'S
COGNITIVE PROCESS

Although Paula Heimann opened up the possibility that the analyst's feelings might provide valuable clues to the patient's inner world, she also advanced the idea that the analyst's *cognitive processes* made a substantial contribution to the psychoanalyst's understanding (Heimann, 1977). By cognitive processes, she meant something much more complex than the analyst's avowed theoretical orientation. Her definitions cut across the common distinctions that are drawn between the affective and cognitive levels of psychoanalytic work (between clinical practice and metapsychology). In the context of the three perspectives on countertransference presented in this chapter, Heimann's views sometimes cross over the main distinctions. Nevertheless, these distinctions remain useful in that they highlight aspects of countertransference that are easily obscured by the complex nature of this subject. This section focuses on the analyst's use of theory as an aspect of countertransference.

Samuel Stein (1991) discusses the influence of theory on countertransference. He observes that the analyst's use of theory can occur independently of both the patient's motivation and transference and the analyst's internal dynamics. Theory plays an "unobtrusive" role in the analyst's work whereby

what transpires in a session draws the analyst's theory out of the woodwork where it was only temporarily residing. . . . This way of working soaks into the analyst's responses. The analyst's reactions are so immediate that one can be seduced into believing that the patient's unconscious is directly *perceived* by the analyst [p. 326].

Stein focuses on the role the analyst's theory may have in eliciting feelings of despair, irritation, frustration, and the like and that, when the analyst is unaware of this relation between theory and countertransference, he may mistakenly attribute his negative feelings to the patient's projections.

Stein also makes a useful and controversial comment on the reported successes of second analyses. He observes that a blocked first analysis may not result from either failures in the analyst's empathic/affective processes or his personal psychodynamics; the problem may have "resided in the theory, which soaked through cognitive, perceptual and affective processes in the analyst" (p. 329). Stein recalls that if candidates at the time he trained had "confided that they felt confused in a session, felt they were unable to think or even felt they were going mad," they would probably not have been allowed to continue the course. Now, however, reports of "not being able to think" or of "feeling profoundly confused" are signs of the analyst's potency (p. 328). Stein attributes these changes in reported countertransference to changed theories.

As noted throughout this book, the relationship between theoretical orientation and clinical practice is itself complex and obscure. It is not as if theory, once learned, is directly applied. This aspect of countertransference, the role of theory in the analyst's clinical practice, has been a topic of recent discussion. Obviously, there are as many different approaches to technique as there are distinct schools of thought—Kleinian, Winnicottian, self-psychological, and so on. But, although in formal presentations analysts describe their clinical work both from within a particular framework and, at times, in order to demonstrate the validity of the framework, these manifestations of theoretical commitment reflect a small portion of the many sources of influence on the mind of a particular analyst. Much more will be going on preconsciously. Joseph Sandler (1983) describes the preconscious constructs that guide clinical work as "partial theories, models or schemata, which have the quality of being available in reserve . . . to be called upon whenever necessary" (p. 38). These part-theories may contradict one another but can happily coexist so long as they do not appear in consciousness. Sandler also believes that the analyst's private preconscious theory may make a much better fit with the patient's material than the official public theories to which the analyst consciously subscribes. The analyst "privately knows better." Therefore, Sandler concludes, "the more access we can gain to the preconscious theories of experienced analysts, the better we can help the advancement of psychoanalytic theory" (p. 38).

In a similar vein, Michael Parsons (1992) discusses the "refinding of theory in clinical practice," noting the central role of preconscious thinking in analysts' interventions. Parsons argues by way of clinical example for the analyst's "active, personal engagement with theory . . . rather than the mere application of it as a received body of knowledge" (p. 105). Thus, Parsons emphasizes the analyst's refinding or even recreating of his theory. Parsons presents a case so as to offer "an opportunity to reflect on how, as we listen and respond to our patients, we listen and respond to our theories as well" (p. 105). He describes a situation in which he resorted to theory in order to cope with chronic feelings of bafflement that occurred with a particular patient; this turning to theory set him thinking about what theory meant to him in his clinical practice. Over the course of time, Parsons found himself turning to classical developmental theory in order to make sense of some of the confusion he was feeling relating to levels of oral and sexual material presented by his patient. His personal struggle led Parsons to refind theory that he already knew and to move "from a preconscious conceptual awareness to the rediscovery of theory which can then be consciously put to use" (p. 108).

Parsons discusses the possibility that he was simply applying correctly a theory he already knew and, indeed, had learned in his first year as a trainee. This formulation would describe a relationship between theory and practice in which the well-informed and well-supervised analyst applies a general, impersonal set of propositions in a particular given instance. This description, however, is insufficient. As Parsons observes, his need to refind a theory of child development did not imply a previous failure of knowledge on his part. "The exercise in observing my own use of theory certainly showed me that I was *finding* theory in my preconscious, and not simply applying it as a given body of knowledge" (p. 111). In addition, he became aware that he was not just applying bits of theory in a random way, as Sandler suggests, but, rather, was using theory that was preconsciously available and that was part of a coherent network of ideas.

COUNTERTRANSFERENCE AND IMAGINATION

To return to Heimann's account of the analyst's cognitive processes, these constitute forms of thought that go beyond the analyst's use of theory. Heimann refers to Robert Holt's (1964) extensive definition of cognition that includes perceiving, judging, forming concepts, learning, imagining, fantasying, imaging, creating, and solving problems. To this list of cognitive processes, Heimann (1977) adds countertransference. She states that, with respect to countertransference, the analyst can assume three cognitive "positions": "listening observer," "partner in a special dialogue," and "supervisor" (pp. 301–310). When an analyst supervises himself, he not only sifts through the patient's material and his own affective responses, he also draws on his interests in psychoanalytic theory and technique. These interests encompass various "stimuli" from reading the literature, from discussions with colleagues, and from participation in scientific meetings. In Heimann's view, all these sources can be used as aids to the analyst's *imagination*, which involves both primary- and secondary-process thinking.

By classifying imagination as a cognitive process, Heimann refines more traditional Freudian and Kleinian approaches to imagination in which imagination is frequently equated with fantasy. Heimann frees imagination, and art, from being reduced to the disorderly conduct of primary process and the evacuative aspect of early infantile impulses. In these reductionist formulations, imagination is contrasted with reason. Heimann states:

> I have earlier expressed my misgivings about the view that neglecting the power of imagination makes understanding another person contingent upon introjection and identification. . . . We understand another person by forming a mental image of him, by grasping with our imaginative perception his problems, conflicts, wishes, anxieties, defenses, moods etc. When we identify ourselves with the other person, we experience a change of our ego that *may not at all further our awareness of him* [p. 298].

Artistic psychoanalysts and creative artists are not alone in their defense of the hidden order and form in art. Philosophers have also clarified the essential distinction between imagination, identification, and introjective processes. The philosopher Richard Wollheim (1974, 1984) distinguishes between the processes of introjection, identification, and imagination. Referring to Freud's study of Leonardo in which Freud linked Leonardo's homosexuality with his identification with his mother, Wollheim (1974) states:

> In identifying himself with his mother, Leonardo imagines himself doing this or that, but what he imagines himself doing is determined not by his knowledge of himself, but by his knowledge of her. And this goes for all cases of identification: in all such cases the person who identifies himself with another may be assumed to imagine himself doing those things the other would be expected to do, or would naturally do [p. 75].

Wollheim (1974) further distinguishes the different ways in which I can be said to imagine being another person. He draws an essential distinction, unrecognized in the psychoanalytic literature, between centrally imagining *myself* being someone and centrally imagining *someone else* doing or being something.

> For instance, I try to imagine how a friend would behave in certain circumstances, and my knowledge of him is such that at each stage I seem not to be at liberty in what I imagine him doing or feeling next. If it is my friend whom I imagine entering a room, filled with such and such people, painters and old ladies, then I have no choice in what I must imagine him doing, and what he will say to each group, and when. My

knowledge of him establishes a repertoire for him in my imagination. And the same can happen with . . . a fictitious character. . . . For once the cluster of properties I have endowed him with is sufficiently profuse—once it takes in, let us say, his attitude towards himself, his marital situation, his relations to his father, his memories and aspirations—then I am likely, at any rate for much of the time, to find myself lying as it were passive to my imagination [p. 70].

Wollheim observes that because I place even characters of my own invention in a particular situation, there is no incompatibility between being *passive* to my imaginings and my *initiating* my imaginings. Having mapped out the various stages through which my imagining must pass from the initial imagining, Wollheim describes the way in which *identification can attach involuntarily and secondarily to the act of imagination.* Whilst I imagine another person, I necessarily share in the feeling of the character whom I centrally imagine. I may then take the further step to identify myself with some of the characteristics that fall into the repertoire of my central character.

To exemplify this sequence, Wollheim returns to Freud's Leonardo: "In the identification of himself with his mother, the imaginings in which Leonardo indulges, and which, as we have seen, are modeled not upon his but upon her thoughts or upon her feelings, are conceived of as a means by which he can take her into himself and thus lovingly merge with her" (p. 75). Here, Wollheim points out that there is something accompanying the act of imagination that results in identification: in other words, imagining someone in order to take him or her into oneself. Psychoanalysts do not ordinarily distinguish a specific use of imagination from a generalized concept of identification that encompasses imagination, internalization, introjection, incorporation, projective identification. It seems to me that the interviewed analysts were thinking preconsciously or implicitly about ideas related to the aspects of identification and imagination just discussed. Yet it is interesting to note that none of the analysts talked about imagination. Those analysts who did integrate the affective and cognitive aspects of the analyst's countertransference seemed to assume that understanding was rooted in identification, either empathic, introjective, or projective.

Wollheim's account of the processes through which I imagine myself into another character, playing out the daily events and dramas of his life, corresponds with a view of countertransference that emphasizes the play element in the psychoanalytic exchange. From the three perspectives discussed in this chapter, play and imagination are necessarily connected: in playing, we use our imagination. And, in the writings of analysts on play, play is used in its double sense, as a dramatic play and as the ordinary play that we associate with children. Many of the most influential nonmedical analysts—Ella Freeman Sharpe, Marion Milner, Joan Riviere, Charles Rycroft (who did obtain a second degree in medicine)—had backgrounds in literature and art. In describing the analytic attitude, these writers do not use medical metaphors and analogies, for example, that of a surgeon or of abstinence and neutrality. If the mind is conceived as a theater in which the patient plays a drama, conferring roles on the dramatis personae in his present life, then it follows that the analyst will become a key player in the unfolding drama.

Sharpe (1930) observed that, when the analyst is "lucky enough," he is able not only to enter the play but also to interpret it by saying, "It is all yours. You made the plot, you invented the characters. It's your show, you must be the showman and the stage manager. You must command these creatures, not they you" (p. 27). These literary (I use literary in contrast to medical) analysts emphasized the technical importance of the analyst's acquaintance with the different *modes of representation* in which patients expressed their ideas and feelings. They saw form and content as inextricably bound up with one another, thus challenging the traditional epistemological division between form and content, and language and the world.[1]

A while ago I referred to the writings of literary-minded psychoanalysts who associate the analytic setting with the provision of a stage for the unfolding of the patient's internal drama. On this stage, both patient and analyst are involved in a dramatic exchange of roles: the patient is given the freedom to play out his transferences, and the analyst uses the play of his countertransferences in the service of imaginative understanding. As Heimann (1960) noted:

> The analytic situation is a relationship between two persons. What distinguishes this relationship from others is not the presence of feelings in one partner, the patient, and their absence in the other, the analyst, but the *degree* of feeling the analyst experiences and the *use* he makes of his feelings, these factors being interdependent. The aim of the analyst's own analysis is not to turn him into a mechanical brain which can

---

[1] It is interesting to note that only two of the 65 analysts mentioned the work of Ella Sharpe. One was an Independent analyst in London and the other an eclectic analyst in Los Angeles. Both had undergone three personal analyses with analysts of different orientations, alerting them perhaps to the ways that different modes of representation inform clinical understanding.

produce interpretations on the basis of a purely intellectual procedure, but to enable him to *sustain* his feelings as opposed to discharging them like the patient" [p. 152].

I now turn to the other meaning of play, not the enactment of an internal drama with all its dramatis personae, but the playing that Winnicott—pediatrician, child psychiatrist, and psychoanalyst—talked about. Winnicott (1971), drawing on his observations of mother–infant pairs and his appreciation of the arts, emphasized the analyst's capacity for playing; this ability created the third area between patient and analyst—the "overlap of two areas of playing" (p. 38). In the play area, neither partner is fully conscious or unconscious, play belonging to neither primary nor secondary process. Winnicott's later writings on play and the third area of the mind constitute a development of the approach presented in his pioneer paper, "Hate in the Countertransference" (Winnicott, 1949). In this early formulation of countertransference, Winnicott attempted to understand the meaning and usefulness of powerful feelings of hate and anxiety evoked by patients in states of regression to dependence. At that time, Winnicott focused more on the origins and use of affective responses *within* the analyst in contrast to the "potential" or "transitional" space *between* analyst and patient.

The idea of the analytic encounter as a play-space takes countertransference as an imaginative encounter to its ultimate limit. Now the analyst plays at imagining the patient, just as the patient plays at imagining the analyst. This kind of reciprocal imagining is not ordinarily discussed, although Winnicott certainly talked about the interplay between patient and analyst. Contemporary intersubjectivists also emphasize the overlap between the two subjectivities of patient and analyst, but, again, no explicit reference is made to the play of imagination or to the creative engagement with the other, which are essential aspects of empathy. Nevertheless, a subliminal play between the participants can be discerned in the responses of a number of interviewed analysts to the subject of countertransference. But this subliminal play does not seem part of the conscious repertoire, or public formulations, of contemporary psychoanalysts. For example, during the process of designing the interview protocol, I ran a number of pilot studies in which I raised the topic of play in relation to the "as-if" quality of transference. In this context I referred to Winnicott's term the "overlap of two play areas." This question, however, seemed to draw a complete blank, particularly from the British Kleinian therapists who participated in the pilot studies. As with the question on "free association," I dropped the notion of the play, or interplay, of transference from the final interview protocol. The research study dictated standardized procedures in the interview design that were accessible both to statistical analysis and to the application of a reliable rating instrument.

It is not surprising that analysts who are actively involved in artistic endeavors, in literature, music, painting, as well as with the drawings and play of children, place a high value on imagination. Mirroring the ways that artists can feel constricted by analytic interpretations of their work, these analysts often disagree with the classical Freudian approach to the artist and his works. Psychoanalysts, tending to ignore the work of, and in, art, have focused instead on the illusory or fantastic origins and content of works of art. It seems to me that imagination has fallen between the two principles of mental functioning that have tended to dominate psychoanalytic thinking since Freud. Like Freud's preconscious, the imagination seems to have lost its place in analysts' models of their work. Imagination uses the real in order to create something not-real, just as, at other times, it draws on fantasy or illusion in order to fully apprehend the real. As noted earlier, it works with primary- and secondary-process thinking; the products of the imagination are surely also the creations of preconscious thought. The preconscious emerges implicitly in the work of analysts who work with the "third area," with the "transitional" or "intermediate" space. For in the preconscious transferences and countertransferences, we find a mixture, or interplay, of emotion and reason, of the fanciful and the rational.

INTERVIEW/DISCUSSIONS ON
COUNTERTRANSFERENCE

Classical Freudians

In this section, the interview excerpts are organized according to geographical location and theoretical orientation although associations between these classifications and countertransference were not clearcut. I begin with the group that expressed the most cohesive set of responses, the classical Freudians in San Francisco. Here are the views of Dr. Friedland, the highly consistent Freudian analyst in San Francisco:

"I think the word countertransference is really useful only because it designates that it is the transference of the analyst to the patient, whatever that patient was trying to do. Everybody says the patient 'is *trying* to do all of those things . . . the patient *wants* me to think a certain way.' . . . Well, anybody who speaks to me wants me to think a certain way, they don't have to be seriously disordered. That is the purpose of communication of any kind—why don't you see it my way? So the analyst's response is necessarily a compound of what somebody is trying to do to the analyst, or wants the analyst to be, or perceives the analyst to be. And the analyst experiences that, and, on good days and in most optimal ways, he responds in terms of the patient's needs and conflicts, etc. But there is the additional fact, which is there for a lifetime for anyone who is seriously working at being an analyst, that he or she is stimulated, triggered, affected, etc. It is not just that somebody is trying to get you to feel a certain way; you do feel a certain way, or variety of ways. What the analyst has to do every day, part of the mental hygiene or working preparation of the analyst, is to be aware of how his response is dictated by the necessities and realities of the situation, on one hand, and how, on the other, it may be intruded upon by his own continuing conflicts, susceptibilities, vulnerabilities, preoccupations, etc. Countertransference, then, is not something which occurs only on bad days. It depends on what you do about it.

"So, I am not of the school that says, 'Well it is a wonderful thing because, when it occurs, it tells me all sorts of things about the patient. . . . And then I really know because, after all, I have no problems, I am just an empty vessel and so when I feel this way, I know they are trying to make me do something'—which is lovely. I sometimes like to think that, but you can't get away with it for too long. It may be that the patient totally accidentally used a particular word that was of little significance to the patient but of great significance to the analyst because it triggered some memories or fantasies. And there is my countertransference interfering with my really listening to the patient. So I do subscribe to the broader definition in the sense that countertransference is omnipresent, but that does not mean that you are disabled continually. The whole point is, how well does the analyst cope with all of the things which occur to one person when they are speaking to another? The difference is that one hopes that the analyst is sufficiently resolved that he can do what needs to be done without visiting his own transference, *including his resistance to doing analysis, which is also omnipresent*, on the patient."

Another San Francisco classical Freudian analyst explicitly linked countertransference with *unneutrality*.

"The analyst has to be neutral, or he can't analyze. And when he begins to get a little unneutral, that is a countertransference moment, and that happens in every analysis. You can't help it, a little bit of unneutrality. And you think, why am I feeling this way? You don't tell the patient. You think about it for a second, and you work something out. You can straighten yourself out in an analytic hour and become neutral, and then you know how to make the correct interpretations, especially if your unneutrality came, as it must have, from something in the patient.

"I will give you an example: I had a patient I saw in analysis which ended, and then I saw him a second time. He had narcissistic and psychopathic qualities, antisocial; his superego was missing a lot. And I really just did not like the guy. Finally we ended for the second time. This time, it was friendlier. The first time, I abruptly ended the analysis. Then, when he came back, I tried to work with him and it was a little better. But I told myself I would never see him again. He called up last week and asked for an appointment. I was in a hurry on the phone and I said, 'I don't have any free time. I can't see you.' I was very abrupt with him. He said, 'Don't you even have an hour?' I really thought I shouldn't be the one to see him because of my feelings about him. But I didn't explain that adequately on the phone. I just said, 'I'll give you a couple of other names.' And he wrote me an angry letter saying, 'How dare you think I wanted to come back to see you? I hate you, I would never dream of it, but why couldn't I have a consultation? Are you so damned busy that you didn't have one hour?' He was right, I should have listened a little more closely and asked him, why are you calling? Then I could have explained to him, maybe, that it would be better if he consulted with someone else. My own remaining countertransference made me more abrupt with him than I should have been, and when he said, 'You could have at least consulted with me,' I thought, yes, maybe I could have. He said, 'You owe me an apology, but I won't insist on it. I won't call you and ask for it.' He's right, I owe him an apology, but he was so nasty to me, I am not going to give it to him."

When I asked this analyst whether he saw his reaction as a blind spot or as a response to a role the patient was pressuring him to take, he replied without hesitation:

"Yes, yes, absolutely, a blind spot. I mention this instance because I have no doubt that everybody has blind spots, not necessarily this way with this particular guy, but there is no human being that can treat everybody. *If you can't be neutral, you shouldn't see the person.* I think neutrality would mean that I could take what he said without feeling anything but the mildest positive or negative feelings. But I wasn't neutral with him, so I do think that there are feelings which are personal to the analyst."

Although these two San Francisco analysts defined countertransference in terms of the analyst's blind spots or personal transferences, the first analyst saw countertransference as pervasive and "omnipresent," whereas the second analyst viewed it as a temporary deviation, "a little bit of unneutrality," from the path of neutrality.

A number of the New York Freudian analysts took a more cognitive approach, referring to the work of David Beres and Oskar Isakower on listening, empathy, and the analytic "instrument." All assumed the primacy of identification over imagination. Dr. Braun, at the center of the New York classical Freudians, replied:

"I disagree with the wide definition very sharply. The basic process is one of empathy; you put yourself psychologically into the other person's position. You think you feel what he feels. That is the aesthetic part of the interchange. But then you realize that your feelings are a response to what the patient is telling you. Once you are stimulated by that particular identification and have an awareness that this is what that patient has generated in you, then, out of the scope of consciousness, you begin to organize all the pertinent things, or many of them, that you have learned about the patient over the course of time. That is the process of intuition. And, as a result of introspection, something from that process comes to consciousness. You have been stimulated, in the same way that the patient is stimulated in the course of an analysis, to free associate. You then look at the material you have, you see where it fits, and you make an interpretation. It all happens very quickly.

"But these are the steps. What happens? We are *identified with* the patient. The patient brings up certain conflictual material. He hesitates to go deeper into it. It stirs up the same kind of feelings in us. Now, we can respond in either way: we can linger at the identification, or we can break off the identification and realize this is what the patient is doing to us. We can either stay at the level of identification and be stimulated—the patient feels erotically aroused, we feel erotically aroused; the patient feels angry, we feel angry—or we break it off. But we may not want to hear what the patient is evoking in us, so we may turn the topic somewhere else. *Most countertransference results from lingering with the identification with the patient and not breaking off the empathic identification.* Most countertransference problems I have observed with candidates take the form of becoming emotionally excited and then making interventions in such a way as to divert the analysand away from the topic. It is as if to say, I don't want you to think about it anymore than I want to think about it, you for your reasons, me for mine. As a rule, we listen to a patient, and at the end of the session, or during it, we find ourselves engaged in some kind of fantasy or experiencing a certain kind of mood or attitude, either angry at the patient or erotically aroused, or confused or perplexed, or depressed or disappointed, or feeling inadequate. With all of these things, we have to ask ourselves, is this not perhaps what the patient intended us to feel? That he has organized the material so that we should feel this way? Now, that in my mind is *not* countertransference. At that point, we are not using the patient as an object of any drive or wish of our own. Rather, this is a form of communication and, of course, it is the kind of communication that artists and patients do all the time. It is part of the aesthetic aspect of the psychoanalytic dialogue that Beres wrote about. For example, a patient starts the session saying, 'I got up early this morning, 5.30. It was grey and dark outside. Everybody was asleep. It was cold. It was winter.' Are you beginning to feel depressed? Well, he is communicating his depression to us. So we start thinking he is depressed."

Dr. Braun does not refer explicitly to imagination in his discussion of empathy and identification; nevertheless, imagination is implied in what he calls the "aesthetic" aspect of psychoanalytic dialogue. As with many analysts, the imaginative element is eclipsed by Dr. Braun's focus on identification. If, by contrast, we take "centrally imagining" (Wollheim, 1974) as one of the analyst's primary tasks, then identification involves the additional step of taking the person into oneself. Perhaps this additional step is essential to analytic understanding, which is why analysts tend to give identification priority, bypassing the preliminary role of imagination. When I asked Dr. Braun about the next stage of the process, how he would move from monitoring his reactions to making an interpretation, he continued:

"That is not the way it happens. What happens is that something suddenly comes into your mind. First, there is an integrative

process of the observations of the data that you have made intuitively—that is, you have made outside of consciousness. Then,
intuitively, an idea appears in your mind. And then you have to
examine that. Why do I feel that the patient is a son of a bitch?
He made me feel that way? What did he do? And then you look
back and you realize . . . and the next thing is, Oh my God, that
has to do with this, this, and this. A lot of what people place
under countertransference is just part of the interpretive process.
That is how we communicate. Anybody who has had the experience of somebody trying to seduce him or her will understand
that. That is what the transference is. Transference is a kind of
seduction. Do it my way. Make my dream come true."

Dr. Smith, the London classical Freudian analyst, also supported the
narrow view, though, again, for different reasons:

"Well, there again, I'm a very old-fashioned, classical analyst. I
hold for the old definition: it is the analyst's unconscious reaction to the patient's transference, maybe not even just to the
patient's fantasies, but that the patient represents something for
the analyst. And so usually this will come out in, let's call them,
inappropriate but human thoughts, fantasies, wishes, fears in the
presence of the patient. Usually if these are strong, you become
aware that this is influencing you, especially if you've been well
analyzed or are being analyzed while you're doing analysis. But if
you are well analyzed, I think you can get a sense of when you've
got an inappropriate unconscious reaction to a patient. My feeling is that you should count to a thousand and say I'm not going
to do anything with this, in fact I'm going to be careful that this
doesn't influence what I say and my interpretations until I've
thought this over. And so I would take this as something coming
from my unconscious and that it could be an interference in my
understanding of, and way of relating to, the patient. I wouldn't
see it in the modern way as something the patient put into me.
This is something from my own past and unconscious and the
patient didn't do it. The old-fashioned way of treating it is that
you assume it's your problem.
    "Now, if you define countertransference as a whole range of
feelings you get when you are listening to a patient and watching
them, then obviously you can feel a whole range of feelings—for
example, My God, I can see why that father was getting irritated
when that mother said that because I feel like that right now.

That is useful because the emotional reactions that develop as you listen are probably a reflection of how that patient affected other people, their parents, and so you get a better insight into what the patient was doing to people. I might use these reactions although not in a revealing way, like saying for instance, 'You're making me feel very irritated in the way you keep asking or saying this and that.' I would disguise it a bit as an interpretation: 'This must have been why your father really walked away from you, just couldn't take your constant going on about. . . .' And, if pressed and if the patient said, 'Well, it has probably annoyed you too,' I would reveal, 'Well, I would have been a little annoyed there too.'

"I like, though, Sandler's view of the role relationship and its actualization because I think it is related to the feeling that you get a sense of the patient's transference when they are trying to get you to be like father, grandmother, brother, etc. and you feel the pressure. But, again, I wouldn't reveal this but use it in an interpretation. I realize that this is contradictory to what I said first. But you have to make an internal distinction between this situation and the one when listening to a patient reverberates with something of your own, for example in your own analysis or something rather sensitive involving events in your own past. But I don't agree with the idea that your reactions take up directly the unconscious in a patient. The projective identification idea, to me it's like some funny form of ESP. How do they get across two yards of air, through doors and things? I mean I just have a skeptical view of this."

AMERICAN ECLECTIC ANALYSTS

A number of American analysts distinguished between countertransference and the real relationship between analyst and patient. The two elderly pioneer analysts (Dr. Furnham and Dr. Nathan) interviewed in Los Angeles, both of whom had been influenced by Franz Alexander and interpersonal approaches, emphasized the quality of the relationship as distinct from countertransference. Unlike the classical Freudians, neither subscribed to the concept of analytic neutrality but distinguished countertransference from the centrality of the specific relationship and attachment between analyst and patient. Dr. Nathan:

"It is essential that the analyst constantly monitor his own impulses, feelings, and reactions because they do get communicated *covertly* and often nonverbally and the patient reacts to them. If the analyst is not aware that the patient is reacting to something in himself, then the analyst will assume that the patient's reaction is totally intrapersonal. And another reason why I think that the analyst's monitoring of himself is so important is that we are constantly communicating our feelings, our approvals and disapprovals, what we like and don't like about what the patient is doing, only we do this by means of an interpretation. And this cannot be avoided. What we actually decide to focus on is a manifestation of one of our own attitudes, and the things we decide not to focus on are those attitudes and behaviors we consider more mature or realistic or rational. That is already a manifestation of our attitude. When you point out to the patient something that you consider to be an irrational reaction that is harmful, you have already manifested something from your own value system. And I think it is important for the analyst to realize this and to be aware of it.

"So I think of countertransference in a very limited way: we react unconsciously, either positively or negatively, to the patient's nonrational, so-called transference, attitudes toward us: in other words, strictly countertransference. I don't find it useful at all, as some analysts do, to regard everything that the analyst does or doesn't do as a countertransference. And everything that the patient does or does not do as transference. I find that much too general. I think it is important to distinguish countertransference from something characterological in the analyst: his attitudes and reactions that are part of his character and his values. Some of these attitudes are idiosyncratic to the analyst, they are not countertransference, and it is important for the analyst to be aware of these."

Dr. Furnham, the most "widely influenced" of the American analysts, answered:

"Let me say something about interpretations. I think insight is a very helpful thing, but I don't think our insights are what cure the patient. One of the things I have observed over half a century of analytic, dynamically oriented work is that patients will often improve with a variety of theoretical insights given to them, from the viewpoints of Melanie Klein, to John Bowlby, or to Karen Horney. To the extent that we can talk of cure or of facilitation or adaptive growth in patients, what cures the patient is the nature of the patient–therapist relationship. And that depends on corrective emotional experiences much more than it does on intellectual-cognitive insights. In terms of the effectiveness of cognitive insights, even incorrect or inexact interpretations, as Glover pointed out many years ago, if they make sense to the patient it is because they occur in the context of a positive and constructive emotional, transference–countertransference relationship. Then they will be helpful. But it isn't the insight that cures the patient; it is the patient–therapist relationship."

A well-known eclectic training analyst at the Columbia Institute in New York discussed the way that such concepts as countertransference become useless through overextension:

"The word has become almost useless. Because I think there are a lot of things going on and, with every patient, one has a background of feelings. Some you like more, some you like less, some you love to see, some you wish you didn't have to see first thing on Monday morning. So that is always there. That seems to me to be countertransference. There are situations in which one has powerful feelings which are brought about by the patient and are actually empathic and accurate registrations of what the patient wants us to know about what they are feeling. And, often, we also have powerful feelings which are designed to defend us from experiencing what the patient wants us to experience. And we use all our techniques to support our own defensiveness. These responses are all countertransference, and I don't think that the term distinguishes between them. But I think there is always a countertransference background and it shifts from day to day, or week to week, or month to month with patients. I like Sandler's role-responsiveness idea too, I think people can induce feelings in us. They behave in ways which make us feel the way that they have, or the people around them have, felt. But I don't like the projective identification idea. We are also quite capable of reacting from our own difficulties to things patients do. Sorting that out is very hard, and one of the things I object to with some of the Kleinian experiences I have had is that Kleinians seem to take it for granted that they can sort this out rather easily, that most of the time when they feel something, they know what the patient is feeling. I believe that is not true."

Yet another group of analysts discussed countertransference in relation to the analyst's unique background and culture. One eclectic Los
Angeles analyst observed:

"I feel there is a broader issue which is never clearly distinguished
from countertransference. I think of this as the broader subjective
involvement of the analyst in the analysis which fuses with, but is
different from, countertransference. The overarching concept is
the analyst's subjectivity, subsumed under which, but not coequal
with, is countertransference. I believe that you can't have an
analysis without a massive subjective involvement by the analyst,
which is often very inconvenient and messy but it is part of the
reality of the analysis. It is interesting that you are British because
I often give the example of myself which is the opposite of the
British. I bring to an analysis the ineradicable memories of
poverty, of ideological, religious, economic isolation in my experience of the world around me, and of sexual issues relating to this.
The alternative example is of the unflappable Eastern establishment, and by Eastern I mean British, the British person who is so
securely self-effacing; this is not the self-effacement of the neurotic, but of a person who is presumably so secure that he can be
self-effacing. Now, it is easy to call somebody like me neurotic and
the other healthy, and to then say that the secure type of self-
effacement is not countertransference. But the point is, if one tries
to stand back, the first is one human type, the second another.
And they will create different kinds of analytic experiences, but it
is not correct to say that one is countertransference and the other
is not. These value judgments creep into the analytic position.

"So I do think countertransference is a useful concept but I
think its range should be very, very limited. It is really a question
of how active is the neurotic meaning of the analyst's reaction—
how intense, powerful it is for the analyst. But the notion that
you are really striving to get back to a state of minimal countertransference is also illusory. I think countertransference is used to
maintain a fictive theory which is the intrapsychic theory."

A senior classical Freudian analysts in San Francisco also referred to
the background, characterological countertransference of the analyst
to his or her analytic work:

"I think there are certainly neurotic problems within the analyst
independent of the patient that can get played out in analytic

work in all kinds of ways. Not only transference responses to the patient, like the patient reminds me of my younger brother, with whom I was always competitive so I am going to be competing with the patient in being cleverer than he is. There are also neurotic problems in relation to the process of doing analytic work, quite apart from the patient. Analyzing can be an exhibitionistic act, it can be a sadistic act, it can be a voyeuristic thing; it can have all of these meanings to the analyst, which are quite different from what a particular patient evokes. It is a general reaction to being in this situation. But I certainly don't think either, as Langs does, that everything that goes on in analysis are the countertransferences of the analyst. That for me is a totally one-sided view."

Although, until recently, the analyst's social background and character have not featured in discussions of countertransference, these influence his perceptions, including his affective and cognitive responses to his patients. Ricardo Bernardi (1992) and Donald Spence (1993) suggest that the analyst's choice or change of theory may be influenced by the analyst's history and personality. The research described in this book indicates that the analyst's culture includes not only his sociofamilial history but the highly charged "residual transferences" and "transference eruptions" (Glover, 1942a, p. 598) that result from training with key figures, such as analysts, supervisors, and fellow students. Many years ago, when schisms broke out amongst the second generation of analysts in Britain, Glover stated that the major source of controversy in the British Institute emanated from "training transferences" (Glover, 1942b, p. 614).

LOS ANGELES SELF PSYCHOLOGISTS

For the self psychologists interviewed in Los Angeles, ideas of countertransference were related to the overarching concept of intersubjectivity. Some explicitly rejected the term countertransference because of its historical, and Freudian, connotations. The intersubjective perspective is exemplified in the following excerpt:

"Countertransference is no different from transference. Transference is a process by which the patient assimilates the analytic relationship into the patient's unconscious organizing principles. Countertransference would be the ways in which the analyst assimilates the analytic relationship into the analyst's unconscious organizing principles. I see them as being no different. I don't make that distinction between 'blind spots' and what the patient is trying to make the analyst feel, because I see the analytic process as a continual interplay between the organizing activities of both participants. The transference reactions of both patient and analyst emerge in the intersubjective interaction. I feel strongly against concepts that attribute the analyst's unwanted and unwelcome reactions to projective mechanisms in the patient.

"While I think that there are nonverbal communications that can evoke strong countertransference experiences, I'm not sure that the person is *trying* to communicate them. I think of these situations as defensive structures or inarticulable hopes that the patient is not yet at the point of articulating, but which come through in their demeanor, or their dress, or whatever. I definitely don't think that ultimately the patient is trying to get the analyst to enact a role. I think in fact that that is usually what the patient most fears, that the analyst will enact a familiar role that is going to disappoint or hurt in some way."

Los Angeles self psychologists who had shifted from a Freudian to a Kleinian to a Kohutian perspective expressed strong disagreement with both the projective identification and the role-responsiveness approaches to countertransference. The following excerpt is taken from the interview with one of the analysts who had changed orientation:

"Once the analyst is experiencing the patient, he is assimilating that experience into his own background, into his own theory, and there is no way he can disarticulate himself from that. I have my own affective reactions to what is taking place, and I have to recognize these and, very often, patients come to experience my reactions as an intrinsic part of their experience. I am very alert to taking this up not as a projection but as an anticipation of an anxiety that would inhibit a process of *self-revelation, self-articulation*, or expression of differentiated experience and unconstricted affect.

"I don't find Sandler's definition useful. The idea of a role relationship attributes an intentionality to the patient and focuses on a presumptive area of the unconscious that derives from the analyst's view rather than from the subjective experience of the patient. It is an attempt to diminish the contribution of the analyst, and it is not to his benefit to diminish that. He doesn't need to apologize for it. All he needs to do is to be aware of an area of vulnerability of his own in the situation. Once he can accept that and use it self-reflectively, he does not need to explain it by resort to, 'this is what the patient is consciously or unconsciously doing in order to repeat a situation, and in order to bring that situation to life so that it can be analyzed.' That is a tortuous explanation. It clutters things up; it is unneeded. *All the analyst has to do is to be himself and the patient herself*, and, human situations being limited, the situation is going to be repeated. The repetitive aspect of it lies in the meaning, not in the experience itself, but in the unconscious meaning that structures and shapes the patient's experience. There is no need to contrive anything."

The raters found that, with the exception of a subgroup of younger British Kleinian analysts, the analysts who held the clearest views on countertransference were the older analysts. Their interviews were the simplest to rate. All the foregoing excerpts are from interviews with senior training analysts in the four cities I visited. If we consider the range of psychoanalysis' basic concepts, countertransference could be counted amongst those which have undergone a radical transformation and expansion.

BRITISH KLEINIANS

The views of the younger British Kleinian analysts on the communicative value of countertransference were unanimous: all regarded countertransference as an indicator of the *patient's* thoughts and feelings. They seemed relatively unconcerned with the idea of countertransference as indicating a blind spot in the analyst and regarded countertransference feelings as an instrument for understanding. The following examples demonstrate this high degree of consistency:

1. "I tend to see it as a response to what the patient is doing, to what is going on. Although I try to be open to the idea that the intensity of my response might have to do with me. But I would first think of it as communication, that's where I would look first."

2. "On the whole I see my countertransference as crucial, important, and worth looking into, as opposed to my own misuse of it insofar as I was not able to pay attention to the patient. I think of it as mostly relevant to what is going on for the patient,

and it is something that is going on all the time. I think more in terms of projective identification, although you may be being pressurized into acting something out."

3.   "I think of Bion's notion of projective identification as a form of communication, that there is a normal stage of projective identification where the infant does need to feel that there is an object that will be available and, in that sense, does allow the infant to get inside the object, or be part of it. I've got a very disturbed child in analysis, he's been very violent. When, for instance, he is spitting, I can say that he is desperate to feel that he can have something taken in although he feels so much that that won't be available to him. He has often been very responsive to that kind of interpretation. It works, rather than saying how destructive he is being. One doesn't have to go along, or collude, with the destructiveness, but to find a way to say how desperately a person might need to feel that there is someone in their life that they can feel is really part of them, that they can flow into or whatever. So, although there are times when one feels that one is having a reaction that one feels very unhappy about, nevertheless the rest of the time it's part of the data."

In sharp contrast to these younger Kleinian analysts, Dr. Roberts, the senior Kleinian training analyst, took a more cautious position. His emphasis on perception resonates with the ideas of Heimann (1950, 1960, 1975) described earlier. Dr. Roberts:

"Oh . . . [shudder] . . . use but not overuse. Oh yes, I have a great respect for the idea of blind spots. I still think that is an extremely useful way of using the word countertransference. But I think it is worth extending the term to cover the feelings of the analyst which are aroused by the patient and which the analyst can then use, and not act out. That is where we really are, I think. But it is so much overused, and people are saying, 'Ah, I knew from my countertransference . . .' when they ought to be able to tell what is going on from something else. It isn't just that the patient is letting the analyst know things, or that you [the analyst] have sniffed out cleverly through your countertransference that the patient's voice went up, or that the patient made a little dig. The patient has given you clues, and that is not all countertransference. There is empathy, understanding, insight, perception. The overuse is dangerous. I agree with Sandler on

role responsiveness; only I would call that projective identification, whereas he would call it nudging or pushing you into a role,
but it is much the same thing."

BRITISH CONTEMPORARY FREUDIANS AND INDEPENDENTS

The majority of British Contemporary Freudian and Independent analysts distinguished between countertransference as emanating from a
problem in the analyst and the analyst's "affective responsiveness" as
defined by Pearl King (1978). Some were particularly alert to the distinction drawn by Heimann (1950, 1960, 1975) between the analyst's
perception of what is going on in the patient and the patient's unconscious communication of thoughts and feelings to his analyst. The following excerpt is from the interview with a senior Independent analyst
who was also a child analyst:

"About this question of communication, I don't agree with
Rosenfeld's idea of projective identification as an attempt at
communication. One can perceive something: one hears the
baby crying because the baby has got a tummyache. But the baby
might be crying in order to yell at mother. And the baby might
be crying in pain and the mother hears it. *Something is perceived
that hasn't been intended as a communication.* One learns about the
patient from the way one feels about the patient. This is a truism.
I am describing a patient I saw and that patient was depressed.
You derive that from your perception of the patient and your perception includes your feeling about it—what Pearl King calls
affective responsiveness. It is part of what Freud called free-float-
ing attention."

The perspective of another Independent analyst, who was also a
group analyst, was unique amongst British analysts although his views
are similar to those of some of the American eclectic analysts presented earlier. According to this analyst, the term countertransference
does not define the analyst's blind spots but refers to his "personality
structure":

"For example, I'm very poor at spotting anality, a kind of ignorance about the material. It has not played a large part in my own

analysis. I'm not that familiar with it. That's not part of the strict
definition of countertransference. This is where group therapy
can be so good, because within the eight people in a group, you
will find that each is more countertransferentially sensitive to
some issues than others. In groups, much more is visible in the
room. This is something that one analyst can't do; analysts just
can't be everything. I also object to the terms 'pressure' or
'manipulate' because they imply a sort of semiconsciousness. The
patient is doing the only thing he knows how to do, which is to
engage in a kind of dance or dialogue or setup with you which is
what he always does. But what takes place goes on interpersonally, even though it may be felt subjectively and very much as if
the patient has put his feelings into me. But I don't believe in
magic. The patient may well have a fantasy of putting something
into me, but there is always something that goes on interpersonally. 'Manipulate' implies a sort of deviousness, and I don't think
it is devious at all. If I think of the people who produce no countertransference response in me except a kind of puzzlement, then
the relationship is fairly inert, intellectual, or slightly schizoid.

"About projective identification as a communication as well as
a getting rid of, I think that is very complicated indeed because it
partly depends on how tolerant the patient is of having an experience *put back to them in the form of words*. Now, if the patient is
tolerant of that, then it is awfully easy to say, 'Oh well, they did
it as a communication. They just needed to be understood, and
now I've understood it, everything's fine.' And, if they reject the
interpretation, it is tempting to say, 'Oh, it was an evacuation of
an intolerable bit, and they are just getting rid of it, and they
won't have it back.' But, actually, I suspect that there isn't any
difference between those two processes. You have just got to
work on your technique. It is too easy when the patient does not
accept your interpretation to take a slightly moralizing tone and
to say it is an evacuation and they are just incapable of dealing
with it. Actually, I think it has much more to do with the analyst's skill in the timing and the phrasing, as well as the amount
and length of time they can stand containing the patient."

The elderly Freudian analyst described in previous chapters brought
her characteristic historical perspective to the topic:

"Well, I was a student and just becoming an analyst when this
whole development took place. In my early student days, it was

seen very much as Freud did, that countertransference is a negative thing which interferes. It was not taught then as the *instrument* that gives one the subtle understanding and insight into the patient. For myself, this later development began via Winnicott. That is where I learned about it and when it became part of my own work. At present, it plays a very, very big part, especially in supervision. And with students who are still in the early stages of their analyses, it is most important to make them aware from the start what a very valuable and essential part countertransference plays—as well as the dangers."

Two British Freudian analysts who were classified in the Independent group expressed views on countertransference that differed from the American classical Freudians. One of these analysts replied:

"I think both the narrow view and the contemporary view of countertransference as communication are wrong, I am closer to Paula Heimann's notion. For instance, I heard somebody speak from the rostrum in the British Society—this analyst said he couldn't remember the name of the patient's husband and that that was the result of an attack on his thinking. I think Pearl King has made an important contribution in her definition of the analyst's affective response and also her notion of the reversed transference. For instance, say you are with a patient and they are treating you in such a way that you are literally screaming: if you can interpret this as a transference reversal, there is less danger of acting out. I think you are much more at risk of acting out your countertransference if you believe that the patient has actually put something into you in some sort of malignant way. I don't actually believe that."

The second Contemporary Freudian analyst, who worked at the Portman Clinic, described specific reactions to sadistic patients that he believed were normal and natural and not, strictly speaking, countertransference:

"It's the reaction that almost anybody would have to a particular kind of behavior. If, for instance, a patient is being really nasty to the analyst, my guess is that the analyst is having the natural response to that. Like, if you get a sadistic patient who is trying to torture you, there is a *natural* response. That may be quickly repressed by the analyst, or he or she may make use of it and build an interpretation on it. It's not a pathological response. It's a natural response to particular stimuli, and, if the analyst didn't react in a normal way, there would be something wrong with him. The patient is actually relying on you to react normally, this is particularly true in the case of sadistic patients."

CONCLUSION

The various examples from the interview/discussions on countertransference demonstrate a lack of consistency in the use of this concept. Nevertheless, all the definitions seem to address the interpersonal nature of self-knowledge. Some analysts view this interpersonal dimension as unfortunate and as something that should be avoided. To this end, they aim for neutrality and the neutralization of affective responses. Other analysts, on the other hand, accept their emotional reactions and use them as a "tool" or "instrument" for a more expanded analytic understanding. For analysts who think relationally, countertransference is a natural occurrence. As the Balints (1939) noted, countertransference and transference are the analytic counterpart of ordinary human relatedness.

Although the self psychologists tended to define countertransference within a symmetrical intersubjective relationship, most analysts stressed the asymmetry of self-knowledge within the analytic situation. Since the analyst has undergone analysis, he has experienced the problems and pleasures of acquiring knowledge of himself. The patient, however, is acquiring this special kind of knowledge, perhaps for the first time. Self-knowledge, being self-referring, invokes all the paradoxes and pitfalls of self-referring systems, specifically a tendency toward self-deception. The analytic relationship is unique in its exclusive focus on the expansion of the patient's self-awareness in the service of healing. The analyst is not only a transference figure, he or she is also a new object or person, one of whose tasks is to reflect back to the patient those persons and the narrowed world view he repeatedly transfers onto the analyst and the analytic situation. The analyst recognizes these transferences through acts of imagination and, very often, identification. The tricky nature of countertransference as a source of self-knowledge is captured in the following quotation from Aristotle's *Magna Moralia*:

It is both a most difficult thing . . . to know oneself, and also a most pleasant thing (for to know oneself is pleasant)—moreover, we cannot ourselves study ourselves from ourselves, as is clear from the reproaches we bring against others without being aware that we do the same things ourselves—and this happens because of bias or passion, which in many of us obscures the accuracy of judgments; as, then, when we ourselves wish to see our own face we see it by looking into a mirror, similarly too, when we ourselves wish to know ourselves, we would know ourselves by looking to the *philos*. For the *philos*, as we say, is another oneself. If, then, it is pleasant to know oneself, and if it is not possible to know this without having someone else as *philos*, the self-sufficient person would need *philia* in order to know himself (Aristotle, *Magna Moralia*, 1213a, 10–26).

If, following Aristotle, we acknowledge the interpersonal or intersubjective basis of self-knowledge, then it follows that the analyst also recognizes some of his selves in his patients. As no human being ever achieves complete self-knowledge and as our knowledge of other people is limited by our self-knowledge and life experiences with specific people, the analyst is always discovering himself or herself in the "new objects" of his patients. Each analyst is involved in a continual process of self-analysis; once out of personal analysis and supervision, he works on his self-understanding through his experiences with his patients, particularly those which (as King, 1978, observes) are least ego syntonic. As noted by Heimann, the only advantage he has over his patient is his greater self-knowledge acquired through training, and his commitment to sharpen his self-awareness in his daily practice. This, of course, is both a pleasurable goal and one that is hard to achieve.

Chapter 10

The Analyst's Model of Change

Kierkegaard wrote in a journal entry in 1843: "It is perfectly true, as philosophers say, that life must be understood backwards. But they forget the other proposition, that it must be lived forwards" (quoted in Wollheim, 1984, p. 1). Expanding on Kierkegaard's thought, Richard Wollheim (1984) reflects: "A person leads his life at a cross-roads: at the point where a past that has affected him and a future that lies open meet in the present" (p. 31). As long as we exist, we live at a crossroads; it follows that no analysis is ever complete. But we can think of living at a crossroads in two ways: one as a potential space or a transitional area from which paths lead into the distance and, two, as a place of immobility. People usually come to analysis in the second position. Unable to move forward or look backward, they turn to analysis as an agent of change. How does analysis work? How does the analyst view himself and his task?

In this chapter, I address these questions from a number of perspectives that converge on the subject of psychic change. During the interviews, I did not ask the analysts directly, "What do you think causes, or leads to, psychic change?" Rather, I posed a number of subsidiary questions about the aim and function of their interpretations. One set of questions addressed such issues as the following: Do you usually formulate your interpretations in terms of conflict? When interpreting, do you usually focus on the main, underlying anxiety, or on another central affect? When making interpretations, do you feel that an observing or reflective part of the patient must be available? A second set of questions addressed the organizing role of the past in interpretation: When you make transference interpretations, do you usually refer to the past, or do you mostly take up feelings and thoughts in the here-and-now

223

transference relationship? Does reconstruction play a central role in your interpretations? If so, do you see the present transference relationship as recapitulating relationships in the past? Or, on the other hand, do you see the past as constantly modified and transformed throughout development? Are your interpretations aimed at the recovery of memories?

Discussion of these aspects of technique clarified the analysts' explicit and implicit models of change. Kierkegaard had remarked on the tendency to forget that our lives must be lived forward. Psychoanalysts value the examined life, overestimating perhaps the understood life relative to the future-orientated way most ordinary people lead their lives. Looking back to the origins of psychoanalysis, we could say that psychoanalysis was at first backward looking; but, once the dynamics of transference revealed themselves, present interactions took the floor. Nowadays, many analysts—and the majority of those I interviewed—pay almost exclusive attention to the here-and-now transference relationship, and to the construction of a coherent narrative of psychic reality, occasionally casting a glance at the sequence of lived events in the past. History taking has also receded. But what about the future? Do we pay sufficient attention to the specific stage of the life cycle in which a patient is situated? Freud believed that adults over the age of 40 were not amenable to change through the psychoanalytic method. Others have suggested that this method is inappropriate for adolescents. In the last 20 years or so, however, a number of analysts have published papers describing work with middle-aged and elderly patients. These accounts address both the potential for change, and the specific changes and developments sustained by older patients undergoing psychoanalysis. In addition to their value in alerting us to the potential for change in later stages of the life-cycle, these clinical studies focus our attention on psychoanalytic notions of change, time, and timelessness. For, even though we lead our lives in unconscious ways that trick us into a sense of timelessness, our life span is timed. Our place in the average expectable life span surely affects our sense of the future.

It also affects our sense of the past. Unless we believe there is one crossroads of life on which all future transitions are modeled—for instance, the infantile neurosis or the early mother–infant feeding relationship—the examined life of a young person will look very different from that of someone in middle or old age. As compared with people in these later stages of the life cycle, an adolescent lacks a product, that is, a life led on which to retrospect and reflect. The ratio of life to be understood backwards is small as compared to the decades that lie ahead waiting to be lived.

Intersecting with issues of the relevance of past and future is the nature of desirable personality change. When theorizing about psychic change, psychoanalysts attempt to define the criteria for delineating the kind of change that is sought. For instance, Freudian goals might include the resolution of the Oedipus complex or the castration complex as these complexes relate to the primal scene; or structural change in terms of psychic equilibrium among Freud's three agencies; or the development of insight. Object relational goals might include the restructuring of internal object relationships leading to new identifications; or the achievement of the depressive position combined with a weakening of persecutory anxieties and a reorganization of primitive defenses. Self-psychological goals might include a capacity for affect regulation, the establishment of a "selfobject tie," or the restoration of the self. Winnicott suggested the development of a capacity for playing and a sense of "continuity of being" ("going-on-being").

Very often, psychoanalysts' models of change reflect favored theories of child development. Almost all analysts agree that the childhood years are the most formative period of a person's life. Melanie Klein emphasized the first six months of life, which culminated in the achievement of the depressive position. Margaret Mahler stressed the "separation-individuation" phase from 18 to 36 months. Contemporary infancy researchers focus on mother–infant attunement in the first year of life. These notions are drawn from models of early development and are sometimes applied clinically with little developmental perspective on the patient's present age and stage in the life cycle. And here again, perhaps, Freud's distinction between psychic and material reality plays a part. In psychic reality, time does not matter; for, in the unconscious, everyday realities of time and place, of consistency and noncontradiction, do not exist.

But how do these models of change translate in clinical practice? What do analysts consider to be the most effective agents for achieving the changes they value? Here we encounter an important shift in the technique of contemporary psychoanalysts of varying persuasions. This can be summed up in the choice analysts make between focusing on the here-and-now analytic relationship and fostering a greater understanding of the past. This antithesis was already implicit in Freud's later theory of transference. In his pivotal paper on transference, Freud (1912) distinguished between the "mechanism" and the "dynamics" of transference. Psychoanalysts continue to debate the relative significance of the repetitive aspect of transference stemming exclusively from the patient's past (the intrapsychic), on one hand, and, on the other, the intersubjective interplay of transference and countertransference experiences in the present analytic situation (the interpersonal). As the interview excerpts indicate, most contemporary psychoanalysts choose to focus their interpretations on the here-and-now analytic relationship.

This choice of emphasis, however, does not simply dispose of the past. Fine distinctions are made in the ways that present and past reflect one another. Some analysts see the here-and-now analytic situation as nonetheless isomorphic with past developmental processes. What those analysts may fail to note is that the past that is repeated in the present is a past that preconsciously reflects their favored theories of child development. (This preconscious or unconscious link is discussed in some of the interview excerpts. It also relates to the analyst's "countertransference to theory" discussed in the previous chapter.) It is possible that those analysts, who interpret almost exclusively in terms of the patient's psychic reality, are more likely to adopt the isomorphic view of present and past. As noted earlier, linear progression and chronological time are not features of unconscious thinking.

At the same time, as the interviews also indicate, there are analysts who are suspicious of this collapse of past and present. Taking in both regressive and progressive aspects of growth and change, they emphasize a more linear aspect of development. To these developmentalists, the past is reached only in highly derivative forms. These analysts may see change as occurring in the here-and-now and formulate their interpretations accordingly, yet refer to the past under specific conditions. This approach is illustrated by a number of the analysts in the developmental Freudian group. Other Freudians conceive of change as an essentially intrapsychic process that, to varying degrees, involves memory and reconstruction.

HISTORY, RECONSTRUCTION, AND THE HERE-AND-NOW RELATIONSHIP

Although group affiliation, influences by leading thinkers, and geographical location played some role in delineating analysts' attitudes to these questions, associations were not as clear-cut as in discussions of other topics. The majority of analysts of all theoretical persuasions focused their interpretations on the here-and-now transference relationship and minimized the frequency, and importance, of references to the past. Associations between the different types of response and these variables were for the most part of low statistical significance. Only nine of the 65 analysts stated that they would refer to the patient's past history more often than they would to the here-and-now relationship with the analyst. The majority of these nine analysts were of a classical Freudian orientation. None of the classical and developmental Freudians were rated as interpreting the here-and-now as isomorphic with the there-and-then. With reference to the P.O.Q., the responses of the Freudian group to this part of the interview indicated a high correlation with the influence of ego psychology. It seems that, although many Freudians tend to focus their interventions on the here-and-now analytic relationship, many value the process of reconstruction. Several spontaneously referred to the important process of working through. They noted that this aspect of Freudian technique was no longer a subject of current technique.

In contrast to these Freudian approaches, influences by Bion and Klein contributed significantly to the isomorphic point of view. On the P.O.Q., the responses of Kleinian analysts to this part of the interview showed negative correlations with influences by ego psychology, Merton Gill, Roy Schafer, and hermeneutic writers. Clearly, the ego-psychological thinking of Hartmann, Lowenstein, and Rapaport contributed to new ideas of adaptation and narrative truth put forward by such writers as Gill, Schafer, and Spence.[1] A significant proportion of British Independent analysts focused on the interpretation of internal object relationships and the early infantile fantasies associated with these relationships. In this respect, their interpretations were similar to those of Kleinian colleagues even though differences occurred with respect to content and origins of these phantasies.

The main reason analysts gave for focusing on the present transference was to avoid "intellectualization" and the "dilution of the transference" and to capitalize on "the heat of what is going on between the patient and the analyst." In the words of one analyst, "The test which should be applied is whether or not the reference to the past augments or diminishes the degree or power of the interpretation." These technical explanations reflect analysts' beliefs in the centrality of *affect* as an agent of psychic change. In addition to therapeutic efficacy, however, discussions revealed a number of implicit beliefs about how access to, and retrieval of, the past might occur. In turn, these assumptions overlapped with ideas about the nature of event memory, construction, and mental structure. For instance, some self psychologists substituted the

---

[1]In terms of the factor analysis of the results of the P.O.Q., two factors were significant: attitudes of developmental Freudians contrasted sharply with those of Kleinians; to a lesser extent, the hermeneutic point of view contrasted with that of the British object relations analysts, both Independent and Kleinian.

concept of invariant organizing principles that are repeated over and over again in the present for event memories or details of personal history. But this reformulation suggests yet another distinction between content and process—as if somehow process could be filtered out from the sequence of ideas and emotions of which it is composed.

Reflections on the contribution of the past to psychic change evoked a multitude of preconscious beliefs, psychoanalytic concepts, and theories. The analysts' statements about these questions were often somewhat contradictory and unclear, resulting in part from a reevaluation of many of Freud's theoretical formulations and analogies. For instance, in comparison with the ways we talk about feelings, we tend to think of memories and perceptions as having a more cognitive, dispassionate connotation. Many of the contemporary analysts seemed to contrast affective experiences with thoughts or memories of the past. Memory was often portrayed as something absent, where affect had paled with the passage of time. In contrast, the present relationship was imbued with intensity of feeling. But this is not always the case. For, in addition to conveying information, memories of specific events in a person's life carry dramatic conviction; a memory sweeps the person up in an emotional storm. The memory has psychic force, imploding events in present time. As Wollheim (1984) observed: "The effect is not simply that we live under the influence of the past—how could we not, if we have one?—but it is that the past influences our lives through *obtruding* itself into the present" (p. 131). Similarly, peering backward, as it were, from the present, there is surely no way to retrieve past memories except through the influence of the present. As we stop in our tracks, consumed perhaps by a memory of the past, life presses on. Our past cannot be severed from the mental and physical space we inhabit today. Memory, severed from present time, would require specific conditions—for example, sensory deprivation or hypnosis—conditions that promote states of heightened awareness but also suggestibility.

In a beautiful essay on memory and its depiction in literature, Joan Riviere (1952) diffuses the contradiction between past and present. Past and present experience are but two aspects of one phenomenon: "Memory, relating to external events and to the corporeal reality of loved figures as beings distinct from ourselves, is one facet of our relation to them; the other facet is the life they lead within us indivisible from ourselves" (p. 320). Riviere then qualifies this statement in an important way: absent loved ones lead their lives *around* rather than *within* us. Quoting a verse from Samuel Rogers's *Human Life*, Riviere emphasizes that the figures that inhabit our inner worlds are experienced not so much as within us as living around us as we lead our lives.

"At moments which he calls his own,
Then, never less alone than when alone,
Those whom he loves so long and sees no more,
Loved and still loves—not dead, but gone before—
He gathers around him."

The past is not always behind us; rather, it surrounds us.

BRITISH KLEINIANS

The following excerpts are from interviews with the Kleinian analysts. These illustrate the preferred focus on the present transference relationship both because of its affective pull and also because of the belief that the here-and-now transactions are the enactments of the past. The implication is that the past can be lived out in the present provided the analyst creates the setting for this potential to be actualized and eventually understood. I first quote from the interview with Dr. Roberts and follow with short excerpts from interviews with younger Kleinians:

"Oh no, I would not go to the past, I would only build up very slowly to that because, so much of the time, it just *breaks up and deflects and takes away from the internal reality of the transference.* You see, I think the transference actually gives one so much more of a feeling of how things may have happened as well as of what is going on now, and it is only slowly that you can build up a picture of the past. And just to say, 'You hate me as you hated your mother' seems to me cheap. I don't think that people actually say that; it is a bit of a caricature. But it is what some of our patients want us to do, isn't it? For example, I have a patient who is extraordinarily careful to fit in with me, then almost has a row with me, then stops again. Now, I think the whole picture of someone trembling to fit in, furious and so on, does really connect somewhere with his mother. That bit I would eventually reconstruct, but first I would get it played out and played out with me. Only when it was no longer hot in the transference would I reconstruct one bit, but only that bit. I wouldn't say, 'This is why,' or anything. I wouldn't start on an explanatory system. Some people like to look at an explanatory system; I don't. I like to leave the whole thing fluid. How I envy that kind of analysis."

When I asked Dr. Roberts about his views on memory, he replied:

"If the memories belong to lost pieces of *psychic reality* that are important, then I think memory is important. Then reconstruction can give a sense of wholeness. I wouldn't be happy just to deal with it only in the transference. One of my patients is just discovering what she thinks her mother is like, which she has never discovered before. She had a beautiful, pretty picture of her. And her mother is turning out to be ever so different. Very important, it accounts for so much of her difficulties. Not that the mother was or was not x, but that the patient had to hide it from herself. About early memories, I don't know. Some people have them, but very few. I notice that even children in analysis forget what has gone on earlier in the analysis. For instance, I think of the analysis of a five-year-old child who had a special animal that we talked about a lot; by the time that child was 10, and I used the name, she had forgotten it."

The younger Kleinians seemed skeptical, even self-deprecatory, about using historical interpretations but took a more assertive stance about the efficacy of here-and-now transference interpretations.

1.   "Certainly I would only make an interpretation relating the present to the past if it was emotionally significant to the patient. It takes a long time to learn about the past and, as I have only been qualified for four years, I haven't got patients who have been in analysis for very long. I don't think one ever knows what it was like, only what it felt like. I don't agree with Professor Sandler's thesis that the past is always updated, rewritten, etc. I think there are fundamental things that remain the same, and these are what one is trying to make contact with. One of the things that I certainly feel I am only beginning to do is to really build up a picture of an infant, or rather *to conceive of my patient in infantile terms* and to conceive of the relationship with the mother. It takes time to develop, both in terms of one's own experience as an analyst and also with a particular patient. If you are Dr. Segal, she can do it in—I don't know—10 minutes, but us mere mortals take much longer! I don't like the idea of constructing a narrative, that you are working together to build up a

story of what happened. What I was trying to say before is that memories are often unverbalized; they are happening in the present. This is what Freud said, that transference is a repetition rather than a memory. When people believe that they actually retrieve memories, my impression is that they have been told, 'You did this' or 'That happened when you were five,' etc."

2.   "Well yes, I do [make frequent references to the past], and I suspect I do it too much. Again, I am trying to be honest. I think I do it sometimes to take something off the boil. I am trying to shift it off me a little bit. That is *a terrible temptation* I fall into. I would never consciously try to get to verbal memories. That wouldn't be the right kind of memories. Rather, they would be sensations, probably pain, memories in feeling, bodily sensations. For example, a patient who says, 'Something you said made my stomach contract.' That kind of memory is of an infantile feeling, an undifferentiated kind of panic attack."

3.   "I always start with the present. I would never go to the past. If I do, *I am getting away from something.* What is most valuable for the patient is that they relive the past in the present. I would also be much more on the side of *the present being very similar to the past* than Sandler's view. The past means the patient's experience of it. I definitely think people have memories of when they were four or five years old. I have some data that supports infantile memories of four or five months. I can't prove this, but I have been amazed when something has come up in the analysis and the patient has gone and asked the mother, and their memories were then confirmed."

The following excerpt is from the interview with the younger Kleinian training analyst whose responses to the P.O.Q. indicated that she was influenced to the same degree by Freudian and Kleinian models. Her approach to the relation of past to present differed from that of her contemporaries.

"I think references to the past have different kinds of functions. I might say something like, I am being this kind of mother, or you are being this kind of mother, but it is a way of referring to the past as a way of clarifying the present. Now, reconstruction, actually going back to the past, has a very different function to interpretations about now because *reconstruction doesn't change the internal world.* It has the function of giving the patient a story more than a history. I think it is a story, a text; as we know, history changes tremendously with analysis. It is important for the analyst and patient to build that up. It is one of the functions of analysis, that there is this coherent, not *defensively* coherent, but *truthfully* coherent story or stories that more or less go together and make sense of things. I don't think that is what cures though.

"I think there are significant memories, in Freud's sense, for people who have suffered *trauma*. But for people whose lives have been vaguely traumatic as a whole, where we are not talking about events or particular facts, but about a whole life situation or family situation, I don't think it happens very often that people have memories. There are *feeling-memories* obviously that are there all the time, but there is a big difference between feeling-memory and factual memory. Factual memory has much more to do with specific psychopathology and trauma."

Dr. Shaw, the analyst who had changed orientation, was perhaps the most "classically" Kleinian in his approach to these topics. His view is very close to that put forward by Klein (1952) in her classic paper "The Analysis of Transference."

"I would say that what one is analyzing are the internal object relations as they manifest themselves in the transference. These internal object relationships derive from *the infantile past*, the original objects about which, as the transference unfolds, one begins to have a much clearer perception. I certainly don't agree with the view that the past has to be present in an interpretation. One of the dangers of prematurely going to the past is that the past changes as the analysis progresses. The picture you got originally turns out to be quite different. Patients are actually liberated by the analysis to see people as quite different from what they originally thought. Personally, I don't think one comes across memories that often. Where there has been repression of traumatic events, then I think the recovery of what actually happened is probably very important and curative. Examples have been very rare. The narrative changes as a result of an exploration of the internal world in the transference, and then one gets to the narrative; one gets closer to what the original narrative was through looking at the transference."

These examples illustrate a fairly homogeneous approach to interpretation, namely, that the here-and-now transference recapitulates, or is isomorphic with, the infantile past. Consistent with this approach, many Kleinians distinguished between "memories in feeling," which are memories of infantile body states, and event-memories, which are seen as rare and linked to the specific psychopathology of trauma. Since, under optimal conditions, the here-and-now transference repeats the infantile past, reconstruction becomes a relatively insignificant aspect of technique. Nevertheless, after dispensing with historical "facts," several analysts talked about getting closer to the "original narrative" or "undefended truth" through the immediacy of the transference relationship. Enactment in the present is the effective agent of psychic change.

BRITISH INDEPENDENT ANALYSTS

Although Independent analysts anchored their interpretations in the here-and-now transference, their approach to history contrasts with that of their Kleinian colleagues. Three of the Independents whose interview excerpts follow either had trained or worked at the Anna Freud Centre, or had undergone Freudian analysis. Their respect for history reflected these Freudian influences and had important technical consequences. In the first place, all valued reconstructive interpretations; moreover, some stated that extratransference interpretation of the patient's past can effect deep psychic change. Second, most held a developmental view so that the here-and-now was viewed not as an isomorphic enactment of the infantile situation, but rather as a highly modified derivative. Third, the version of the past constructed during the history of the analysis was not deemed more correct or truthful than earlier versions. Fourth, most analysts valued the *link* between present and past as contributing to psychic change.

Dr. Stevens, the "widely influenced" British analyst classified in the American eclectic cluster, observed:

"You know David Malan's 'triangle of conflict,' after Menninger, the triangle with the three corners: T-O-P. T meaning the therapist in the transference, O meaning the other outside, and P meaning the parent and the past. Whenever a patient is talking about one corner of the triangle, try and work out the other corners. But don't feel that you have to bring them all in. The old, elaborate, full-blown interpretation seems to be relatively rare.

"I think most memories are derivative. I don't think one is conducting a detective hunt for buried memory. And this has a lot to do with the issue of seduction. The whole subject has changed. We don't just dismiss such memories as fantasies. Patients feel freer to talk about such things. But I am always struck by how giant the loss of childhood memories can be. I do a lot of assessments for the Health Service, and most people don't remember anything before the age of 11 or 12. But this leads into quite difficult philosophical areas about the nature of history. What is the nature of historical history? History is always a history of the present. I believe in Rycroft's phrase that the analyst is the assistant autobiographer. The analyst is inviting someone to help them construct a narrative story. On the other hand, autobiographies can be just novels. There are different sorts of biographies. We rewrite history every century; we reconstruct, but presumably *we expect it to have some correspondence with what went on*. It's not either-or. It's quite interesting the way people in analysis go and check things out with surviving relatives. They look up photographs. I don't invite people to do that; some analysts do, particularly child analysts. People will go to Somerset House to find out who their real parents were if they were adopted. They conduct their own historical search."

Dr. Matheson, the "classical" Independent analyst with highly consistent views, disagreed with the Kleinian position on extratransference interpretation:

"Most of my interpretations would not be in terms of the past. But I do think that reconstructions have a place at specific points in an analysis, when the patient is trying to understand what happened. Why do you think that those people reacted in the way they did, and why did you react the way you did? What might the early family dynamics have been? This is what I would call extratransference interpretation in terms of the past. It enables patients to understand something they have never understood before. And very often that makes an enormous difference to a patient, brings *great psychic change*, when a patient realizes something about their past which they never appreciated before."

Two other senior training analysts in the Independent group spoke of the dimensionality of time, relating this to reconstruction:

1.   "I don't think a transference interpretation is a full transference interpretation unless there is some reference to the past—if not about a real event or person, at least an internal object. Something like, 'You mean me' is only a bit of a transference

interpretation, not the whole network. And I think that only *the here-and-now can be defensive against the past.* I am such an inveterate 'go back to the past-er,' I can't see how anybody can enjoy themselves without that—which is not a very good reason. *The here-and-now makes everything too two dimensional, indeed less than two dimensional.* It just seems to be cardboard-making; the depth is lost. We have four dimensions if time is a dimension. I make reconstructions as I go along. I don't think it happens that often that people have memories of things that really happened that suddenly reveal themselves. I do believe in body-memories, affect-memories that are shut off, blotted out, and do need to be refound. But they are so wispish; they mean a hell of a lot to the person himself but they are so quiet."

2.   "*I believe very much in the historical view.* All that has gone on under this magical label of here-and-now. It started off as a good idea, but in the last 20 years, it has been perverted into some sort of ridiculous absurdity. Really, I don't see how anybody can work without taking into account a historical view. I have never met a single person, patient or not, who is not saying all the time, 'That's how I found it last year' or 'That's how I found it 10 years ago.' I remember arguing with my first supervisor when I said that a patient had an experience for the first time. The supervisor sort of laughed at me and said, 'How many times in your life have you lain on an analytic couch?' The point was that although lying on the couch was something novel, I reacted to it in accordance with previous similar experiences. For instance, in the South American country I come from and trained, I would take off my jacket before lying down on the couch. Not only because of the hot climate but out of respect. You go into a room, shake hands, and then take off your jacket before sitting down. Here, unfortunately, my analyst never got the point. To her, it was a question of getting ready for a fight and all sorts of stupid things like that. But I had never lain on a couch before and when I did, I did it in accordance with my previous experience."

BRITISH FREUDIANS

Interview/discussions revealed striking affinities between the British Independent and Contemporary Freudian views on reconstruction and here-and-now transference interpretation. Analysts of both orientations valued a historical approach and saw the here-and-now as a derivative of the past that is transformed through experiences at different developmental stages. Approaches to the recovery of childhood memories were somewhat idiosyncratic and reflected personal experience. British Independents also emphasized the force of interpretations that explicitly linked past and present.

Dr. Smith's attitude to these questions was more "classically" Freudian than that of many of his British Freudian colleagues, particularly those who used the Sandlers' (1984) approach to here-and-now transference interpretation and reconstruction. Consistent with those described in previous chapters, Dr. Smith's views were often closer to those of the Americans than to the British Freudians.

"The here-and-now is a modern focus, and here I would disagree with both English groups, the Contemporary Freudians, who follow Joe Sandler in this shift, as well as the Kleinians. The Sandlers' 'present unconscious' doesn't bother me so much, but what bothers me is this model of the here-and-now. It goes against the model I am trying to create of *the benign listener*, which creates a very different atmosphere from the one where you are commenting on the analytic relationship all the time. I see this as changing the basic character of the analytic relationship. I see it as very unanalytic; to me it is artificial. It is as if you and I were in an conversation and I say, 'Well, I see you are nodding for some reason. Why are you nodding?' 'Gee, I don't know.' I say, 'Well, think about it.' Then, 'Now you are laughing. What are you doing? Now you are fiddling with your hair.' Jesus, you know, it ruins the situation. It gets the patient and the analyst in some funny game of interpreting each other. I am completely against it. It isn't that I don't see that there is something to it, but it goes against the whole atmosphere of what I am trying to create. And, of course, neither of my two analysts were anything like that at all. When I hear it, it makes me very uneasy. It is like group therapy where people are nodding and everybody is analyzing everybody's movements. It is a terribly tense, funny situation. *I think the analytic situation should have a very natural feel*, it is a very important, serious thing we are trying to do, not just analyzing each other's immediate interactions. I don't understand why so many people are going over to this way of analyzing.

"Sure, I use the old model in which you are trying to reconstruct the past and its influence on the present personality and problems. This is part of my conception of 'working through.' In the first months or so of analysis, you might make a reconstruction of a person's childhood influences. It could seem very convincing to the patient and myself. A few months later, a different element comes up. The patient, or maybe I, would go back to the same childhood period and this time see it from a different angle. And so there is a different story. You could get *a hundred different versions*, all different sides of seeing childhood phases, traumas, etc. In a way, they are all correct; it is the way a person tried to understand at the time. I see the working-through process that way. You go over and over it until you have covered a thousand different angles and until you have a feeling, well, that it is worked through."

Like many of the Independent analysts, Dr. Smith viewed the process of reconstruction very differently than most Kleinian analysts. In the foregoing quote, Dr. Smith states his opinion that there is no correct, or truer, version that is reached through the analytic transference but, rather, a working through of the past where understanding builds on a cumulative process. Dr. Smith continued:

"And memories came out in my own analysis. I actually had some very clear memories from about a year and a half, a few scenes that were very significant. I happen to have a very good childhood memory, so there were many things before the age of three that I remember very vividly. I had them all before analysis, but I did not give them much significance. But when you go through them in analysis, they become very significant. I think it is possible for a child to retain visual memories, at least between one and a half and two years. Nevertheless, I have found that very few patients have many memories before the age of three. And, when they do, they are mixed with, 'My grandmother told me this and that.' I think early memories are very rare, and, God, some patients don't remember anything before the age of 10 or 11. I can hardly believe it, but it is true.

"Now, about the Kleinian point of view, they talk about very early memories in the first months. I am very doubtful that experiences from that early period are recorded in the memory system. I think in terms of the Hartmann-Rapaport model—what is the infant brain capable of? I think adults can reproduce bodily patterns, for instance, if a patient cleans his ears or something. It might be useful to point out, 'You probably pulled your ear as a baby when you were tired or nervous.' This is the Kleinian and English point of view, about the retention and usefulness of *infantile phantasy development.* This is a major difference with all classical analysts. It is not really even an argument. It is like saying, 'The moon is black.' I simply don't think the moon is black or that there are these infantile phantasy developments."

The frequency with which Freudians referred to the concept of the "past and present unconscious" introduced by Anne-Marie and Joseph Sandler (1984) seemed to distinguish a group of older British Freudians, who made more frequent references to the past, and the more contemporary group, who focused on the here-and-now transference relationship. Analysts in the second group also believe that the past that is reconstructed in analysis is always derivative of early experience and never isomorphic with it. The following excerpt illustrates this position:

"I come from the Sandler stable. I think that going to the past is used to take the heat of the moment off the boil. Ernst Kris said—I think in the 50s paper on reconstruction—that even about trauma, it is so rarely 'the afternoon on the staircase.' There will always be something cumulative as well as how the trauma evolves in the person's experience. It is the same with the affective experiences that are repeated in the transference."

One of the more widely influenced British Freudians, well read in American literature as well as Kohut's work, observed:

"I think, nowadays, everyone interprets the transference in the here-and-now. There are differences between the groups in this, but all the groups recognize that one works in the here-and-now. Sandler, Gill, Schafer have also written about it—it is like many roads lead to Rome. I really think that the genetic link is not necessarily a deep interpretation. The here-and-now situation is the most threatening, the closest, the one that patients find most difficult to handle because they are actually bringing their transferential feelings very close. When I deal with the past, it is more in the way that the Sandlers think—in terms of the 'child within.' For instance, 'when I am speaking to you, I feel that there is a little boy you who is listening.'

"On the other hand, I sometimes think that the older analysts knew their histories better. They really took notice of every little event from the patient's childhood, whereas we tend not to do that. It can be very burdensome to have a history, to remember every detail of childhood. I wouldn't like to say that we have embraced the here-and-now because we are lazy, but I think that the older analysts, the first- and second-generation analysts, really had these early childhood experiences and they remembered them. In terms of reconstruction, we have moved away from the view that the present is virtually the same as the past. The current Kleinian position is actually a very classical Freudian position in this respect. And yet the Kleinians don't take very close histories in the way the older analysts did. I have heard Kleinian papers where the analyst doesn't even know whether the person has brothers and sisters. I don't think of reconstruction anymore. Sandler's recent paper is really quite a classic on this.

"In terms of memories, I am really very oriented toward memory retrieval. But whether this is the same as reconstruction, I don't know. I am not clear about the definitions, and therefore the difference between the interpretation of a memory and reconstruction. I really do believe that people remember events before four or five years, though I think these are isolated memories. I am certain I have had memories of myself as a two-year-old. Kohut has a very interesting way of talking about it: he talks about the telescoping of genetically analogous experiences. You get a sort of telescoping of events that take place at different developmental levels."

AMERICAN FREUDIANS

In discussing the current preoccupation with here-and-now transference interpretation, American Freudians did not direct discussion toward Kleinian techniques but rather to the recent work of their American colleague and former bastion of the classical point of view, Merton Gill. (In his two-volume monograph with Irwin Z. Hoffman, *Analysis of Transference*, Gill [Gill and Hoffman, 1982] revoked his earlier stance on reconstruction and strongly propounded the here-and-now approach to transference interpretation. It is to the 1982 work that most of the analysts in this sample referred rather than Gill's later publications in which he made a number of changes and modifications). When talking about the retrieval of childhood memories, American Freudians differed from their British counterparts in the frequency with which they spontaneously talked about Freud's concept of infantile amnesia. None of the British Independent or Kleinian ana-lysts referred to this idea, and, when the concept was introduced during discussion, younger Kleinian analysts were completely unfamiliar with the concept.

The Los Angeles classical analyst who trained with Ralph Greenson disagreed with the views propounded by Merton Gill in *The Analysis of Transference*:

"I disagree with Merton Gill that you only interpret the present. I do both. I first attempt to interpret what is going on in the pre-sent. If I do that clearly and successfully enough, the patient will usually make the reconstruction. If the patient doesn't, then I make it. *The object of the treatment is to convince the patient that cer-tain things happened to him that affected his current strategies.* Your hope is to change the old-time strategies to new ones that are more effective. And, to me, it is more convincing if the patient can see why he established the strategies he did. For that, mem-ory is very helpful. *I do believe in the concept of infantile amnesia.* Very often it is lifted through analysis. Sometimes you may have to make a reconstruction as to what you imagined happened. For example, my own situation. My analyst was Ralph Greenson. I had a very bad accident when I was two. I knew about it, but I could not remember it although it had profound effects on my development. Greenson knew about my history, and he inter-preted various dreams I had as clearly relating to the accident. I was shocked when he did that although it seemed perfectly cor-rect even though I remembered nothing."

In parts of the interviews discussed in previous chapters, several San Francisco analysts referred to the strong influence of Merton Gill dur-ing their training at a time when he was an integral and powerful pres-ence in the San Francisco community. His views were of continuing interest to those analysts with whom he had personal or supervisory contact, even when they were not in whole-hearted agreement. A few examples follow:

1. "Gill takes a straw-man position against the presumed exclu-sive preoccupation with the past, apparently something he had experienced with one of his previous analysts that he is trying to undo with a vengeance. He does it with a vengeance in that he

becomes totally preoccupied with the present in a way that makes exploration of the past impossible."

2. "I agree with Gill up to a point. But I see the analytic process as being a focus on those areas where there is the most anxiety, where a person is trying to ward off something and will talk about all sorts of other things to avoid the anxiety. So I follow the anxious trend and the defensive trend."

3. "I agree with Gill. I fell into what Gill criticized everybody for. I was just talking about childhood this and that. It really didn't mean much. I believe we all should make reference to the past carefully but only after it has been explicated in the present. Freud was confused about this, but he did say in many places, 'You can't kill an enemy in effigie or in absentia.' That is not reconstruction; it means the enemy is alive and that is here-and-now. So, reconstruction? Freud liked figuring it all out, but look what happened with the Wolf Man! He figured it all out, but the Wolf Man didn't get analyzed."

The one San Francisco analyst who was classified within the American eclectic group referred to the past in terms of the future. In this respect, he was the only analyst to take up the "forward-looking" direction in which we live our lives described in the quotation from Kierkegaard at the beginning of this chapter.

"I make a lot of *references to the future*. And when I do that, I am referring to the past. 'Is it going to be a repetition of the past, or are you going to do something different?' So I am big on the past, and I do it with reference to the future. I agree with Sandler that everything is continually being revised in memory and that is why we make reconstructions. It doesn't mean that you are right, but you are aiding the analytic process by giving the person a sense of a life story. *The closer it is to being correct, the better.* But it is valuable to people even when it is wrong. I tend to put memories in schematic terms. It is interesting but not vitally important whether the mother put shoe polish on her nipple to wean the baby. More to the point, and the way I would put it, is, 'We understand what the pattern is now about x, y, z and it might give us a bit of a platform to understand x, y, z if we knew where this pattern came from. You have this memory and that memory, and general human nature suggests that perhaps your mother was feeling frustrated and stymied, not malevolent and murderous, but she was in this kind of conflict when she put the shoe polish on.' Then you can get the insight that develops into, 'Gosh, my mother was a human being with conflicts, not just a murderous monster.' That shift comes out of a great softening of the person's attitude and leads to an open door into a whole new reworking of the entire life story. You know, that 'My mother was a conflicted young woman in a dilemma rather than an omnipotent witch-goddess.' *The purpose of reconstructions is to have that working-through process*. I expect people to *imagine* their pasts—imagine what this would be like now with your adult mind and your child memories. It is new construction, new learning, new reworking. And it is more fun!"

A number of the San Francisco analysts who used the theories of Roy Schafer and Donald Spence held mixed models of narrative and historical truth. The eclectic analyst quoted earlier talked about the making of a life story, but at the same time talked about the closeness of fit between this story and some "x" that is correct. The same ambiguity occurs in two other excerpts:

1. "I still do make references to the past whenever possible. I still have that strong bias. I definitely feel that the past deeply enriches the analysis and the person's whole sense of who they are, what they are afraid of, etc. I don't confuse reconstruction with history. The more I develop, the more I think that the reconstruction is not a *historical* reconstruction, it is more of an *intrapsychic* reconstruction. Yes, I understand Spence's idea. I think that all humans need a story to maintain their psychic integrity. We all have our story, our own narrative. I don't think memories play much of a part unfortunately. Affects yes, or affect-memories, that kind of memory does enrich or give one a sense of continuity."

2. "Oh, I start very much with the here-and-now. If an analyst says to a patient who is mad with them, 'Oh, it's not me, it's your father you are really mad at,' that is exculpating yourself and taking yourself out of the intensity of the transference. And when I do refer to the past, I put it in terms of, 'This is the way your past *could* have been and how you could have experienced it, given that it has been modified by all that has come after.' I do agree with Spence, but not fully, because, carried to its extreme,

Spence says any narrative is as good as any other. But *some narratives are better than others, and they are better because they fit better with the facts* of the case, given that the facts of the case can never be exactly and fully reached. They are always interpreted, but some interpretations are better than others. In that sense I don't fully subscribe to the hermeneutic position.

"And one can certainly conduct an analysis successfully without retrieving infantile memories buried behind the *infantile amnesia*. For instance, I had a patient whose father committed suicide when he was four years old. A good part of the analysis was preoccupied with reconstructing the circumstances of the suicide. A lot of material. There were two alternative versions of how it had happened. Bits of the material fitted in with each version. He was not told about his father's death when he was four; he was told his father had gone away on a long trip. But at school, other children said to him, 'Your father is dead.' A year later, his mother acknowledged that it was true that his father was dead. There was so much uncertainty. During the analysis, since his father was well known, he went through all the newspaper files for that period. But he found nothing. We never heard the true story. But the analytic work got done."

Dr. Friedland, the most highly consistent of the San Francisco Freudians, stated categorically:

"Here-and-now does not make any sense unless it is connected with there-and-then. *You may as well narrate a football game.* You can't understand the meaning of anything otherwise. Any description of an intelligent process—whether Gill said it or not—would necessarily begin with what the person is expressing now to you, transferring to you, repeating with you. And repeating it because they repeat it all day and every day whether they are in the room with you or not. You would have to begin with whatever they are saying. Now that can be vulgarized as understanding. The vulgar version of the fact that you have to start from what the patient is expressing now is to always begin a session with the fact that somebody is a minute late, or did something in the waiting room, or saw you do x, or reacted to something as they came in the door. That is interesting. It is O.K. There is nothing wrong with it, but it doesn't really represent what would be a very useful way of understanding the here-and-now. What a person is expressing in the here-and-now is not necessarily about this room, or our transactions. *The here-and-now is a disguised version of the there-and-then.*

Dr. Friedland's views were very similar to those of the New York analyst at the center of the classical Freudian cluster who viewed the current emphasis on here-and-now interpretation within a cultural context:

"I feel very strongly about the historical point of view and linking up to the past. *We are historical beings*, we make sense of our lives, we think historically. I think the emphasis on the here-and-now is also part of the times, that is to say, of the culture. Part of that is to try to reject history. Everything is in the moment. I think it can lead to a very closed, stuck situation."

AMERICAN SELF PSYCHOLOGISTS

The self psychologists gave different reasons for focusing on the here-and-now relationship than did the Freudian and Kleinian analysts. Because of their emphasis on the intersubjective field and the curative value of "selfobject" ties, the *new* experience was valued as an agent of change. All the self psychologists described a developmental or transformational view of the remembered past.

1. "I still think the best interpretation is the one that includes something of the present, something of the transference, and something of the past. I don't see the present as being a complete representation of the reactivated past. I think we bring our past into the present, but it is also *a new experience* that is being looked at and organized from our previous experience. So that, hopefully, there is an opportunity to grow. *The present isn't ruled by the past, it is affected by the past.*

2. "The past I am concerned with is not the objective past anyway, it is *the subjectively experienced past.* That is what is reconstructed and undergoes transformation. Indeed, it is already a product of transformation when it is experienced. Also, my idea of transference is not that a concrete experience is literally being replicated, but has to do with the principles organizing the present experience which are derived from repetitive experiences in the past. I am more concerned with the way the person *structures* their experience than with a specific *content.*"

3.   "Yes, I think that the past is modified. It is not that there is a baby in the room, but that there have been transformations which have taken place. I think the recall of memories is very important. It is like *regaining lost parts of the self.*"

4.   "I get more analytic mileage out of the here-and-now. But, when it is not defensive on my part, I like to tie things to the past because I think that, as analysts, we can provide the sense of the pattern of the person's history. I do think that there is *a great similarity between the past and the present.* There are times when the situations are remarkably similar. I understand that you might be dealing with a 40-year-old rather than a four-year-old. But, you know, you are really talking about their affective experience, and I am not sure that that really has evolved, changed, or been modified or anything like that."

One of the Los Angeles self psychologists, who had *changed* orientation more than once, replied:

"The whole point is whether reference is made to the past because of some program that the analyst has in mind. My own preference is to let things evolve and not to try to get at what the antecedent situation was but, rather, patiently to enable the patient to recognize the *invariant principle leading to the repetitive experience* that is happening over and over again. For example, I try to allow the anxiety to subside so that the patient himself comes to reflect, 'Well, how come I keep feeling this way?' Then he may have a dream or a memory of a time when he felt an enthusiasm for something he wanted to do and there was some calamitous response to it."

AMERICAN ECLECTIC ANALYSTS

Because of the emphasis on the interpersonal, transformative context in which the past emerges, the views of some of the New York interpersonal analysts were remarkably similar to those of the intersubjective perspective of many of the Los Angeles self psychologists:

1.   "That is another misconception people have about the interpersonal point of view, that we only concentrate on the here-and-now. But *the here-and-now is simply a medium* that is valuable

to the extent that it opens up the past and connects the patient up emotionally with whatever he needs to discover. If working in the transference and countertransference is effective, once that is flowing, it is going to stir associations to the past. If you end up stuck in the here-and-now transference, something is wrong. I am not comfortable either with the view that the here-and-now is an almost exact repetition of the past. That is too glib. At different points in the analysis you get a different history, events that are remembered with great anger at one time may now involve great sadness. In other words, we are in *the realm of emotional truth* which changes with internal changes."

2. "I don't see the relational approach as denying or overlooking childhood or development. I think my technique about reconstruction has changed. If someone says, 'But we have talked about that. I know all that and it hasn't changed anything,' I no longer think, 'Well, it is because we have overlooked something.' I just think we have to work more on it. I am not really involved in this whole issue of hermeneutic truth and reconstruction. I have a more *pragmatic* point of view. It is more like 'If it is not working well, then let's keep at it until we figure something that works.' On the other hand, I have met the families of patients whom I have seen for many years, say at the end of an analysis. It has been fascinating to me. I have rarely been surprised, when the family walks in. Boy! They are very recognizable people. So I suppose you could say we did arrive at some truth."

An eclectic New York analyst, a member of one of the new I.P.A-affiliated American institutes and strongly influenced by American and British object relations as well as by the works of John Bowlby, responded:

"No, I don't agree with the current focus on just the here-and-now. The Gill influence has been useful, and I find it very useful in supervision to help beginning candidates become aware of the fact that the patient is really talking about them, and to confront them more with the immediacy of the relationship. That strengthens the candidate's confidence. But, quite frankly, I think Gill nags his patients. He is forcing them into contact with him too early before a relationship has been clearly established. I think that Gill is too enthusiastic about this. Same with Robert Langs's communicative approach and his works on the interpersonal field, where Langs says that the patient is always talking about the analyst, so everything is interpretable within the analytic frame. Rangell points out that the constant here-and-now interpretation makes the patient dependent on the analyst and also does not encourage the patient to work. I think it can be useful to say to patients, 'You probably know more what is going on than I do.' That encourages separation from the analyst. Also, with reference to reconstructions—take Spence's book. It think it is very easy to make a story, that view goes too far. I guess I am very conservative. I do think that memories are very important and that people do remember very accurately."

A second eclectic New York analyst stated:

"My best answer about this issue is that it all depends on what you want to achieve. If you want to permit the transference and all the feelings to come to the fore, then you have to be very careful not to use anything like a link to the past that can be used as an intellectualization. But, for instance, when I work in a general hospital doing crisis intervention, it can be very useful to bring in the past. There is an intervention formulated by Dr. Milton Viederman called 'The Psychodynamic Life Narrative,' which is designed to be used as a defense! It is a construct that I use early on in the crisis with a patient which demonstrates the logic of his current emotional situation as a product of the past—'How could it be otherwise but that you would be depressed or anxious in this specific situation because this happened to you?' It is enormously relieving of anxiety, and it is specifically designed to help the patient defend."

Dr. Furnham, the widely influenced Los Angeles pioneer analyst, also emphasized that the past recovered in analysis is derivative of early childhood experience:

"I don't think there is any mystique about the past, you know the old assumption that, until you uncovered the critical core of the past, the analysis wasn't going to work. I think it works in the here-and-now, but I do believe very much in *the developmental approach to personality*, so that whenever I can, I illustrate or uncover the past events that contributed to a current distortion in the here-and-now. It helps the patient realize that he or she wasn't always this way, wasn't born this way, but that there has been a developmental process. That is why I believe in psycho-dynamic developmental theory. The past is constantly transformed. It is not an object that remains like a stone in our lives; the past is a constant dynamic process that is going on all the time. And *that is why people get better in life too, even outside the analyst's office!*"

CONCLUSION

In this chapter, analysts discuss their views on the respective roles of reconstruction, the interpretation of memory, and here-and-now transference interpretation in relation to the overall goal of psychic change. A majority of the analysts interviewed from all the groups affirmed the greater technical power of interpretations that focused on the present transference interactions between patient and analyst. Those analysts who did use reconstructive interpretations felt they were important adjuncts to the development of a sense of self and continuity of being. Views on the retrieval of memories versus the creation of a satisfactory life narrative were often unclear and even contradictory. The concepts of memory, memory retrieval, and narrative fit clearly relate to the superordinate theories of truth and reality discussed in earlier chapters—specifically, the correspondence, coherence, and pragmatic theories of truth. The whole subject of memory—of "procedural" and "declarative" memory, of "true" and "false" (narrative or reconstructed) memory—is a topic of intense research and evolving theory among cognitive psychologists, neurobiologists, psychotherapists, and neuropsychologists. It is not much wonder that a parallel conglomeration of ideas emerged when these topics were discussed in the interviews with the analysts in this sample. Many of the analysts seemed uneasy with their statements and moved somewhat inconsistently between beliefs in the possibility of retrieval of event-memories, on one hand, and a constructivist position, on the other. Discussion of the past raised epistemological questions about the status of memories and the reconstructive process as well as implicit or preconscious beliefs concerning the nature of truth and reality.

Chapter 11

————— ·§·§· —————

The Reparative Process

I n this chapter, I focus less on the form and content of interpretations aimed at psychic change and more on the nature of the reparative process that interpretation sets in train. How does repair occur? Is repair a process of restoration, of reparation, or of both? Again, the analysts were asked specific questions that might elucidate implicit or preconscious ideas about the healing process. For example: Do you think interpretation plays an important role in the "undoing" of developmental arrests? Do you think that interpretation can heal "basic faults"? Does interpretation build up new "psychic structures"? Does the idea of a "new beginning," or "new relationship" with the analyst, play a central role in your interventions? Are issues of separation a central theme in your interpretations? Do you think that the process of mourning is an important factor in psychic change?

More than on any other of the topics covered during the interviews, the analysts' views on psychic change and the aims of analysis emerged from discussions of the practical applications of the concept of developmental arrests. These discussions also clarified the analysts' explicit and preconscious models of normal development. Obviously, deficit models—models that use the terms arrests, basic faults, states of privation—imply notions of sufficient, or good-enough, development. It is these models of normalcy that direct analysts' understanding of the reparative process. Does repair involve reparation for past damage, an attitude of forgiveness or revenge toward the depriving object (internal or external)? Does reparation invoke the restoration of a hidden and sequestered self, or the reclamation of disavowed good experiences in the past? Does psychic change build upon these *lost* functions or

249

parts of the self, or on entirely *new* experiences? And if, as children, we were unusually deprived, do we have "holes" or "gaps" in our being, or do we bypass these deficits so that development proceeds along alternative pathways? If so, who is to say that these alternate routes are deviant?

Another way of looking at the analysts' approaches to this topic is to consider the question, what does/can analysis provide? The contributions of such pioneer figures as Michael Balint, Anna Freud, Melanie Klein, Heinz Kohut, Margaret Mahler, and Donald Winnicott played a key role in the analysts' convictions about what analysis could, or should not, provide. Statistical analysis of responses to this part of the interview highlighted important differences in the interpretive attitudes of adult and child analysts. For the most part, child analysts expressed a more hopeful attitude toward the analytic potential for new development, a "new beginning," and for the restructuring of internal models of self and other through the analytic relationship. It is possible to conjecture that adult analysts who are trained in child analysis feel more at home with regressive states and, therefore, hold more favorable opinions about their potential for psychic change. The majority of the Kleinian analysts, however, including those who worked with children, challenged the value of therapeutic regression to dependence. Generally speaking, Kleinians regarded regressive states as expressions of primitive, omnipotent defenses against separateness. It follows that the concept of mourning for an illusory state of fusion or control over the other person is central to Kleinian views on psychic change.

Although experiences of separateness and separation are not identical, feelings and thoughts about separateness frequently arise in the context of separation. Many of the analysts articulated their thoughts on the therapeutic impact of the mourning process when discussing separation. Although 50% of the analysts interviewed believed that issues of separation were important, Kleinian analysts and self psychologists were much more likely to interpret interruptions in the analytic relationship. Twenty-five percent of the sample of 65 analysts stated that they rarely made these interpretations. The analysts took two broad approaches to this topic: one group, most of whose members were of a Freudian orientation, took up the theme of separation if and when material arose in sessions that linked with the patient's past separation history; a second group, most of whom were Kleinians or Kohutians, focused on the separation process as this was experienced in the context of breaks or ruptures in the analytic relationship. Clearly, they made separation interpretations with greater frequency.

Although the results of various statistical analyses linked the Kleinians with the self psychologists, however, analysts in these two orientation groups gave very different reasons for their emphasis on separation. Self psychologists focused on disruptions of the "bond" or "selfobject tie" as this related to the analyst's empathic failures; Kleinians were concerned with the capacity to tolerate the loss of control involved in the rupture of phantasy links forged through processes of projective identification.

In addition, cultural factors played an important role in the analysts' focus on separation. American and British analysts differed in their approach to the interpretation of separation. Given the historical background of British analysis and its development over two world wars, as well as the importance of child analysis in the work of many British pioneers (Anna Freud, Susan Isaacs, Melanie Klein, Marion Milner, Donald Winnicott), this result is not surprising. In addition, analytic practices concerning frequency of sessions and predictability and length of vacations differ between the two countries. Most British analysis is conducted on a five-times-per week basis, with one break over the weekend. Holidays are considerably longer than those taken by Americans and for the most part follow the academic school year.

Statistical analyses of the influences of specific sources listed in the P.O.Q. on attitudes toward the concept of developmental arrests were also highly significant. It seems that the acknowledgment of strong influences by Freud's *drive* and structural models, as well as any influence by French psychoanalysis (including Lacan), resulted in negative attitudes toward the potential for a "new beginning" through the experience of an affective relationship with the analyst. In this one area of analytic work, however, Anna Freud's views on development contrasted sharply with those of adult Freudian theorists. As indicated in the interviews both with Dr. Martin and with one of the older British Freudians who had trained with Anna Freud, Anna Freud's ideas on developmental lines and developmental arrests had grown out of her experiences in the Hampstead War Nurseries. She and her colleagues found that, among the refugee children who had suffered traumatic breaks in their development, many were able to move forward and resume processes of maturation when they were given the opportunity to attach themselves to a secure, reliable, and loving figure. Thus, with respect to the part of the interview on the topic of developmental arrests, influences by Anna Freud, the Balints, and Kohut converged on a similar therapeutic approach. Presumably, this unusual consistency of approach among analysts influenced by these three thinkers resulted from two basic concepts: one, the idea of an arrest, or basic fault; two, the idea of a new beginning, or resumption of development, through the unique analytic situation and relationship.

On the other hand, the approaches of the American classical Freudians and British Kleinians were highly consistent with one another and contrasted sharply with the approaches of the self psychologists and those influenced by Balint and Anna Freud. The association of the two orientation groups can be explained in part by the value of drive theory to analysts in both the classical Freudian and Kleinian groups. The use of drive theory also accounts for the unique influence of Lacan's ideas on this aspect of technique. It seems that strong a belief in Freud's drive theory radically affects analysts' models of change as well as their views on the power of the new analytic relationship to effect psychic change. In terms of geographical location, the Los Angeles analysts differed significantly from analysts in the other three cities. This geographical difference may, however, simply reflect the fact that all the self psychologists interviewed worked in Los Angeles.

KLEINIAN ANALYSTS

As noted in previous chapters, the younger Kleinians expressed very similar views on many of the topics discussed in the interviews. This reflects the influence of teachers, supervisors, and fellow students during training as well as participation in ongoing postgraduate seminars. In terms of the topics of this chapter, the analysts in the younger group were somewhat hesitant in expressing their opinions on developmental arrests, and they were unfamiliar with the self-psychological literature. Consistent with Melanie Klein's views on the recapitulation of infantile internal object relationships in the here-and-now transference relationship, all the Kleinian analysts interviewed believed that so-called new experiences in analysis are built on bits of previous good experiences that have been lost or overlaid with bad experiences and destructive defenses.

Discussions of mourning, of separateness, and of experiences of fusion or selfobject transferences provide some fascinating examples of the ways analysts of different groups both attempt to translate between one analytic "language-game" (in Wittgenstein's sense) and another, and tend to stereotype terms that are foreign to their preferred conceptual scheme. Here is an excerpt from the interview with Dr. Roberts, followed by quotes from younger Kleinian analysts that illustrate both group cohesion and coherence of ideas:

"I think separations are important, but very many patients have such a capacity for denial, you have to go along with it. The interpretations that used to be given—'You are angry because of the weekend'—are really rubbish. *About developmental arrests, I don't know what you mean.* Does it mean a not good-enough environment? [I expanded on the idea of missing psychic structures related to something having gone wrong in the early environment.] Yes, that is what I thought, basic faults. Really, it depends on the degree. There are some children who have had the most terrible environments that you will never be able to make good. Sometimes, these sorts of questions contain the idea that a good-enough analyst ought to be able to give the patient what is missing, which is something I do not accept. *I think the idea of 'new' developments through analysis is a problem. I think most patients have got bits and pieces of good experience which very often have got lost and which have been overlaid by all the bad experiences.* I think patients can *rediscover* the lost bits of good and build something in that way, but I also think that really the traumas may have thrown up such awful defenses, made the patient so paranoid and so on, that actually they can never be put right. My theory is that, if a patient really has nothing good to build on that he can rediscover in the transference, then even if he thought he had hope, that hope collapses, and that patient discovers it was only an idea, and he is left with the paranoia."

In this passage, Dr. Roberts clarifies his belief that when rediscovery does not occur through the transference, then real change is impossible. Any hope of change is illusory and leads to collapse back to a fundamental paranoid position. Dr. Roberts continued:

"A 'selfobject' tie, I don't know that. I am terribly sorry to be so ignorant, training analyst and all. [I translate by reference to Winnicott's term the 'subjective object' and Kleinian ideas of normal 'projective identification.'] This is something that may well develop, the idea that the patient feels that he is *inside* you or something. I think that would need really careful analyzing without it being biffed or knocked down. *I don't think you should encourage it, because you then would go over to Winnicott and encourage regression, which I am not happy about in any way.*"

Consistent with the concept of projective identification as the psy-chic representation of the earliest form of relating and communicat-ing, most Kleinians, following Dr. Roberts, translate states of at-oneness or selfobject unity into the metaphor of container–con-tained. An individual experiences herself as inside, rather than con-tinuous, or in communion, with another.

On reading over the interviews, it was fascinating to notice that a number of younger Kleinians spontaneously focused their discussion of separation on the ways patients enter into and exit from the analyst's room. Some examples are given below:

1. "Some patients take offense at interpretations of separations because they immediately assume you are making a bookish interpretation. But I think that *most of analysis is about separation,* I can't think of anything more important really. But what I find enormously complicated also are people's patterns of coming late or early. I would like to read more about this because I find it is one of the things that is most unchangeable and terribly mean-ingful in a primitive way. You can coerce your patient into always coming on time if you make enough superegoish interpreta-tions—well, of course, it is always wrong to interpret superego-ishly—and that patient will probably come on time in the end. But, if you are really interested in the meaning of it instead of interpreting it from the outside in terms of 'You are destroying the analysis' or whatever, I find these kinds of patterns are terri-bly, terribly rigid. I mean the patterns of going in and going out, of going to the door, they are completely set forever. They reveal a set relationship to a particular you in a particular state of mind. The patient I am thinking about always comes a few minutes late. He is able to come inside my room only when I am completely ready and when everything else has gone out of my mind so that no barrier exists at all. If he comes two minutes late, then he can feel this complete going in without any kind of mental barriers. It is easy to make interpretations about destructiveness or how 'You hate to be kept waiting so you think I am going to be kept wait-ing' etc. I don't think this kind of interpretation helps.

    "*I don't think I really know anything about developmental arrests.* I would hope that some analysis would change things rather dras-tically, but I don't know that way of thinking at all. Now, about mourning leading to change, I think there is truth in that, except that I also think that there is work which has to do with the *recovery* of good experiences, which is not quite the same as mourning. This can be experienced as giving something new, although presumably it isn't new, but just *the capacity to make use of something which was there but is now brought to life*. I don't think you can give a wonderfully good experience to somebody who for 40 years has lived in terrible deprivation. That person is going to *internalize* a bit of something good, but I still think that internalization is directly connected with recovering bits of something which survived and which have actually allowed that person to grow. What helps is *making use* of good experiences and not being stuck in bad experiences."

The foregoing passage clearly describes the view that mourning and internalization involve, first, the recovery of good memories or experiences within and, second, the capacity to make use of the good rather than the bad in the analyst and analytic situation. The following two excerpts are also from interviews with younger Kleinian analysts:

1. "I do think separations are important, I slip up by not interpreting them enough. But I also often try to draw on the way the patient comes in and leaves a bit more than the actual weekends—what the sensation is as they come in and go out, that feels more immediate. I would not feel that I really knew enough to say anything about this idea of developmental arrests. I would have to say, 'Ask me in 15 years.' I think, though, that the more that I see of these things, the more I feel that it is regrettable that *nothing achieved through a selfobject tie is on a secure foundation. It is only the working through of separateness that is secure.*"

2. "I don't think arrests in development can be fully overcome. I don't think analysis is so powerful that it can replace what is missing in a whole lifetime. I can't think of any instances, but *I would see the work of reparation as coming to terms with oneself really.*"

The following two excerpts are taken from interviews with two Kleinian child analysts who expressed somewhat different views, translating the concepts of Anna Freud and Kohut into terms that are current in British analysis:

1. "The idea of developmental arrests is unfamiliar . . . [pause] I mean . . . is that a bit like the idea that by nurturing a patient, the analyst can make up for a deficit? I don't think one can. Through

mourning, yes. Another way of putting this is, 'Can you ever modify people's *internal objects?*' And, put that way, I think you can, but you can't ever undo the experience of the bad or depriving object. And you can only modify it by *allowing an experience in the present to live alongside the bad experience*, or the deprived experience, so that the present experience can almost attach itself to that. It is an experience in the present of being with someone who can tolerate the situation, who can bear it with the patient and help the patient face it. It is modified through the sense that something has been contained."

2. "I am a bit familiar with the 'selfobject' tie idea. I find it difficult to know, though, because I immediately translate the idea into my own language. I do think that Bion's notion of projective identification as a form of communication, a normal stage of projective identification, is important. This is a stage where the infant does need to feel that there is an object who will be available and who will allow the infant to get inside his or her object or be part of it. Like this child I see—the one who spits—who is desperate to feel that he can have something taken in and he feels so much that that person won't be available to him."

In chapter 5, I described Dr. Martin, the child analyst who was the most "widely influenced" of the Kleinian analysts. His views on the topics of this chapter were unique. Dr. Martin was younger than the most senior group of Kleinian British analysts (most of whom were in their late 60s and 70s) but had trained a few years earlier than the group of younger analysts described earlier in this and in previous chapters. With respect to the effects of institutional affiliation, he had worked for many years at the Tavistock Clinic, from the time when John Bowlby was director of training until more recently when the orientation of the Department for Family and Parents became dominated by the Kleinian-Bionian thinking of Donald Meltzer. He was fully conversant with the Anna Freudian literature. Dr. Martin:

"Yes, I do know what you mean. You see, if you are in the process of helping a patient come to terms with distortions or lacks in development—and, by the way, I use the word 'distortion' because you are never quite certain what part was real failure in parenting and what the patient made of that—then *the whole process of analysis can be seen as becoming a corrective experience.* I don't mean by that that if there has been a failing in mother's nurturing, then you are actually taking on the job of mothering, but I am talking in terms of *mental* functioning or ego functioning. Hopefully, the whole analysis is a good experience. Corrective sounds a bit like a probation officer, corrective detention or something! I think of introducing and instating, *not reinstating*, within the ego of the patient elements that were not there previously. I don't think these are just *identifications with* the analyst. This has to do with a capacity to value aspects of the analyst's ego and to establish them within the patient's ego as valued ways of *managing* stress, anxiety, affects, and object relations. *So, I think that actually you can make up the deficit.*

"One has to remember too that children actually can make up the deficits; just think of the work of Anna Freud in the Hampstead nurseries. I think the people who worked in the war nursery showed very convincingly that you can make up for the deficits and trauma. But, as well as the analytic work, I think you do have to have an environment that can forward that movement. Obviously, for children, that is important anyway, but I think it is important for adults too. I think it is always much more difficult for very isolated, schizoid patients in analysis to find the resources around to help in that restorative work. Sometimes you find yourself thinking, 'I hope that patient has a bit of luck.' At this point in time, something has to come in and fill the gap which can't be filled from the analyst, a little bit of real object satisfaction which can help them with the next step on."

Dr. Martin introduces alternative ways of looking at development. First, he emphasizes the idea of distortions rather than deficits in development, indicating the notion of a deviant pathway as opposed to a gap or lack. Second, his awareness of Anna Freud's work supports the belief that therapy introduces, rather than reinstates, new experiences. Third, by discussing the ways in which the patient establishes self-regulatory organizations, he expands on traditional notions of internalization of, or identification with, the analyst's containing capacities.

The last excerpt is taken from the interview with Dr. Shaw, the Kleinian analyst who had changed orientation from the Independent group:

"Separation interpretations would seem to be one of the realities of the whole procedure. It is very important. The whole procedure is affected by weekends and holidays. I don't think you can undo basic faults. I think you inevitably relive them with your patient, and you inevitably struggle with the ways the patient coped with these traumas. Hopefully, the patient will gain greater insight into the more *destructive* ways in which he or she coped with them. But I don't think the trauma is ever done away with or changed. The idea of building new mental structures, this is the area the Americans call the 'corrective emotional experience.' I think there is a corrective emotional experience, but it is through *finding an object in the analyst* who is capable of helping the patient develop a greater awareness of how they coped with the past so that disastrous defenses will be less strong. There is reparation in that sense I suppose, finding an object that can face things. But I certainly don't think that is achieved by the analyst being the good object the patient did not have. It is achieved by the analyst being able to face what is going on in the present, which is a *heightened recapitulation of the trauma*.

"I don't know what a 'selfobject tie' is. *I would interpret the patient's avoidance of separateness.* There are some patients where it is actually pernicious that they want nothing separate, only the original illusion, which is based on a form of thinking which has a quite psychotic quality. It is when that is questioned that all hell breaks loose. If the patient is actually to develop in any way, then they have to see that that sort of tie is an illusion, and, in some cases, that would turn out to be a complete catastrophe. It depends on whether you agree that there is some ego distinction from the object at birth. Of course, Freud did not think so, but I do."

In this passage, Dr. Shaw underlines a critical difference between Kleinian and Freudian/British Independent concepts of the development of the ego. When the ego is conceived as a separate entity from birth, experiences of fusion are illusory and grandiose always involve control over the other person.

INDEPENDENT ANALYSTS

In contrast to the British Kleinians, the analysts in the Independent group had little difficulty in translating Kohutian concepts into those of Balint and Winnicott. Clearly, some valued therapeutic *regression* as an agent of change. Like the majority of British analysts, all emphasized the interpretation of separation as well as the crucial role of processes of mourning in psychic change. Following the theories of earlier object relational thinkers, both Independent and Kleinian, the focus was on the interpretation of internal object relations. Many Independents used Winnicott's concept of "the use of an object" to articulate beliefs in the development of a separate self as well as the sense of others existing outside the self in the larger cultural environment. The following excerpts illustrate those aspects of technique that characterize Independent analysis.

Dr. Matheson, the senior "classical" Independent analyst, spoke clearly on the benefits of therapeutic regression:

"I don't think in Kohutian terms. I think in Winnicottian and Balint's terms, which are very similar, that is, *in terms of the basic fault and therapeutic regression where, in the analysis, the patient gets back to much earlier states of development, perhaps to traumatic or pretraumatic states.* And working with those states, both in terms of experiencing and in terms of interpretation. Very often, it is the noninterpretation that is as important, the experience of the analytic situation. And also it can be very important not to interpret because interpretation, particularly transference interpretation, can take the patient out of a state of regression. It is better to allow the patient to experience what it is like to be in that state and for you to be in the regression with them. You might also interpret quite a lot when a patient is in a state of regression, but you would be careful to interpret in terms of the place where the patient is at the time. I think it would be wrong, absolutely wrong, to make interpretations about separateness when a patient is in that state. You should do everything you can to keep yourself as 'unobtrusive,' in Balint's phrase, as possible. You are just there to be used and to try to help the patient understand where they are in that state, at the moment, both way back in the past or as acted out in the present. I wouldn't want to destroy that fantasy state in the present under any circumstances."

A second senior Independent analyst made a similar point, translating self-psychological concepts into Winnicott's terms:

"One has to live with one's history. It is like getting down to some kind of bedrock and then being able to build on that rather than on some kind of illusory structure. When I hear people talk about a selfobject tie, I think of Winnicott's 'Use of an Object'

paper, the distinction he draws between object relating and
object usage. Object relating I think covers what the self psychologists mean by a selfobject tie, where the reality of the object
is of little consequence as compared with the internal object relationship. The qualities of the internal object relationship so
determine the perception and function of the object—the object
is not separate, it is just a projection. I haven't ever had this sort
of debate with a Kleinian, so I don't know whether Winnicott's
distinction between object relating and object usage means much
to them. I think the object has to be allowed to be *an autonomous
separate entity*. I am not sure how transitional phenomena fit in
with this, but I would tend to think that transitional phenomena
are regressive, but, then, *I think we probably need all kinds of regressive phenomena in order to restore ourselves.*"

The following excerpt is taken from the interview with the
Independent analyst who was very familiar with Kohut's work and who
had been a close associate of both Anna Freud and John Bowlby. He
too translated Kohut's selfobject concept into Winnicottian terms:

"You know, Balint said, 'out of the wounds' can come a scar. But
he meant that as a metaphor. The wounds will have certain influences forever. But I do believe that mourning builds up new
structures, as does the integration of our maturational development. *All maturation processes are new structures, including the analytic process.* And yes, of course, the selfobject tie is important as
leading to healthy narcissism. And I would not necessarily see
that as a defense against separateness. That process needs to be
worked through. Ultimately, we aim at separation and a separate
object relationship. I think of the process in Winnicott's terms—
'putting the object outside the area of omnipotent control'."

This next excerpt is from the interview with the Independent analyst who was rated as falling on the edge of the Kleinian cluster. His
discussion exemplifies a Kleinian approach to the interpretation of
separation and an Independent view of the value of the new relationship with the analyst. As indicated in earlier chapters, this analyst is in
the same peer group as the younger Kleinians and participated in postgraduate clinical seminars with senior Kleinians as well as in case discussions with colleagues at the Tavistock Clinic. Like the other
younger Kleinians, he gave the following example to illustrate the
close attention he pays to the ways patients enter and leave the con-

sulting room. With reference to developmental arrests, however, his views are closer to those of his Independent colleagues:

"I think of a carpenter. One day I collected him a minute early for his session. He spent a lot of time during the session describing hanging a door. He said, 'When you really make a door beautifully and you put it in its jam perfectly, then you have got a millimeter clearance all the way round the edge of the door. The door opens and stays at any position at which you open it. When you close it, you have got this beautiful one-millimeter line all the way around it.' I interpreted that he was very aware of the fact that I had collected him fractionally early for his session so that the session didn't fit inside its frame in the way he wanted it to fit. On that occasion, the interpretation was spot on. Of course, that is not a separation . . . but it is connected.

"*I do think the experience of the relationship with the analyst is of immense importance.* It can't alter the past, but it does provide another experience. I do not like this phrase 'coming to terms with one's past.' '*Coming to terms with*' *implies a kind of resignation, not an internal change.* From within the analytic relationship, the patient may understand his past in a different way and come to have different feelings about it. Yes, it has to do with giving up illusions, idealizations, phantasies, but actually you gain something else. What you gain is a structure, a new structure inside you which somehow incorporates the object that is the analyst as well as everything that that analyst is for you."

Two Independent *child* analysts raised interesting theoretical questions about the concept of psychic change:

1. "I don't think you can 'undo' the past. But that does not answer the question as to whether you are just helping the patient come to terms with the status quo ante or whether you can produce new structures? *You can produce new attitudes.* For instance, take a patient who, before analysis, didn't know how to be a father. Now, he has got three children. He has given a lot of evidence lately of being able to play and relate to his children. Now, is that a new structure? Does that reflect an internal psychic change? I noticed in your questionnaire that you stayed clear of the question what is meant by internal change! Would my example be a new structure? His behavior is surely a sign of growth. The other thing that has changed is that he has *stopped*

looking so compulsively to turn other people into a good father. Now,
is that also a new structure?"

2. "This is an area of intensive research. I don't know the
answer. Whether you call it a 'basic fault' or a 'developmental
arrest,' so much depends on what you are referring to. *So much of
it has to do with the picture you have of how a human being should be.*
Then, if you find something missing in that picture, you say, 'Ah
hah, that's what is missing.' I believe we are moving into an era,
an age, where we're gradually recognizing that some of us don't
have all the cogwheels we were meant to have. This takes me
back to the work I do with children. I see some children where
I'm not really convinced that all they have relates to some
arrested development. I get very suspicious when I hear about
analysts fostering certain sorts of development."

BRITISH FREUDIANS

This section illustrates the ways in which British Freudians think
about separations, mourning, and the analysis of deficits and developmental arrests. As one Freudian remarked, "There isn't anyone in the
British Society who doesn't think seriously about separations." Most of
the Freudians had no difficulty with self-psychological ideas of deficit
and developmental arrests and readily translated these terms into the
more familiar ones of Anna Freud, Michael Balint, and Donald
Winnicott. With the exception of the elderly child analyst who had
worked in Anna Freud's wartime nurseries, the Freudians were more
pessimistic than their Independent colleagues concerning the potential for psychic change in the area of the basic fault. In this respect, the
British Freudians were closer to the American Freudians influenced by
ego psychology in the ways they conceptualized structural change in
terms of the *adaptive* functions of the ego. A typical response was, "My
experience is that with developmental arrests or deficits, the best we
can do is to help the patient come to deal with them and to learn new
adaptive ways of relating."

I first quote from the interview with the elderly British Freudian who
had trained and worked with Anna Freud in the wartime nurseries:

"I have war nursery experiences, two very interesting ones which
have been written up. Both cases were illegitimate boys who
never knew their father. I don't know if the mother of one used

him sexually, but she always had him very close to her physically. She herself was quite uneducated, a country girl who had hardly been to school and was not very intelligent. When the boy went to school, and when we met him, he was extremely slow at learning to talk. Everyone just had the feeling that he was slow like his mother. He became very attached to me and then had an analysis. When the war nursery closed, he was already quite good at school. He then got into a very good grammar school. There a male teacher took a great deal of interest in him. He was the first man to make a relationship with the boy. This teacher said that he was a highly gifted actor. We had always called him an actor because he copied our Austrian accents so well. He copied Anna Freud. She loved him very much. He made us all laugh. *What really mattered was partly the attachment but, very largely, the two analyses.* He had one analysis when he was about five or six, and then he came back for another analysis when he was a teenager. In the second analysis, he worked on his whole problem with his mother, the sexuality, and not knowing who his father was as well as his mother never telling him about his father. All this, the knowing and the being able to talk about it evidently made this absolute change in him. So the poor functioning of his brain which we first believed, and the trouble he had learning to read and write, all that was left behind. The second child couldn't get through school at all, but he emigrated to Australia and did awfully well. He now has a complicated job as a chartered accountant in a big firm. He had an analysis in Australia, and here we couldn't get him through the simplest things."

This analyst immediately translated Kohut's concept of the selfobject tie into Margaret Mahler's concepts:

"I haven't really taken the trouble to understand Kohut's ideas, but certainly the idea of the selfobject is based on Mahler's original concept of symbiosis. I am very interested in Mahler's concept, and I have had a lot of experience of the simultaneous analyses of mother and child at the Anna Freud Centre. This was Dorothy Burlingham's original idea, based on the experience that if one just analyzes the child, it does not always lead to good results. But, with the simultaneous analyses, we came across a great deal of interaction in which *the child was not really allowed by the mother to develop into a separate being.*"

A second child analyst, also trained at the Anna Freud Centre, observed:

"I look at this differently from some other analysts. I feel that there are certain structures and ways of mental functioning that have a very rigid quality to them. Analysis does *reduce the rigidities*, but it does more than that. The importance of these experiences is lessened so that the repetitious quality diminishes *because the investment shifts*. Something else is invested in and takes its place, or something else is found that was already there but not attended to. *I don't think the deficits are put right through analysis. There is a fabric with a flaw that remains, but the clamor for compensation, for the flaw to be put right, changes.* And that often comes up in the context of separation. I think people have a right to go on about what went wrong. That is what I would want and I would be impressed by that. But I would then want to find a new way of thinking about it. It is like mourning. With trauma, I would not want to interpret that there is something missing which analysis can't provide. If you interpret that, all that means to patients is that you are rejecting what they want and long for. But I know fully well that I can't provide what was missing."

Dr. Smith described his approach to separations and basic faults from an American Freudian perspective:

"About weekend separations and breaks, I would hold what I call Greenson's position. There is a lot of variation, and some patients do see the weekend as, 'Whew, thank God, a break from work and homework, a little holiday before school again.' I very much agree with Balint and Anna Freud concerning developmental arrests, severe traumas, fixations, lack of development, basic faults, etc. I would see basic faults as 'beyond words.' It is like accepting that we are going to die. And I would work toward this sort of experience from a basic assumption that it was first some childhood conflict, or repression, something more standard. But if I gradually came to feel that the experience was a basic fault, a wound or lack of development, I would change my approach. For example, if a person's mother died at the age of one or two and there was no good substitute, I wouldn't say that nothing could be done. I would certainly keep the analysis going and try to heal the wound. *In other words, the person has got to compensate for it, accept it.* So I would take a more tolerant, sympathetic view that this is something that you have got to learn to accept and come to terms with.

"And about the old Alexander idea, I am not so opposed as others to this corrective view. I would not consciously set about to create a corrective experience. I think it is inherent in the stability of the analytic relationship that the analytic, calm stance would help heal these wounds. *I like Joe Sandler's idea that you never can erase the past, but you can get some better ways of handling it.* When you start out and you are young, you think you can correct and erase these childhood traumas by a brilliant interpretation, but I don't think so. And with Kohut's selfobject transferences, the mirror and merger transferences, I have read the book, but I must say that Kohut's kind of thinking goes right through me, in the same way that projective identification goes right through me. I can't really get a grip on it. But, if I understand the use of these terms as saying that there is a need to have a loving, positive relationship where you feel the analyst respects and admires you, and thinks you are a good person, then there is certainly something to that, and something that you should not tear apart."

AMERICAN CLASSICAL FREUDIANS IN NEW YORK AND SAN FRANCISCO

The American Freudians tended to use developmental concepts drawn from the ego-psychological literature in contrast to the works of Anna Freud. Beyond insight into intrapsychic conflicts, the younger, third-generation Freudians also emphasized the concept of the real relationship and the affective experience of the analyst. Few focused on the interpretation of separation and mourning. I first quote in detail from these parts of the interview with the elderly Freudian analyst at the center of the classical Freudian cluster, Dr. Braun in New York:

"Oh, the English interpret separation because of this same error, which I call the phenomenological error in which *unconscious content is assigned to manifest phenomenology.* The content is assigned according to the preferred paradigm of pathogenesis held by the analyst. *I don't interpret separation. I interpret what the patient says to me in context, in sequence, in metaphors, in similes. You interpret the text of the patient's associations.* If and when I had the text of a patient's associations, then I could decide whether the analyst was superimposing a preconceived paradigm or whether the interpretation was in keeping with what the patient was talking about. The Kleinian does not have to be wrong because he makes that interpretation. What I am cautioning against is the superimposition of preconceived paradigms of pathogenesis.

"Take an easy example. The patient begins to feel anxious as the summer vacation approaches. The interpretation is given that this is separation anxiety. Manifestly this is true. But that is not what we mean by separation anxiety. Separation anxiety refers to a specific situation in which an infant feels bereft of maternal support and care and feels threatened by overwhelming needs and the anxieties of unpleasure created by the danger of such a situation. The content of separation anxiety is the idea of being abandoned, not being able to survive without a supporting, sustaining figure. And that is supposed to be due to some untoward set of circumstances, bad mothering during the early years of life. Now that could be what is behind the separation anxiety, but it also could be the mechanism known as the protector under protection. That is, the analyst goes away and the patient becomes anxious: 'Maybe the analyst will die while I am away, so I have to know where the analyst is in order for me to feel comfortable.' The anxiety might stem from a conflict over the analysand's death wishes toward the analyst so the analysand has to be sure that the analyst is alive. Or, at a particular point in treatment, the analyst may represent the controlling, modulating, superego influence that has been projected onto him and the patient unconsciously thinks, 'When the cat's away, the mice will play.' So the patient may be anxious because the separation evokes certain dangerous patterns of acting out, or fantasies that have been forbidden."

Analysts in both the American classical Freudian and British Kleinian groups viewed separation anxiety as a derivative of other unconscious, latent conflicts. Nevertheless, although they assigned a different content to the unconscious fantasies underlying the manifest anxiety evoked by separation, Dr. Braun's analysis is not so different from the kind of interpretation that might be given by a Kleinian. Again, perhaps, cultural stereotypes of analysts in different groups do not always reflect actual clinical practice. The clinical example given by Dr. Braun seems to suggest that the preconscious thinking of

American classical Freudians and British Kleinians on separation anxiety is not that dissimilar. Dr. Braun continued:

> "*Talking about deficits is like asking someone, 'Have you stopped lead-
> ing your life?'* because that viewpoint makes a certain assumption
> about the role of developmental arrests in the process of patho-
> genesis. That leads to another question about whether analysis is
> a replacement therapy, whether I can make up for this or that. I
> don't look at it that way: not because there aren't developmental
> arrests which happened in childhood to do with mothering, etc.,
> but the point is how that individual's mind tried to cope with
> these different real factors. Somebody is born with palsy, that
> person will have certain developmental problems, the inability
> to use the left or right hand. But what does the individual do?
> How do these real factors contribute to the apprehension and
> response to reality, to sensory perception, object relations, and
> the conflicts generated? Now, that is talking about anatomical
> deficit. That is one thing, but the concept is used now in the
> sense of deficits in ego structure. That is a difficult concept to
> work with. *I think that sometimes the idea of deficit is used as a court
> of last resort.* We don't know why we are not able to budge this
> particular aspect of the patient's conflict. Perhaps he has a deficit
> way back when. . . . This is an example of how some of the obser-
> vations and concepts of developmental psychology have been
> extrapolated and transformed over the years and inserted into
> adult psychopathology without taking into account all the trans-
> formations that take place in the intervening years."

Two of the third-generation training analysts at the Columbia
Institute in New York took a more liberal approach to these ideas.
They were clearly conversant with, and used, concepts outside those of
the classical Freudian and ego-psychological repertoire and emphasized the curative power of the analytic relationship:

1. "You mean Kohut's 'transmuting internalization'? I would
   call that by the old term 'corrective emotional experience.' I
   think, within reason, we sometimes do a lot of that. *I think that the
   idea of psychic change through the new relationship is absolutely important.* When somebody has had an incredibly traumatic experience and you treat them with dignity, respect, and consistency, it
   helps. Do you eradicate the early flaw? I am less sanguine. I am
   thinking of a patient with a horrendous childhood: well, she has

come to grips with the fact that something dreadful happened, but whether we can undo it, I don't know. This is where the relationship makes the difference. She said, 'You know you are the first person in my life who has treated me with the amount of respect you have given me in this analysis.' "

2.   "I am not sure, I am never sure what basic defects are unless they are very obvious defects of intelligence—not even traumas. *I don't think of trauma as a defect.* There are some people who have suffered what I would think of as very severe traumas but who have developed quite extraordinarily and have neurotic problems. It is hard to say that they are suffering from a defect. A *disturbance*, yes. And other people come with troubles which you might think were minor and you work in analysis with them without much possibility of major change. *Yes, I think change occurs through the analysis and the analytic work, but the relationship to the analyst should be a new experience.* This is an experience of being able to examine, to look at or inquire into, all the conflicts and difficulties that you have not been able to deal with before."

The following excerpts are taken from interviews with San Francisco analysts, all of whom were rated as belonging to the classical Freudian cluster despite some acknowledgment of the value of relational and self-psychological concepts. Few believed in the deficit model of development, stating instead that development always proceeds although it make take alternate, less desirable, pathways. Dr. Friedland, rated as close to the center of the classical Freudian cluster, responded dismissively to these questions:

"Well, as you can hear in your framing of the question, you just had to use several phrases that attach to unknown variables. *Developmental arrests, basic faults, etc. I strongly distrust all of them as being indicators that really measure a reality that has any implications for treatment or outcome. I am afraid they are wastebasket terms like the borderline diagnosis.* That started out candidly enough. We didn't know quite what the entity was, which is why we called it 'borderline.' Now we know exactly what a borderline is, and we have all these definitions to prove it. It is the same with these other things—deficits, developmental arrests, etc. It has become fashionable to talk about a deficit and not a conflict. But I see very little basis for that. There are people who are inaccessible for a variety of not easily known reasons. But there is no positive evidence to say, 'Well, the trouble is that you have this deficit and I will show you in the history where that deficit was, because your mother was x, y, or z.' I mean terrible things happen to people, and there are terrible consequences. But it is certainly far from clear that those terrible things result in some kind of imprinted, ingrained, irreversible blank spot which is then inaccessible to future understanding. There are plenty of people who can be shown to be suffering from the most superficial and trivial sort of silliness of whom one might be tempted to say they are untreatable. What is your alibi? The analyst was not skillful enough? The patient was frightened even though the pathology can't be shown to be earth shaking?

"Anyway, this is a profoundly skeptical consumer of such terms that you are talking with right now! I hope I made it clear, it is not that I underestimate the serious consequences or that I am saying, 'Oh, that is all nothing.' But I suggest that the kind of categorization of events into static concepts of faults, or losses, or deficits, or arrests, says less than could be said. We may just as well say, 'There are terrible things that happen, and so we suppose that terrible things eventuate.' I don't like these concepts, which basically rule somebody out. To me, they say, 'Well, there is no use really trying to analyze them unless you contain, or hold, or ally, or support. You certainly can't do analysis with them, or interpret them.' This is not helpful or useful conceptually. It is an explanation. It is conceivable it might be right. My knowledge of a person's history, and their knowledge of their history, is ultimately extremely important, but I had better not make up my mind that, given this history, this person can only go so far. That seems to me counterproductive. It is an educated, or a foolish, defensive, guess. It is sort of mapping without exploring. Maybe we haven't been able to explore. We will never be able to explore, so why draw the maps? You know, it is a dark continent, so there you are!"

Additional examples from the interviews with San Francisco Freudians follow:

1. "To me, *self psychology is an outgrowth of a reaction against the lack of recognition of the influence of the interpersonal aspect.* I remember once at a conference, someone—a social worker, I think—said, 'But what about the humanistic point of view?' I said, 'Well, I hope we all have a humanistic point of view, but I want to

introduce this particular psychoanalytic point of view, which is not antithetical but an implementation of the humanistic point of view.' I think self psychology is also based on some really fundamental differences about the nature of technique, the idea of restoring, healing, of being a good parent, I think it's overdoing that. But that is not because I deny the significance of the analytic experience. I think that development can occur through the relationship, and only partly as a result of the interpretation of the analytic process. When I was in training, it was *verboten* to say that. Obviously, I don't agree with the corrective emotional experience. I don't think the analyst should play a role, but just being who you are is a corrective emotional experience. It is part of what happens in the transference. It is the experience of having this fantasy with affect, whatever the impulse, and then learning about it in the safety of the analytic situation.

"*In fact, I put less and less emphasis on insight and more on the experience of the analysis.* I haven't found, either with the people I have seen, or those whom I am seeing for a second analysis, or myself, or colleagues, or family—I have not been overwhelmed by the profound insights. Changes yes, but not through insight. I think it is analogous to what happens in development. Say, you ask a person aged 21, 'Tell me what you've learned. Tell me of your insights into life now that you are 21.' They can't. Analysis is a condensation of that. Things happen in the experience, I hope largely through the analytic process, but patients can't necessarily articulate what happened. And some that do tend to overintellectualize anyway."

2.   "*I think we may be presumptuous in thinking we can ascertain what is a developmental deficiency which is the contemporary term for basic faults.* I don't know if there really is such a thing as a developmental arrest, because development does proceed. It gets distorted. I don't think it is possible to produce the building blocks that were needed at a later point in time. I think the problem comes in making the assumption that a building block is missing in the first place. What you are seeing is the consequence of a severe neurotic conflict and not necessarily a developmental deficiency. I have seen some remarkable things happen that, on the basis of this distinction, I would never have expected. I don't attribute the positive outcome of the analysis to making up for a developmental deficiency but to its having previously been wrongly understood. I do think, though, that a certain degree of

conviction helps one work. And this conviction is conveyed in the Kohutians' belief in building new structures. After a few more years, we will be able to assess more of the results."

In the following excerpt, the analyst puts forward a good case for adaptation in contrast to change in psychic structure:

"I think some people come a long way. The people I have seen that have had these horrendous mothers and traumata, what they do is they develop a sense of irony. I agree with the Kohutian concept of irony and wit. I see that in older patients too, or people who have been chronically ill. Two people I think of, one a chronic diabetic since childhood, and another, a woman whose mother died of Huntington's disease. Both were deeply upset and embarrassed and would try to hide the disease or not think about it. But much later these terrible thoughts and feelings became the subject matter of jokes.

"So, do people get better? Yes, they get better, but they don't really get better. They come to grips with the meaning of their life. You know, we all get married and have children and live happily ever after. We are all well analyzed, except what do we do? We are more anxious and depressed than we ever were before we started. But we know what it is about, right? The quality of life and the pursuit of happiness is the pursuit of as much freedom, daring, and courage to deal with things as you can. *So this business of character change, what is the outcome of a successful analysis? It is probably adaptation.* That is of therapeutic benefit, rather than a change of structure or a resolution of transference. What is resolution of transference? Probably an increased capacity for transference without anxiety. Look at all these follow-up studies: people continue to have transference reactions, even the most 'well-analyzed' people. So I don't see people as getting better, I see them as just basically understanding more and then having more options and being able to utilize those options."

In the next set of interview excerpts, the American Freudian analysts directly discuss their approaches to separation:

"Well, of course, separations are important, but there is such a thing as an *art* of interpretation, just as a baseball pitcher has to have different kinds of pitches. An analyst has to have different kinds of interpretations, or else you bring about an iatrogenic resistance. It has become a joke. *About psychic change, we are simply dealing with concepts. It is impossible not to reify something like structure. Nobody can find out whether that changes.* I would not know how to approach it. I think change depends a great deal on how recent certain kinds of disturbance are. I love the title of Robert Gardiner's book *Self-Inquiry.* It captures the sense that, at the end of analysis, you have the ability, the willingness, the discipline to be able to ask yourself, 'Why in hell have I done this? Or think, or feel this?' *Mainly, the result of analysis is a constant self-analysis.* I don't mean this in a disparaging way but, if you can achieve this, you do have some control."

Earlier, I described a number of the American analysts as internationally minded. This description referred to those analysts who were active in the International Psycho-Analytical Association as well as the American Psychoanalytic Association. These analysts seemed particularly aware of the thinking of their British colleagues as demonstrated in the following excerpt from the interview with a senior San Francisco analyst:

"*The focus on separation reflects a difference in region.* The British emphasize it more; the Americans are more casual about it. But for a particular reason. America is a very large country, and then meetings of the American Psychoanalytic Association are held twice a year for a week. So there are periodic interruptions that are in the scheme of things. You make less of them each time they come up than when interruptions are more rare events. Also, in America, don't forget, analyses are four times a week; very few people see patients five times a week. In England, it is still five times a week. But when it is four times, many people may come Tuesday through Friday, or Monday through Thursday, but for others there may be an interruption in the middle of the week. So there is less focus here. Also, in England they take these long school holidays, six weeks in the summer and two weeks at Christmas and Easter. Everyone takes their break at the same time. Americans are much more individual about breaks. One person takes four weeks, another eight weeks; one takes it in July, another in October. And so there is all this variability here, and it gets reflected technically in this way. Now, Bowlby and others would say we don't pay enough attention to separations."

"This argument over conflict versus deficit has been a spurious argument. To me, there is always a conflictual side to every aspect of functioning. All we can do is focus on that and interpret it and then the patient comes to the best possible adjustment they can with whatever built-in capacities they have. The shadow is always there, under stress it can always be reactivated. But it can become less peremptory, less dominant in behavior."

Lastly, it is interesting to contrast the views of these New York and San Francisco analysts with those of the classical Freudian in Los Angeles who had been analyzed by Ralph Greenson. In terms reminiscent of Ronald Fairbairn, he emphasized the working through of guilt feelings that children have about their parents' deficiencies:

"I believe that the new object that the analyst represents can establish an atmosphere in which the patient can grow again and rebuild that which he had lost. This happens through a clarification of what happened, through removing the sense of guilt. You know, children all tend to feel guilty for their parents' misconduct. And I think it is through the new experience with the analyst that the deficits can be worked through."

LOS ANGELES SELF PSYCHOLOGISTS

The high level of consistency of the self psychologists on these topics was notable. All expressed hopeful attitudes toward the undoing of traumatic deficits through the integrative and new selfobject functions provided by the analyst. Two examples follow:

1. "I think that interpretations are particularly valuable in the areas of developmental arrest or basic fault, not only because of the insights they convey, but because of the transference meaning that the interpretations have for patients. For example, when the analyst interprets a disavowed affect state, it is not only the insight that is valuable, but that the patient is having an experience in the transference of a longed-for object who can tolerate and welcome that affect and understand that affect state. In other words, *I see interpretations as being part of the analytic bond and as serving selfobject functions for the patient. And, yes, I do think that analysts can undo, or at least unstall, developmental arrests and help development to resume.* But I would rephrase it a bit. I think that much of the curative action of psychoanalysis results from the integration of previously unintegratable painful affects,

including mourning. But there are other sorts of painful affect that get integrated through the analytic process and through the analyst's providing this integrative function."

2. *"The way I think about psychic change is that it is the interpretations that establish a bond that are necessary and essential. It is through the bond that new experiences can be elaborated.* And I do think that these new experiences can build new mental structures. I think, though, that a lot of effective analysis takes place in the interpreting of the preexisting structures that have been erected because of what didn't happen. And the interpretation has to do with getting through those structures, so that something new can then occur."

In the following excerpt, a self psychologist illustrates the way in which he interprets separations in relation to the *analyst's* needs:

"I think separation responses are important, and the danger of not taking them up has more to do with the analyst not wanting to take up his own needs as these affect separations, for example, not working seven days a week. In my case, I tend to work back to back, and sometimes I will be a few minutes late and the range of responses is pretty wide. It really doesn't bother some people, some people are not even aware of it, and some people feel it proves that they don't matter to me. One of the most profound aspects of the patient's experience is the genuine feeling that the analyst is there—or not there—for them. I don't mean that the analyst is available seven days a week or always on the phone, but much more the feeling that the analyst was there for them. I have heard this said by two patients in analysis with a prominent self psychologist in town. He was 'always present'; that was the most salient feature of the experience. I would like my patients to be able to say that."

The last excerpt is taken from the interview with one of the Los Angeles self psychologists who had *changed* orientation. This analyst underlined the importance of an undisrupted bond between patient and analyst:

"One of the most important processes that analysis offers a patient is the encouragement and facilitation of the resumption of a process of reflection and articulation of self-experience of things that the patient was not able to think before. As long as the bond is in good working order, it serves as a facilitating medium to enable the patient to undertake the work of self-reflection, self-articulation, and self-definition, and of understanding the various interferences to her being able to maintain her own psychological functions, the interferences that impair her from sustaining a positive and resilient sense of her own self. For example, these interferences often emerge when such a patient becomes involved with another person and that person gets upset with the patient. That upset *activates developmental malstructures* by virtue of which the patient is inclined to accept the other person's idea that she has done something wrong and to lose connection with the motivating forces within her that were in operation before the upset. This is a whole area of analytic work that has been bypassed heretofore and that I am extremely enthusiastic about. The role of the analyst in this work is background, very restrained. I have often gotten the impression that I am not doing enough active work. What am I doing? But I recognize these doubts as emanating from some organizing principle of my own whereby I need some demonstration of my wisdom and talent and impact in order to assure myself. And that constitutes much more of an interference in the bond, in the ongoing process, than a help."

AMERICAN ECLECTIC ANALYSTS

Like British Independents, the American analysts who were rated as independent or eclectic emphasized the curative value of the relationship with the analyst. One of the New York Freudian analysts who was affiliated with the Columbia Institute, influenced by Sullivanian ideas and rated as falling close to the center of the cluster of American eclectic analysts, linked reparation with unrelenting desires for vengeance:

"I don't take up separations. In fact, if anything, I perhaps underplay separation. I don't fish for it, probably not as much as I should. About change, I think probably change occurs through insight but also through the analytic relationship. You see, I don't think that there are simple developmental arrests in that the patient stops at some point, or regresses back and then develops normally. I think development proceeds more or less normally or abnormally. I think it is also the case that we don't do perfect analyses. I don't think we create new people out of old ones. I have never seen an analysand who did not retain the capacity to reproduce his old neuroses under the right circumstances. *In terms of building new structures, I am closer to the Kleinian view of reparation through mourning.* I think neurotics are enormously involved in vengeance and desires for endless reparation. They give up their neuroses with extreme difficulty because nobody is going to pay them back for the evils done to them; that is part of all analyses. I don't think of regression back and then progression forward to full development. More a giving up of a grudge, nobody gives up a grudge easily."

A New York interpersonal analyst at the very center of the eclectic cluster linked the interpretation of deficits with resistance:

"I find the concept of deficit very useful. There is something really missing, although I do not make a sharp distinction as to whether it was based on conflict, or fixation, or deficit. The therapy with these patients is different. It is much more 'here-and-now,' more in the reality of the relationship. With the more analytic patient, you really can stay back and let the analytic process proceed, and intervene only when you have something to say. But with a patient with a deficit, it is much more tumultuous. *The reason I think the deficit concept is useful is that it does not focus the analyst on resistance,* because resistance assumes that the patient really does have a little motor in there but he is just not using it. It would almost be sadistic to think of deficit as resistance. I personally don't use the concept of resistance in my work. What I would say with phenomena that others call resistance is something like, 'I guess what we are talking about makes you very uncomfortable so you don't want to talk about it.' The concept of building new structures— that to me is a spatial concept, I don't have a spatial model, so I don't think of change in those terms."

The Los Angeles eclectic analysts were, for the most part, hopeful about the potential for psychic change through the analytic relationship. The influence of Greenson on the Freudians in the Los Angeles Psychoanalytic Institute and of Franz Alexander on the more eclectic analysts at the Southern California Institute seemed to have set the climate for this more positive view of the outcome of analysis. Despite important theoretical differences and many other personal influences, it is possible that the climate in Southern California was already ripe for the developmental models and techniques of self psychology. The eclectic analysts from the Southern California Institute clearly preferred the theoretical and practical implications of Alexander's notions of psychic change in contrast to the deficit models implied by Kohut and self psychology. Views of the two elderly pioneer analysts follow. First, Dr. Furnham:

"I think much of the separation reaction is iatrogenic. If you see a patient five times a week, you create a certain kind of dependency, so the patient is going to feel as though he or she is being deserted if you are away for two days. If, however, from the beginning of your work, you interpret these dependencies and you encourage autonomy, you find that the negative effect of temporary separations is minimized to a great degree. Franz Alexander wrote about this in his book *Psychoanalytic Therapy.* I recommend it to you very strongly. A lot of the anxiety that patients feel about separations is a measure of their dependency, and, if that dependency is interpreted from the very beginning instead of being fostered as the classical technique does deliberately, then patients not only handle separation but sometimes grow during the separation so that it becomes a positive experience for them.

"Certain basic developmental faults are as hard to move as a rock. We have to get away from the assumption that we are omnipotent. I think one of the problems of the early analytic environment is that it promised more than it could deliver. And that was part of the omnipotence of the early analysts. We do the best we can, and we try to get patients to accept certain limitations. In that, we are no different from other therapy modalities. You have to learn to live with it, within its limits. I think the idea that the 'selfobject bond' can be curative is old wine in a new bottle. In early analytic theory, we talked about introjects. I don't attach the same mystique to the term selfobject as the self psychologists do. I think what they are describing is a kind of introject that is a living presence in significant relationships. I have no quarrel with the self psychologists, I just don't find that it has added anything revolutionary to my approach."

Dr. Nathan, the second pioneer analyst, stated:

"I don't think analysis changes the patient; what does is the experience with the analyst. A very important part of the analytic process is the actual experience the patient has with the therapist as a real person, the interaction and the transaction. *As I see it, the analyst is a parental figure, and here I am not talking about transference. In reality, the analyst has a parental attitude and behaves in many ways like a parent.* The patient has a new and different experience with a different kind of parental substitute. One of the things I resent about Kohut and all his followers is that they never mention Alexander's concept of the corrective emotional experience, and yet that is what they are describing. But that is another thing. The whole concept of *structures* bothers me. I am kind of simple minded, and to me a structure is something concrete, mechanical, like a table. But I don't have any doubt that changes occur. There is no question that changes occur in the character-traits. And this is through the relationship with a new kind of figure. This includes not only the actual experience with a new parental figure but the incorporation of some of the attitudes of this new parental figure toward the patient. What are these attitudes? We are talking about someone who has a genuine interest and concern for the welfare of that patient, which is exactly what a good parent does. Sometimes that does not occur. Because, sometimes, the analyst is not really genuinely, sufficiently involved with the welfare of that patient because he is involved with doing analysis and analyzing according to his theoretical model of analysis. When the analyst is overly involved in doing analysis, then he is usually not sufficiently involved either with the patient or with what is really going on."

Three other analysts, also training analysts at the Southern California Institute, felt that the analyst's image of the patient as suffering a deficit had a diminishing effect:

1. *"I don't think we fill in the faults. We give people some other ways of dealing with them, but the vulnerability stays.* I realize that when I started interpreting deficits people would be offended because in a way it was saying, 'You are diminished.' It was confirming their suspicion that they were defective. It took away their hope. Instead, they begin to get in touch with their feeling-self, which was repressed, denied or disavowed. So that self was still there; no person is without a self, and so they find what they had lost and that strengthens them."

2. "About deficits, I think of scars and structures. I liken those very early scars to driftwood. *The early trauma is indispensable to the*

development of individuality. To be normal is not a goal. We are not computers. The human experience involves the uniqueness of each creature, and that uniqueness is probably maximized by the impact of the unique traumatic exposures and the distorting influences. I don't think you want to 'undo' anything, transform perhaps. If you try to undo, it is like amputating a part of someone's being. We are what we eat; we are the blows that we endured, the genetic defect that we incorporated. I think Kohut's basic notion is too quantitative."

The third analyst in this group of training analysts at the Southern California Institute had undergone several analyses, including Kleinian analysis and supervision, and seemed at home with concepts from the different theoretical models:

"Oh yes, definitely, analysis produces internal change. It is a corrective experience, *Franz Alexander's term again.* One can have corrective experiences in analysis, and I go along with Kohut's concept of the development of new structures. I think that happens. But I also see the 'depressive position' develop in analysis, and that is usually a sign that the patient is becoming more integrated. Thus it is not only a corrective emotional experience but also a new integration process, which adds to the coherence and strength of the psyche as it develops during an analysis."

CONCLUSION

Differences in the approaches of the orientation groups to the topics of this chapter were clear-cut and statistically significant. Whereas the majority of the analysts in the different orientation groups agreed on their approaches to here-and-now transference and group differences on this topic were of low statistical significance, the subject of developmental arrests clearly reflected radically different models of early development. As one of the British Independent child analysts observed, "So much has to do with the picture you have of how a human being *should* be."

It seems that the interview/discussions distinguished between those analysts who held a relational model of development—the British Independents, the American eclectics and interpersonalists, and the self psychologists—and those who take an internalist view of early infant development. In this respect, although Klein's theory is clearly presented as object relational, the classical Freudians and British

Kleinians took a similar view, focusing almost exclusively on the intra-subjective dimension. As noted in previous chapters, with the exception of a few child analysts, analysts in these two orientation groups did not acknowledge the influence of contemporary theories of infant development. Freud's concept of primary narcissism and Klein's concept of the paranoid-schizoid position were basic to their theories of normal child development and colored their theories of therapeutic change. For the classical Freudians the object is the object of the drives, and for the Kleinians the relationship is with an internal object. Since neither the classical Freudians nor the Kleinians believe in the intersubjective, or real, relationship between analyst and patient, analytic change cannot occur through the new relationship or new experiences in the analytic situation. The classical Freudians viewed psychic change as resulting from insight and *adaptation*, and the Kleinians linked change with mourning, *reparation*, and the achievement of the "depressive position." As Dr. Braun observed, our theories of pathogenesis and the potential for analytic change recapitulate models of normal development. This connection was clearly demonstrated in discussion of this part of the interview protocol.

Chapter 12

❧❧

Dream Interpretation in Contemporary Psychoanalysis

It is hard to imagine how we can talk of human beings without a concept of the Inner. And as soon as we talk about Inner and Outer, we introduce spatial terms. The idea of the Inner, however, need not refer to some private space, hidden behind or separable from, the observable behaviors of human beings. We relate to, and perceive, human beings not as a sum of discrete behaviors or mechanical movements but as live beings, capable of self-expression, who find each other in language. If, for instance, a psychoanalyst describes someone's "inner state" as one of anger, we imagine someone being angry—that is, behaving in recognizable ways, having specific feelings and sensations, and uttering specific words and exclamations. If we say that the angry person does not show his anger, this is because other things he says and does tell us otherwise; we can, though, predict with some certainty that he is indeed angry.

Now, one of the sources of our interest in other human beings has to do with the randomness, uncertainty, and individuality of their behavior—the "unprovoked bursts of rhythm" described by the biologist and infant researcher, Colwyn Trevarthen. Trevarthen (1978) asks:

> How, physically, could the infant mind identify persons? What features of their behaviour are diagnostic of them? Intentional behaviour has a number of features that are not shared with inanimate things, and so an intentional agent may be equipped to respond to others like itself. . . . Inanimate movement runs downhill, oscillates in simple ways, bounces, but it does not surge in self-generative impulses. Anything that tends to make unprovoked bursts of rhythm, like a spot of reflected sunlight,

281

seems alive. This rhythmical vitality of movement is the first identification of live company [p. 101].

The unknown aspect of human behavior is another way of describing
what we call the Inner. If we could predict the behavior of human beings
with certainty, we would have little need for the concept of the Inner.
Indeed, it is hard to imagine that human beings, devoid of "unprovoked
bursts of rhythm," would sustain the same level of interest for us.
Psychological concepts reflect this variation among human beings in the
ways they express emotions. Take, for instance, grief: a person can be numb
or wild with grief, speechless or driven mad with sorrow. And yet the range
is not infinite; there are behavioral and linguistic criteria for identifying
these psychological states. Most of the time, most of us get on pretty well
without rigidly defined criteria for the use of psychological concepts.
Flexible criteria do not mean no criteria.

Contemporary infancy research affirms the directness of our relationship to specific human expressions and behavior. Most infants
have no difficulty in identifying the human smile. Later, doubt enters
in through the recognition of the variation in smiling faces as well as
the contexts in which smiles occur. Researchers have described the
puzzled look that infants express in the first weeks of life. With increasing awareness of the idiosyncrasies of human expressions, life becomes
more complicated, calling forth the interpretive process. Uncertainty
increases. Initially, however, we seem to have a kinship with other
people, which allows us to relate to their behaviors unmediated by
conscious or preconscious interpretation. Our concept of another
human being develops to include the idea that we cannot know
exactly what he or she is thinking and feeling. Our sense of others
reflects their spontaneity and absence of simple regularity. It is this
sense that enters into the idea of the Inner.

In this chapter, I describe psychoanalysts' notions of the dream as
they emerged in the interview/discussions. The analysts' responses to
dream interpretation reflect conscious and preconscious models of the
mind, of the Inner, and of the place where dreams and thoughts take
up residence. Surely, a dream is the most private of experiences, inviting entrance to the inner sanctum. Dream images are unique and their
conjunctions seem random and idiosyncratic. Yet, according to Freud,
dream-formations follow rules. Many contemporary practicing analysts, particularly those with backgrounds in developmental and cognitive psychology and in neurobiology and neuropsychiatry, disagree
with Freud's rules of dream formation and interpretation. For these and

other reasons, some analysts no longer regard dream material as offering privileged access to unconscious mental states.

What rules, if any, guide contemporary analysts in their interpretation of dreams, of the dreaming process, and the telling of dreams? Has there been a shift away from depth and content to breadth and process? And does this reflect a change in technique from focusing on entry into the inner sanctum and its contents to a concentration upon the current relationship? I think so. The focus on the here-and-now transference interpretation has changed analysts' use of dream material. When dreams are interpreted as manifestations of disguised thoughts and feelings about the present transference relationship, dreams are understood along a horizontal as opposed to vertical dimension. Relational, present-time interpretations flatten and extend laterally the condensed and dispersed associations to dream content. The dream, like the mind, loses depth both historically and as an imaginative elaboration of everyday experience. And with this loss, the fragility, specificity, and complexity of dreams disperse into more simple affective and relational transactions. That none of the analysts in this sample talked about imagination as an ingredient of empathy and understanding reflects, perhaps, the contemporary approach to the interpretation of dreams as part of the transference traffic of everyday analytic life. If, also, analysts are no longer concerned with the detailed histories of their patients, the idiosyncratic imagery of dreams has less to reveal about the mind of one of the two participants in the analytic relationship. And perhaps that means that imagination is, after all, less central to the analyst's creativity than is his capacity for empathic or projective identification. He is no longer called on to delve into the strange contents of a mind so different from his own.

Discussions with the 65 analysts about their attitudes to dream interpretation indicate that contemporary analysts have indeed moved away from Freud's original model. The topography of dreams has changed. With the exception of a handful of the Freudian and British Independent analysts, the majority of analysts in all the orientation groups noted that they no longer focused on gathering associations to individual elements in the dream. It seems that relational theories and theories of affect (for example the self-psychological concept of self states) have introduced an entirely new approach to symbolism and interpretation. This is particularly true when the analyst interprets the dream as representing the affective state of the dreamer.

The topic of dreams was discussed at the end of the interviews. The analysts were asked whether they looked at dreams "as any other material in the session" or whether they regarded dreams as providing "privileged access" to the patient's unconscious mind. The interpretation of "manifest" and "latent" content was also discussed, particularly as it related to the technique of free association and the interpretation of dreams within the transference. The analysts' reflections on their technique of dream interpretation were idiosyncratic and often personal; this lack of homogeneity is particularly interesting in the light of the preeminence Freud originally accorded to dream interpretation. For example, the following statements were made by two British Freudian analysts: "Most dreams mystify me, most of the time. . . . To the extent that I can use them, I see dreams as bits and pieces of ongoing work. I rarely understand them." And, "I personally don't think I am very good at dreams. Some people are, but it may be because I am not that I don't go much for latent content." Others, on the other hand, responded with enthusiasm: "Well, I love dreams. They are the royal road to the unconscious. I think they are wonderful, and my patients know that. So they bring lots of dreams."

These personal and heterogeneous approaches were confirmed by the statistical analyses. When the frequencies of the different categories of dream interpretation were associated with orientation, the responses were heterogeneous for all five orientation groups. Neither the orientation factors nor the 20 individual sources of influence listed on the P.O.Q. were meaningfully related to the analysts' responses to dream interpretation. Geographical location was not significant either, although there was slightly more consistency in the approaches of the San Francisco Freudians and the older London Freudians. In terms of orientation, the views of the classical Freudians and the British Kleinians also showed slightly more consistency than the other orientation groups. Apart from differences in approach to the content and telling of dreams, it is interesting to note that, with the exception of the self psychologists, the American analysts for the most part expressed more articulate and explicit views than did their British colleagues. This might be explained by the fact that, until recently, mainstream American training has been organized around two fairly coherent schools of thought, Freud and ego psychology. For Freud, of course, dream interpretation was the foundation of psychoanalysis. Object relational ideas have been part of the British scene for at least 50 years, and this may account for a rather looser approach to dream interpretation, particularly among some of the Independent analysts with backgrounds in literature. Analysts with backgrounds in literary criticism, for example Ella Sharpe and Marion Milner, have challenged Freud's theories of symbolism and symbol formation. The views of the British Independents are more congruent with the current trend in American psychoanalysis toward a relational bias when formulating interpretations.

Because of the highly individual nature of responses of analysts in all the groups, this chapter is organized around qualitative differences in approaches to dream interpretation. The main distinction is between those analysts who regard dreams as "special" and those who treat them "as any other material." Those taking the latter approach often felt that dreams were meaningful and worth pursuing, but they did not think of dreams as a unique mental process, following its own rules of formation and elaboration. This second group of analysts tended either to emphasize the centrality of the transference relationship in dream interpretation or to view dream products from a more ego-psychological point of view. From the latter perspective, dreams, symptoms, and transference manifestations are all "compromise formations" between conflicting intrapsychic forces. For the sake of clarity of presentation, the examples in the two sections of this chapter are organized according to geographical location and orientation group, although this organization is not indicative of statistical significance.

THE DREAM AS "THE ROYAL ROAD"

Only 9% of the analysts were rated as believing that dreams give "privileged access" to the unconscious. However, 30% felt that dreams were in "some sense special," although the majority of these analysts acknowledged a markedly reduced focus on the latent or hidden content of dreams. Despite these ratings, there was little consistency in the reasons given by the analysts for taking this particular approach.

American Freudian Analysts

The first three excerpts are taken from interviews with the San Francisco Freudian analysts. The first analyst, also a child analyst, was one of the few analysts to talk about the "play" element in dreams and dream interpretation.

1. "I do still think of dreams as special, but perhaps that is because I like to *play*. There's a puzzle side to it, but I also think that dreams are *creative*, they really are. In the literature, a lot of people disagree with those who say dreams are creative acts, but

I think there is a creative process involved in the dream itself. Secondary revision enters into it for sure, but it is very important if you can get a person to play with the dream by bringing in their associations and catching onto a theme in the dream. I also do not discount the manifest content. Since it incorporates the secondary revision, it brings in the defenses. There are many different configurations in a dream. I will also think, What is the transference load in the dream? And sometimes the transference is weighing right in there. I like dreams, and the people who are in treatment with me, they catch on. So I have to watch out for that because someone will say, 'I've got a dream for you.' And then dreams become distance-making.

"Then, there is another aspect to dreams which is very like play with a kid. Sometimes I would rather a kid is able to use toys or drawings than coming right at me because then there is often not enough elbow room. The excitement pops up too strongly, and I want to have a thought process going on. If the kid is right into it at my body, then it's not going to work well for them. It's the same with a dream, you can sometimes handle the situation through dreams before the person gets to more immediate and primitive actions. Then there is also the powerful, regressive side of dreams. The dream takes them to a regression but acts as a modulator so that you can go back and then glide away."

2.   "Greenson wrote this paper 'On the Exceptional Position of the Dream.' It is a rejoinder to a paper of Ernst Kris written in the 1960s in which Kris said in essence that dreams were like anything else. Greenson presented his paper in New York and then tore apart someone from Kris's study group, saying, 'The problem with you is that you don't understand dreams.' Now, I don't go over every bit piece by piece like Freud did. But I think dreams are fascinating, and they give us a window into unconscious material. We get to this in other ways, but the dream is one of the best places to find it. If you are a patient of mine and you want to get me to talk a bit, you start talking about dreams! I think we do useful work around dreams, but it might be slightly iatrogenic because people learn you are more interested in some things than others. I like to think about my own dreams, the whole idea of trying to fathom what all this means. I don't think that it is an accident that Freud first thought of the interpretation of dreams. From antiquity, people have been fascinated . . . 'What the hell is all this about?' "

3. "I am changing my thinking a little in the past year or two in view of recent comments, particularly those of Charles Brenner, whom I respect. I think Brenner leans too far in saying dreams are the same as any other material. That is wrong. I still believe that the dream is the royal road to the unconscious. My whole analytic life, I have paid so much attention to dreams, I do find them very valuable and I spend extra time on a dream; even doing a little instructing. Because no patient wants to interpret his dream; what the patient wants to do is to explain and get away from his dream. *Universally people use the dream as resistance.* They will report a dream and then say, 'Well, that dream means so and so.' Now, that is a resistance, because they don't have the faintest idea what the dream means. And so, sometimes, I still say, though less than previously, 'Well, you know the dream had a lot of parts. Tell me about some of the parts.' This is to get the old-fashioned associations to the dream elements. Then the patient unrepresses the day residue that they were not thinking about. Then they say, 'You know, two days ago, I had a fight with my wife' . . . or 'Oh, I remember, I saw that little scene on TV.' Well, that is the day residue that was dynamically unconscious or preconscious, but the patient is not thinking about it until the analyst works on the dream. Then he says, 'That guy on the TV show, he looked like my brother. I haven't thought about my dead brother in 20 years.'

"What I have not read anywhere is this sequence I am talking about: the patient puts together the dream element, the day residue, and the memory of the dead brother from 20 years ago and then adds, 'Oh, you know, by the way, I sometimes think you remind me of my brother.' That sequence really happens, and there is no more powerful demonstration to the patient of the unconscious than this sequence of events. That is why I like dreams, their power to demonstrate the unconscious."

One of the American Freudian analysts practicing in New York focused on the process of secondary revision in dreams:

"I focus on the secondary revision. But I do have a different way of viewing it. I think the dream is not the same as anything else in the session in one simple respect—it occurs in sleep whereas the other material occurs in waking. I have been very interested in *states of awareness.* Dreams and secondary revisions are one of the areas on the *borderline between consciousness and unconsciousness,* waking and sleeping. This is particularly fascinating to me. In dreams, you can see the actual process of the secondary revision occurring."

A Freudian child analyst practicing in Los Angeles stated:

"I do feel dreams are special. When patients give me dreams, I usually write them down because of the *words of the dream*. I don't write notes when patients are sitting face to face but if they tell me dreams, I do. I don't always think I can make sense of them, and I always approach a dream with a bit of anxiety. My first response when a patient tells a dream is always, What in the hell could that be about? What in the name of heaven? I just don't know. Then if you have a patient who is really working, it gradually becomes clearer. But, with patients who can't work that way, I would rather not try because I am probably going to be way off. And with a patient who never dreams, I think there is something really missing in the treatment. What does it mean that a patient doesn't dream?"

British Freudians

The first three excerpts are from interviews with British Freudians in the younger group (qualified over two years, but not yet training analysts). Excerpts 4 and 5 are from experienced training analysts aged 50–65. The last two are from interviews with two senior Freudian analysts, both of whom trained with Anna Freud. These analysts clearly focused more on the interpretation of latent content than did the younger, more recently qualified, Freudians.

1.   "I see dreams as a bit more special than other material, not a run-of-the-mill type of thing. I see dreams as giving very quick, immediate clues to what has been going on which you can't get in the ordinary material. Yes, I interpret the latent content in terms of *condensation, displacement, and reversal*, but I also take up both manifest and latent content in terms of transference."

2.   "I think dreams are very special because people can become much more aware of how *overdetermined* everything is through dreams than with any other material. The interpretation of dreams is one of the most mutative of analytic experiences."

3. "I certainly see dreams as different and special, and also as very obscure and *coded*. I don't think it is very easy to understand dreams. Dreams can also be used in a defensive way, for instance if a patient constantly brings dreams and does not bring in their current life at all."

4. "I'm relatively suspicious of the manifest content of any dream, and I almost always wait for the patient's associations before interpreting. If the patient does not associate, then I'll use what went on before or after the telling of the dream as the associations. I follow John Klauber's views on this, the way he talks about the whole session as an association to the dream. I still don't quite understand why there is so much focus on the manifest content of the dream and also on the transference. What I think people miss is the essence of what Freud was talking about, *the disguising function* of the manifest content and the *wish* buried underneath that."

5. "I try not to get too absorbed in the manifest content of dreams. But, so far as latent content is concerned, I personally don't think I am very good at dreams. Some people are, but, because I'm not, I don't go so much for the latent content. I think more about the way dreams show a pattern, a wish, or motive. The Kleinians are very good at manifest content. Often, though, I find that fragments of dreams are very good, and I can use them and that can be more helpful. For example, 'I remember I was alone in a room. It was like a casino' . . . that sort of fragment can be marvelous and lead to all sorts of associations. Dreams that go on for more than 10 minutes, you just can't use them. Nobody does the sort of Sherlock Holmes-type of dream interpretation now, following up all the elements. Also I think it is not just the dream that is important but the reporting of the dream, because whatever the dreamer tells is already subject to *secondary revision*. In the telling, dreams are linked with all sorts of other material in the session."

The next excerpt is from the interview with Dr. Smith:

"I would have the old-fashioned or Freudian view that interpreting the dream is a very special, royal road into the unconscious. I would try to get associations to the manifest content and see how the dream linked to the previous day or to the more distant childhood past. Then you get to what Freud called the latent themes. Once you have gained more experience with the patient, you don't have to go through the details every time. The only time I see the dream as fitting in the transference is when the dream is very obviously about the analyst. Just as with any important areas of life, the patient will begin to dream about the analyst. Sometimes you can see the disguise and displacement in that a figure in the dream probably represents the analyst. That happens once the patient gets into the transference neurosis stage, then they frequently dream about the analyst. But, by English standards, my interpretations of dreams would be classified as extra-transference. I would interpret the dream as *intrapsychic*, as a very complex message from the person's unconscious which I would see as relatively independent of me just as it is in thousands of people that are dreaming but not in analysis. It is the old Freudian approach of interpreting the unconscious as it emerges in dreams."

The elderly analyst who had trained and worked with Anna Freud noted:

"No, I don't take up dreams in terms of the transference. I find dream interpretation very important and different. The transference plays its part, but I think the central point is the association to the *dream content*. And something which is on the decline in the teaching of dream interpretation is the essential linking of the content with the day-residue. If you link the dream to the *day residue*, the dream opens up so much more. People who interpret without the day residue are simply losing the main reason for having a dream. The day residue was at the very heart of Anna Freud's seminars. Anna Freud believed that you could not understand what the dream was about if you ignored such a little thing as the day residue. For instance, a patient says, 'Gosh, yesterday somebody trod on my foot in the underground,' and this patient was furious but felt he had to be polite. His whole conflict was in the dream but is filled out by the memory of the incident from the day before."

Those seven excerpts show the ongoing relevance of a number of Freud's principles of dream interpretation: the interpretation of latent content according to the rules of condensation, displacement, reversal; the disguising function of dreams; dreams as disguised wish fulfillments; the principle of overdetermination of mental phenomena; the central importance of free association to analytic interpretation; the process of secondary revision in the telling of dreams; the investigation of day residues; the meaning of not dreaming in analysis; the link between dreams and regression; the modulation of primitive material through dreams; the mystery of dreams since antiquity; and the creativity of dreams and the play element in dream interpretation.

American Eclectic Analysts

The eclectic analysts use a variety of models. These are reflected in the excerpts from the interviews with analysts in the three different cities. One of the New York interpersonal analysts observed:

"I love dreams. They are the royal road to the unconscious. I think they are wonderful and I find them very helpful. How do I deal with them? That is the question. I do regard them as giving special information. I try to stay as closely as possible to the *manifest* data. Then we have the associations. If the dream makes utterly no sense, I will ask more traditional questions like, 'What were you thinking of?' 'Why this?' If the patient is just opaque about it, there will be something in the session that will at least set off an association of mine to the dream. It will bring the dream back again. Obviously, the patient associates to the dream, but I also have no trouble from a technical point of view in myself associating to the dream. I will see the patient as being every person in the dream, and sometimes the transference elements will be the focus. The reason I stay closely to the manifest content is so that we don't get lost too much in esoteric symbolism."

A Los Angeles analyst:

"I do think they are special, but not that they are utterly sacred. I just proceed from the obvious. They are *created and experienced in a different mode of consciousness*. They are encoded and need to be understood as Freud did. They are a sort of 'window to the soul.' And there is much more than that. Dreams bear the imprimatur of an individual's style, his ego functioning, even though they occur in a different state of consciousness. Dreams are readily identifiable; each person's dream is different. They are virtually the only data that I transcribe. I have two patients who do not want me to record their dreams; they feel that my writing is an interference. Others protest, but I disregard their protests. I also think that dreams have a very special power of organizing and communicating important issues. Self psychologists don't highlight dreams. Therapy can occur without dreams, but I feel that it tends to be more inelegant, amorphous, more adrift. Despite their phantas-magoric quality, dreams give a coherence and order to therapy. They are nodal phenomena and also epiphanic—from dreams new directions often occur. I think that those analysts who want to reduce dreams to any other associative or transferential material are mistaken. Dreams include those things, but they are unique forms of representation, containing the most intimate kinds of meanings and dilemmas in the individual's life. They are a special form of intersubjective communication too. *Those who don't dream, don't remember, report, or work on dreams, they are the most resistant patients. In my experience, such patients correlate with resistance.*

"Latent and manifest content—these are relative terms. An analytically experienced person who dreams of a policeman is much different from a more naive patient who dreams of a police-man. The first might say, 'Well, there you go again. What are you clubbing me for?' Is that latent? The second might think much more about the policeman as a superegoish, punitive, menacing figure, and for that patient the transference is much more con-cealed or submerged. And so I think of all these things—rela-tivism, relativism, relativism."

Dr. Furnham stated:

"I treat dreams differently from other material. They are the royal road. But each analyst has a different way of working with dreams. I pay a lot of attention to the manifest content. I will go over it in order to fix it. I try *to identify the main action* in the dream. The main action is the clue I start with as to what was going on that night for that patient. And I mean I start with a clue. It is not settled yet. Then, from paying a great deal of atten-tion to the manifest content, you get associations and therefore more clues as to what is actually going on."

British Independent Analysts

Although the views of the British Independent analysts on dream interpretation showed some variation, nevertheless the overall per-spective of this group was more consistent with that of the British Freudian than that of their Kleinian colleagues. All the Independent analysts quoted in this section had had some training or supervision either with Anna Freud herself or with analysts trained at the Anna Freud Centre. In answering the P.O.Q., all acknowledged considerable influence by Anna Freud.

1.   "I do think that dream interpretation has changed a lot, but *the point is that patients themselves value dreams.* They bring them in as special. I certainly don't agree with the people who treat dreams just as any other kind of material."

2.   "I think I am more classical. Some people just interpret dreams as any material, but I think the dream is what you might call privileged. I don't like to interpret a dream without associa-tions, although I will sometimes say, 'I will tell you what this dream reminds me of . . .'—more of a sort of to-and-fro."

3.   "I don't treat dreams as exactly on a par with any other mater-ial because I think that *the form of representation* in dreams is impor-tant in its own right. They are structured and developed quite differently from day material. And there are times when dreams have much more to do with the *presentation of a piece of history* than the present state of the analytic relationship and transference."

4.   "Dreams as communication, that's Kleinian. I sometimes feel that the patient uses the dream as communication, but at other times the patient wants to work with the analyst toward under-standing the dream. And then it is not just communication. As long as you believe in the dynamic unconscious, there are latent meanings. But I don't ask for associations to bits of the dream. Only very occasionally do I ask, 'What do you think that means?'"

5.   "I'd say for a start, and I think my patients would agree with me, that dreams are not my forte. But, still, I do try to get to the latent content, because I do think they are a different form of communication and that they follow rules of their own."

The following excerpt is from the interview with a child analyst who had worked for many years at the Anna Freud Centre and the Tavistock Clinic:

"I'm just interested in dreams, so my patients tend to get influ-enced by my interest. But I try to link them up with the whole session and the series of sessions that have preceded the dream. But the link could be a *developmental link to a childhood scene*. And I would take up the transference aspects of the dream more often than not. And about this, I am interested in the *analyst's undisguised appearance* in a dream. One patient repetitively brought me into his dreams over at least three years. He kept returning to me in his dreams. I think there is a very close association with *trauma* when a patient persistently dreams about the analyst. Also, these dreams are often linked with *separation*, rather crucially. The patient is summoning the analyst to them in the dream. Not that they are doing analysis in the dream, but they are having tea, or having a chat, or showing the analyst around the house. The summoning of the analyst is very closely related with separation, anxiety, and of course control. If you have created a break and the patient can summon you, then the patient has got that much more control. There is an infantile aspect to these dreams."

It seems that free association remains an important feature in the interpretive approach of British Independent analysts. In addition to the more classical Freudian emphasis on free association, this focus is consistent with Independent concepts of "psychic space," "transitional space," and a "play" area. Unlike many of their Kleinian colleagues and analysts who interpret from a relational perspective, the British Independents seemed to value a more "private" area of the self, along the lines developed by Balint, Kahn, Milner, and Winnicott. The acknowledgment of a "hidden" and "private" self is consistent with the attitude expressed by a number of the Independents in the study toward the value of *silence* in relation to free association. The question of the analysts' technique in responding to silences on the part of the patient was discussed in the interviews. The analysts' opinions on the value, or lack of value, of silence emerged in relation to discussions of dream interpretation. In keeping with some of Balint's observations on technique—for example, his emphasis on "the unobtrusive analyst"—the Independents were less likely than the Freudian and Kleinian analysts to take up silence as resistance. A number of the Independent analysts stated that, in comparison with their Kleinian colleagues, they were more ready to wait and listen before jumping in with transference interpretations. They also saw themselves as expressing more respect toward the dreamer of dreams, that is, their patients, than analysts who interpreted dreams as resistance or transference enactments.

American Self Psychologists

A number of analysts of different orientations commented on the lack of attention they felt self psychologists paid to dream material. It seems that self psychologists tend to define latent content in terms of the patient's "unconscious organizing principles." A number of the self psychologists also referred to "self-state" dreams as describing affective states of mind. Although the self psychologists did seem to interpret dreams very differently from analysts in the other orientation groups in this study, nevertheless many did believe that dreams are privileged. And, in this respect, their views were not unlike those of colleagues in the other orientation groups.

1. "I would try to take up dreams in the transference, and I still think of dreams as having a somewhat special quality. This is because of the proximity of dreams to experiences that might be difficult to talk about. I certainly don't see them as worth spending four sessions on or as something toward which I would bias someone's experience. I pay some attention to latent content, though what interests me is the kind of *self-state* implications of dreams."

2. "I still think that dreams are special because I think of them as unfettered psychological products par excellence. They provide a special access to the patient's *unconscious organizing principles*. That is what I think of as latent content."

3. "I think of dreams as special. Things are disguised in dreams, but, because they get through the censorship, they are revealed. I would look at the latent content more than the transference. Some dreams are what are called 'self-state' dreams. To me that means descriptions of states of mind. This is the essential part of the dream. But, even with self-state dreams, there are specific, idiosyncratic elements, why a person chose a particular picture, etc. I don't focus on that all the time, but I think there is more to dreams than just the surface content."

4. "I think they are special and that a special meaning is associated with the dream that may not be revealed in any other material. *They often come unrevised.*"

5. "I am more interested in *the patient's experience of his dreams than the content.* To what extent does the patient recognize that

the dream is significant or illuminating? Where does the dream fall in the ongoing process? I am not interested in any concept that dreams are the royal road. There are patients who do feel that way, especially ones in the creative field. I have one very depressed patient and when he begins to emerge from the depression, he begins to dream. He is also creative. Other patients do not have this facility and that is not because of resistance. I apply the same procedure as with any material: what part do dreams and dreaming play in the patient's subjective experience? I do not impose an artificial framework on the dream.

"I do think dreams represent, in general, the patient's organizing activity in a relatively pure form. What is called latent content is the part played by the *invariant organizing principles* that are reflected in the dream. An example: a patient dreams of going into a room and everything is in a mess, all piled up. The feeling of the dream is that it is a hopeless task to clear things up. That is purely subjective. The patient feels that what he has to do in order to amount to anything or to find a place for himself in the world is hopeless. That is an organizing principle at work. Or a patient dreams he is driving a car and all of a sudden the car stops and begins rolling back. This is the organizing principle reflected in the dream as well as specific elements of his experience. This is an organizing experience, an accelerating psychological process of perceiving some obstacle, not being able to go any further and then an unmodified slip backward, falling into a pit. The manifest elements are reactive to the events and preoccupations of the day, and these appear in some form or other.

Freud had the courage, understanding, and time to mess with dreams. That was what he was interested in and his patients cooperated with that. Whether it did them any of the good he thought it did, that is questionable. It might be a worthwhile endeavor to try to understand why the elements take the form they do. But that is a creative enterprise. And it would also require a particular patient in treatment, and I would never be sure that that patient was not complying with me."

British Kleinian Analysts

Only three of the Kleinian analysts interviewed regarded dreams as privileged; they focused on associations to latent content as well as transference. Two of the analysts (excerpts 1 and 2) were child ana-

lysts. The first excerpt is from the interview with Dr. Martin, the analyst who was the most widely influenced of the Kleinian group:

1. "I think dreams are great, basically. If a patient can bring
dreams and really work on them and look at the latent content,
they are a marvelous part of analysis. I think they are tremendous. They do reveal to both analyst and patient bits of material
which are vital to understanding the psychic make-up of the
patient. One is also aware at the same time of why that patient is
bringing a dream at a particular time. But that is combined in the
associations."

2. "Well, as a matter of fact, I'm actually more with Freud on
that. Obviously dream interpretation has changed in that one
has always to be ready to look at how a dream might be being
used. They can be *lures* and *attempts to get the analyst to do something*. . . . But I think they are really the royal road to the unconscious, really useful. And if you can get to the latent content, I
would treat that in a sense as any other material, but dreams do
have a quality that is a bit different."

3. "I still think in terms of latent content and not just taking
the dream up in the transference. How much I focus on dreams
depends so much on what else is going on in the session. For
instance, how much the patient goes back to the dream and
whether I think he is avoiding something more important, or getting stuck. I might just leave a dream and we might come back to
it a few days later, or perhaps never. It is more haphazard. I never
think, 'Have I done this or taken up that?' Sometimes, at the end
of a session, I will say to myself, I wonder what he meant? I never
asked him and he never said."

In describing themselves as taking a "more Freudian approach,"
these Kleinian analysts seemed to mean that they still interpreted
latent content in contrast to the here-and-now transference relationship. Other aspects of Freudian technique, for example, the interpretation of the day residue or free association, did not seem to be of
particular interest. In two of the excerpts just quoted, dreams are
described as "lures" and "attempts to get the analyst to do something."
These terms are consistent with the contemporary Kleinian view of
dreams as enactments and forms of action. Dreams are regarded as
"acting in" in the transference.

THE UNPRIVILEGED DREAM

This section covers the approach of those analysts who broadly take up dreams "as any other material." In other words, although they regard dreams as important, they do not think that dreams offer a uniquely privileged access to the unconscious mind. These analysts tend to interpret dreams within the overarching context of the here-and-now transference relationship. In presenting examples of the second approach, I follow the same order as the preceding section: American Freudians, British Contemporary Freudians, American eclectics, British Independents, and British Kleinians. Self psychologists are not represented in this section; although they tended to interpret dreams as representing immediate affect states or self-states, they did believe that dreams offered a unique access to unconscious material.

American Freudian Analysts

The first five excerpts are from interviews with Freudian analysts in San Francisco. All were strongly influenced by ego-psychological ideas as well as Freud's three models. Many of the senior San Francisco training analysts had been supervised or taught by Erik Erikson and Merton Gill. Additional individual sources of influence were the New York analysts Charles Brenner and Martin Stein.

1. "Dreams are no longer the royal road to the unconscious and, anyway, you know Freud never really said that they were. What he said was that dreams are the *royal road to the understanding of how the unconscious works*, which is quite different. The misinterpretation is more relevant to creative people than to analysts. I think that dreams are used much like other material. And anyway transference and resistance are much more applicable to the analytic process than dream interpretation. Historically, when Freud wrote *The Interpretation of Dreams*, analysts were interested in content. Now there has been a significant change, and the *focus has shifted more and more from content to process* so dreams are not necessarily seen as useful. I said this at a public meeting, and I got a letter from somebody who was furious at my suggestion, 'Dear Sir, You Err'."

2. "My approach comes more from my American training, the American school, which is yes, dreams are important material

but they don't have a special character that makes them the preeminent road in the way Freud believed. In Freud's day, there was less concern with character, ego functioning, the defensive apparatus. My approach is that dreams are material, and so are fantasies, the events of yesterday—whatever the patient brings. Freud wrote the Dora case to illustrate his theory of dreams. I am also influenced by Erik Erikson's paper on the dream specimen. In that paper, Erikson reanalyzed the Irma dream to show how much you can do with the manifest content. Erikson pointed out that our preoccupation with unraveling the dream work to get to the latent content has made us bypass all that is there in the manifest content and structure of the dream. To me, of all his work, Erikson's dream paper is the most brilliant. Many of those who have made a cult of Erikson don't know this technical, clinical, analytic paper. It is an extraordinary paper."

3.   "I think that dreams are extremely valuable in relation to transference. There are many facets to dreams, but the one common thread is the way that dreams reveal transference phenomena, transference needs, which can't be expressed directly. But these can be said in quotes as it were through dreams. It is like, 'Let me tell you about a movie.' The dream is a compromise formation like every other communication. It has both the expression and the defense. So, primarily, dreams inform me of what is going on in the transference. They are much less valuable from the standpoint of genetic reconstruction. Also, there are big differences between patients in terms of their work on dreams. But I find them very informative. I find my own dreams informative. Now, they are not being analyzed because nobody can analyze himself. But you can learn something just because the dream is a little bit ahead of you sometimes. You think, Aha! Now I know what was bothering me."

4.   "I still take a midway position; dreams are like any other material and they are special. What I find incredibly intriguing about dreams is how to work with a patient on them. I don't just do resistance interpretations about the elements they are or are not interpreting. *I let the patients go with it.* I am very respectful of dreams being a special way in. But I am also tremendously respectful about fantasies or breaks in the flow, when someone stops talking. Or when suddenly there is a little

tension in someone's voice. These breaks are exciting to me. I think of them as the dreams of the hour. There is always a spot in the hour where something breaks down, or the person slips into primary process, and that is where I wake up. And I make a distinction between the dream that you start the hour with and that is elaborate—'This is an important dream that I want to tell you'—versus the dream that comes up that was forgotten. You have made an interpretation and the patient says, 'Oh yes, that reminds me. . . .' Then I am off into left field, excited about that."

The last excerpt is from the interview with Dr. Friedland, the San Francisco Freudian analyst:

"Well, from everything I have said, I am sure that you would deduce that I look for the latent in everything. The dream is a good place to look, but so is every place else. I wouldn't look a gift dream in the mouth, as they say! But my attention is always to what somebody is expressing. I am not focused on getting a dream. Most analysts aren't anymore, you know, taking notes and trying to get to the true dream. Because if there is anything we should really know by now, it is that people love to tell dreams because dreams have got nothing to do with them. 'There is the dream that came to me, and I can't remember it.' Or, 'I do remember it now from my notes, but it makes no sense to me. You do something with it.' Or, 'I would be glad to free associate all day long about the dream and when we finish, it will be an interesting dream.' Or, 'Here is this fragment of a dream, but there is no use talking about it because it is only a fragment and the dream escapes me.'

"So, my attention is to what someone is telling me, whether they are telling me a dream or not. The text of what they are telling me is distorted whether by sleep or in waking. I am willing to take advantage of a dream if I can understand something. But the upshot is, no, I don't make much of a distinction between dreams and other material. In fact, I feel that, more often than not, *dreams are a source of intense resistance*, or rather an expression of resistance. The source was there a long time ago. It is there all the time. But in the shared interest in dreams, resistances can be exploited, misread, and remain unidentified. It is good stuff, like working on a jigsaw puzzle together, and it is certainly a holding environment! I don't want to seem too skeptical or cynical. I respect dreams as much as anyone, but I don't enshrine them. It is a good hobby, writing down dreams. Someone may learn something, but then the question is, are they really learning? Or are they not learning more from some apparently trivial thing that happened during their waking life. I see hallowing the dream as hallowing a resistance to self-observation. If you asked me, 'Do you think it is worthwhile to observe myself closely walking, standing, sitting up, or lying down?' Well, yes, I try to do that. Writing it down does not do it for me. Look at me analyzing my dreams or someone else's dreams does not necessarily say that I am a closer observer of what can be observed."

Dr. Friedland's views on dream interpretation were characteristically skeptical and somewhat dismissive. The following two excerpts are from interviews with New York Freudians. The first analyst is one of the third-generation training analysts at the Columbia Institute who had experienced considerable exposure to British ideas, particularly those of Herbert Rosenfeld and Donald Winnicott:

"We had a study group with one of my supervisors to look at the function dreams were playing in analytic work. We all came up with the feeling that the most useful purpose of the dream was that it enhanced our sense of conviction about the interpretation of certain material. Very often, I may have a hunch, and then when I see certain material emerging in the dream associations that I was playing with a week ago, I will interpret. But I think you can also be seduced by dreams like any other material."

The following excerpt is from the interview with Dr. Braun, the senior New York Freudian analyst:

"If you deal mostly with the transference, you fall into the danger of imposing a set of interpretations on a dream where it may not be relevant, or where the transference element is not the central issue. In this context, we should look at a well-forgotten statement of Freud: he said, 'Transference appears in the course of an analysis as a resistance.' What did he mean? At that time, he meant it in a special sense, that the therapeutic task was to get the patient to remember the traumatic events. He said that as the patient is getting closer and closer to the traumatic event concerning something that happened with the primary object, in place of that primary object, the analyst is mentioned in a similar context. So, sometimes the dream deals with the primary object, and sometimes with the specific defense called transference. People who just impose transference interpretations miss the whole significance of transference."

British Freudians

The following two excerpts illustrate the thinking of the Freudian analysts, the minority in the British Freudian group, who value dreams but nevertheless interpret them in much the same way as any material in the session:

1. "I think they are special in that they are a more undefended aspect of psychic life, but I take them up as part of the material of the session. I don't have the technique or the patience to interpret dreams in the way Freud did. I've found that dreams are often used defensively. A patient dreams and dreams and does not associate but just plops them down and says, 'O.K., you do something with this.' I would take up what the patient is doing with the dreams, not the content."

2. "I interpret the dream as occurring within the session, not as a more profound or deeper phenomenon. I don't make the distinction between latent and manifest content. I look for *the anxieties* that are being expressed. We don't interpret the wishes so much now. I do look at dreams as providing a picture of the primitive mind, the early structure of development. But you can't use that picture much. I don't ask for the associations. Recently a patient said, 'You are not interested in my dream.' I see that as part of the association. I am often free associating, I rely a lot on my own free associations."

American Eclectic Analysts

The first excerpt is from the interview with a Los Angeles analyst who had undergone a classical training, then worked for many years at the Menninger Clinic, before undergoing Kleinian analysis and supervision.

"I think of dreams as both special and as expressing the transference relationship. I do think of them as a window into the
unconscious depths. But I don't make any special emphasis on
the elements of the dream. I interpret when and why they come
up in sessions and also what was going on in the sessions before
the dream. I don't know how latent dreams are anyway. Take a
dream where the patient is in his mother's kitchen, stuffing a
turkey, banging into the turkey's opening with his fist. He
demonstrates the movement in the session. Well, apart from the
manifest content of the mother's kitchen, the eating, etc., there
is the aggression, the punching into the turkey. You could say
latent but it is not very latent, it is very close to the surface."

The next excerpt is taken from the interview with a Los Angeles
analyst strongly influenced by self-psychological ideas, specifically
those of Bernard Brandchaft and Robert Stolorow.

"I view all material as a dream in a sense. In essence, I always
look at the day residue in terms of the feelings evoked. I look at
dreams as a process. *It isn't the meaning of the elements in the dream
but rather the process of trying to discover the meanings that I find
useful.* I think dreams are in a sense privileged in that they con-
dense what is going on in a particular moment. But I don't do a
lot of dream interpretation. When I think of the way Kohut
interprets dreams, I realize I do less of that. I find his interpretations comprehensive but long winded. When interpretations are
so detailed, they are distancing. I just hear a dream as another
association in the hour so I don't particularly focus on the latent
content."

The following excerpts are from interviews with two New York analysts who, although classically trained and well-known members of the
American Psychoanalytic Association and the International Psycho-
Analytical Association, were classified within the American eclectic
cluster. Interestingly, both analysts link their lack of focus on dreams
with personal lack of interest, or difficulty, in working with dreams.

1.   "*Most dreams mystify me, most of the time.* What I end up doing
with most dreams is picking on those pieces that are available for
work that has been ongoing and in relation to which the dreams
provide us with some in-depth commentary. That commentary
might be transferential, but I don't have to drag in that the dream

relates to me. So, to the extent that I can use dreams, I see them as bits and pieces of ongoing work. I rarely understand them."

2. "No, I don't see dreams as a special communication. I see them as part of free association because they are so mired in secondary elaboration. I always try to get to the day residue. To me, the day residue is as important as the analysis of the dream. If you get to the day residue, then you have a real conflict to anchor the dream on. I also have to say that I am not very good at dream interpretation. I am not as good at it as I would like to be, and, therefore, I make less use of dreams than other people. I can't offer an explanation for that. *I think Freud's notion of the dream as the royal road is a questionable concept.* The dream as transference? I have made use of that idea, but I don't emphasize transference very heavily. If you were to criticize my work, it would be that I don't work as intensively as I might on dreams. Maybe it is because patients have a great deal of difficulty working with dreams—at least mine do—that there are very few dreams I have been able to work on to any reasonable conclusion."

British Independent Analysts

Members of the British Independent and Contemporary Freudian groups are not well represented in this section for the reasons discussed earlier. The views of these two groups were consistent with one another in that both groups accorded privileged status to dreams. Both valued the process of free association and a relatively unobtrusive stance on the part of the analyst. At times, this stance was communicated through a silent presence. The silence indicated that the analyst felt it seemed more important to wait for the patient's associations, than to connect dream material to the transference relationship. Dr. Matheson, whose views bridge both Freudian and Kleinian approaches, follow:

"I would want to have a certain amount of association to a dream. I would want to know what it means to the patient, whether it can take the patient back into the past so that he can recover aspects of the past in order to help the patient rediscover more of himself. But the function of the dream in the relationship between us is also extremely important. Nowadays, both are vital. But, on the whole, I think I usually focus more on what is going on in the analysis. Nowadays, there is much less attention to getting back to the past and we think it is much more difficult to get access to it."

British Kleinians

Although the associations between approaches to dream interpretation and group orientation were statistically significant, not a large proportion of the Kleinian analysts disagreed with the view of dreams as privileged. As already noted, they placed greater emphasis on transference and enactment than on free association. Clearly, dreams were linked to, and viewed as expressions of, the psychotic parts of the personality. As such, a number of Kleinians viewed them as more real, or "ordinary," than waking life. It is in this primitive area of the mind that the Kleinian analysts expect to do their most effective analytic work. Here are some examples from interviews with younger Kleinians:

"Actually I would turn it around. *I only treat dreams as ordinary material*, but then I think it is helpful to think of a patient's communication as a kind of dream sequence. I take up why the patient is bringing the dream at this time, what it is telling me about the transference."

When I questioned this analyst about her approach to latent content, she seemed vague and eventually answered in a hesitant manner, "Yes, yes . . . if I understood it, which I don't always do."
Two more examples from interviews with younger analysts:

1. "My training has been a more quick way, not like Freud, who would work at a dream over many sessions. In terms of latent content, I try to see if I can arrive at some alive meaning about the dream. But one also has one's resistances to things like dreams and the operation of the unconscious. Maybe, then, we can learn from Freud."

2. "Yes, I do think the emphasis has changed and now is much more on the transference. I would try if I could to take up both the function and the content. But *patients use dreams completely defensively, to project into, to get rid of things*, etc. It is interesting, though, that some people have dreams that are saner than their daily life. They are saner in their dreams and more insightful about their dreams. Normally, you would think the other way

round, that people are crazier in their dreams, but for some people the saner kind of thinking which they don't acknowledge goes on in their dreams."

Dr. Roberts, the senior Kleinian training analyst described earlier, commented:

"Yes, I do think we concentrate less on isolating a dream and analyzing it as a thing in itself. Some American analysts who visited the Institute recently accused me of just interpreting from the manifest content. I was terribly offended. I didn't think I was doing that. I always encourage my patients to bring associations, and I believe I use them. That was why I was amazed by the Americans. But I also see the dream as belonging to a particular session and as probably *acted out* in the session. But I still think in terms of latent content. I think there have been two moves in relation to dream interpretation. One is the concentration on the dream as if that is the most important element in the session and let's exhaust every little element in it. Freud was brilliant at that and, God, I am glad he did it, but we have moved a bit away from that. The second move is that we see the material of the dream as belonging essentially to the transference. And, perhaps, there is the risk of people analyzing the dream too glibly from the manifest content."

Lastly, the views of Dr. Shaw, the Kleinian analyst who had changed orientation from the Independent group:

"I always give dreams some kind of priority because they arise *uncontaminated* within the patient's psyche. They are definitely the most free from external things. So you get the effects of the internal world in its purest form in dreams. Dream interpretation has altered very considerably since Freud's day. Most of us believe that dreams give us very important clues about what is going on in the transference. I would give dream imagery precedence in providing me with clues about what is exactly going on in the patient and between the patient and myself. I don't think I would think that manifest content was so very different to latent. I don't think of manifest content as this sort of obscure, heavily disguised expression of a wish. I think of it as an expression of the nature of internal object relations. I wouldn't go in for long and extensive sequences of associative links."

CONCLUSION

The interview excerpts show the variation that exists in the approaches of analysts of different orientations toward dream interpretation. What was once taken as the hallmark of the psychoanalytic method seems very largely a personal matter. Many analysts no longer view dreams as special in the sense that they offer privileged access to the unconscious mind. And those who do believe that dreams offer the "royal road" do so for a variety of reasons.

Afterword

W hat is pluralism in psychoanalysis? How does a pluralist practice? What distinguishes the pluralist from the monist? Discussions of central aspects of analytic technique carry information about these questions. The analysts we meet in these chapters reveal a great deal not only about what they believe but about how they believe. They tell us what matters to them, and what matters is intimately tied up with what works in the consulting room, as well as personal experiences with their own analysts, supervisors, and colleagues. They indicate whether a few beliefs are important to them, or whether they have a preference for, and facility with, a variety of perspectives.

Early on in the research project that furnished the interview data presented in the book, I was struck by the relevance of analysts' beliefs about the external world, about reality as distinct from illusion or distortion, and about the truth conditions that apply in psychoanalysis. These beliefs came to the fore in discussions of the internal world, psychic truth, and concepts of transference. The results of the various statistical analyses of the interviews strengthened these philosophical hunches and were reflected in the two principal dimensions that emerged from the factor analysis of the rated interviews. These were called "Total transference versus relative view of transference" and "Identification of psychic truth versus interpretations as hypotheses." An analyst who takes a total transference approach will tend to focus on the here-and-now transference to the analyst and the analytic situation; in contrast, an analyst who believes that transference is a relatively circumscribed aspect of the analytic relationship may distinguish between the transference and the real relationship, and between distorted and correct perceptions.

It was possible, again using statistical measures as well as many readings of the research findings, to think about the ways that these philosophical assumptions linked both with theoretical orientation and
approaches to interpretation on one hand, and, on the other, with the
overall *pattern* of an individual's beliefs. Patterns of belief were
described in the second chapter; three basic patterns were distinguished
that encompass the range, force, and content of the beliefs held. Beliefs
were categorized as "circumscribed," "wide," and "changed"—a third
pattern specific to individuals who had changed theoretical orientation. It was this investigation into the nature of analysts' belief systems
that revealed that pluralism in psychoanalysis is not simply a matter of
divergence among analysts, but also a mode in which some individual
analysts attempt to operate.

Overt and implicit patternings of belief clearly relate not only to the
contemporary debate on "one psychoanalysis or many," but also
implicitly to how analysts of different persuasions contemplate the historical evolution of their field. As historians have pointed out, Freud
held divergent views on many topics; his theories are not internally
consistent. Nevertheless, when we take a retrospective look over the
hundred years' of psychoanalysis, the field seems to have shifted from a
relatively unified, monistic position dominated by Freud to a diversi-
fied one accommodating the different viewpoints of other charismatic
figures. The interview discussions, especially those described in the
later chapters of this book, indicate how much the central tenets of
psychoanalysis have shifted. The beginning chapters focus on the
stronger, discriminating beliefs about reality and truth as these affect
specific approaches to technique: attitudes, for example, toward the
real relationship, analytic neutrality, the identification of psychic
truth, and the acknowledgment of mistakes. These technical
approaches can be seen as crystalizations of polarities and ambiguities
in Freud's thought. Subsequent chapters reflect an increasing diversity
of opinion and, moreover, suggest that some of the guiding principles
of the psychoanalytic method no longer seem relevant. Free association, the interpretation of the Oedipus complex and the erotic transferences, reconstruction, and the development of a transference
neurosis did not engage the attention of the analysts. The final chapter, on dream interpretation, exemplifies the personal and somewhat
idiosyncratic ideas about what was once considered the royal road to
the understanding of unconscious life.

Using these interview discussions to think about the ways the field
of psychoanalysis has shifted, I am struck by the contemporary emphasis on the emotional relationship between analysand and analyst.

With the exception of a few of the more "classical" Freudian analysts, all the analysts seem to focus their attention on the here-and-now transference relationship, on immediate affects, and on the analyst's responsiveness. This scrutiny of exchanges occurring within the relationship has moved analysis onto a more horizontal, transparent plane. Gone is the search for the mysterious, for the inner, for the latent, and for historical fact. Analysts ask, What is going on now between us? What feelings are we inducing in each other? Analysts seem less interested in the individual elaboration of language and imagination as this is manifested, for instance, in dreams, daydreams, and other flights of fancy. We don't hear much nowadays about symbolism, about the medium or modes of representations in which patients express their thoughts and feelings.

It seems that attachment—both between patient and analyst and between analyst and his close colleagues—preconsciously dominates the psychoanalytic domain, even though, in comparison with other mental health professionals, psychoanalysts have been slow to recognize the relevance of attachment theory and research. But, through the literature and practice of object relational analysis as well as through contemporary infancy research, attachment ideas seem to have seeped through. Strangely, what seems to have been overlooked is how systems of attachment also organize the analyst's own professional and theoretical identity. Analysts form attachments to specific theories, to key figures, and to encompassing ideas that provide the analyst with a measure of security. These preconscious attachments can be seen as providing a secure base from which analysts undertake an uncertain, often treacherous, journey. More than any other professionals, perhaps, analysts must become masters in the "management of uncertainty" (Marris, 1991). In linking the fields of psychology and social science, Marris observes that learning to manage the early attachment relationship is at the same time learning to understand order and control. He notes that the management of attachment is the starting point for understanding every kind of order. The childhood experience of attachment is also a product of the attachment patterns of a particular culture. This experience affects whether we tend to see order as natural and secure, and as something to learn about, or, rather, as the imposition of human will on chaos and destructive impulses. Human beings express conservative urges toward the familiar but are constantly vulnerable to the uncertainty evoked when relationships change and become contradictory. Analysts presumably also develop different strategies to manage the uncertainties of their immersion for often eight to ten hours a day in the intense emotional field of the analytic relationship.

To do their job, analysts press up against the unknown, both in their analysands and in themselves. They cannot sit back and take a break from emotional engagement. Perhaps none of the attachment patterns described in the attachment literature can capture the peculiar nature of the analyst–patient relationship. The analyst is expected to provide security for the patient even when the analyst is felt to be a traumatizing or negligent person. The analyst is expected to draw security not from his patient but from his understanding of his own reactions through his personal analysis, training, supervision, life experience, and knowledge of other people who are different from himself. My study of the effects of training, reading, clinical conferences, and geographical location indicates that analysts form close professional ties that affect their clinical work with all patients, but particularly with those who then join the psychoanalytic profession. These ties lead to attachments that affect the future theories and practices of analysts, and of those analysands they subsequently treat and train.

It would be interesting to investigate the kinds of attachments analysts form to their preferred orientation, theories, and techniques. Referring to the main attachment patterns that have been delineated in the attachment literature, we might attempt to link range and force of belief with differing forms of attachment. Would we find that a person who holds a strong and relatively circumscribed set of beliefs can practice with greater freedom and security just because he is rooted in an all-embracing, highly consistent theory? Or, on the other hand, would he be protecting an insecure and ambivalent attachment pattern by directing all his criticism toward another set of beliefs? While his particular set of beliefs is right, the others are wrong-minded. Similarly, the analyst who changes orientation might be engaged in the resolution of an ambivalent attachment toward a previous analyst or belief system. He might seek greater security through attaching himself to the new theory, thinker, or set of beliefs. And what about the pluralist? What kind of attachment might he express toward the analytic enterprise? Does he have greater security because he feels free to use a number of theories, or does he express an insecure attachment since he has no single set of beliefs on which to anchor himself? These are speculations that may add a useful dimension to thinking about the preconscious ways that analysts organize their theoretical and clinical understanding.

In reflecting on these questions, it occurred to me that it might be pertinent to describe what it was like to interview this group of 65 analysts in the two different countries. My personal experiences of talking with analysts about what matters to them clinically and theoretically might shed light on the transmission of a unique kind of relationship.

The chapters on the nature and content of belief already give some indication of how both the more highly circumscribed and the more pluralistic analysts think. Clearly, the more consistent thinkers expressed strong attachment either to their theory or to certain interpretive practices that they found essential—for example, the analyst who felt that he could not interpret perversion without a concept of the death instinct. If I ask myself whether, in general, these highly consistent thinkers were more difficult to interview because they were less open, the answer would be no. Very occasionally, a strong believer brought a powerful affective charge into the discussion, either by dismissing the topic at hand or by behaving in a testy or irritated way toward me for raising it. Yet altogether I experienced only five or six interactions of this nature.

For the most part, the circumscribed thinkers were a pleasure to interview. They were clear and succinct in expressing their opinions about the areas of clinical practice that were familiar and central. When asked to consider approaches that were less familiar to them, they did so; for example, the British analysts who simply said that they did not understand the meaning of a self–object tie. In fact, the British Kleinians and the Los Angeles self psychologists, both relatively circumscribed in their views, entered into the project with greater eagerness and interest than many of the British Independents and American eclectics. By contrast, it was hard to coax some of the more pluralist thinkers into participating in the project; perhaps they felt a particular antipathy toward something as circumscribed as a semidirected interview. Similarly, I encountered some initial difficulty in finding the 10 British Freudians I needed for my sample, but it is fair to say that the Freudians in both countries were well versed in other theories as well as highly articulate and thoughtful about their own theory.

If I think now of my interview experiences from a more cultural or geographical viewpoint, I would say that the American analysts were more articulate and displayed greater verbal facility. Though it is hard to convey exactly what I mean by this, it seemed that, as they reflected on a given subject, those reflections were put into words. The British analysts paused more, seeming to go away in thought, before reentering the conversation. They "picked their words," whereas with the Americans the flow of thought and speech was as one. As a group, the San Francisco analysts were the most responsive both to the request for interview and during the interview-discussions. They engaged with great concentration and enthusiasm on all the areas discussed. This quality is particularly interesting, since the San Francisco analysts were the most consistent geographic group and at the same time very widely read and open to other ideas. I felt I was being invited into an ongoing study group. They were particularly gracious and respectful toward me and toward their colleagues in the San Francisco community. It is possible that the presence in the community of a number of well-known analytic researchers—L. Bryce Boyer, Mardi Horowitz, Harold Sampson, Joseph Weiss, and Robert Wallerstein—significantly affects the attitude of clinicians toward research.

I particularly enjoyed the interviews with the older analysts in all the orientation groups in both countries. They conveyed the sense of another time and place, when analysts were less pressured by the constrictions of the 45-minute hour or the insurance companies, as well as a sense of adventure into territories where few had gone before. In the countries where these older analysts had settled, they seemed happiest in close-knit circles of colleague/friends where they could exchange fresh ideas. In Britain, the older analysts had enjoyed the early days of practicing within the National Health Service, when psychoanalytic psychotherapy was valued as an effective form of treatment. Similarly, in America, psychoanalytically trained psychiatrists were once valued in hospital settlings. These older analysts wanted to pass on their experiences of training in the early days of psychoanalysis and of their participation in then entirely new, psychoanalytically oriented social programs such as the Hampstead wartime nurseries and the Tavistock Clinic in London, and the Menninger Clinic in the United States.

Finally, I would like to try to describe some of the ways that this project, particularly the personal encounters with the analysts, has influenced my own thoughts about the field of psychoanalysis as well as my clinical practice. The project has had far-reaching effects on my views about psychoanalytic theory, about the relationship between theory and practice, and about analysts of orientations different from my own. It has fundamentally altered my picture of the field. When people ask me to describe the experience of the interviews, usually they want to know what it *felt* like to do such an extensive survey. My first feeling was undoubtedly one of anxiety. The prospect of interviewing a large enough sample of analysts for a statistical study was indeed daunting. I had been warned that analysts did not make good "subjects." They were not used to being questioned about themselves and about their beliefs; and some of those who have opened up to investigators of the field—to historians, biographers, and journalists—feel that they have been poorly or wrongly portrayed. Thus, I expected considerable resistance. In fact, I came up against very few obstacles from those who responded to my request. Perhaps resistance was expressed by those who did not answer my letters asking for their participation. As I noted in the introductory chapter, most of the analysts appreciated the personal attention that was given to what they thought and felt about their work. Many, like me, were anxious at the outset of the interview and, of course, it was my job as the interviewer to lay their anxieties to rest.

In tandem with the anxiety with which I approached each interview, I was constantly surprised and stimulated by the complex ways ideas and clinical practices interconnected with one another. Once I got the hang of interviewing, I was alerted to the logical ways in which analysts connect their ideas. Eclectics usually were not "woolly-minded"; they too were logical. Many stereotyped assumptions that I had built up over the years were challenged. When I did come up against some rigidity, it was usually unexpected. For example, in the first interviews with American analysts of a self-psychological perspective, I had no idea that questions about conflict or the therapeutic alliance would arouse the scorn that they did. Nor did I expect that some British Kleinian analysts would take similar exception to the concept of holding. The cross-cultural aspect of the interviews also alerted me to the difficulties of translation. How does one translate a foreign term to a stranger who has not participated in the forms of practice and discourse in which a particular term is embedded? How does one describe the differences between two concepts when there are no definitions to compare with one another? By the time I had supplied the definition, I had already done the translation.

Close to the end of the 65 interviews, one analyst asked me, "Well, what do *you* think?" "I really don't know," I replied. "I have been listening to so many people and imagining myself into the minds of so many analysts, thinking myself into so many ways that I never thought of before, that I can no longer say, This is what I think, or This is the kind of analyst I am." I felt that I was indeed without orientation. Some days everyone seemed to have a point. Although initially perplexed, I would see how a strange idea could be used effectively in a particular clinical setting. Then over the months and now years, I began to surface from the immersion in the "subjects" of my research with whom I felt a special, even intimate, tie. I transcribed nearly all the interviews myself, which was an arduous and time-consuming task. But the advantage of this labor was that the atmosphere of the interviews and the presences of the various analysts were reevoked over and over again. With the passage of time, however, I found sufficient distance to discriminate areas of difference and agreement.

I first became aware of the effects of the project on my analytic thinking when participating in psychoanalytic presentations—scientific meetings, clinical conferences. While listening to presentations or reading papers in psychoanalytic journals, I realized that I now had a map. This map orientated my listening and enabled me to detect where one territory—cluster of ideas—separated from, or bordered on, another. Although, of course, the various statistical analyses that I performed after the interviews were completed had highlighted patterns of association, I was surprised how often, within a few sentences, I could predict the association of ideas. Not that the presentation was not informative, but, given one or two key words, others seemed to follow naturally. And, even though aspects of psychoanalytic theory and practice have changed in the five years since I completed the interviews, my map still alerts me to these changes. It makes me question, Are those changes central or peripheral? How far do they reverberate across discrete networks of ideas?

Perhaps my background in philosophy led me to pay particular attention to consistencies and contradictions between networks of concepts; undoubtedly, philosophical assumptions organized the "clusters of belief" that emerged from the literature review that preceded the empirical study. All psychoanalysts bring to the field a previous training. Medical doctors, professors of anthropology, history, literature listen and read differently. They would likely discern alternative patterns of linkage to myself. Wittgenstein (1980b) stated that, although philosophy is not a privileged source of truth or knowledge, people who have never carried out an investigation of a philosophical kind might not be equipped

> with the right visual organs for this type of investigation. Almost in the way a man who is not used to searching in the forest for flowers, berries, or plants will not find any because his eyes are not trained to see them and he does not know where you have to be particularly on the lookout for them. Similarly, someone unpracticed in philosophy passes by all the spots where the difficulties are hidden in the grass, whereas someone who has had practice will pause and sense that there is a difficulty close by even though he cannot see it yet [p. 29].

It was some time before I felt able to articulate how the project had affected my clinical practice with clients. Those effects of which I am most conscious are somewhat paradoxical. The project has inspired me to try to practice more consistently at the same time as it has enabled me to feel greater security about being a pluralist. First, consistency. My British training was eclectic. I would call myself, and am thought of by British colleagues as, an Independent. My analyses, supervisions, and classes have been Freudian, Independent, and Kleinian. I also enjoyed an enduring friendship with John Bowlby from my student days until his death in 1990. Attachment ideas are embedded in my analytic attitude. But this British training was often atheoretical, at times even antitheoretical, in keeping with the tradition of British empiricism. As students, we were supposed to approach the "clinical material" uncluttered by theory. Certainly, I preconsciously gathered all sorts of concepts, practices, interpretive styles during the 15 or so years that I practiced in Britain. In addition, since I have worked in Los Angeles for the best part of 20 years, I have learned and assimilated many of the practices of my American colleagues. Whereas, in England, I might have been happy to muddle along using whatever seemed helpful or effective, I think I have been influenced by the more heavily theoretical bent of American analysis. And my research indicates that even eclectic analysts work systematically. The result is that I am more aware of what I draw on in my work with a particular client, although I continue to practice in the apparently atheoretical way that I have always done. But the research has affected my reflections about what I do. I am more worried about my use of bits of theories, more aware of the ways that part-theories do not fit one another and can be confusing over time even if they seem apt within the intensity of a session.

In terms of practicing pluralistically, however, the research has enabled me to feel more secure about not belonging to a particular orientation group. A British colleague once described me jokingly as "a mongrel." He commiserated with the sense he thought I might have of not belonging to a particular group. Not being a Kleinian or a Freudian, or a self psychologist/intersubjectivist here in Los Angeles, can create a feeling of not belonging. This is particularly so when, in my clinical work, I face uncertainty over a long period. For instance, if I find a client particularly difficult to understand, and if also that client is particularly hostile or rejecting, I find myself thinking So and So would know exactly what to say. Or, if I were So and So, I would interpret this way. Trouble is that I don't. For the most part, however, the project has helped me to feel freer of an analytic superego, of the feeling that "we," the Independents, Kleinians, or whoever, really know. Nobody *really* knows. Even the more consistent thinkers practice inconsistently and in ways that are personal and idiosyncratic. There are many uncertainties. Nevertheless, psychoanalysts do bring a wealth of observations and clinical expertise to the understanding of human behavior and to unconscious processes in particular. My hope is that the book will take the field one step closer toward both the articulation of pluralism and the tracing of unanimity within that pluralism.

APPENDIX
TRANSFERENCE INTERVIEW QUESTIONNAIRE

(Note to raters: the questionnaire numbers and headings are correlated with the same numbers and headings on the rating scale. Look for answers to item 1 on Rating scale in the introductory definition below, and in section 1 on nontransference and section after item 2 headed MUTATIVE.)

DEF. OF TRANSFERENCE — Some analysts have said that the tendency to form transferences is universal. Others have defined transference as a uniquely analytic phenomenon. They would say that transference develops in consequence of the conditions of the analytic setting. How would you define it—both in a more general sense and as something more specific to the analytic situation?

1. NON- or EXTRA-TRANSF. — Some analysts tend to take up whatever the patient talks about in terms of what the patient is feeling toward the analyst in the present; other analysts, however, feel it is important to maintain a firm distinction between feelings and thoughts that belong to people in the patient's life outside the analysis without necessarily interpreting these as relating to the analyst. Do you feel this distinction is an important one?

What do you think about nontransference interpretations, including interpretations of relationships with other people outside analysis? For instance, some analysts believe that nontransference interpretations can act as "feeders" for transference interpretations in that they can lead to transference interpretations. Others think that this is not their only use.

Do you usually make nontransference interpretations in order to get to a position where you can make a transference interpretation?

Do you think that it is important to make nontransference interpretations for other reasons?

2. REAL RELATIONSHIP — Some analysts think that it is important to refer their interpretations, to what has been called the real aspect of the patient–analyst relationship (e.g., Greenson and A. Freud, who said that we should leave room somewhere for the realization that analyst and patient are also two real people, of equal adult status, in a real personal relationship to each other). How much do

you think the patient develops a relationship with you which is over and above the transference—more of a "real" relationship? For instance, do you think that all the patient's feelings about you during and after the analysis would be transference? Some analysts think that the transference can be resolved only when the patient develops a "real" relationship with the analyst. What do you think about this?

3. VALIDATION OF CORRECT PERCEPTIONS

Connected to the question of the "real" relationship—some analysts think it is important when making interpretations to distinguish between the patient's transference "distortions" of them and what they call the patient's correct perception of them (e.g., Greenson's example of a patient who told him that he always talked a bit too much and tended to exaggerate. Greenson explicitly validated this perception because he thought it was correct). Other analysts do not make such a definitive distinction and would not corroborate a patient's so-called real perceptions. What do you think about this—is this something you would ever say to a patient?

MUTATIVE (in item 1 on rating scale)

Some analysts believe that there are "effective" or "mutative" interpretations and have described the specific characteristics of these interpretations in different ways. Do you agree strongly with the view that transference interpretations are the most effective or mutative type of interpretations—bring about psychic change?

Left out later

(Do you sometimes feel that you have made an incorrect interpretation?

How do you deal with the occasions when you make an interpretation which you think is wrong/incorrect?)

4. SURFACE/DEPTH

Analysts who take up most of their patients' material in the transference have different approaches. Some analysts consider it appropriate, for instance, to make a transference interpretation when transference is just below the surface. Others feel that no matter how deeply unconscious the transference element is, it is very important to take it up in the transference. They would tend to make direct transference interpretations no matter what the patient says. Do you usually make transference interpretations when you feel the transference elements are fairly well below the surface?

So much has been written about the interpretation of unconscious thoughts, feelings, fantasies, impulses, etc., but much less about the interpretation of preconscious or even conscious material. In your interpretations, do you think it is important to include references to thoughts and feelings of which the patient is conscious even though he is not telling you about them?

5. CONFLICT

Some people try to follow the rule of looking for and interpreting conflict while others tend to take up the underlying fantasy or anxiety or wish that is seeking expression. What is your view on these two positions—would you usually try to take up conflict in your interpretations? (e.g., think of a patient wanting to kill you—would your interpretation be of the form "I think that your feelings about me are mixed . . ."?)

These questions not on rating scale, but responses usually occur at this point in interview

There are analysts who feel it is important to refer in their interpretations to the child part of their patients—or, as some have put it, the "child within" the patient. They would say something quite explicit like, "The little child in you wants to . . ." or "There is a part of you who wants to behave as a little child. . . ." Other analysts would tend to say, "you" when making interpretations to a patient, even if the "you" referred to feelings or actions of which the patient was quite unaware. In your interpretations, do you explicitly refer to the child within or the child part of the patient?

Do you have any particular phrases you use when talking to your patients about this?

When you interpret the child aspect of the patient, do you usually also talk about the "adult" or "grown-up" part of the patient?

Why do you think this is important? Or, if person says not usually or rarely, ask if any reason why they do not do this.

6. OBSERVING EGO

A similar point: Some people refer to the "adult" part of the patient; others think more in terms of the "reasonable" part of the patient—for instance, the patient's "observing ego" or a part of the patient that is able to listen. Is this an important aspect of your technique—do you usually address your interpretations to this aspect of the patient?

DEFENSE (This question not on rating scale but occurs at this point in most interviews.)

When interpreting a patient's defenses do you usually distinguish between defenses that the patient is employing in the present in relation to yourself—for instance, defenses against sexual material—and the repetition or transference of defense mechanisms used by the patient during his childhood? Do you think this is an important distinction?

Do you feel it is important that you also convey to the patient that you see his defensive behavior as the best possible solution to his difficulties at the time even if no longer useful?

7. POSITIVE & NEGATIVE TRANSFERENCE

Analysts vary in the way they take up their patients' destructive fantasies about them. Some feel it is important to interpret these whenever they are in the material; others tend to interpret only when the patient is directly in touch with these feelings. Would you usually wait to interpret destructive fantasies until the patient could express these directly toward you?

Analysts differ in the way they take up the positive and negative transference. Some feel it is better to take up negative feelings first because many patients feel more uncomfortable about the direct expression of negative feelings. Others disagree and point out that many people are as afraid of direct expressions of love as hate. There are pitfalls in not taking up one side or the other. If both are present, are you more concerned to take up negative feelings toward you than the positive transference?

8. & 9. HOLDING & CONTAINMENT

A great deal has been written in recent years about the importance of creating a "holding" environment in analysis. This has been put in various ways—some talk about holding, others talk in terms of containment where the analyst tries to contain the primitive feelings of the patient. Do you feel at home with this point of view? Do you feel these terms are very useful?

Do you think it is important to differentiate the terms holding and containment?

Could you say a bit about how these beliefs might influence your technique?

(This question not on rating scale, but asked in most interviews.)

Some analysts have paid considerable attention to the maintenance of the analytic setting particularly when seeing very disturbed or regressed patients. They would focus less on making interpretations and more on keeping the boundaries of the setting intact. They might be very outspoken and confrontative about the patient's efforts to disrupt the safety of the setting. They might openly express their anger with the patient. Others disagree with this approach and feel that interpretation is the only effective method. Do you think it is ever appropriate in these situations to confront patients without making an interpretation?

10. BORDERLINE & PSYCHOTIC (Note: no analyst currently seeing psychotic patients.)

Do you ever take on borderline or psychotic patients in analysis?

If answers Yes to both, or to psychotics only or borderlines only, then ask: Some people think that special types of intervention are required for the analysis of borderline or psychotic patients. Other analysts aim to make the same type—by which I mean form rather than content—of interpretations across the whole range of patients in their practice. Do you usually use the same type of interpretation with borderline/psychotic patients as with your other patients, or do you introduce special parameters?

11. PSYCHOTIC AREAS OR PARTS IN ALL PATIENTS

Some people believe that everyone has a "psychotic" or "borderline" part of their personality. Is this something you would agree with?

Would you say that an analysis was incomplete if this level of the personality was not reached?

(This question asked only at beginning of interviews— aroused a hostile response.)

Some analysts think it is helpful, and might even give relief to a patient, to talk quite directly to them about the "mad" part of themselves; others would never use these words with any patient. Do you ever use these words when talking to your patients?

(This question also not on rating scale but asked in most interviews)

Some analysts feel that it is important to use a more concrete language, a sort of body language, when talking to their patients about their most primitive feelings and would explicitly refer to parts of the body in their interpretations. Others disagree with this view since they feel that this encourages the patient to think concretely about himself. Do you make interpretations using a part-object language?

12. DEATH INSTINCT

Some analysts who work with very disturbed patients see their withdrawn or destructive behavior as an expression of the death drive or instinct. Of course, they do not talk to their patients using these terms, but they do feel that this concept is a useful aid to understanding and to formulating interpretations. They give clinical examples in order to demonstrate the practical implications of the concept. Others disagree. Do you find the concept of the death instinct is useful in formulating interpretations?

How do you think this belief affects your technique?

13. QUALIFYING STATEMENTS

Do you ever preface your interpretations with qualifying words such as perhaps, maybe, I think you might be feeling . . . . Some analysts think this is not a helpful way of talking to their patients and would rarely use these words. Do you often use these or similar qualifying words in your interpretations?

Do you have any ideas as to why this is necessary/not necessary?

(This question not on rating scale but asked in most interviews.)

Some analysts try to make their interpretations as plausible or convincing to the patient's conscious mind as possible. Others are not particularly concerned with this issue. Do you usually formulate your interpretations with this in mind?

14. SILENCE

Some analysts have written about the value of silence during the analysis of their patients; others say very little about this issue. Do you see silence as having a value?

Could you tell me why you think silence is valuable/rarely helpful?

Would you ever let a whole session go by without saying anything if your patient was completely silent?

According to answer, ask why would you do this?

15. NEUTRALITY

As you know, Freud wrote about the value of the analyst's maintaining a "neutral" stance toward his patients. Analysts have understood this statement in different ways. Some see it as meaning that the analyst should say very little or that the analyst should act as much as possible like a mirror to the patient. Others feel that analytic neutrality is not about whether the analyst says very little or tries to act as a mirror; they may engage in a dialogue with their patients, talk with them; for them, the important issue is the analyst's attitude of "tolerance" toward whatever the patient brings.

With which view of neutrality do you feel most comfortable?

Can you say how you convey an attitude of neutrality in your work—what this analytic attitude means to you?

16. TRUTH

Some analysts try to avoid using such terms as truth or reality, which imply an absolute standard. Others feel that this is not always feasible. For instance, if a patient were to deny or disavow his feelings or perceptions of important events in his life, the analyst might say to the patient that he was "evading reality" or "avoiding the truth." Do you ever use these words when interpreting your patients' defensive behavior?

(This question may amplify the one on truth but not on rating scale. Responses often occur in interview in discussions of Kohut.)

Some analysts try to formulate their interpretations so as to convey to the patient that their view is just as subjective, no less relative, than that of the patient. In formulating interpretations, they would try to attune themselves to their patients so as not to disrupt the intersubjective flow of experience. Other analysts disagree and say that the analytic relationship is inherently unequal or assymetrical because of the analyst's greater self- knowledge and training. Do you agree with this view of the analytic relationship?

17. REFERENCE TO PAST/HERE-&-NOW INTERPRETATION

Some analysts feel that it is essential when making a transference interpretation that they also make an explicit reference to a figure of the past. Others think that it is not essential to bring in the past. Do you usually make a reference to the past when making a transference interpretation?

Some analysts have emphasized the defensive use of the past by both patients and analysts. For example, they point out that both may flee from the heat of the here-and-now relationship between analyst and patient. Others disagree with this emphasis and point out that the present can also be used to defend against the past? Do you think it is generally preferable to focus on the here-and-now relationship when making interpretations?

18. RECONSTRUCTION

Analysts have had different views about the ways patients repeat past relationships in the here-and-now relationship with the analyst. Some see the current relationship as a reenactment of relationships in infancy or early childhood. Others feel that past relationships are always transformed so as to make them appear more appropriate to the present. Would you ever make interpretations in which you describe the present relationship as virtually the same as the past?

Some analysts see the function of reconstruction in terms of gaining access to memories. Others think of reconstruction more as the attempt to construct a coherent and meaningful account of how the patient leads his life. When making reconstructive interpretations, do you aim to retrieve memories of events?

The issue of the interpretation of memories is obviously complicated. What do you think about early memories—do you think people can remember—i.e., offer accurate information about—events before the age of four or five?

19. SEPARATIONS

Many analysts think it is very important to pick up planned separations—for instance, the end of sessions, weekends, and holidays/vacations. Others pay less attention to these breaks and bring them up to remind the patient of the gaps or specific dates or only when prompted by the patient. In your practice, is this something which you take up very frequently—for instance before every weekend—or only on occasion?

On a similar topic, some analysts do not put much emphasis on unplanned or small changes in sessions times—for instance if a session had to be changed by a few minutes or if the analyst or patient was a few minutes late or early. Others would always take up these changes, however minute—for instance if the analyst was five minutes late or the patient arrived a few minutes early. Would you always take up such changes, however minute?

20. DEVELOPMENTAL ARRESTS/BASIC FAULTS

There are analysts who think that interpretation can have an important function in undoing or repairing what have been called deficits or "arrests"—"basic faults"—in the patient's development. Others believe that interpretation helps but that basic defects or arrests are never completely overcome. Do you think that interpretation can undo or repair arrests?

Do you think that the experience of the relationship to the analyst can bring about psychic change in the patient's internal world?

Some analysts believe that patients have to come to terms with the fact that they have been hurt, that things have gone wrong which can't be put right. In formulating and making interpretations, they would focus on mourning for what cannot be repaired. Reparation in the present is thus intimately connected with the work of mourning. Other analysts disagree with this view of reparation and believe that interpretation can do more than this—that through analytic interpretation, the patient can build new mental structures. Do you agree strongly with this view?

Some analysts believe it is very important to phrase their interpretations so as not to disrupt a kind of bond in which the analyst exists as part of the patient's internal world or subjective experience— Kohut refers to this bond as a "selfobject tie," perhaps linked to Winnicott's use of the analyst as a transitional object. Others feel that it is not usually helpful to let this sort of bond develop and would interpret the patient's avoidance or intolerance of separateness. Do you usually take up your patient's attempts to merge, or be part of you, as a defense against separateness?

21. EROTIC TRANSFERENCE

Analysts interpret their patients' erotic feelings toward them in different ways. Some might see the expression of sexual feelings as indicating a lowering of resistance and a capacity to get in touch with sexual feelings for the analyst. Other analysts tend not to take up erotic feelings in this way and focus more upon the defensive use of sexuality—e.g., as a defense against feelings of emptiness or depression. Would you say that you tend to find yourself taking up the defense aspect more than the sexual feelings toward you?

22. IDEALIZED
TRANSFERENCE

If a patient were talking to you in a very idealizing way—he saw you as very powerful, successful, and kind—would you ever think it was important to accept his view of you without pointing out the idealization? Some analysts might go along with this, thinking it represents an important developmental step. Others would strongly disagree with this approach. They would tend to see and interpret idealization as largely defensive. Do you usually take up a patient's idealized view of you as defensive?

What value do you think/not think an idealizing transference can have? Do you think that idealization necessarily leads to a depletion of the self and increases envy of the analyst?

23. COUNTER-
TRANSFERENCE

Analysts have different approaches to the painful or very uncomfortable feelings their patients arouse in them. Some tend to see and interpret these responses as what the patient is trying to make them feel or do; others tend to see their own discomfort as a sign of their own unresolved conflicts in response to the patient's material. Do you usually understand such feelings as a sign of your own unresolved difficulties—what have been called the analyst's "blind spots"?

(All the following questions included in one item on countertransference.)

Do you ever think of your countertransference as something entirely personal and not related to the patient?

Some analysts see their countertransference feelings as indicating that a patient is trying communicate with them in a very primitive—nonverbal—way. The patient communicates by the projection of feeling rather than by words. Others focus more on the patient's attempt to get rid of his feelings into someone else.

Would you usually use your countertransference to interpret to your patient that he is trying to let you know what or how he feels, i.e., as a response to communication?

Do you think of your countertransference as a response to the way a patient is trying to pressurize or manipulate you to enact a role from a past object relationship where you have a part to play in the externalization of an internal drama? Or would you tend to think of it as a response to patient's attempt to project unwanted parts of the self into you?

Some analysts think of the countertransference as a sort of running commentary on what the patient is talking about and feeling. Others do not think that it is such a constant process but that it occurs under specific conditions. Do you think of countertransference as something which goes on all the time or as a specific, even rare, occurrence?

24. MISTAKES &
FAILURES

Some analysts openly acknowledge their mistakes to their patients. They will talk about their failures in empathy or understanding. Others do not think this is a good idea. Do you at times acknowledge your mistakes to your patients?

A related question. Some analysts believe it is important also to give their patient an explanation or an apology for why they failed to understand something; others think this is not a good idea and might even burden the patient or make him feel guilty. Would you ever give an explanation or apologise to a patient for a mistake?

Analysts who do acknowledge their own mistakes do so for a number of reasons. Some interpret these as revealing important failures in the patient's childhood—in the way Winnicott did. Others focus more on their own failure of empathy in the present as conveyed in a previous interpretation. Would you tend to see and interpret analytic mistakes as repeating failures in the patient's past?

(This question rarely asked.)

If you were fairly sure that a patient had had a very unhappy or deprived childhood, would you ever talk to him directly about how his parents had failed him? Some analysts feel that this can be important; others feel that is is not usually helpful and that it can lead to a sort of blaming of the parents. Is this something you would usually take up with a patient with this kind of background?

ACTING-IN (This question not on scale, asked rarely.)

As you know, much has been written about patients' "acting-out" both as a form of transference and as an avoidance of transference. In addition to enactments outside the sessions, do you usually look for and interpret the ways your patient "acts in" in sessions?

25. TREATMENT
ALLIANCE

Some analysts believe that it is important to establish an alliance with their patients before proceeding to work with transference material. Others think it is more helpful to interpret right from the beginning and that an alliance is fostered by the sense of being understood. Do you usually try to establish some sort of alliance with your patients before proceeding to transference work?

How do you think of the concept of treatment alliance—e.g., do you mean the motivation to work together with the analyst against resistance?

(Omitted usually.)

Some analysts (notably Sterba) have thought that the treatment alliance could be fostered by the use of the pronoun "we" rather than always addressing the patient as "you." Do you think it can be useful to formulate interpretations using the pronoun "we"—is this something that you say?

(Not on rating scale but asked—may amplify item on treatment alliance.)

Some analysts tell their patients very little in the first session about the analytic arrangements and will tend to interpret the patient's behavior from the moment the patient comes into the consulting room. Others think it is important to explain the procedure to the patient before they make interpretations. For instance, they might tell the patient that it was important that he or she try to tell the analyst whatever thoughts or feelings they had, however silly or embarrassing these might seem. In addition to setting the fees and times of sessions, do you usually explain the analytic procedure to your patient before making transference interpretations?

26. TRANSFERENCE
    NEUROSIS

Do you feel there is a difference between transference and transference neurosis—a firm distinction or a question of degree?

27. DREAMS

Some analysts believe that the view of dream interpretation has changed radically since Freud's day and that many analysts treat dreams in the same way as any other analytic material in the session. This has various consequences. One is that there is a shift from interpretations of the content of the dream to interpreting its function in the analysis, i.e., how the dreamer intended the dream to impinge upon his relationship with his analyst. Do you usually take up dream material in relation to the transference? How important do you think it is to also interpret the latent content of a dream rather than/in addition to taking up the act of telling the dream?

RATERS' SCORE SHEET

Code Name:

	++	+	0	–	––
1. EXTRA/TRANSFERENCE					
2. REAL RELATIONSHIP					
3. VALIDATION OF PERCEPTIONS					
4. SURFACE/DEPTH					
5. CONFLICT					
6. OBSERVING EGO					
7. NEGATIVE/POSITIVE					
8. HOLDING					
9. CONTAINMENT					
10. BORDERLINE PARAMETERS					
11. PSYCHOTIC AREAS					
12. DEATH INSTINCT					
13. QUALIFIERS					
14. SILENCE					
15. NEUTRALITY					
16. TRUTH					
17. REF. TO PAST/HERE-&-NOW					
18. RECONSTRUCTION					
19. SEPARATIONS					
20. DEVELOPMENTAL ARRESTS					
21. EROTIC TRANSFERENCE					
22. IDEALIZING TRANSFERENCE					
23. COUNTERTRANSFERENCE					
24. MISTAKES/FAILURES					
25. TREATMENT ALLIANCE					
26. TRANSFERENCE NEUROSIS					
27. DREAMS					

FACTOR ANALYSIS OF ORIENTATION & INTERVIEWS

FIVE PRINCIPAL DIMENSIONS OF ORIENTATION QUESTIONNAIRE

1. Developmental Freudian v. Bilonian-Kleinian.
2. Classical Freudian v. Kohutian-self psychology.
3. Hermeneutics (narrative truth) v. British object relations (unconscious fantasy focus).
4. Interpersonal or external reality influences.
5. French psychoanalysis.

SEVEN PRINCIPAL DIMENSIONS OF TRANSFERENCE INTERVIEWS

1. Total transference v. relative view of transference.
2. Psychic truth v. interpretations as hypotheses.
3. Neutrality.
4. Interpretation of surface manifestations of positive feelings.
5. Separation emphasis.
6. Use of qualifying phrases.
7. Dream interpretation.

References

Aristotle. *Magna Moralia*, Book II, 1213 a, 10–26. *The Complete Works of Aristotle*, Vol. IX. Oxford: Clarendon Press, 1925.

Balint, A. & Balint, M. (1939). On transference and countertransference. *Int. J. Psycho-Anal.*, 20:223–230.

Balint, M. (1957). The three areas of the mind. In *The Basic Fault*. London: Tavistock.

Bateson, G. (1972). Metalogue: What is an instinct? In *Steps to an Ecology of Mind*. New York: Ballantine.

———(1979). *Mind and Nature*. New York: Dutton.

Bennett, J. (1985). Critical notice of *Inquiries into Truth and Interpretation*, by D. Davidson. *Mind*, 94 (373): 601–626.

Berlin, I. (1992a). The pursuit of the ideal. In *The Crooked Timber of Humanity*. New York: Vintage.

———(1992b). The decline of utopian ideas in the West. In *The Crooked Timber of Humanity*. New York: Vintage.

Bernardi, R. (1992). On pluralism in psychoanalysis. *Psychoanal. Inq.*, 12:506–525.

Bollas, C. (1989). The dialectics of difference. In *Forces of Destiny*. London: Free Associations Books.

Bowlby, J. (1958). The nature of the child's tie to his mother. *Int. J. Psycho-Anal.*, 39:350–73.

———(1969). *Attachment*. London: Hogarth Press.

———(1978). Psychoanalysis as art and science. In *A Secure Base: Clinical Applications of Attachment Theory*. London: Routledge, 1988.

Brafman, A. (1989). Infant observation. *Int. Rev. Psycho-Anal.*, 15:45–59.

Budd, M. (1993). *Wittgenstein's Philosophy of Psychology*. London: Routledge.

Cavell, M. (1993). Mind, body, and the question of psychological laws. In *The Psychoanalytic Mind*. Cambridge, MA: Harvard University Press.

Fenichel, O. (1941), *Problems of Psychoanalytic Technique*. New York: Psychoanalytic Quarterly.

Freud, S. (1900). *The Interpretation of Dreams. Standard Edition*: 4 & 5. London: Hogarth Press, 1953.

————(1909). Five lectures on psychoanalysis. Fifth lecture. *Standard Edition*, 11:52–53. London: Hogarth Press, 1957.

————(1910). The future prospects of psychoanalytic therapy. *Standard Edition*, 11:144–145. London: Hogarth Press, 1957.

————(1912). The dynamics of transference. *Standard Edition*, 12:99–108. London: Hogarth Press, 1958.

————(1914). Remembering, repeating and working-through. *Standard Edition*, 12:145–156. London: Hogarth Press, 1958.

————(1915). Observations on transference-love. *Standard Edition*, 12:159–171. London: Hogarth Press, 1958.

————(1917). Mourning and melancholia. *Standard Edition*, 14:217–258. London: Hogarth Press, 1958.

————(1937a). Constructions in analysis. *Standard Edition*, 23:255–269. London: Hogarth Press, 1964.

————(1937b). Analysis terminable and interminable. *Standard Edition*, 12:209–253. London: Hogarth Press, 1958.

Gill, M. (1993). One-person and two-person perspectives: Freud's "Observations on Transference-Love." In *On Freud's "Observations on Transference-Love,"* ed. E. Person, A. Hagelin & P. Fonagy. New Haven, CT: Yale University Press, pp.114–115.

————& Hoffman, I. (1982). *The Analysis of Transference.* New York: International Universities Press.

Glover, E. (1942a). Introductory memorandum. In *The Freud-Klein Controversies 1941–45*, ed. P. King & R. Steiner. London: Routledge/Tavistock, 1991, pp. 597–601.

————(1942b). Edward Glover's response to memorandum by James Strachey. In *The Freud-Klein Controversies 1941–45*, ed. P. King & R. Steiner. London Routledge/Tavistock, 1991, pp. 611–616.

Greenson, R. (1967). *The Technique and Practice of Psycho-Analysis.* New York: International Universities Press.

Grünbaum, A. (1984). *The Foundations of Psychoanalysis.* Berkeley: University of California Press.

Hamilton, V. (1993). Truth and reality in psychoanalytic discourse. *Int. J. Psycho-Anal.,* 74:63–79.

Hanly, C. (1992). *The Concept of Truth in Applied Psychoanalysis.* New York: Guilford.

Heimann, P. (1950). On counter-transference. In *About Children and Children No-Longer,* ed. M. Tonnesmann. London: Tavistock/Routledge, 1989, pp. 73–79.

————(1960). Counter-transference. In *About Children and Children No-Longer,* ed. M. Tonnesmann. London: Tavistock/Routledge, 1989, pp. 151–160.

————(1977) Further observations on the analyst's cognitive process. In *About Children and Children No-Longer,* ed. M. Tonnesmann. London: Tavistock/Routledge, 1989, pp. 295–310.

Holt, R. (1964). The emergence of cognitive psychology. *J. Amer. Psychoanal. Assn.,* 12:650–655.

Hopkins, J. (1988). Epistemology and depth psychology: critical notes on *The Foundations of Psychoanalysis*. In *Mind, Psychoanalysis and Science*, ed. P. Clark & C. Wright. Oxford: Blackwell.

Jahanbegloo, R. (1992). *Conversations with Isaiah Berlin*. London: Halban.

King, P. (1978). Affective response of the analyst to the patient's communications. *Int. J. Psycho-Anal.*, 59:329–334.

Klein, M. (1952). The origins of transference. *Int. J. Psycho-Anal.*, 33:433–441.

Kohut, H. (1971). *The Analysis of the Self*. New York: International Universities Press.

Leibniz, G. von (c. 1689). A letter on freedom. In *Leibniz Philosophical Writings*, trans. M. Morris & G. Parkinson. London: J. M. Dent & Sons, 1973, pp. 113–114.

Marris, P. (1991). The social construction of uncertainty. In *Attachment Across the Life-Cycle*, ed. C. Murray-Parkes, J. Stevenson-Hinde & P. Marris. London: Routledge, pp. 77–90.

McGuire, W., ed. (1974) *The Freud/Jung Correspondence*. Princeton, NJ: Princeton University Press.

Parsons, M. (1992). The refinding of theory in clinical practice. *Int. J. Psycho-Anal.*, 73:103–115.

Rangell, L. (1988). The future of psychoanalysis: The scientific crossroads. *Psychoanal. Quart.*, 57:313–340.

Reyner, E. (1991). *The Independent Mind in British Psychoanalysis*. Northvale, NJ: Aronson.

Riviere, J. (1952). The unconscious phantasy of an inner world as reflected in examples from literature. In *The Inner World and Joan Riviere*. London: Karnac, 1991.

Rorty, R. (1991). Priority of democracy to philosophy. In *Objectivity, Relativism, and Truth*. Cambridge: Cambridge University Press.

Sandler, J. (1960). The background of safety. In *From Safety to Superego*. London: Karnac/New York: Guilford, 1987.

———(1983). Reflections on some relations between psychoanalytic concepts and psychoanalytic practice. *Int. J. Psycho-Anal.*, 64:35–45.

——— & Sandler, A-M. (1978). On the development of object relationships and affects. *Int. J. Psycho-Anal.*, 59:285–296.

——— & ———(1984). The past unconscious, the present unconscious and interpretation of the transference. *Psychoanal. Inq.*, 4:367–399.

Schafer, R. (1992). Five readings of Freud's "Observations on Transference-Love." In *On Freud's "Observations on Transference-Love"*. New Haven, CT: Yale University Press.

Sharpe, E. (1930). The analysand. In *Collected Papers on Psycho-Analysis*. London: Hogarth Press, 1978.

Spence, D. (1993). The hermeneutic turn: Soft science or loyal opposition. *Psychoanal. Dial.*, 3:1–10.

Stein, M. (1981). The unobjectionable part of the transference. *J. Amer. Psychoanal. Assn.*, 29:869–892.

Stein, S. (1991). The influence of theory on the psychoanalyst's countertransference. *Int. J. Psycho-Anal.*, 72:325–334.

Stern, D. (1985). *The Interpersonal World of the Infant*. New York: Basic Books.

Stone, L. (1961), *The Psychoanalytic Situation*. New York: International Universities Press.

Trevarthen, C. (1978). Modes of perceiving and codes of acting. In *Psychological Modes of Perceiving and Processing Information*, ed. H. Pick. Hillsdale NJ: Lawrence Erlbaum Associates, pp. 99–136.

Winnicott, D. (1941). The observation of infants in a set situation. In *Through Paediatrics to Psycho-Analysis*. London: Hogarth Press 1982.

———(1949). Hate in the countertransference. *Int. J. Psycho-Anal.*, 30:69–74.

———(1953). Transitional objects and transitional phenomena. In *Playing and Reality*. London: Tavistock, 1971.

———(1971). Playing: A theoretical statement. In *Playing and Reality*. London: Tavistock.

Wallerstein, R. (1988). One psychoanalysis or many? *Int. J. Psycho-Anal.*, 69:5–21.

Wittgenstein, L. (1980a). *Remarks on the Philosophy of Psychology*. Vol. 1, ed. G. Anscombe & G. von Wright (trans. G. Anscombe). Oxford: Blackwell.

———(1980b). *Culture and Value*. Oxford: Blackwell.

Wollheim, R. (1974). Imagination and identification. In *On Art and the Mind*. Cambridge MA: Harvard University Press.

———(1984). *The Thread of Life*. London: Cambridge University Press.

———(1993). Desire, belief, and Professor Grünbaum's Freud. In *The Mind and Its Depths*. Cambridge, MA: Harvard University Press.

Zetzel, E. (1956). Current concepts of transference. *Int. J. Psycho-Anal.*, 37:369–376.

INDEX

337